CELTIC
the encyclopaedia

previous books by the authors

Tom Campbell:
Glasgow Celtic (1945-1970) Civic Press
The Glory and the Dream [with Pat Woods] Mainstream
Rhapsody in Green [with Pat Woods] Mainstream
Dreams and Songs to Sing [with Pat Woods] Mainstream
A Celtic A to Z [with Pat Woods] Greenfield Press
Celtic Football Club 1887-1967 [with Pat Woods] Tempus
Jock Stein; the Celtic Years [with David Potter] Mainstream
Celtic's Paranoia – All in the Mind? Fort Publishing
Ten Days That Shook Celtic Fort Publishing
Tears in Argentina Fort Publishing
Charlie Tully, Celtic's Cheeky Chappie Breedon Book;

George Sheridan:
An Alphabet of the Celts (with Eugene MacBride and Martin O'Connor)
ACL& Polar Publishing
The Essential History of Celtic (with Graham McColl)

CELTIC
the encyclopaedia

Celtic's first team 1888

compiled by
Tom Campbell & George Sheridan

ARGYLL✤PUBLISHING

First published in September 2008 by
Argyll Publishing
Glendaruel
Argyll PA22 3AE
Scotland
www.argyllpublishing.com

**British Library Cataloguing-in-Publication
Data.**
**A catalogue record for this book is available
from the British Library.**

ISBN 978 1 906134 15 0

Printing: Bell & Bain Ltd, Glasgow

This book is dedicated to the women in our lives
who continue to forgive our love affair with Celtic with a baffled patience:
Pauline, Robin and Dana Campbell;
Marie, Claire and Julie Sheridan.
And with affection to the memory of
Eugene MacBride and Tommy Burns:
Eugene, longtime editor of *The Celt*, who was himself an encyclopaedia of Celtic
and who shared his knowledge and insights so generously;
Tommy, born and raised within yards of the club's birthplace
and who represented in his person and life everything that was good about Celtic.

Acknowledgements

We have to acknowledge the help and advice given to us by several people throughout the compiling of this encyclopaedia. Without their assistance the book would have been infinitely less comprehensive and accurate:

the Celtic historians Pat Woods and David Potter for their encouragement and for knowledge given so generously;

the Celtic enthusiasts Patrick Reilly and the late Eugene MacBride for sharing their insights into their passion;

Paul Lunney for his contribution to the planning of the book and for help with several units;

Frank Glencross for providing photographs and programmes from his collection;

Billy McNeill for contributing the foreword;

and to Argyll Publishing – and especially Derek Rodger – for unfailing patience and cheerfulness in accepting additions, changes of mind and corrections up to the very last minute.

All reasonable efforts have been made to locate copyright holders of photos and other images. Should the holder of rights on any image have been overlooked, please make contact with the publisher so that any oversight or mistake can be rectified in future editions.

Tom Campbell and George Sheridan

Contents

A view of the Celtic fans (above) and an extract from a newspaper feature in 1970

The story of one of football's great clubs.
GLASGOW CELTIC

CELTIC FOOTBALL CLUB began in 1887, when a team was formed with the aim of raising money to feed needy children. A year later, the club was properly founded. In 1890 they helped to form the Scottish First Division.

One member of the original team was Willie Maley. He later became Celtic manager, and was connected with the club until 1938, a period of 50 years.

Right from their earliest days, Celtic have been winning cups and trophies—right up to the most sought after trophy of all —the European Cup in 1967.

Jack Thomson was one of Celtic's greatest goalkeepers. After his death following an injury on the field, a folk song was written about him.

One of Celtic's all-time greats was Jimmy McGrory, centre in the 1930's. He scored 550 league goals, many with his head.

Bobby Evans, Celtic and Scotland skipper, was one of Celtic's top half-backs. Bobby won 73 caps for Scotland in an international career lasting eleven years from 1949-1960.

1967 was a big year for Celtic. They made a clean sweep of the Scottish honours and won the European Cup. When Celtic returned to Glasgow, a 30,000 crowd packed Celtic Park to see their heroes parade with the European Cup on a specially-decorated lorry. 7.3.70

FOR THE RECORD
LEAGUE DIVISION I CHAMPIONS
1892-93, 1893-94, 1895-96, 1897-98, 1904-05, 1905-06, 1906-07, 1907-08, 1908-09, 1909-10, 1913-14, 1914-15, 1915-16, 1916-17, 1918-19, 1921-22, 1925-26, 1935-36, 1937-38, 1953-54, 1965-66, 1966-67, 1967-68, 1968-69.

SCOTTISH F.A. CUP WINNERS
1892, 1899, 1900, 1904, 1907, 1908, 1911, 1912, 1914, 1923, 1925, 1927, 1931, 1933, 1937, 1951, 1954, 1965, 1967, 1969.

LEAGUE CUP WINNERS
1957, 1958, 1966, 1967, 1968, 1969, 1970.

EUROPEAN CUP WINNERS   1967.

Ground: Celtic Park, Parkhead, Glasgow.
Record Gate: 92,000, v. Rangers, Div. I, 1938.
Colours: Green and white hooped shirts, white shorts.
Record Win: 11-0, v. Dundee, Div. I, 1895.
Record Defeat: 8-0, v. Motherwell, Div. I, 1936-37.

Celtic's team in their first season – even before the Hoops

Foreword

I have been a Celtic supporter all my life, and I consider myself fortunate to have played a part in the unfolding history of this great club as a player, as a captain and as a manager.

It is a sobering thought to think that when you put on a Celtic jersey, the world-famous 'Hoops', you are following in the footsteps of some of the greatest players who have graced the Scottish game – men like Alec McNair, a legendary and ice-cool figure at right-back, Jimmy McStay, an inspirational centre-half, Patsy Gallacher, a magician with the ball, Jimmy McGrory, the greatest goal-scorer ever in Scottish football, Malcolm MacDonald, reckoned by many to be the club's most complete footballer; and modern stars like Jimmy Johnstone, incomparable and unforgettable at outside-right, and Henrik Larsson, a genuine world-class player who delighted in playing for Celtic. . . The list is simply endless.

Magnificent players and performers, a passionate and faithful support, a club which, while providing entertainment on the football field, has never forgotten its roots and continues to acknowledge its charitable origins, Celtic is an institution within Scotland and further afield.

It is also a club which has been well served by its chroniclers down the years: Tom and George, who have compiled this encyclopaedia, Pat Woods, that most dedicated of researchers and historians, Eugene MacBride and so many others.

This book is a most welcome addition to the Celtic bibliography and will be the sort of authority which will end arguments – and perhaps start others. It's not just a dry-as-dust collection of facts. I was surprised to learn that at one time – during World War 1 – Celtic were nicknamed 'The Huns', that Kinnaird Ouchterlonie is the Scot with the longest name to play for the club, that only one Celtic player has ever missed a penalty in a Scottish Cup final during regular play. . .

Read it for yourself, and enjoy it, as I did.

Billy McNeill

Celtic captain Billy McNeil scores against
Dunfermline in the 1965 Scottish Cup final –
and ushers in a new era for his club

NOTE: Match results are set out in this
book so that Celtic's goals are always first
whether home, away or neutral venues.
So, if 3-2 is given as the result, that means
Celtic scored 3 and the opposition 2,
regardless of the venue.

A

ABANDONED GAMES

The most recent Celtic match to be abandoned was the league fixture against Aberdeen at Celtic Park on 15 January 1994. Referee Hugh Williamson (Renfrew) called a halt to a scoreless contest in 61 minutes when the fog became so bad that spectators 'were yelling that they couldn't see the play'. The re-arranged fixture was completed on the following Wednesday (19 January) with the admission prices reduced. The teams fought out a 2-2 draw in heavy rain: Paul Byrne opened the scoring for Celtic in 30 minutes, but goals from Irvine and Jess had put the visitors in front before a volley from Paul McStay levelled things at 60 minutes.

Just over sixteen years had elapsed since the previous abandonment of a Celtic match – the league fixture against Clydebank at Kilbowie Park on 26 November 1977. The referee, Douglas Downie (Edinburgh), after consultation with his linesmen, halted the match at halftime with the game tied 1-1. The officials were in agreement that the frozen, slippery underfoot conditions had become too dangerous. However, players and officials of both clubs felt that the conditions were no worse at halftime than at the start, and it reflected credit on the

10,000 present at the all-ticket encounter that they departed quietly with 'only the odd rumblings of discontent' – and without any hope of a refund. When the fixture was re-scheduled on 26 April 1978, the result was another 1-1 draw. The match was an end-of-the-season affair played before only 4,800 spectators and Mike Conroy scored Celtic's goal; Clydebank were already doomed to relegation and Celtic were playing out a trophyless season – Jock Stein's last in charge.

On 19 October 1975 Mr.R.H. Davidson called a halt to a league fixture at Parkhead between Celtic and Hibernian because of poor visibility after 83 minutes with Hibernian leading comfortably 2-0 but in the replayed match Celtic gained a 1-1 draw, the goal being netted by Dixie Deans, a prolific scorer against the Edinburgh side.

On 6 December 1958 Celtic were coasting to a 2-0 win over Motherwell on a fog-shrouded Celtic Park when the referee had to curtail the league match with only seven minutes left. In the re-scheduled fixture Motherwell escaped with a 3-3 draw, thanks to two late goals.

On 23 August 1948 a Glasgow Cup tie against Partick Thistle was halted when a

thunderstorm made further play impossible. Celtic and Thistle were level 1-1 at
the time and Celtic won the re-match 2-1.

Another fixture against Partick Thistle
was abandoned at Firhill on 2 November
1940. Rain and sleet had made conditions
virtually impossible in this wartime
Southern League match and two minutes
after Thistle equalised Frank Murphy's
earlier goal for Celtic the referee tactfully
stopped the proceedings at 61 minutes.

In the modern era, once they have started,
matches are very seldom abandoned.
Improved playing surfaces has been the
principal factor, as well as early pitch
inspections. However, in the early days of
organised football, abandoned games were
frequent and crowd control – when only a
rope separated spectators from players –
was the major problem.

Celtic and Hibernian was a fixture
often bedevilled by crowd trouble, the Leith
side's supporters remembering that Celtic
had poached several Hibernian star players
to help in their first season. On 20 October
1888 when Celtic were leading by 3-0 in
Edinburgh in the second half hostile home
supporters invaded the pitch three times.
In fact, the referee blew for time with ten
minutes left – with the approval of both
teams – in order to forestall any further
trouble.

In 1890 the Scottish Cup tie against
Queen's Park at the first (and primitive)
Celtic Park was delayed at the start and
interrupted frequently by crowd invasions.
The game ended as a 0-0 draw but the re-
match was ordered to be played at the more

established Hampden Park where Queen's
Park won 2-1.

In 1891 Celtic travelled to Larkhall for
a Scottish Cup tie against Royal Albert but
the match was halted a few minutes from
the end with Celtic leading by 4-0; in an
effort to force a replay the local supporters
invaded the pitch. Despite the score and
the circumstances, the SFA ordered a replay
and Celtic won again, this time by 2-0 at
Ibrox Park.

In 1892 the Scottish Cup final between
Celtic and Queen's Park was held at a
recently modified Ibrox Park with a record
crowd in attendance. Frequent crowd
invasions and a treacherous field caused the
clubs to play the match as a 'friendly'
unknown to the majority of the crowd and
it was won 1-0 by Celtic. Celtic also won
the replay (5-1) to gain their first Scottish
Cup.

In 1898 the New Year's Day Old Firm
fixture was abandoned with fifteen minutes
left to play, and the game tied at 1-1.
Repeatedly, some of the record crowd
(officially 44,000) encroached upon the
field, causing the players to leave it for their
own safety. The re-arranged match ended
in a 0-0 draw, but Rangers and Celtic
disputed the division of the 'gate', a
disagreement which caused considerable
friction.

In 1899 a Scottish Cup tie at Hampden
against Queen's Park was abandoned after
70 minutes because of poor light with Celtic
leading by 4-2. The replay was switched to
Celtic Park to accommodate a larger crowd
and Celtic won 2-1.

Another cup tie against Queen's Park,

Celtic Football & Athletic Club

Celtic Park, Parkhead
(Corner of Dalmarnock and Janefield Streets)

Patrons: His Grace the Archbishop of Glasgow and the Clergy of St. Mary's, Sacred Heart and St. Michael's Missions, and the principal Catholic laymen of the East End.

The above club was formed in November 1887 by a number of the Catholics of the East End of the City. The main object of the club is to supply East End conferences of the St. Vincent de Paul Society with funds for the maintenance of the 'Dinner Tables' of our needy children in the Missions of St. Mary's, Sacred Heart and St. Michael's. Many cases of sheer poverty are left unaided through lack of means. It is therefore with this principal object that we have set afloat the 'Celtic', and we invite you as one of our ever-ready friends to assist in putting our new Park in proper working order for the coming football season.

We already have several of the leading Catholic football players of the West of Scotland on our membership list. They have most thoughtfully offered to assist in the good work. we are fully aware that the elite of football players belong to this city and suburbs, and we know that there we can select a team which will be able to do credit to the Catholics of the West of Scotland as the Hibernians have been doing in the East. Again there is also the desire to have a large recreation ground where our Catholic young men will be able to enjoy the various sports which will build them up physically, and we feel sure we will have many supporters with us in this laudable object.

Reproduction of Original Poster (1887)

this time in the Charity Cup in 1900, ended in confusion when the referee whistled for time ten minutes too early. Many in the crowd had been unhappy with the official's performance – he had awarded Celtic two dubious penalty kicks – and stormed on to the pitch. They refused to disperse when the teams attempted to restart the match after the referee had been advised of his timekeeping error. Celtic won the replay 6-1.

In 1903 Celtic and St. Mirren could not be separated after two Scottish Cup ties: 0-0 at Celtic Park and 1-1 in Paisley. A decider was held at Ibrox Park but had to be stopped after 75 minutes through bad weather with Celtic leading by 1-0. A fourth match, also at Ibrox, ended in a 4-0 win for Celtic.

ABERDEEN

Celtic have enjoyed a harmonious relationship with the Dons for many years.

Before Aberdeen joined the Scottish League's top division for the 1905/06 season, Celtic had toured the region on missionary work and those tours did much to get the relationship off to a good start. During that season Celtic, eventually the league champions, defeated Aberdeen 1-0 at Celtic Park on 9 December 1905 thanks to a goal from Jimmy McMenemy but Aberdeen gained revenge on 3 March 1906 with a 1-0 win at Pittodrie on Celtic's first competitive visit to the ground.

Like Rangers and Celtic (and Inverness Caledonia Thistle), Aberdeen have never been relegated from the top division in

The late Phil O'Donnell heads for goal against Aberdeen at Hampden in 1994

Scottish football. Their record against Celtic in league competition is a respectable one to date (end 2007/08 season): 64 wins, 59 draws and 128 defeats.

Similarly, the record in the Scottish Cup makes impressive reading: 9 wins, 6 draws and 13 losses.

Several players have played for both clubs: Roy Aitken, Tommy Bogan, Jimmy Delaney, Joe Miller, Steve Murray, Billy Stark, Paddy Travers. etc. Billy McNeill has been manager of both clubs.

ADDRESS

Celtic Football Club
Celtic Park
Glasgow
G40 3RE

A view of Celtic Park in the 1950s shows its position in Glasgow's East End in the midst of industry and housing.

AGGREGATE SCORES

Celtic's highest ever aggregate score in proper competition came in a European Cup first round tie in 1970 when they thrashed the Finnish side KPV Kokkola by 14-0. Celtic won the first match at Parkhead 9-0 on 16 September 1970 before a crowd of 41,000. At halftime Celtic led 6-0, and eased up in the second half although substitutes Paul Wilson and Vic Davidson scored three goals between them. Harry Hood netted a hat-trick within thirty-six minutes, his first goal coming inside the very first minute. It might be worth noting that Celtic struck the woodwork five times and were criticised for missing half-a-dozen 'sitters'.

Celtic: Williams, McGrain, Brogan, Murdoch, McNeill, Hay (Wilson), Johnstone, Connelly, Hood (Davidson), Lennox, Hughes.

Scorers: Hood 3, Hughes, McNeill, Johnstone, Wilson (2) and Davidson.

In the second leg Celtic emphasised their superiority by winning comfortably 5-0 in Finland before a crowd of 5,096 after leading 2-0 at the interval. Celtic: Fallon, Craig (McGrain), Brogan, Murdoch (Dalglish), Connelly, Cattenach, Davidson, Wallace, Chalmers, Callaghan, Lennox. Scorers: Wallace (2), Callaghan, Davidson, Lennox. Nine players had shared in the fourteen goals scored, and Celtic had made nine changes for the second leg, an indication of the depth of the squad.

The League Cup used to provide two-legged contests and Celtic's largest win in that competition came in 1968/69 in a quarter-final against Hamilton Academical. At Celtic Park on 11 September 1968 the home side crushed the Accies by 10-0, with both Stevie Chalmers and Bobby Lennox scoring five times. Two weeks later Celtic travelled to Douglas Park to register a 4-2 win, merciful in the circumstances as Jock Stein chose an understrength side for the occasion with debuts coming for goalkeeper Bobby Wraith and Kenny Dalglish as a substitute.

11 September 1968
Celtic: Simpson, Craig, Gemmell, Brogan, McNeill, Clark, Macari, Lennox, McBride, Chalmers, Hughes (Johnstone)
Scorers: Chalmers (5), Lennox (5)

25 September 1968
Celtic: Wraith, Craig, Gorman, Connelly, Hay, Clark, McMahon, McBride, Quinn, Gallagher (Dalglish), Macari.
Scorers: McBride (2), McMahon, Clark

In the Victory Cup of 1946 – a one-off tournament held to replace the Scottish Cup, put aside during World War II – the first round was held on an aggregate basis with Celtic beating St. Johnstone 8-2 at Muirton Park, and then by 5-0 at Celtic Park. The experiment seems to have been abandoned for the subsequent rounds of the competition

The lowest aggregate score for Celtic in European competition was achieved by two 0-0 draws against the Italian side Inter Milan in the European Cup in April 1972 – with Celtic being eliminated after extra time on penalty kicks at Celtic Park on the 19th.

ALL-TIME APPEARANCES
(MAJOR COMPETITIIONS)

Billy McNeill	790
Paul McStay	677
Roy Aitken	672
Danny McGrain	663
Pat Bonner	641
Alec McNair	604
Bobby Lennox	589
Bobby Evans	535
Jimmy Johnstone	515
Jimmy McMenemy	515
Tommy Burns	508

Paul McStay – second in the list of all-time appearances for Celtic

ALL-TIME SCORERS
(MAJOR COMPETITIIONS)

Jimmy McGrory	468
Bobby Lennox	273
Henrik Larsson	242
Steve Chalmers	219
Jimmy Quinn	217
Patsy Gallacher	192
John Hughes	188
Sandy McMahon	177
Jimmy McMenemy	168
Kenny Dalglish	167
Adam McLean	148

Jimmy McGrory – the all-time highest Celtic scorer with 468 competiive goals

AMATEURS

The definition of 'amateur' is 'a person who engages in a pursuit as a pastime rather than as a profession' or as 'a player who does not receive remuneration from an organisation for playing football'.

In the beginning of the association game all football was amateur; indeed, Scotland's oldest club Queen's Park, formed in 1867, remain so to this day.

However, with the growth in popularity of the game in the 1870s and 1880s football changed from being a middle-class sport played by amateurs and gentlemen into a virtual opiate for the working-class. Inevitably, business and commercial interests were attracted to enterprises which could attract large crowds, presumably with money to spend on their passion. England was the first to make Association Football a money-making activity with the introduction of professionalism in 1885 and the inevitable formation of the Football League in 1888.

All footballers in Scotland were nominally amateur until the legalisation of professionalism in 1893 but the reality was otherwise. Why should any working-class boy with football skill play in Scotland for nothing when he could 'work' in England for at least double the average working wage? Frankly, they did not play for nothing: payments had to be disguised or hidden.

One Celtic player – James Kelly – an apprentice joiner by trade came to the club from Renton and had also been sought after by Hibernian. Why did he chose Celtic, a new and unproven club? The fact that he ended up owning three public houses – allegedly on his savings as a joiner – may have had something to do with it.

Celtic in essence have always been a professional club since they were founded in 1887 and enticed Hibernians' best players west in 1888. It is not surprising that Celtic's committee-man and later chairman J.H. McLaughlin was the leading advocate for both professionalism in Scotland and, exactly as in England, the formation of a league.

That notwithstanding, Celtic Football Club have occasionally had amateurs on their books. The most famous of these 'puritans' was the Welsh international goalkeeper L. R. Roose. A doctor by profession, Leigh Richmond Roose's only appearance for Celtic was in a Scottish Cup tie against Clyde at Shawfield in 1910. Celtic lost by 3-1 but the main talking point came after fifty-five (55) minutes when Chalmers scored a third goal for the home side. At that moment Dr. Dick lived up to all the principles of the amateur code – and his own reputation as a sportsman – by chasing after the goalscorer to congratulate him. It was such a gracious and unexpected gesture that an elderly Clyde supporter could vividly remember the moment more than seventy (70) years later in an article for a Sunday newspaper.

After an initially rocky start, Celtic and Queen's Park have enjoyed a friendly relationship. This was aided in part by Celtic's unwritten agreement not to poach any of the amateur side's promising players. The most notable Celtic signing from Queen's Park must be Willie Lyon who went on to captain Celtic to several honours in the late 1930s.

Jackie Jordan, former Queen's Parker who served with the Scots Guards, played three league matches for Celtic at outside right in 1946/47 and scored one goal

Three other Celts have represented Scotland at amateur international level while with the club: Tony Hepburn: vs Ireland, Wales 1953; Malcolm Slater: vs Ireland 1959; Tommy Henderson: vs Ireland 1960.

Tony Hepburn could play on either wing, and made six league appearances at outside-right in 1952/53; yet, Scotland chose him as an outside-left for his two international appearances against Ireland in Belfast (0-1) and against Wales in Wrexham (1-0) in 1953. Educated at St., Aloysius College and at Glasgow University, and hailed as 'a dandy dribbler', Tony subsequently played with Dumbarton, Ayr United, Morton and Boston United. He also won an Irish Cup medal when Distillery defeated Glentoran by 1-0 after two previously drawn games. His career as a footballer was secondary to his profession as a lawyer, and he went on to establish his own legal firm. He died in November 2000 at the age of 68.

Another winger, Malcolm Slater played in a 0-0 draw between Scotland and Ireland at Coleraine on 21 February 1959. Born and bred in Buckie – whose Thistle wear the same green-and-white hoops as Celtic – Malcolm joined the Glasgow giants in November 1958 as a right winger and made five appearances in 1959, but following a family bereavement, he rejoined Buckie Thistle in 1960. He played also for Inverness Caledonian and Montrose before venturing into England where he appeared for Southend United, Leyton Orient and Colchester. Away from football Malcolm was a tax officer stationed in Aberdeen.

Raised in Larkhall, Tommy Henderson played for the Scottish Schoolboys Under 15s against England at Wembley in 1958. His friend Billy Bremner also played in that team and both boys signed for Leeds United. However, young Henderson was homesick, returned to Scotland, and joined Celtic in 1959. Diminutive and very direct, he never did make any first-team appearances but while at Celtic he was chosen to play for Scotland at Hampden Park against Ireland in 1959/60 and helped his country to a 2-0 win. Freed by Celtic, he joined Hearts in 1960 and was transferred from them eventually to St. Mirren for £2,000 in December 1961 and played in the Scottish Cup Final against Rangers in 1962. Later in his career he played in England with Bury, Swindon Town, Stockport County – assisting them to the Fourth Division title – and then to Altrincham.

ANGLO-FRANCO-SCOTTISH FRIENDSHIP CUP

Invitations to appear in this somewhat bizarre and down-market competition were based on league performances in the 1959/60 season. Hearts, Rangers and Hibernian had qualified for the major European competitions, Kilmarnock were scheduled to appear in a New York tournament – and Ayr United were unable to accept their invitation because they had no floodlights.

That left Clyde Dundee, Motherwell and Celtic – the ninth-place club – to represent Scotland.

Eight French sides and four English teams made up the roll call along with the four Scottish clubs. Celtic's French opponents in a home-and-away format were U.A. Sedan Torcy from the country's North East, and the first leg was played there on 6 August 1960 in odd circumstances. No representatives of the Sedan club materialised until a mere three hours before the kick-off, and it was obvious that nobody there had heard of Celtic. Even worse only 3,000 turned up for the match, and allegedly there was only one Celtic supporter present.

The part-time French outfit – wearing blue jerseys – outplayed an inept Celtic side to win 3-0, all their goals scored within the first thirty minutes.

Celtic's line-up was Haffey, MacKay, Kennedy, Crerand, McNeill, Peacock, Carroll, Chalmers, Mochan, Kelly, Auld. John Kelly, a new signing from Crewe Alexandria, was making his debut.

The second match was played eventually at Celtic Park on 18 October 1960 and Celtic's team was:

Haffey, MacKay, Kennedy, Crerand, McNeill, Peacock, Chalmers, Fernie, Carroll, Divers, Auld.

It appeared to be compulsory for Celtic in those seasons to make wholesale changes in the forward line for every game.

A crowd of 27,000 turned up and they were shocked when Sedan scored in the first minute, a rather cheeky back-heel past Haffey. John Divers equalised quickly but the visitors were much more inventive and led by 3-1 with two goals from long range which deceived Frank Haffey. In the closing stages Celtic rallied, and Steve Chalmers scored in 70 and 87 minutes; Bertie Auld had missed a penalty kick early in the second half. The match became towsy in that second half, and Willie Syme – a Scottish referee – had to caution four players, three of them French.

Despite Celtic's paltry contribution of one point for the draw at Parkhead, Scotland headed their league table with eleven points as Clyde and Motherwell won both their matches against French competition. The competition attracted little interest – at least in France, where only 14,000 spectators showed up for the four matches involving Scottish clubs.

Celtic did agree to participate in the next season's competition but were unable to agree suitable dates with their opponents Reims. The concept was quietly shelved to everybody's relief.

ANGLO-SCOTTISH CUP

A short-lived experiment mainly for clubs not eligible for European competition.

Celtic's participation in 1978/79 appeared half hearted and ended with an embarrassing capitulation to Burnley, a lower-division outfit. The fixture at Turf Moor was marred by crowd trouble.

3 August 1978 Clyde H 2-1 Conn, Burns

5 August Clyde A 6-1 Conn (2), McAdam (2), Glavin (2)
12 September Burnley A 0-1
27 September Burnley H 1-2 Lynch

ANNIVERSARY DATE

Johnny Crum had a busy day on 15 June 1938, the Wednesday after he scored the winning goal against Everton in the Empire Exhibition tournament. During the morning he got married to Miss Mary Allan, in the afternoon he attended a reception at the City Chambers along with his Celtic team-mates to collect the Charity Cup, and in the evening was a guest at the club's celebration of its fiftieth year at the Grosvenor Restaurant.

ANNOUNCEMENTS

Almost every stadium worthy of the name has a P.A. system designed to keep spectators informed of those issues that might affect their enjoyment of the entertainment on view: team line-ups, notification of substitutes, half-time scores, safety procedures, future happenings etc. In recent years many clubs employ some form of local 'celebrity' to jazz up such information (but with varying results).

In the 1950s an odd-looking structure decorated the back of the Rangers End of Celtic Park. This was the half-time board – which resembled some form of gallows. The matches were designated by letters (A, B, C, etc) and a man on a ladder was sent out to put in the scores shortly after halftime.

On one occasion, a Scottish Cup tie, the crowd was so dense that the man could not get through. The P.A. system came to the rescue, and read out the scores:

'A 1-0, B 1-1, C 1-2 . . .'

Apparently the announcer was not authorised to divulge more information because the list of games was published in the match programme (price 3d) and the club did want to jeopardise the number of sales.

On 16 April 1955 Aberdeen, who had clinched the league championship a week earlier after a close race with Celtic, came to Parkhead. The stadium announcer asked the crowd of some 45,000 to give the Dons 'a real Celtic welcome'. To their immense credit waves of generous applause greeted the appearance of Aberdeen on the pitch a few minutes later.

Similar sportsmanship is extended by Celtic's P.A. man on the pitch on European nights when he invariably welcomes the visitors and their supporters to Glasgow and Celtic Park.

On 18 April 1992 the stadium announcer at Airdrie's Broomfield read out Celtic's line-up, having prefaced the announcement by calling the visitors 'Cambuslang Celtic' – a sarcastic comment about Celtic's plans to redevelop their ground at Cambuslang. The visiting fans were not amused.

At St. Mirren Park in 2007 the stadium announcer pointedly asked the home support not to imitate or respond to what he referred to as 'the sectarian chants' from Celtic's supporters.

The role of the stadium announcer is an important one and the perils can be illustrated by the misguided effort of the one at Linfield's Windsor Park during the match between the home side and Belfast Celtic on 26 December 1948.

During the first half a Linfield player was carried off after a clash with Celtic's

Jimmy Jones. At the interval the Linfield secretary announced over the P.A. that he had been taken to hospital with a broken leg. Immediately after the game ended, Linfield supporters invaded the pitch to attack Jones and other Celtic players. Jones' leg was broken in several places, and Belfast Celtic decided to close down.

Silence can be golden.

ANNUS MIRABILIS

In 1966/67 Celtic won every competition they entered: the European Cup, the Scottish Cup, the Scottish League Championship, the League Cup and the Glasgow Cup. The manager Jock Stein joked that they could have lifted the Epsom Derby if they had thought to enter Bobby Lennox for it.

League Championship

10 September 1966 Clyde 3-0 A Chalmers, McBride, Hughes

17 September Rangers 2-0 H Auld, Murdoch

24 September Dundee 2-1 A Lennox, Chalmers

1 October St. Johnstone 6-1 H Johnstone (2), Lennox (2), McBride (2)

8 October Hibernian 5-3 A McBride (4), Chalmers

Celtic's all-conquering 1966/67 team with manager Jock Stein won every trophy they entered including the European Cup and committed Celtic fans can usually recite their names effortlessly:
Simpson, Craig, Gemmell,
Murdoch, McNeil, Clark,
Johnstone, Wallace, Chalmers, Auld, Lennox

15 October Airdrie 3-0 H Lennox (2),
    McBride
24 October Ayr United 5-1 H Johnstone (2),
    Lennox, Hughes, Gemmell
2 November Stirling Albion 7-3 H McBride
    (3), Chalmers (2), Johnstone, Auld
5 November St. Mirren 1-1 H Gemmell
12 November Falkirk 3-0 A McBride (2, p),
    Auld
19 November Dunfermline Ath. 5-4 A
    McBride (2, p), Murdoch, Johnstone,
    Auld
26 November Hearts 3-0 H McBride (2, p),
    o.g.
3 December Kilmarnock 0-0 A
10 December Motherwell 4-2 H Chalmers
    (3), Murdoch
17 December Partick Thistle 6-2 H Wallace
    (2), Chalmers (2), McBride, Murdoch
24 December Aberdeen 1-1 A Lennox
31 December Dundee United 2-3 A Lennox,
    Wallace
7 January 1967 Dundee 5-1 H Wallace (2),
    Murdoch, Johnstone, Gallagher
11 January Clyde 5-1 H Chalmers (2),
    Gallagher, Gemmell, Lennox
14 January St. Johnstone 4-0 A Johnstone
    (2), Chalmers, Lennox
21 January Hibernian 2-0 H Wallace,
    Chalmers
4 February Airdrie 3-0 A Johnstone,
    Chalmers, Auld
11 February Ayr United 5-0 A Chalmers (3),
    Johnstone, Hughes
25 February Stirling Albion 1-1 A Hughes
4 March St. Mirren 5-0 A Wallace (2),
    Lennox, Hughes, Gemmell (p)
18 March Dunfermline Ath. 3-2 H Chalmers,
    Wallace, Gemmell (p)
20 March Falkirk 5-0 H Chalmers (2), Auld,
    Hughes, Gemmell (p)
25 March Hearts 3-0 A Auld, Wallace,
    Gemmell (p)

27 March Partick Thistle 4-1 A Chalmers (2),
    Lennox, Wallace
8 April Motherwell 2-0 A Wallace, Gemmell
    (p)
19 April Aberdeen 0-0 H
3 May Dundee United 2-3 H Wallace,
    Gemmell (p)
6 May Rangers 2-2 A Johnstone (2)
15 May Kilmarnock 2-0 H Wallace, Lennox

Appearances:

Gemmell (34),	Hughes (19),
Clark (34),	O'Neill (18),
McNeill (33),	Craig (17+1),
Simpson (33),	McBride (14),
Murdoch (31),	Gallagher (11),
Chalmers (28),	Cushley (1),
Auld (27),	Fallon (1),
Lennox (26+1),	Young (1),
Johnstone (25+1),	Brogan (1s)
Wallace (21),	

Scottish Cup

28 January 1967 Arbroath 4-0 H Murdoch,
    Gemmell, Chalmers, Auld
18 February Elgin City 7-0 H Lennox (3),
    Wallace (2), Chalmers, Hughes
11 March Queen's Park 5-3 H Chalmers,
    Wallace, Murdoch, Lennox, Gemmell
    (p)
1 April Clyde 0-0 N
    6 April Clyde 2-0 N Lennox, Auld
29 April Aberdeen 2-0 N Wallace (2)

Appearances:

Clark (6),	Chalmers (5),
Gemmell (6),	Johnstone (5),
McNeill (6),	Lennox (5),
Simpson (6),	Craig (4),
Wallace (5+1),	Gallagher (4),
Auld (5),	Murdoch (4),

Hughes (3+1),
Cattenach (2)

LEAGUE CUP

11 August 1966 Hearts 2-0 A McBride (2, p)
17 August Clyde 6-0 H McBride (3, p),
    Lennox (2), Chalmers
20 August St. Mirren 8-2 H McBride (4, p),
    Lennox (2), Auld, Chalmers
27 August Hearts 3-0 H McBride (2, p),
    Chalmers
31 August Clyde 3-1 A McBride (2, p),
    Gemmell
3 September St. Mirren 1-0 A Murdoch
14 September Dunfermline 6-3 H Auld (2),
    McNeill, Hughes, Johnstone, McBride
    (p)
21 September Dunfermline 3-1 A Chalmers
    (2), McNeill

Joe McBride was Celtic's leading goalscorer during their great season 1966/67 although missing out on the second half of the season through injury

17 October Airdrie 2-0 N Murdoch, McBride
29 October Rangers 1-0 N Lennox

Appearances:
Clark (10),
Gemmell (10),
Johnstone (10),
McBride (10),
McNeill (10),
Murdoch (10),
Simpson (10),
Chalmers (9+1),
O'Neill (9+1),
Auld (9),
Lennox (7),
Hughes (4),
Craig (1),
Gallagher (1)

GLASGOW CUP

22 August 1966 Rangers 4-0 A Lennox (3),
    McNeill
10 October Queen's Park 4-0 H McBride (2),
    Lennox, Gallagher
7 November Partick Thistle 4-0 H Lennox
    (3), Chalmers

Appearances:
Clark (3),
Gallagher (3),
Gemmell (3),
Lennox (3),
McBride (3),
McNeill (3),
Murdoch (3),
Auld (2),
Johnstone (2),
O'Neill (2),
Simpson (2),
Chalmers (1),
Hughes (1),
Martin (1),
Young (1)

European Cup

28 September 1966 Zurich 2-0 H Gemmell,
    McBride
5 October Zurich 3-0 A Gemmell (2, p),
    Chalmers
30 November Nantes 3-1 A McBride,
    Lennox, Chalmers
7 December Nantes 3-1 H Johnstone,
    Chalmers, Lennox
I March 1967 Vojvodina 0-1 A
8 March Vojvodina 2-0 H Chalmers, McNeill
12 April Dukla 3-1 H Wallace (2), Johnstone
25 April Dukla 0-0 A
25 May Inter Milan 2-1 N Gemmell,
    Chalmers

Appearances:
Clark (9),   Murdoch (9),
Chalmers (9),   Simpson (9),
Gemmell (9),   Auld (8),
Johnstone (9),   Lennox (7),
McNeill (9),   Craig (5),

Hughes (5),   Gallagher (2),
O'Neill (4),   McBride (2).
Wallace (3),

Goalscorers (All Competitions):

McBride 38   Auld 12
Chalmers 37   Hughes 8
Lennox 32   Murdoch 8
Wallace 21   McNeill 4
Johnstone 16   Gallagher 3
Gemmell 16

Celtic line up in Montevideo for the deciding match against Racing Club in the World Club Championship (November 1967)

Jimmy McMenemy who played between 1902 and 1920 had 456 league appearances for Celtic.

Jimmy Quinn

APPEARANCES

Length of service is one measure of a player's contribution to his club, and perhaps the number of league appearances – 'the bread-and-butter' of the schedule – is the best guide.

The table below lists those players who have made over two hundred (200) such appearances for Celtic. It should be noted that substitute appearances – if the player actually participated in the matches – have been included.

APPEARANCES – LEAGUE

Alec McNair: 583 (1904/05–1924/25)
Paul McStay: 515 (1981/82–1996/97)
Billy McNeill: 486 (1958/59–1974/75)
Roy Aitken: 483 (1975/76–1989/90)
Pat Bonner: 483 (1978/79–1994/95)
Jimmy McMenemy: 456 (1902/03–1919/20)
Danny McGrain: 441 (1970/71–1986/87)
Patsy Gallacher: 432 (1911/12–1925/26)
Charlie Shaw: 420 (1913/14–1924/25)
Jimmy McStay: 409 (1922/23–1933/34)
Andy McAtee: 406 (1910/11–1923/24
Willie McStay: 399 (1916/17–1928/29)
Alec Thomson: 391 (1922/23–1933/34)
Jim Young: 391 (1903/04–1916/17)
Bobby Evans: 385* (1946/47–1959/60)
Jimmy McGrory: 378** (1922/23–1937/38)
Adam McLean: 367 (1916/17–1927/28)
Joe Dodds: 352 (1908/09–1919/20)
Peter Wilson: 344 (1923/24–1933/34)
Peter Grant: 338 (+26) (1983/84–1996/97)
Tommy Burns: 324 (+32) (1974/75–1989/90)
Bertie Peacock: 318 (1949/50–1960/61)
Jimmy Johnstone: 298 (+10) (1962/63–1974/ 75)
Bobby Lennox: 297 (+50) (1961/62–1979/ 80)
Tom Boyd: 296 (+10) (1991/92–2002/03)

Celtic 1956/57

Bobby Murdoch: 287 (+4) (1962/63–1972/73)

'Peter' McGonagle: 286 (1927/28–1935/36)

'Chic' Geatons: 285* (1928/29–1939/40)

Bobby Hogg: 278* (1932/33–1947/48

Murdo MacLeod: 274 (+7) (1978/79–1986/87)

Jimmy Quinn: 271 (1900/01–1914/15)

'Jean' McFarlane: 268 (1919/20–1928/29)

'Joe' Kennaway: 263 (1931/32–1939/40)

Paddy Connolly: 260 (1921/22–1929/30)

Willie Loney: 254 (1900/01–1913/14)

Stevie Chalmers: 253 (+10) (1958/59–1970/71)

John Hughes: 252 (+3) (1960/61–1971/72)

Tom McAdam: 251 (+7) (1977/78–1985/86)

Davy Adams: 247 (1903/04–1911/12)

Tommy Gemmell: 247 (1962/63–1971/72)

Jackie McNamara: 221 (+16) (1995/96–2004/05)

Davy Hamilton: 221 (1902/03–1911/12)

Bobby Collins: 220 (1949/50–1958/59)

Willie Fernie: 219 (1949/50–1958/59)

Henrik Larsson: 218 (+3) (1997/98–2003/04)

Willie Fernie takes on Stewart (East Fife)

Bobby Hogg leads out Celtic for a Scottish Cup tie at Dens Park in 1947

Jimmy Hay: 217 (1903/04–1910/11)
Charlie Tully: 215 (1948/49–1958/59)
John Collins: 211 (+6) (1990/91–1995/96)
Derek Whyte: 211 (+4) (1985/86–1992/93)
Peter Johnstone: 211(1908/09–1916/17)
John Browning: 210 (1912/13–1918/19)
Jim Brogan: 208 (+5) (1963/64–1974/75)
John McMaster: 204 (1913/14–1922/23)
Willie Cringan: 203 (1917/18–1923/24)
Kenny Dalglish: 200 (+4) (1969/70–1976/77)

* This player also made appearances for Celtic in 'unofficial' Regional Leagues during World War II.

** Jimmy McGrory went to Clydebank on loan during season 1923/24

APPEARANCES – OTHER COMPETITIONS

In other competitions the players with the most appearances are as follows:

Scottish Cup: Billy McNeill 94
League Cup: Billy McNeill 138
Europe: Billy McNeill 69
Charity Cup: Alec McNair 30
Glasgow Cup: Alec McNair 45

Some pundit once claimed, 'You don't win leagues with kids.' Well, this would be a highly experienced side (with almost 6,400 appearances among them):

Bonner,
McNair, McNeill, Aitken, McGrain,
Evans, Murdoch, McMenemy, Burns,
Johnstone, McGrory.

Tommy Bogan's international career (when with Hibernian) lasted only one minute as he was injured in collision with England's goalkeeper Frank Swift. He had not touched the ball once in the match at

Danny McGrain is congratulated by his manager after his debut against Morton (1970)

Billy McNeill blocks a shot against Airdrie in the 1975 Scottish Cup final (his last game for Celtic)

Celtic in their trophy-winning 1987/88 Centenary season
(back) McGhee, Stark, Baillie, McCarthy, Rogan, Whyte;
(middle) Scott (physio), Traynor, Burns, Rough, Bonner, Andrews, McAvennie, Archdeacon, Craig (asst manager);
(front) Miller, Grant, Aitken, McNeill (manager), McStay, Morris, Walker

Hampden Park on 14 April 1945.

Joe Craig was another international oddity in that he scored on his debut against Sweden on 27 April 1977 after coming on as a substitute. His goal (and first touch) came with a header, and he too had not kicked the ball up to that point.

APPLAUSE

Celtic prefer the method of honouring a recently deceased person by staging a minute's applause (rather than silence). It is believed the club introduced it in September 2005 to honour the twentieth anniversary of Jock Stein's death.

ARGENTINA

Celtic have played only one match in Argentina, the second fixture in the World Club Championship of 1967, and lost by 2-1 to Racing Club of Buenos Aires in the Avellaneda Stadium. The game was played in a most hostile environment, the Celtic goalkeeper being injured by a missile before play had started. (*See World Club Championship*)

ART

In the Scottish National Portrait Gallery in Edinburgh there is a study of former Celtic captain, Danny McGrain by Mark I'Anson done as a drawing. There is also a painting of McGrain by Humphrey Ocean in the same gallery. The frame has a motif of football boot studs or cleats and the player looks very impressive in his kilt.

Also in the same gallery is a portrait of Michael Kelly, former Lord Provost of Glasgow and Celtic director. It has been donated to the Gallery.

Mark I'Anson • Danny McGrain • Scottish National Portrait Gallery

Seton Airlie, who played for Celtic in the mid-1940s, was stationed in the South of France near the end of World War II and was on speaking terms with the renowned artist Pablo Picasso.

'John, you're immortal!' Bill Shankly, Liverpool's manager, to Jock Stein in the immediate aftermath of the Lisbon European Cup final.

Danny McGrain, born 1950, footballer
The above drawing hangs in the Scottish
National Portrait Gallery. It was made in
2003 and measures 112 x 193cm.

ARTIFICIAL PITCHES

An early attempt to play football on a non-grass artificial pitch was made in 1906 at Olympia in West London, but it ended in failure.

In 1966 the Houston Astrodome introduced Astroturf in an attempt to minimise the effects of the Texas heat on natural grass. Many American Football teams now play on artificial surfaces.

Queen's Park Rangers introduced it in Britain in 1981 with a brand called Omniturf and their pioneering effort was followed by Luton Town (1985), Oldham Athletic and Preston North End (1986), and in Scotland by Stirling Albion in 1987.

Celtic have played on artificial surfaces in friendly games while on tour in North America, but they did play and win a tournament in Hamilton, Canada. This was in 1994 during a Scottish Week in the Ontario city and Celtic defeated Hearts, Aberdeen and Montreal Impact to pick up the Hamilton Cup.

Celtic have also played competitive matches against such opposition as Dunfermline Athletic at East End Park, and most notably against Spartak Moscow in the qualifying round for the Champions' League in 2007.

ATTENDANCES

Celtic, as a well-supported club and renowned for an attacking philosophy, have always attracted large crowds. Celtic share the following record crowds in domestic football;

Scottish League: 118,567 at Ibrox Stadium vs Rangers (2 January, 1939)

Scottish Cup: 146,433 at Hampden Park vs Aberdeen (24 April, 1937). Some sources claim the attendance was 147,365. In either case, it constituted a record crowd.

League Cup: 107,609 at Hampden Park vs Rangers (23 October, 1965)

Scottish Premier League: 69,594 at Ibrox Stadium vs Rangers (30 August, 1975)

Drybrough Cup: 57,558 at Hampden Park vs Rangers (3 August, 1974)

Celtic also hold the attendance record at these Scottish grounds:

Cappielow Park (Morton) 23,500 1921/22 Scottish League

Clydeholm Park (Clydebank) 23,193 1925/26 Scottish League

Ibrox Stadium (Rangers) 118,567 1938/39 Scottish League

Love Street (St. Mirren) 47,428 1949/50 League Cup

Brockville Park (Falkirk) 23,100 1953 Scottish Cup

Recreation Park (Alloa) 15,467 1955 Scottish Cup

Annfield Park (Stirling Albion) 28,600 1959 Scottish Cup

East End Park (Dunfermline) 27,816 1967/68 Scottish League

New Kilbowie Park (Clydebank) 10,605 1977/78 SPL

Broadwood Stadium (Clyde) 7,382 1996/97 League Cup

Excelsior Stadium (Airdrieonians) 8,762 1997/98 League Cup

Caledonian Stadium (Inverness Caledonian Thistle) 7,100 2004/05 SPL

Almondvale (Livingston) 10,024 2001/02 SPL

Celtic Park (1):
Many of the attendance figures for Celtic Park are considered unreliable as, for many years, there was no automatic counting mechanism at the turnstiles.

The estimated capacity of Celtic Park for many years was 92,000 and this figure is regularly cited as the record attendance achieved on 1 January 1938 against Rangers but this is almost certainly wrong. Most newspapers at the time reported the attendance as 83,500 – a much more probable crowd.

In the Scottish Cup the largest attend-

Celtic fans gather at Cathkin Park in the early 1960s prior to a Scottish League Division 1 game against soon to be defunct Third Lanark.

ance attained was the 80,840 who saw Celtic beat Hearts 2-1 after extra time in a replay on 22 February, 1939. Surprisingly, this figure was reached for a midweek match and in winter.

The largest attendance for a European match was 77,240 and that was for a 3-0 win over Fiorentina (Italy) on 4 March, 1970.

The lowest attendance at Celtic Park must be that which watched Celtic play Atletico Madrid on 2 October, 1985. Celtic lost this European Cup-Winners' Cup tie by 2-1. The match was played behind closed doors as a UEFA punishment for crowd trouble at Celtic Park and Old Trafford in the previous season's ECWC ties against Rapid Vienna.

Another contender for the lowest attendance must be the 600 (estimated) spectators who turned up for a Scottish Cup win over Albion Rovers on 13 October 1888. It was, however, considered a respectable turnout for those early days although it fell below the expectations aroused by Celtic's impact on the sport.

On 22 December 1894 a similarly poor crowd assembled to watch Celtic and St. Mirren draw 2-2. The weather that day was atrocious, the rain and stormy conditions causing chaos throughout Britain.

Celtic have been watched by some record crowds, two of which were at Hampden before the modern verion of the national stadium was built –146,433 vs Aberdeen in the Scottish Cup, 24 April, 1937; 133,961 when Celtic beat Leeds United 2-1, April 1970 in what is held to be the record crowd ever to watch a European Cup tie.

Celtic Park (2):

With the change to an all-seated stadium after 1995 the capacity has been reduced to just under 61,000.

The record attendance is the 60,440 who watched Celtic defeat St. Mirren 1-0 to clinch the Premier League champion-ship on 7 April, 2001. Because of security restrictions it is doubtful if any fixture with Rangers will exceed that figure.

Celtic have also played to the largest crowd ever to watch a European Cup tie. In April, 1970 Celtic beat Leeds United 2-1 at Hampden Park before a crowd of 133,961. This was the 'official' attendance but it is believed that several more thousands gained entrance to the ground when a gate was broken down.

Celtic have always maintained a decent average attendance, reflecting the fact that the club and the team can always rely on a

strong core of support. The best season for average attendance at the first Celtic Park is shared between 1948/49 and 1968/69, each with an approximate 37,000. The former season marked the introduction of the charismatic Irish inside forward Charlie Tully, and the latter Celtic's domination of Scottish football under Jock Stein.

In 1966/67 more than two million spectators watched Celtic's 65 fixtures, including 'friendlies'. A little more than one million attended Celtic's 28 matches at Celtic Park.

It is believed that Celtic share in the record attendances for British and European Testimonial Games.

Just after winning the European Cup in 1967 Celtic were invited to participate in the testimonial match against Real Madrid for Alfredo di Stefano, and won that match by 1-0 in the Bernabeu. The

The 'Celtic End' at Hampden Park

A Celtic crowd at Dens Park Dundee for a Scottish Cup tie, 25 January 1947

crowd was estimated at well over 100,000.

On 9 May 2006 Celtic went to Old Trafford to play Manchester United in Roy Keane's testimonial. A crowd of 69,591 attended and Celtic's 23,000 tickets was officially the highest-ever away allocation granted for a game in Britain.

AUSTRALIA

Celtic's contact with Australia has been fairly limited although two strikers have come from the Southern Continent to play for Celtic in recent times: Mark Viduka and Scott McDonald.

However, Celtic have visited Australia on football business. In July 1977 the Celtic party flew to take part in two international competitions – in Singapore and Australia.

On 13 July Celtic defeated a Singapore Select by 5-0 in the National Stadium, packed with 45,000 spectators and the scorers were Alfie Conn (2), Tommy Burns, Bobby Lennox and Johannes Edvaldsson. On 17 July they faced Red Star Belgrade in the final in the same stadium but lost by 3-1 in a match played in stifling heat and humidity. Bobby Lennox scored Celtic's goal from the penalty spot.

In Australia the competing teams were Celtic, Arsenal, Red Star Belgrade and the Australian International XI. Celtic advanced to the final by drawing 1-1 with Red Star Belgrade at the Olympic Park in Melbourne on 21 July when Roddy MacDonald equalised late on, by defeating Arsenal 3-2 at the Cricket Ground in Sydney on 24 July with goals from Paul Wilson (2), and Ronnie Glavin. and by edging Australia again by 3-2 at the Sports Ground in the same city on the 26th. Johannes Edvaldsson (2) and Ronnie Glavin scored on that occasion.

The final was against Red Star in what was virtually a rubber match. The Belgrade side were the betting favourites after their triumph in Singapore but Jock Stein opted for semi-defensive tactics by restricting Danny McGrain's overlapping and the Yugoslavs dominated possession but rarely managed a direct shot on Peter Latchford in Celtic's goal. One minute before halftime Alfie Conn took a corner on the left and his inswinger struck the bar before dropping for Roddie MacDonald to bundle home. Despite pressure on their goal Celtic's Paul Wilson broke away on the right wing beating several defenders in a great run; his cross was met by Johannes Edvaldsson who had deserted his defensive duties in a 70-yard sprint to slide the ball into the net for the decisive killer goal

Celtic: Latchford, McGrain, MacDonald, Stanton, Burns, Glavin, Aitken, Edvaldsson, Conn, Lennox (Doyle), Wilson.

A noticeable absentee was the side's captain Kenny Dalglish who decided to stay in Scotland after an arduous season and to prepare for his subsequent move to Liverpool.

The 'World of Soccer' Cup, picked up by Danny McGrain would be the last trophy gained under the managership of Jock Stein who presided over a barren year in 1977/78 after the defection of Dalglish and injuries to other key players.

AWAY-GAMES

On 28 March 1929 a fire destroyed the pavilion at Celtic Park, destroying equipment and valuable records. Celtic were forced to play some fixtures away because of the damage and their final seven fixtures of the league campaign were played on the road: against Third Lanark (3-1), Partick Thistle (1-0), St. Johnstone (1-1), Hibernian (1-4), Queen's Park (1-2), Falkirk (3-0), and Kilmarnock (3-2). The fixtures against Thirds, St. Johnstone, and Kilmarnock had already been scheduled as away games.

Neil Mochan was signed from Middlesbrough in May 1953. His first four appearances were all at Hampden Park: against Queen's Park in the Charity Cup final (3-1), and against Arsenal (1-0), Manchester United (2-1) and Hibernian (2-0) in the Coronation Cup.

Neil scored four times, and picked up two medals while never playing at home for his new club.

Occasionally, Celtic have had to play European ties on grounds not normally associated with their opponents:

1963/64 ECWC vs MTK Budapest (Fixture was played at the Nep Stadium to accommodate expected crowd);

1965/66 ECWC vs Dynamo Kiev (Match played in Tbilisi, Georgia because of winter conditions in Kiev);

1970/71 EC vs Waterford (Match transferred to Dublin to accommodate crowd);

1970/71 EC vs Ajax (Fixture switched to the Olympic Stadium in Amsterdam to accommodate crowd);

1977/78 EC vs SW Innsbruck (Match ordered to be played in Salzburg as punishment for crowd trouble);

1988/89 ECWC vs Partizan Belgrade (Match ordered to be played in Mostar as punishment for crowd trouble);

1997/98 UEFAC vs Inter Cabletel (Venue switched to Ninian Park, Cardiff to accommodate crowd);

1999/2000 UEFAC vs Cwmbran Town (again switched to Ninian Park for the same reason);

2002/03 UEFAC vs FK Suduva (Venue switched to Kaunas to accommodate crowd).

Several Scottish clubs have had to waive the advantage of home League Cup ties because of the inadequacy of their grounds:

12 August 1992 Stirling Albion 3-0 (Switched to Hampden Park);

10 August 1993 Stirling Albion 2-0 (Switched to Firhill);

4 September 1996 Alloa Athletic 5-1 (Switched to Firhill);

4 September 1997 Berwick Rangers 7-0 (Switched to Tynecastle).

On 14 August 1971 while Celtic's main stand was being renewed, the home League Cup tie v Rangers was switched to Ibrox. Celtic won 2-0. The away match at Ibrox was also won 3-0.

On 22 September 1993, because Hampden Park was unavailable due to reconstruction, Celtic faced Rangers at Ibrox Park in the semi-final, and lost 1-0. Rangers had won the toss of the coin to stage the match at their stadium.

In 1994/95 Celtic played all their 'home' matches at Hampden Park because of the reconstruction of Celtic Park. On 21 September 1994 Celtic defeated Dundee United 1-0 in the quarter-final of the Scottish League Cup at Hampden.

On 8 January 2001 in the Scottish Cup, the game against Alloa Athletic was switched from Recreation Park to Falkirk's Brockville. It ended Alloa 0 Cetlic 5.

AWAY-GOALS

In an attempt to encourage visiting teams to play attacking football UEFA introduced the concept of 'the away-goal' whereby, if the ties finished level, any goal scored in the away leg would count as double. Celtic have had mixed fortunes when the rule was invoked;

Defeats:
1980/81 Politechnica Timisoara (Romania) ECWC H 2-1 A 0-1
1989/90 Partizan Belgrade (Yugoslavia) ECWC H 5-4 A 1-2
1997/98 Liverpool (England) UEFA C H 2-2 A 0-0 2002/03
Basle (Switzerland) EC H 3-1 A 0-2

Victory:
2002/03 Villareal (Spain) UEFA C H 1-0 A 1-2

B

BALLS

Originally, in organised football, the ball was made from leather but in recent decades the cover has been made from synthetic materials. This came as a considerable relief for almost every player who risked concussion in heading a ball that soaked up water and became heavier by the minute. Indeed, some medical and legal opinions contend that frequent heading of such a ball could be a contributory factor in causing brain damage, the effects of which would show later in a player's life.

In a contemporary development the colour of the ball could be varied, and again this was a godsend for spectators watching through the gloom of a late afternoon in winner. The most obvious of the new colours was white, but in recent seasons the colour of the ball has become virtually psychadelic.

Celtic's chairman Bob Kelly was an early and enthusiastic advocate of the new all-weather ball – invariably white – in the early 1950s, presumably thinking that Celtic, with a number of highly skilled players, would have a built-in advantage. He arranged for a container of such balls to be readied for the match referee at Celtic

Park to make a choice; in the vast majority of cases, the new ball was selected.

On one occasion, a row broke out on the field just prior to the kick-off – in the Celtic-Rangers fixture for 1 January 1954 when the two captains (Jock Stein of Celtic and George Young of Rangers) argued with the referee (Mr.J.A. Mowat) about the choice of ball: Young had brought on a brown (and probably leather) one on to the pitch and wanted that used; Stein wanted the white (all-weather) one used. Mr. Mowat tested both and plumped for the white one; Celtic won the match 1-0, and later the league championship.

For the England-Scotland match at Wembley in 1961 an orange ball was used, and England won by 9-3. It was claimed facetiously that the Celtic pair of Frank Haffey and Billy McNeill were unwilling to go near it, while the Rangers defenders Bobby Shearer and Eric Caldow were unwilling to kick it.

After Dixie Deans scored six of Celtic's seven goals against Partick Thistle at Parkhead on 17 November 1973, he was presented with the match ball.

Normally, the match ball becomes the

property of the referee at the conclusion of each half of play. However, Jim Baxter of Rangers, who had tormented Celtic in the 1963 replay of the Scottish Cup final, decided to keep the ball after the whistle. He was later fined by the SFA.

On 12 February 2000 at Dens Park the match was started with the customary ball, mainly white; however, snow fell through-out the second half and covered the pitch and the referee opted for an orange ball to complete the fixture. Celtic won by 3-0.

'BATTLE OF BRITAIN' MATCHES

Clashes between Scottish and English clubs often raise national feelings – at least in Scotland.

3 October 1927:
Celtic 4, Cardiff City 1
Celtic and Cardiff had won their respective cups, the Bluebirds taking the FA Cup to Wales after beating Arsenal 1-0 at Wembley. Both sides concentrated on football but Jimmy McGrory was unstoppable as he scored all four Celtic goals.

16 September 1936:
Sunderland 1, Celtic 1
A splendid match at Roker Park and both sides, champions of their leagues were cheered off the field by an appreciative crowd. Malcolm MacDonald scored for Celtic.

30 September 1936:
Celtic 3, Sunderland 2
In this return match Celtic scraped through by the narrowest of margins with Joe Kennaway saving a penalty kick. Jimmy McGrory (2) and Jimmy Delaney scored the vital goals.

6 October 1937:
Sunderland 0, Celtic 2
A clash of Cup-winners and Celtic triumph-ed again as Jimmy McGrory scored with a spectacular header. Willie Buchan netted the other.

10 June 1938:
Celtic 1, Everton 0 (aet)
Celtic won the unofficial championship of Britain by beating a strong Everton side in the final of the Empire Exhibition Trophy at Ibrox Park. Previously Celtic had defeat-ed Sunderland (again) and Hearts. John Crum netted the winner.

1951 Celtic 3, Newcastle United 3
Both United and Celtic were cup holders and produced a thrilling battle. Celtic fought back to earn a draw. Bobby Evans scored one of his few goals – a raging drive from thirty yards out which beat Ronnie Simpson in the Newcastle goal.

1954 Celtic 3, Wolverhampton 3
Celtic and Wolves had been the previous season's league champions but Celtic struggled in the opening stages and were two goals down after ten minutes. They were saved only by a last minute goal from Bobby Collins.

25 February 1986:
Celtic 0, Manchester United 3.
Both sides were holders of their Cups but the English side were too slick for the Scots. Gordon Strachan scored United's third.

9 December 1986:
Celtic 1, Liverpool 1
Liverpool, English champions, defeated Celtic, Scottish champions, on penalty kicks to win the Dubai Cup.

4 April 1989:
Celtic 1, Liverpool 1
Celtic gained revenge for defeat in 1986 in the same competition by winning on penalty kicks.

All of the above were one-off occasions but Celtic have won outright three tournaments which could accurately be described as the British Championship: the Glasgow Exhibition Cup of 1902 in which the champions and runners-up in both countries participated (Celtic, Rangers, Sunderland and Everton); the Empire Exhibition Trophy of 1928 in which Celtic, Rangers, Aberdeen, Hearts, Everton, Sunderland, Chelsea and Brentford took part; and the Coronation Cup of 1953 to which Celtic, Rangers, Hibernian, Aberdeen, Arsenal, Tottenham Hotspur, Manchester United and Newcastle United were invited

BELFAST CELTIC

The Ulster cousins were formed in 1891 by a group of lads from the Falls Road district in Belfast who had originally formed a cricket club but were then looking to expand their sporting horizons.

The logical decision was to start a football club and the team in Glasgow was their template: the name, the colours, the strip . . . and an identification with a specific community. Celtic, in Glasgow, gave considerable support and encouragement in those early days.

Belfast Celtic went on to become the dominant force in Northern Ireland football but the political, religious and social problems in the province would lead to their demise almost fifty years later.

They won the Irish League thirteen times, including four in a row between 1925 and 1929 and an even more memorable six in a row from 1935 to 1940. During World War II the championship was reorganised and renamed the Regional League and Belfast Celtic won four of the seven competitions held, and their great rivals Linfield the other three. The Irish League resumed in 1947 and Belfast Celtic, starring Charlie Tully, were the first post-war champions.

In addition they won the Irish Cup on eight occasions, the Gold Cup seven times and the City Cup ten. And, in an era when Irish players playing on the mainland were given preference for the limited number of international matches, Belfast Celtic provided thirty players for Northern Ireland.

Like their Scottish counterparts they could point to discrimination. At Christmas in 1912 in a match against Linfield, both neck and neck at the top of the league, they were greeted by a salvo of gunfire as they took the pitch; unsurprisingly, they lost four goals that day but (allegedly) scored four themselves only to have all of them disallowed!

Of interest to Glasgow fans is a piece in a Belfast Celtic programme of 1927 in which *The Celt* gives the words of their song. The first line runs, 'What a grand old team to play for,' and the finishing line ends, 'And the Belfast Celtic will be there.'

Sadly it is for their sudden shocking end for which they are best remembered.

On Boxing Day (!) 1948 they were again at Linfield's Windsor Park. In the first half, following a vigorous but fair challenge from Celtic's centre forward Jimmy Jones, Linfield's player, Bob Bryson, suffered a broken ankle. At halftime the PA announcer informed the crowd that Bryson had been taken to hospital and that he had sustained a broken leg – news that did nothing to calm the situation. In the second half two players (one from each side) were ordered off. Celtic took the lead with ten minutes left from the penalty spot, an award that angered the home support even more; however, Billy Simpson equalised in the second last minute.

At the final whistle a section of Linfield fans stormed on to the pitch and attempted to attack the Belfast Celtic players as they were leaving the field. Most of those players saved themselves by racing for the safety of the pavilion but Jimmy Jones was unlucky in that he was furthest away from the dressing room. He was surrounded by the mob, thrown over a boundary wall, punched and kicked but his most serios injury was a badly broken leg.

The Celtic directors were furious at the lack of protection given to their players at Windsor Park, ironically Northern Ireland's regular home ground considered the best in Ulster, and made the decision to withdraw from football altogether and announced this on 21 April 1949. It was a decision that has adversely affected the standard of play in the Irish League until the present time.

During the close season Belfast Celtic fulfilled a tour of the United States and astonishingly defeated the full Scotland national team (including Bobby Evans) in New York. It was a grand finale to a grand old team.

In 17 May 1952 Celtic Park was opened to admit 28,000 spectators for a charity match involving Glasgow Celtic (captained by Charlie Tully) against a Belfast Celtic Select (captained by Jackie Vernon). For legal reasons the Select played under the banner of Newry Town, a club affiliated to the Irish League. For the record, Glasgow Celtic won by 3-2.

Celtic Park, whose pitch was lovingly maintained for decades, went on to feature greyhound racing but the spirit had gone out of the ground; in 1983 the famous ground – nicknamed 'Paradise' – was demolished to make room for a shopping complex.

Two Glasgow Celtic players, Jimmy Blessington and Jimmy McColl, managed the Belfast club while several players have worn the famous hoops on both sides of the Irish Sea: Billy Crone, Bob Davidson, Jim Foley, Mickey Hamill, George Hazlett, Gerry McAloon, Dan McColgan, Harry McIlvenny, Willie McStay, Con Tierney, John Wallace and most famously the great Charlie Tully.

On 7 May 2001 Celtic defeated St. Mirren by 1-0 to clinch the club's 37th league championship. Northern Ireland's Martin O'Neill was Celtic's manager and several ex-Belfast Celtic players were invited to attend They included Jimmy Jones, Jimmy Donnelly, Leo McGuigan, Ossie Baillie, Alex Moore, and George Hazlett; Charlie Tully Jr. represented his father.

The two clubs – Glasgow and Belfast – met fourteen times over the years, and all the games were played in Belfast:

1897: 4-0;	1927: 2-4;
1902: 1-0;	1929: 7-4;
1904: 0-1;	1930: 2-1;
1910: 1-0;	1932: 3-0;
1911: 1-0;	1936: 2-1;
1925: 3-0;	1947: 4-4;
1926: 3-2;	1952: 3-2.

(Glasgow Celtic's score first).

BIG NAME SIGNINGS

Among the contenders:

Johannes Edvaldsson (18 letters)

Pierre van Hooijdonk (18)

Dariusz Djiekanowski (19)

Jean-Joel Perrier-Doumbe (21)

Jan Vennegoor of Hesselink (23).

Kinnaird Ouchterlonie might well be the Scottish candidate with the biggest name (20 letters).

BLACK PLAYERS

Such players were once considered a rarity in Scottish football and were subject to abuse from opposing supporters.

Fortunately, with greater familiarity, their worth as performers has been recognised by all followers of the game.

Celtic have fielded several players of colour and all have been acclaimed by the support for their skill and commitment, among them Didier Agathe, Gil Heron, Paul Elliott, Bobo Balde, Henri Camara, Mo Camara, Momo Sylla, Evander Sno, Paul Wilson, Regi Blinker, Fernando de Ornales, Bobby Petta, Olivier Tebily, Pierre van Hooijdonk, Tony Warner, Ian Wright.

BRAZIL

Not too many Brazilian players have settled in Scotland and, in common with other clubs, Celtic have had little luck with the South Americans.

Early in his tenure as Celtic's manager Jock Stein gave an extended trial in the reserves to a some young Brazilian 'hopefuls' but they proved unsuitable or were unable to agree on suitable terms. The players were Fernando Consul, Marco di Souza, Jorge Farah, and Ayrton Inacio. Farah appeared to be the best prospect but his representatives wanted a three-year contract for him and the proposed move went no further as none of the current Celtic players was on such an extended contract. At least, the attendance at the reserve side's matches increased considerably with crowds of 11,000 and 9,500 turning up, but the feeling persisted that the experiment was little more than an attempt to generate more publicity for the club.

Rafael Scheidt was a central defender who reputedly cost Celtic £5M in 1999 and who had earned one 'cap' for his country but, plagued by injury, he played only a handful of matches – mostly under an assumed name.

Juninho, the Brazilian World Cup player who came from Middlesbrough, faded after a bright start, and made only fourteen matches as a starter in 2004/05.

Out of favour, he was employed latterly only as a substitute.

Celtic were associated with two further attempts to land Brazilian players but both fell through: Rivaldo, the veteran World Cup forward, was invited by Gordon Strachan to try out for Celtic but his agent termed the proposal as "insulting'; in January 2008 the Corinthians' right back Coelho arrived for a trial but did not impress enough to be offered a contract.

Steve Chalmers played against Brazil at Hampden Park on 25 June 1966 and scored Scotland's only goal (1-1) in the first minute of play.

Ex-Celt John Collins scored Scotland's goal from the penalty spot in a 2-1 defeat to Brazil in the opening match of the 1998 World Cup in France; Tom Boyd was a bit more unlucky as his 'own-goal' gave Brazil the victory.

On 7 August 1988 Celtic arranged a friendly game with Cruzeiro Belo Horizonte, partly to celebrate the club's centenary. The teams competed for the Centenary Cup, a trophy contributed by Strathvale Homes. A large crowd – 41,659 – turned up for the occasion in brilliant sunshine to see Celtic win 4-2, with Andy Walker scoring three times and Frank McAvennie once. Celtic's side was: Andrews, Morris, Rogan, Aitken, McCarthy, Grant (Archdeacon), Miller (Stark), McStay, McAvennie (Christie), Walker (McGhee), Burns.

BIBLIOGRAPHY

This list has been arranged alphabetically within categories. These categories overlap and the titles have been assigned to categories deemed most appropriate to the contents.

Inevitably, this bibliography will be out-of-date by the time this encyclopaedia is published.

ANNUALS/YEARBOOKS:

Baillie, Rodger (editor): *Playing for Celtic Nos. 1–21* (annually, 1969-1989 inclusive), Stanley Paul

Celtic, All Every Bhoys' Fan Needs to Know about the 1998/99 Season Mustard/Parragon, 1999 [Superteams Series]

Celtic Football Club Yearbook 1992/93 Premiere Marketing Services Ltd., 1992 [Review of the 1992/93 season, and believed to be the only one of its type produced by the publisher as a brochure]

The Official Celtic Football Club Annual (annually, 1991 to 2003 inclusive, and with various publishers, initially Holmes McDougall and presently Grange Communications Ltd.)

Official Celtic F.C. Yearbook (Eagle Football Diaries Ltd., annually for seasons 1986/87 to 1990/91 inclusive). Despite the publisher's name, these were not diaries, rather comprehensive reviews of each season, backed by statistics and pen-portraits of players.

Unofficial Soccer Yearbook 1998/99 for Supporters of Celtic, Dempsey Parr, 1998 [One of the 'Superclubs' series]

BOARDROOM/ADMINISTRATION:

Brown, Jock: *Celtic-Minded*, 510 Days in Paradise, Mainstream Publishing, 1999

Caldwell, Allan: *The McCann Years* the Inside Story of Celtic's Revolution, Mainstream Publishing, 1999

Caldwell, Allan: *Sack the Board!* Celtic: the End of a Dynasty, Mainstream Publishing, 1994 [Chronicle of the end of the 'Family' control of Celtic F.C.]

Kelly, Michael: *Paradise Lost* the Struggle for Celtic's Soul, Canongate, 1994 [a former director's account of events leading to the 1994 McCann takeover]

Low, David & Shennan, Francis: *Rebels in Paradise* the Inside Story of the Battle for Celtic Football Club, Mainstream Publishing, 1994 [Events leading to the McCann takeover in 1994]

'CLEAN SWEEP' (1966/67):

Celtic Year of Triumph (a Weekly News Special, published by D.C. Thomson, 1967) [Pictorial review of the 1966/67 season, as a brochure]

Peebles, Ian: *Celtic Triumphant* Stanley Paul, 1967 [a journalist's account of the all-conquering 1966/67 season]

Traynor, John & Griffin, Tony: *A Season in the Sun* Celtic's Wonder Year of 1966/67, Lion Books, 1992

COLOURING BOOK:

The Official Celtic Colouring Book Grange Communications Ltd. 2000 [Colouring-in book for children]

DIRECTORY:

Celtic – Directory of Services Celtic F.C. 1997 [a comprehensive guide to Celtic F.C: stadium, supporters' clubs, ticketing etc]

THE DOUBLE
LEAGUE AND SCOTTISH CUP:

Adams, Jack: *My Team, Celtic* Collins, 1972 [Pictorial review of 1971/72 season]

Champions Celtic Season 1976/77 (a Celtic Player pool publication, 1977, printed as a brochure)

Celtic, a Celebration – the Players' Own Account of the Centenary League-and-Cup Winning Season, John Donald, 1988

EUROPE:

50 Years of the European Cup and Champions' League Pineapple Books, 2005

Boyle, Jack: *Celtic in European Competition* 2004

Celtic – 40 Years in Europe History Newspapers, 2006

Celtic in European Competition 1962–2003 (published by author, and available only from Kollectables, 51 Parnie Street, Glasgow G1 5 LU) [Brochure containing reports of all Celtic's European matches from the outset, up to and including the UEFA Cup final in Seville, and with statistical appendix]

Celtic! Britain's Best – a Souvenir of Celtic's Magnificent Season (Promotional Agency Ltd in association with Celtic's First-Team players, 1970) [Brochure covering Celtic's 1969/70 European Cup campaign]

Cuddihy, Paul & Sullivan, Joe (editors): *The Road to Seville* (Celtic F.C. Ltd. 2003) [an account of Celtic's 2002/03 UEFA Cup campaign]

Dougan, Andy: *The Lisbon Lions*, a Celebration of the European Cup Campaign 1967, Virgin Books, 1967

Alex Gordon/Billy McNeill and others: *The Lisbon Lions the Real, Inside Story*, Black and White Publishing, 2007

The Lions' Roar (Pixall, Corunna House, 1103 Argyle Street, Glasgow G3 8ND) [Pen-pictures of the 1967 European Cup winners and memories of the final, printed as a brochure]

McCarra, Kevin & Woods, Pat: *One Afternoon in Lisbon* Mainstream Publishing, 1988 [Celtic's road to winning the European Cup]

McColl, Graham: *Celtic in Europe* – From the 60s to Seville, Mainstream Publishing, 2003

Smith, Anna/Howden, Simon: *Over and Over – the Story of Seville*, Daily Record, 2003

FICTION:

Montgomery, Douglas: *On Their Way to Lisbon*, Seanachaidh, 1989 [a comic account of six fans on their ways to Lisbon in 1967]

HISTORY:

Archer, Ian: *Celtic* Hamlyn, 1988

Campbell, Tom: *Celtic's Paranoia. . . All in the Mind?* Fort Publishing Ltd, 2001

Campbell, Tom: *Glasgow Celtic 1945 – 1970* Civic Press, 1970

Campbell, Tom & Woods, Pat: *Celtic Football Club 1887 – 1967* Tempus Publishing Ltd, 1998, [Photographs tracing the first 80 years of the club's history]

Campbell, Tom & Woods, Pat: *Dreams and Songs to Sing* Mainstream Publishing, 1996 – updated edition with new material by Tom Campbell, 1999

Campbell, Tom & Woods, Pat: *The Glory and the Dream*: the History of Celtic F.C. 1887 -1986, Mainstream Publishing, updated edition in paperback published by Grafton, 1987

Campbell, Tom & Woods, Pat: *Rhapsody in Green*: Great Celtic Moments, Mainstream Publishing, 1990

(ed) Tom Campbell: *Ten Days that Shook Celtic* (essays about significant events in Celtic's history), Fort Publishing, 2005

Canning, Patrick and Tommy: *The Will to Win!* The Illustrated History of Glasgow Celtic, Mainstream Publishing, 1988

Celtic Glasgow/Benfica Lisbonne [edition L.G.C.E.Sa, 1989] (Combined Celtic/Benfica brochure in 'Les grands Clubs Europeens' series, Swiss/French production)

Celtic – a History from 1925 Historic Newspapers, 2006

Celtic – a Newspaper History Historic Newspapers, 2007

Craig, Jim: *A Lion Looks Back* John Donald, 1998 [The ex-Celt's history of the club from origins in 1887, including an account of his own part in that history]

Forsyth, Roddy: *Fields of Green* Unforgettable Celtic Days, Mainstream Publishing, 1996

Gordon, Alex: *Celtic* Purnell, 1988

Great Moments in the History of Celtic Historic Newspapers, 2006

Guidi, Mark: *The Inner Sanctum* (the story of Celtic's 1997/98 season), Mainstream Publishing, 2008

Handley, James. E.: *The Celtic Story* Stanley Paul, 1960

Kelly, Sir Robert: *Celtic* Hay, Nisbet, and Miller, 1970

Lunney, Paul: *Celtic FC 50 Classic Matches* Tempus, 2007

McColl, Graham: *Celtic, the Official Illustrated History* Hamlyn, 1995; updated in 1996 and 1998

McColl, Graham and Sheridan, George: *The Essential History of Celtic* Headline Book Publishing, 2002

McNee, Gerald: *The Story of Celtic* an Official History, Stanley Paul, 1978

Maley, Willie: *The Story of the Celtic* (published by the author, 1939 and reprinted in facsimile edition by Desert Island Books, 1996)

Marshall, Stuart: *Celtic Football Legends 1888-1938* Stenlake publishing, 1998. [Collection of photographs, postcards, cigarette cards etc illustrating the history of the club to 1938]

Potter, David: *Walk On – Celtic Since McCann* Fort Publishing, 2003

Paradise in the Making, Celtic F.C. 1991/92 [eight-page potted history of the club in booklet form].

Traynor, John C.: *The Celtic Story* an Official History, Grange Communications Ltd, 1998

Traynor, John C: *Former Glories, Future Dreams* Grange Comm. Ltd, 2000

Wilson, Brian: *Celtic, a Century with Honour* – the Official Centenary History, Collins, 1988

Wilson, Mike: *Celtic*, Hodder & Stoughton/Basic Skills Agency, 1998 [Forty-page outline of the club's history].

HUMOUR:

Munro, Michael: *The 'Old Firm' Joke Book* Canongate, 1997

Shields, Tom: *The Celtic/Rangers Joke Book* Famedram Publishers Ltd., 1978

LEAGUE CHAMPIONSHIP:

Into Europe as Champions Celtic Success Souvenir, (a 'Weekly News' Special, published by D.C. Thomson, 1966) [brochure covering Celtic's 1965/66 league season, and also League Cup triumph]

Celtic: World League Record Holders 1965-1974 Souvenir (Celtic F.C. Supporters' Association, 1975 brochure)

Dougan, Andy: *The Glory, Glory Bhoys* Mainstream Publishing Company, 1998 [covers League Championship of 1997/98 and League Cup triumph]

Scottish Premier League Winners 1997/98 – Celtic Dempsey Parr, 1988

LEAGUE CUP:

Burns, Peter and Woods, Pat: *Oh, Hampden in the Sun. . .* Mainstream Publishing, 1997 [the 1957 '7-1' triumph told within its social context]

Potter, David W: *Celtic in the League Cup* Tempus Publishing Ltd, 2002 [Celtic's experience of the competition from its outset (1946/47) up to and including season 2001/02]

MANAGERS:

Barnes, John and Winter, Henry: *John Barnes, the Biography* Headline Book Publishing, 1999; updated edition 2000

Barnes, John and Hill, Dave: *Out of His Skin, the John Barnes Phenomenon* Faber & Faber, 1989 [Biography written while Barnes was still a player, years before he became Celtic's manager]

Brady, Liam: *So Far So Good. . ., a Decade in Football* Stanley Paul, 1980. [an auto-biography when he was a player, and years before he became Celtic's manager]

Campbell, Tom and Potter, David: *Jock Stein, the Celtic Years* Mainstream Publishing, 1998

Crampsey, Bob: *Mr. Stein*, Mainstream Publishing, 1986; republished in 1987 by Signet under the title *Jock Stein: the Master*

Gallacher, Ken: *Jock Stein, the Authorised Biography*, Stanley Paul, 1988

McColl, Graham: *Celtic – the Jock Stein Years* Chameleon Books/ Memorabilia Pack Company, 1999 [contains replica souvenirs from the time]

McColl, Graham: *The Head Bhoys* Celtic's Managers, Mainstream Publishing, 2002

Macpherson, Archie: *Jock Stein – the Definitive Biography*, 2004

Montgomery, Alex: *Martin O'Neill, the Biography* Virgin Books, 2003

Moynihan, Leo: *Gordon Strachan, the Biography*, Virgin, 2007

Alex Murphy: *The Lisbon Lion – the Book of Jock Stein* Naked Guide Ltd, 2007

Potter, David: *Willie Maley – The Man Who Made Celtic* Tempus Publishing, 2003

Smith, Anna and McCarthy, David: *The Martin O'Neill Story* 'Daily Record' 2001

Telfer, Glenn: *Jock Stein, a Scots Life* Argyll Publishing, 1997 [a Scots language biography]

Strachan, Gordon: *My Life in Football* Little Brown Book Company, 2006

See also the following:
The Story of the Celtic Willie Maley, 1939. Also, consult the 'Player Biographies' for Jimmy McGrory, Billy McNeill, and David Hay.

MASCOT:

Hardie, Maureen: *'Hoopy' Comes to Paradise* Celtic F.C. Ltd, 2003 [Adventures of the club mascot, 'Hoopy the Huddle Hound' – suitable for children aged 3 to 7 years, or supporters young at heart]

MEMORABILIA:

The Celtic F.C. Memorabilia Pack, Nostalgic Pack Co., 1992 [Reproductions of programmes for noted matches, of sheet music for 'Celtic Song' etc.

MISCELLANEOUS:

(ed) Bradley, Joseph M: *Celtic Minded* (essays on religion, politics, society, identity and football), Argyll Publishing, 2004

(ed) Bradley, Joseph M: *Celtic Minded 2* (essays on Celtic Football Culture and Identity) Argyll Publishing, 2006

Daly, Raymond / Warfield, Derek *Celtic and Ireland in Song and Story* 2008

McColl, Graham: *The Little Book of Celtic* Carlton Books, 2005

Morgan, Steve: *Celtic – a Rough Guide* Rough Guide Ltd., 2005

Paradise Lost? Or Regained? A Community Group Study of the Impact of Celtic F.C. on the Economy and Environment of the East End of Glasgow, [published by Action for Training and Employment Rights, 1991 as a booklet]

Russell, Douglas: *The Official Little Book of Celtic* Grange Publications, 2005

White, John : *The Celtic Miscellany* Carlton, 2006

Worrall, Frank : *Celtic -United* (Links between Celtic and Manchester United), Mainstream, 2007

Inside the Hoops, Cre8, 2006

The Best of the Celtic View, Headline, 2007

OLD FIRM:

'*The Herald*' *Book of Old Firm Games* a Complete Record of All Old Firm Matches Fought Since the Second World War, Canongate Books Ltd., 1995. [Match reports, most abridged].

Macpherson, Archie: *Blue and Green, Rangers v Celtic*: a Personal look at the Glasgow Derby, 1949-1989, BBC Books, 1989.

Murray, Bill: *Glasgow's Giants: 100 Years of the Old Firm* Mainstream, 1988.

Murray, Bill: *The Old Firm*: Sectarianism, Sport, and Society in Scotland, John Donald, 1984; revised and updated edition, 2000.

Murray, Bill: *The Old Firm in the New Age* Celtic and Rangers Since the Souness Revolution, Mainstream Publishing, 1998.

Bill Murray: *Bhoys, Bears, and Bigotry* Mainstream 2003

PLAY / DRAMA

'*The Celtic Story*' – Teachers' Resource Pack for use with Secondary Schools, Balcony Productions, 1998, [published in conjunction with the stage play].

PLAYER BIOGRAPHIES:

Aitken, Roy and Cameron, Alex: *Feed the Bear!*: the Roy Aitken Story, Mainstream Publishing, 1987

The Packie Bonner Story Copperfield Publications Ltd., 1991. [printed as a brochure]

Black, Jim: *Jinky, the biography of Jimmy Johnstone* Sphere 2007

Burns, Tommy and Keevins, Hugh: *Twists and Turns, the Tommy Burns Story* Sportsprint, 1989

di Canio, Paolo and Marcotti, Gabriele: *Paolo di Canio, the Autobiography* Collins Willow, 2000

Cascarino, Tony and Kimmage, Paul: *Full Time, the Secret Life of Tony Cascarino* Simon and Schuster/TownHouse, 2000

Cooney, Brian: *Celtic's Lost Legend – George Connelly* Black and White Publishing 2007

Crerand, Pat and Peebles, Ian: *On Top with United* Stanley Paul, 1969

Crerand. Pat: *Never Turn the Other Cheek* Harper Scott 2007

Dalglish, Kenny and Gallacher, Ken: *King Kenny, an Autobiography* Stanley Paul, 1982

Dalglish, Kenny and Winter, Henry: *Dalglish, My Autobiography* Hodder and Stoughton, 1996; updated edition by Coronet in 1997. This work also appeared in abridged form as a two cassette audio-book, Hodder Headline, 1996

The Kenny Dalglish Soccer Annual: Brown Watson, 1979. [includes details of his Celtic career]

Docherty, Tommy: *Soccer from the Shoulder* Stanley Paul, 1960

Docherty, Tommy and Peskett, Roy: *Tommy Docherty Speaks* Pelham, 1967

Docherty, Tommy and Henderson, Derek: *Call the Doc* Hamlyn, 1981

Docherty, Tommy and Clarke, Brian: *Docherty* a Biography of Tommy Docherty, Kingswood, 1991

Docherty, Tommy: *The Doc – My Story* Headline 2006

Kelly, Stephen F: *Dalglish* Headline, 1992

Gemmell, Tommy: *The Big Shot* Stanley Paul, 1968

Glanvill, Rick: *The Wright Stuff, the Unauthorised Biography of Ian Wright* Virgin Books, 1996 [covers his pre-Celtic career only]

Greig, Tom: *My Search for Celtic's John* (the biography of John Thomson) Ogilvie 2003

Guidi, Mark and Grahame, Ewing: *You Are My Larsson* a Tribute to Celtic's Goal Machine, Daily Record and Sunday Mail, 2001

Hartson, John: *John Hartson, the Autobiography* Orion 2006

Hay, David and Gallacher, Ken: *Paradise Lost, the David Hay Story* Mainstream Publishing, 1988

Hay, Roy: *James 'Dun' Hay* (life of an early Celtic player and captain) Sports and Editorial Services 2004

Johnston, Mo and Young, Chick: *Mo, the Maurice Johnston Story* Mainstream Publishing, 1988

Johnstone, Jimmy: *Fire in My Boots* Stanley Paul, 1969

Johnstone, Jimmy and McCann, Jim: *Jinky – Now and Then*, the Jimmy Johnstone Story, Mainstream Publishing, 1988

Jordan, Joe: *Behind the Dream* Hodder & Stoughton 2004

Larsson, Henrik and Sylvester, Mark: *A Season in Paradise* the Official Authorised Diary of Henrik Larsson's Glorious Season, BBC Worldwide Ltd, 2001

Lambert, Paul and Clark, Graham: *A Bhoy's Own Story* Mainstream Publishing, 1998

Lennon, Neil: *Neil Lennon – Man and Bhoy* Harper Sport 2006

Lennox, Bobby: *30 Miles From Paradise* Headline 2007

Lennox, Bobby and McNee, Gerry: *A Million Miles for Celtic* Stanley Paul, 1982

McAvennie, Frank and McKay, Reg: *Scoring* Canongate, 2003

McCarthy, Mick and Nugent, Matthew: *Captain Fantastic*, O'Brien, 1990

McClair, Brian: *Odd Man Out, a Player's Diary* Andre Deutsch, 1997

McColl, Graham: *Tommy Gemmell* Lion Heart Virgin Books 2004

McGrain, Danny and Patience, Bob: *Celtic, My Team* Souvenir Press, 1978

McGrain, Danny and Keevins, Hugh: *In Sunshine and in Shadow* John Donald, 1987

Cairney, John: *Heroes Are Forever* (the life and times of Jimmy McGrory) Mainstream 2005

McGrory, Jimmy and McNee, Gerry: *A Lifetime in Paradise* [published by the authors, 1975]

McNeill, Billy: *For Celtic and Scotland* Pelham Books, 1966

McNeill, Billy and Cameron, Alex: *Back to Paradise*, Mainstream Publishing, 1988

Billy McNeill: *Hail Caesar* (life of Celtic's near-legendary captain) Headline 2004

Macari, Lou: *United, We Shall Not Be Moved* Souvenir Press, 1976

Mowbray, Tony and Drury, Paul: *Kissed By an Angel* Bookman Projects Ltd., 1995

Murdoch, Bobby and Herron, Allan: *All the Way with Celtic*, Souvenir Press, 1970

Nicholas, Charlie and Gallacher, Ken: *Charlie, an Autobiography* Stanley Paul, 1986

Petrov, Stylian: *You Can Call Me Stan* Mainstream 2005

David Potter: *Bobby Murdoch, Different Class* Empire Publications 2003

Potter, David: *Jimmy Delaney – the Stuff of Legend* Breedon Books 2006

Potter, David W: *The Mighty Atom, the Life and Times of Patsy Gallacher,* The Parrs Wood Press, 2000

David Potter: *The Mighty Quinn* (the biography of Celtic's legendary centre forward) Tempus 2005

Rough, Alan and Brown, Stewart: *Rough at the Top* John Donald, 1988. [two chapters dealing with his signing and brief career with Celtic]

Alan Rough: *The Rough and the Smooth* Headline 2006

Rowan, Marie: *Dan Doyle* (the life of an early Celtic maverick) Black and White Publishing

Simpson, Ronnie and Herron, Allan: *Sure It's a Grand Old Team to Play For* Souvenir Press, 1967

Saffer, David: *Bobby Collins, 'the Wee Barra'* Virgin Books 2004

Stanton, Pat and Pia, Simon: *'The Quiet Man', the Pat Stanton Story* Sportsprint, 1989

Stubbs, David: *Charlie Nicholas, the Adventures of 'Champagne Charlie'* Boxtree, 1997

Sullivan, Joe: *7: The Official Tribute to Henrik Larsson* Celtic 2003

A Tribute to John Thomson: (John Thomson Memorial Committee, 2001, produced as a brochure)

Tully, Charlie: *Passed to You,* Stanley Paul, 1958

Worrall, Frank: *Roy Keane, Red Man Walking* Mainstream Publishing 2006

Wright, Ian: *Mr. Wright* Collins Willow, 1996, updated 1997 [strictly pre-Celtic career]

Zeman, Michael and Sullivan, Joe: *Lubo Moravcik, a Life Less Ordinary* Celtic F.C. 2001

Zeman, Michael *Lubomir Moravcik* Celtic 2001

PLAYER BIOGRAPHIES/ PEN PICTURES:

Celtic, Your Pictorial Guide to Parkhead's Heroes Magpie Books Ltd., 1996, Superteams' Series, produced as a brochure

Celtic All-Time Greats Parkhead Legends, Siena, 1997, reprinted by Parragon, 1998

Celtic, the Pride of Parkhead Profiled Siena, 1997 – Superteams' Series, produced as a brochure

Hayes, Dean *Celtic: 100 Heroes of the Modern Game,* Mercat Press, 2007

Keevins, Hugh: *Celtic Greats* John Donald, 1988

Keevins, Hugh: *More Celtic Greats* John Donald, 1990

Lunney, Paul: *Celtic F.C. 100 Greats* Tempus, 2005

MacBride, Eugene: *Talking with Celtic, 2001* Breedon Books, 2001 [interviews with ex-Celts]

Potter, David: *Celtic's Cult Heroes* Know the Score, 2008

Traynor, John C: *Celtic Official All-Time Greats* Grange Communications Ltd, Lomond Books, 1999

PROGRAMMES:

McGouran, Tom: *A Collector's Guide to Celtic Home and Away Programmes 1946/47 to 1987/88* (Competitive Matches, (published by author, 1988 and updated in 1995, taking the period covered up to and including season 1994/95)

McGouran, Tom: *A Collector's Guide to Celtic Home and Away Friendlies 1946/47 to 1988/89* (published by author)

QUIZ BOOKS:

A Celtic Legends Quiz Book, Sports Event Management, Aberdeen, 1995

White, John D.T.: *The Hoops Quiz Book* 2008

Woods, Pat: *The Celtic Quiz Book* Mainstream Publishing, 1987

REFERENCE:

Campbell, Tom/Sheridan George: *Celtic, the Encyclopaedia* Argyll Publishing, 2008

Campbell, Tom and Woods, Pat: *A Celtic A-Z* Greenfield Press, 1992

Crampsey, Robert A: *Now You Know About Celtic* Argyll Publishing, 1994. [based on the well-known *Evening Times* Question-and-Answer column]

Docherty, David: *The Celtic Football Companion* John Donald, 1986 [Line-ups and other statistics from 1946/47 to 1985/86 inclusive]

Lerman, Richard and Brown, David: *The Bhoys, Day-to-Day Life at Celtic Park* Mainstream Publishing, 1998 [Use of diary-format, with listing of landmarks in club's history]

Lunney, Paul: *Celtic, a Complete Record 1888-1982* Breedon Books, 1992 [Statistical coverage, line-ups, scorers etc]

MacBride, Eugene, O'Connor, Martin, and Sheridan, George: *An Alphabet of the Celts: a Complete Who's Who of Celtic F.C.* ACL and Polar Publishing, 1994

McColl, Graham /Sheridan, George *The Essential History of Celtic* W.H. Smith 2002

McDermott, Neil: *The Old Firm Guide – Celtic versus Rangers, a Background to Football's Most Celebrated Contest*, Famedram, 1985

Mason, Chris: *Celtic Packed With Information About the Bhoys*, Parragon, 1998. [one of the 'Factfile' series – details on Celtic's history, statistics etc.]

Powter, David: *Celtic F.C. – the 25 Year Record* 1970/71 to 1994/95 Seasons, Soccer Book Publishing Ltd, 1995

Woods, Pat: *Celtic F.C. Facts and Figures 1888-1981*, (Celtic Supporters Association, 1981)

SCOTTISH CUP:

Potter, David: *Our Bhoys Have Won the Cup* 30 Times Scottish Cup Winners, John Donald Publishing Ltd., 1996 [the story of Celtic's triumphs in the competition]

SUPPORTERS:

10 (published by the author writing under the pseudonym 'The Andy Thom Experience' in 1998). [a supporter's view of the Celtic campaign that prevented Rangers winning 10-in-a-row league titles]

Bennie, David: *Not Playing for Celtic, Another Paradise Lost* Mainstream Publishing Ltd, 1995, and updated 1998

Boyle, Raymond: *Faithful Through and Through*, a Survey of Celtic's Most Committed Supporters (National Identity research Unit, Glasgow Polytechnic, 1991)

Celtic Supporters' Association *The Greatest Fans in the World* UFB Publications 2004

Celtic Supporters Club, Carfin – *50th Anniversary Brochure, 1998* [a potted history of the Carfin CSC]

Cuddihy, Paul and Sullivan, Joe [editors]: *Celtic Views* Stories from the Celtic Writing Competition, Celtic F.C. Ltd, 2002. [a collection of fans' stories and poems on 'anything to do with Celtic'].

Dillon, Des: *I'm no a Billy, He's a Dan* Lauth Press 2006

Divers, Jim: *A History of the Celtic F.C. Supporters Association* (Celtic F.C. Supporters Association, 1995, and printed as a brochure)

Larkin, Paul: *The Football Club – Celtic First, Last and Always* (published by the author, 2002.

McGlone, Matt: *Emotionally Celtic* G.D. Communications Ltd, East Kilbride, 1995

McNee, Gerald: *And You'll Never Walk Alone* Impulse Publications, 1972 [Celtic fans' experiences of following the club in Europe]

O'Kane, James: *The Celtic F.C. Supporters' Club, Greenock, Golden Jubilee* – 50 Years of Faithful Support 1945-1995 (Greenock CSC, 1995, and printed as a brochure)

O'Kane, John: *Celtic Soccer Crew* (Memoirs of a Celtic Casual), Pennant Books, 2006

Quinn, John: *Jungle Tales* Celtic Memories of an Epic Stand, Mainstream Publishing, 1994, and re-issued in 1998 with additional chapter

Smith, Anna and Houston, Simon: Over and Over, the Story of Seville 'Daily Record', 2003 [the fans' story of the 2003 UEFA Cup final]

Walsh, Stephen: *Voices of the Old Firm* Mainstream Publishing, 1995. [Old Firm fans recount their memories].

TREBLE:

McKenna, Ron and Alba, Carlos: *Keep the Faith*, the Story of Celtic's Historic Treble-winning Season 2000-01, Mainstream Publishing, 2001

TROPHY ROOM:

Traynor, John and Russell, Douglas: *The Glory of the Green: the Celtic Trophies* Holmes McDougall, 1991

WORLD CLUB CHAMPIONSHIP:

Belton, Brian: *The Battle of Montevideo*, Tempus, 2008

Campbell, Tom: *Tears in Argentina* (Celtic's misadventures in the World Club Championship), Fort Publishing, 2006

BOOTS

Players' footwear has changed dramatically over the decades.

The most famous of the early boots was 'the Hotspur' and players used to buy them a size smaller than their regular shoes, and then stand in the bath wearing them to make the leather expand and mold to their feet. Jackie Milburn, the famous Newcastle United centre-forward, used to wear his new boots down the coal pit and work them in while standing in pools of water.

John Collins, the Celtic midfielder, favoured 'The Predator', and developed expertise in curling free kicks round defensive 'walls'.

BOXERS

At least two World Heavyweight Champions have visited Celtic Park: 'Gentleman Jim' Corbett – whose parents came from Mayo – performed the ceremonial kick-off prior to a match against Hibernian on 26 May 1894, and Mohammed Ali was introduced to the players during a training session in the 1970s.

Scott Harrison, the troubled Scottish fighter, was invited to make the half-time draw at one match.

The tragic Benny Lynch – for three years the holder of the World Flyweight title from the Gorbals and dead at 33 from the effects of alcoholism – was a keen Celtic supporter and fought at Celtic Park against Jim Warnock of Belfast before a crowd of 20,000 on 2 June 1937. It was a preliminary for the World Flyweight Championship, but Lynch weighed in at over the eight stone four pound limit – and eventually lost narrowly on points over fifteen rounds to the Ulsterman from the Shankill.

BRAKE CLUBS

These could be described as the original supporters' clubs.

Some early followers of Celtic organised themselves into groups and travelled to matches on large horse-drawn wagonettes which could hold up to twenty-five supporters. Often these 'brakes', after gathering near the city centre, would form a lively procession as they made their noisy way to local fixtures.

In a manner still followed by many modern-day supporters' buses, the brake clubs identified themselves with a banner (or plaque) which contained a representation of a favourite player. Baird's Bar, it is believed, still displays that of St. Mary's (Calton) which depicts Tom Maley.

Perhaps most unlike present-day supporters' clubs the brake clubs grew out of the League of the Cross, a Glasgow temperance society – and drinking was not approved of by most of the members.

They were idealistic especially at the start and contributed greatly to Catholic charities. In fact, they advocated the fielding of an all-Catholic side to represent Celtic (1897); they pressed for a reduction to their admission charges on the grounds that they were the most loyal of Celtic supporters and, on principle, boycotted a 1908 Scottish Cup tie with Rangers at Ibrox in protest at the doubling of the admission price by the home club.

Their decline started in the early 1920s

Brake clubs were the original supporters' clubs travelling to matches in large horse-drawn wagons. This early photo (opposite) from 1896 shows St Mary's (Calton) with their banner of Tom Maley. This same banner is presently displayed in Baird's Bar in the Gallowgate

with the introduction of motorised transport, and the easy availability of the train as a method of travelling to fixtures. However, by then the once-idealistic brake clubs had also acquired a reputation for disorderly – and drunken – behaviour.

All that remained of the brake clubs, once the most loyal and respectable of Celtic followers, was a reputation for hooliganism.

BREAKS

Jimmy Delaney, Celtic's sprightly outside right, fractured his left arm badly when tackled against Arbroath at Celtic Park on 1 April 1939. His injury was so serious that the hospital surgeon considered amputation. Delaney eventually recovered but was out of the game for almost two seasons.

Henrik Larsson suffered a serious leg

break against Olympique Lyonnais on 21 October 1999 in a UEFA Cup tie. The effect of his absence contributed to the eventual sacking of manager John Barnes. Henrik was also able to recover quickly from a broken jaw, suffered against Livingston at Celtic Park in 2003.

In the 1978/79 season Celtic played Morton at Cappielow on 23 December 1978 and did not play another league fixture until 3 March 1979. In December Celtic were struggling in the championship, but the enforced break – caused by a severe winter – did a great deal of good as the Parkhead men gained the league flag with a memorable last-day victory over Rangers on 21 May.

In the 1981/82 season an official midwinter break was introduced into the Scottish Premier Division. Celtic took full advantage by eventually winning the title.

Bobby Evans, Celtic captain in 1956/57
After the North American summer tour
Evans frequently played with his shirt
outside his shorts

C

CAMBUSLANG

Cambuslang were a redoubtable club in the early days of football in Scotland. Celtic played them four times in league competition:

1890/91
Aug 30 H 5-2 Dowds (3), Crossan (2);
Mar 7 A 1-3 Madden

1891/92
Jan 30 A 4-0 McMahon, Brady, Coleman, Campbell
Apr 16 H 3-1 Dowds, McCallum, Campbell

In the dying months of the ancien regime (1994) at Celtic Park the name 'Cambuslang' turned up again as the possible site of a new stadium for Celtic, but the scheme disappeared without trace as Fergus McCann took over.

'CAPS'

The following Celtic players have made most international appearances while on Celtic's books:

'Packie' Bonner (Ireland) 80

Paul McStay (Scotland) 76

Tommy Boyd (Scotland) 66

Danny McGrain (Scotland) 62

Roy Aitken (Scotland) 50

Henrik Larsson (Sweden) 49

Kenny Dalglish (Scotland) 47

Bobby Evans (Scotland) 45

Johann Mjallby (Sweden) 40

John Collins (Scotland) 32

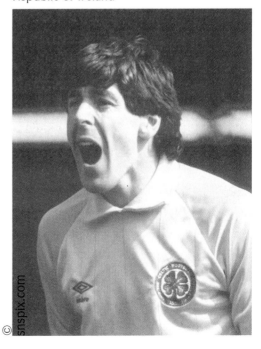

Pat 'Packie' Bonner is Celtic's most capped player having played 80 times for the Republic of Ireland

©snspix.com

CAPTAINS

It is considered an honour to be appointed captain of a famous club and Celtic have had leaders on and off the pitch who have measured up to the responsibility. James Kelly, an attacking centre-half, was signed from Renton and became Celtic's very first captain. Three members of the McStay family have been appointed captains of Celtic, but perhaps the most successful of all is Billy McNeil who, as captain, led Celtic to success in six League Cups, seven Scottish Cups and nine League Championships – as well as being the first British skipper to hold the European Cup in his hands.

Some of the more celebrated Celtic captains are listed here:

James Kelly	1888–1897
Jimmy Hay	1907–1911
'Sunny Jim' Young	1911–1916
Willie Cringan	1916–1923
Willie McStay	1923–1929
Jimmy McStay	1929–1934
Willie Lyon	1935–1940
John McPhail	1947–1952
Jock Stein	1952–1957
Bobby Evans	1956–1957
Bertie Peacock	1957–1961
Billy McNeill	1963–1975
Kenny Dalglish	1975–1977
Danny McGrain	1977–1987
Roy Aitken	1987–1990
Paul McStay	1990–1997
Tom Boyd	1997–2001
Paul Lambert	2001–2004
Neil Lennon	2004–2007
Stephen McManus	2007 –

'CELTIC'

Sometimes Celtic are referred to as 'Glasgow Celtic' – wrongly. However, there have been a number of Scottish clubs at junior level who share the name: Bannockburn Celtic, Blantyre Celtic, Buckhaven Celtic, Buckpool Celtic, Edinburgh Celtic, Inverness Celtic, and Paisley Celtic.

CELTIC BOYS' CLUB

Celtic Boys' Club had its origins around 1965 when a businessman Jim Torbett organised and ran the Mount Street Boys' Club in Glasgow's Maryhill district. For training and fixtures the club used the local Ruchill Park (just north of Partick Thistle's Firhill). Torbett later asked permission of Bob Kelly to use the name 'Celtic' to replace 'Mount Street'. Permission was eventually granted although there never was an official connection between Celtic and the Boys' Club.

The Celtic Boys' Club, wearing the famous Hoops on the pitch and smart dark-green blazers and grey flannels on match days, went from strength to strength in attracting players, winning trophies, and supplying many senior teams with potentially good players.

Celtic captains (opposite, clockwise from top left) Jimmy McStay, Jock Stein, Stephen McManus, Tom Boyd, Paul McStay, Neil Lennon

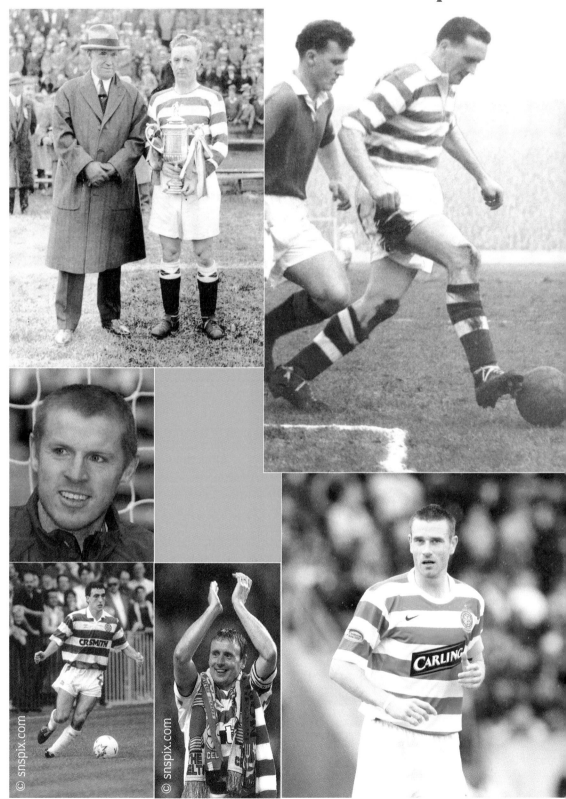

As Celtic and other clubs began to set up their own youth teams, the influence of the Celtic Boys' Club was diluted although it continued to provide a route into professional football for many youngsters.

Graduates of the organisation (not all of whom actually played for Celtic) include the following:
Roy Aitken, Owen Archdeacon;
Jim Beattie, Tom Boyd, Jimmy Boyle, Alan Brazil, Gerry Britton,
Mark Brown; Kenny Campbell,
Jim Casey, Peter Cheney, John Collins, Ronnie Coyle, Danny Crainie,
Gerry Creaney; Raymond Deans, Billy Dolan, Mark Donaghy;
Peter Feeney, Steve Fulton; Peter Grant; David Hay; Steve Kean, David Kenny; Ray Lorimer; Sean McBride,
Chris McCart, George McCluskey,
John McCluskey, Tommy McEntaggart, Dougie McGuire, Jim McInally,
Tosh McKinlay, Mark McNally,
Paul McStay, Raymond McStay,
Willie McStay, Peter Mackie,
David Marshall, Alex Mathie, Joe Miller, Dougie Mills, David Moyes, Jim Murphy; Pat Nevin, Charlie Nicholas,
Paul Nicholas; Brian O'Neil; Alex Rae, Mark Reid, Andy Ritchie;
Tony Shepherd, Peter Shields;
John Traynor; Derek Whyte.

A possible all-star team (4-3-3) might be

David Marshall,
David Moyes, Roy Aitken, Derek Whyte, Tosh McKinlay,
Paul McStay, Peter Grant, John Collins, Pat Nevin, Charlie Nicholas, Owen Archdeacon.

CELTIC CROSS

Celtic were founded after a meeting in St. Mary's Hall in Abercromby Street in the Calton. When the building was razed after demolition, a Celtic Cross was designed out of the stone. It was presented to the club by the Roman Catholic diocese at the time of the inauguration of the statue of Brother Walfrid outside the ground on 5th November 2005.

CELTIC'S FIRST ELEVEN

An eleven chosen to represent the new club turned out for Celtic against Rangers Swifts on 28 May 1888 (a Monday) was comprised of players who, although 'attached' to other clubs, were free as amateurs to join the new Glasgow club.

It was a happy occasion, as Celtic won 5-2, with Neil McCallum scoring the first goal in front of a splendid crowd of 2,000.

After the match both teams and their committees were whisked down to St. Mary's Hall for a Social Evening with food and entertainment.

CELTIC:
Dolan (Drumpellier), Pearson (Carfin Shamrock), McLaughlin (Govan Whitefield), W. Maley (Cathcart), Kelly (Renton), Murray (Cambuslang Hibs), McCallum (Renton), T. Maley (Cathcart), Madden (Dumbarton), Dunbar (Edinburgh Hibs), Gorevin (Govan Whitefield).

CELTIC LADIES

This all-female team was formed in June 2007 and became members of the Scottish

Women's Premier League. The first game was lost 1-2 to Hamilton at Barrowfield before an attendance of 200 on 12 August 2007. The first-ever Celtic Ladies team was:

O'Donnell, Cheshire, Davies, Dalziel, Jones, Watt (Quigley), Murray, McCallum, Cunningham, Curley (McInally), Stokes.

Becky Stokes had the signal honour of scoring the first goal for the Celtic Ladies. Ten days later, in their next match, the side accomplished its first win – a 4-3 result over Kilmarnock on 22 August at Glasgow Green.

An early meeting of Celtic Supporters' Association

CELTIC PARK CUP FINALS

The Scottish Cup final has been played at Celtic Park on five different occasions:

1902: Celtic 0, Hibernian 1
1903: Rangers 2, Hearts 0
1913: Falkirk 2, Raith Rovers 0
1993: Rangers 2, Aberdeen 1
1998: Hearts 2, Rangers 1

CELTIC SUPPORTERS' ASSOCIATION

The CSA was founded at a most unlikely time – in September 1944 while the Second World War was still raging on all fronts.

Celtic had virtually given up competing for the honours in wartime Scottish football (a period dominated by Rangers) and the supporters were most unhappy; in twenty-one Old Firm clashes, to take one example, Celtic had lost fifteen.

Willie Fanning, 27 years-old and a Celtic supporter, first thought of the concept as he witnessed Celtic lose by 6-2 to Hamilton Academical at Douglas Park. On 5 September he sent a letter to Waverley's column in the *Daily Record*, ending with these words: 'Would any Celtic supporters interested in a Supporters' Club please write me?' Although he received a substantial amount of mail, only fourteen people turned up at the first meeting which was held in Shettleston.

A steering committee was formed, Willie Fanning chosen as its president, and the idea took off. It received a boost when Waverley, probably the most respected journalist in the country at the time,

approved of the fledgling association's aims: 'to promote closer contact among the management, players and supporters, and to halt the decline of a once-great football club.'

The second meeting was held on 24 September 1944 at an Ancient Order of Hibernians' Hall and it was realised quickly that the building was not big enough for the crowds pouring into it. The meeting adjourned to an open space on Wishart Street, an air-raid shelter providing a make-shift platform.

The football club recognised the potential role that the Supporters' Association could play in achieving mutual objectives and were relieved that the CSA would not be discussing the merits and/or demerits of the team and its individual players. Willie Fanning stated: 'We are not emotionalists, flag-wavers, or bottle-throwers. We have the welfare of the club at heart to discuss any methods to raise the club from the degenerate state into which it has fallen.'

The first step was a practical one – to outfit the ball-boys at Celtic Park with uniforms. Celtic were able to provide the money but, in those days of rationing, members of the Association contributed clothing coupons. The uniform was a neat one: light-grey jerseys with a broad green band across the chest.

The first crisis was the proposed transfer of the club's star player Jimmy Delaney to Manchester United in February 1946. Delaney was acutely aware that he had a family to provide for and that wages in England were higher – and Celtic seemed unwilling to offer any great increase in wages. The Association attempted to mediate in the growing rift and were prepared to subsidise the player's wages themselves. . . but to no avail.

Within a year the Association had to confront the fact that Celtic Football Club, saddled with an ailing chairman (Tom White), was not capable of turning the football fortunes round. More in sorrow than in anger, the CSA tabled a list of rhetorical questions for the directors and shareholders to consider. It was a mature response to the continuing mediocrity at Parkhead.

The new organisation had already proved its expertise by giving a hand to other supporters' associations including those of Rangers, Clyde, Partick Thistle, Third Lanark, Falkirk and Kilmarnock. Similarly, it was the Celtic Supporters Association which instigated the Scottish Federation of Senior Supporters Association – the forerunner of the Scottish National Federation of Supporters Clubs. Unsurprisingly, Joe Regan, president of the CSA, was elected to a similar position within the national federation.

In accordance with the club's founding interest in charitable works, the Supporters Association embarked on a programme of helping the wounded servicemen recuperating at Erskine Hospital. Despite the handicap of operating within a nationwide system of rationing, the CSA was able to make many of the servicemen honorary members and to transport them – despite their serious wounds – free of charge to Celtic Park on match days. The club itself helped in the work by reserving two rows of seats immediately behind the directors' box for their use. After the match

Their finest hour – Celtic supporters at the UEFA Cup Final in Seville 2003

the servicemen were transported to 'a tea and social' in one of two local halls: the Orange Hall in Campbellfield Street (hired with no problems whatsoever) and Granny Black's Hall in Hart Street. The day out was rounded off frequently by famous Celtic players of the past dropping in at the venues to mingle with the servicemen.

By October 1946 the association had expanded to twelve branches in central Scotland. The Glasgow Branch, the first and largest, had swollen to gigantic proportions; for a day outing to the Trossachs in June 1946 it had to hire eleven coaches and limit its contingent to the 1947 international against England at Wembley to 650 applicants.

In the immediate post-war period most people still worked on Saturday mornings and the departure of buses from George Square was timed to be as late as possible. Journeys in the days before motorways and bypasses lasted much longer then, and the trip to Aberdeen was more akin to an expedition.

One feature of away-matches in Fife was the frequent visits to the graveyard in Cardenden to honour the memory of the Celtic goalkeeper John Thomson, fatally injured at Ibrox in September 1931.

Doubts about the behaviour of the supporters travelling on the coaches were quickly dispelled, as the report of the secretary of the Cowie (Stirlingshire) Branch suggests:

'Bus companies weren't too eager to do business, but one or two journeys without the expected rowdiness boosted the club high in their estimation. The custom of taking old-age pensioners and treating them to a seat, free bus ride, and the proverbial 'half and a pint' has also swayed a number of the community who had frowned with disdain with 'the wait-and-see-what-they-do' manner. The children of this district will also benefit by a Christmas treat. . . '

CENTENARY CUP

Celtic invited Cruzeiro Belo Horizonte of Brazil to participate in the club's centenary season by competing for the Centenary Cup at Celtic Park on 7 August 1988.

The Brazilian side, of whom so much had been expected, proved a disappointment and Celtic quickly established a two-goal lead within the opening twelve minutes with goals from Andy Walker and Frank McAvennie. Cruzeiro pulled one back one in twenty-five minutes from a penalty kick. Walker quickly restored Celtic's two-goal advantage but Cruzeiro were given another penalty kick for a handling offence. In the second half Andy Walker completed his hat-trick in sixty-eight minutes and Celtic coasted to a 4-2 win made easier when a Brazilian defender was ordered off.

The attendance was a splendid 41,659 who watched the contest in brilliant sunshine.Interestingly, Cruzeiro bought on Roberto Carlos as a substitute.

CHARITY CUP

The Glasgow Merchants' Charity Cup was introduced in the wake of a controversial Scottish Cup tie between Vale of Leven and Queen's Park in 1876. The Dunbartonshire side won the match, but Queen's Park were angered that the Vale of Leven players had used spikes on the soles of their boots – a practice outlawed at the time.

Relations between the two clubs became strained and a group of prominent Glasgow business men funded a trophy, the proceeds to go to charity. It was anticipated that the same two sides, the strongest in the country would contest the final and the occasion would be a profitable peace-making exercise. But Vale of Leven declined to play Queen's Park and were replaced by Rangers although the Amateurs prevailed 4-0.

The tournament was held at the end of the season and initially was not confined to the Glasgow clubs with Vale of Leven, Dumbarton, Renton, St. Mirren and Hibernian contesting Charity Cup finals. For a number of years the players participating were not paid – the money going to charity – and indeed it was widely believed that the participants paid their own way into the ground.

A unique feature of the competition (until shortly after the end of World War II) was that the outcome of drawn matches after ninety minutes was settled by counting the number of corner kicks; if that was inconclusive, even after thirty minutes' extra time, the result was determined by the toss of a coin. In 1930, for example, Rangers defeated Celtic on the toss of the coin which meant that the Ibrox men gained a clean sweep of all the honours in Scotland that season.

In 1921/22 Celtic lost to Rangers by 10 corners to 6 after reaching the final by beating Partick Thistle on corners after a 3-3 draw at Firhill.

Celtic gained the trophy in 1911/12 without actually winning a match or scoring a goal; they eased past Partick Thistle at Firhill by 5 corners to 2, and lifted the cup by gaining 7 corners to the Bully Wee's 0. Shortly after World War II the Glasgow Charities' committee decided to replace this method altogether, replacing it with a toss-of-the-coin.

When World War II ended in Europe in May, 1945, the Glasgow Charities Committee staged a one-off match for the V.E. Trophy. Celtic and Queen's Park battled to a 1-1 draw, but Celtic gained the trophy (permanently) by outscoring the Amateurs by 3 corners to 2.

Celtic have won the Charity Cup on twenty-seven occasions, including an impressive run of seven successive wins between 1912 and 1918.

One famous occasion was the 1950 final at Hampden Park when more than 81,000 saw the zany American comedian Danny Kaye presented to both Old Firm teams.

However, ten years later only 12,000 were present in the same stadium to watch Celtic and Clyde draw 1-1 and both clubs were declared joint holders. This match turned out to be the last in the tournament's traditional format as the Charity Cup had become the inevitable victim of an expanded schedule, including European competition.

For a time an annual show-game involving a Glasgow Select against top English sides was held in the pre-season. The last such fixture was Glasgow versus Leeds United in 1966 when Bobby Lennox scored the home side's goal in a 1-1 draw.

In a bizarre development it transpired that the trophy, generally considered one of the most handsome in football, had simply disappeared. Had it been misplaced, or stolen, or melted down?

CORNER KICKS

Corner kicks were used in some competitions to determine the result when the match finished level in goals after extra time. The thinking was that the team with the more corner kicks had attacked more, and therefore deserved the win.

Charlie Tully, an immensely gifted footballer, was celebrated for his corner kicks

The most famous corner kick in Celtic's history had to be taken twice – and both times Charlie Tully scored with it. It was at Brockville in the 1953 Scottish Cup and Celtic were two goals down shortly after the interval when they were awarded a corner on the left at the Railway End of the ground. Tully took it and 'scored' with his inswinger, but the referee disallowed it because Tully had placed the ball outside the arc.

Tully asked the linesman to place it for him for his next attempt, and did exactly the same, his cross deceiving the Falkirk keeper again. Not surprisingly, Celtic went on to win by 3-2 before the record crowd of 23,100. A later rule change would have meant a goal kick being awarded to Falkirk after Tully's infringement.

In the same year Bobby Collins scored directly from a corner kick at Hampden Park against Arsenal in the Coronation Cup when his swerving cross deceived George Swindin, the Gunners' veteran goalkeeper. Celtic went on to defeat the Londoners by 1-0 in a major upset before a crowd of 59,000.

In the 1955 Scottish Cup final Celtic conceded a corner on the right with little more than a minute left. Archie Robertson took the kick and his high floater into the penalty area was mis-handled by Celtic's John Bonnar for Clyde's equaliser. Celtic lost the replay on the following Wednesday.

Billy McNeill enjoyed lots of luck with Celtic corner kicks in important matches:

1965: With eight minutes left in a pulsating Scottish Cup final and Dunfermline Athletic and Celtic level at 2-2, Charlie Gallagher's corner from the left was met by a McNeill header for the winning goal;

1967: Seconds were left in the European Cup quarter-final against Vojvodina Novi Sad when Celtic gained yet another corner, this time on the right. Charlie Gallagher flighted over a perfect cross and once more Billy McNeill's header found the back of the net for the winning goal;

1967: At Hampden Park in the Inter-Continental Club Championship against Racing Club of Buenos Aires Celtic were finding it difficult to break through against a determined and brutal defence. In 70 minutes Celtic forced another corner on the right and Billy McNeill rose majestically to head home John Hughes' deep corner kick;

1969: In the Scottish Cup final against Rangers, Billy McNeill was astonishingly left unmarked for Celtic's first corner kick in only ninety seconds and the captain rose alone to head Bobby Lennox's corner kick into the net to send Celtic on the way to a 4-0 rout of their great rivals.

CORONATION CUP

To celebrate the crowning of Queen Elizabeth in 1953, the football authorities arranged a knock-out competition involving top clubs from Scotland and England: Aberdeen, Celtic, Hibernian and Rangers; Arsenal, Manchester United, Newcastle United and Tottenham Hotspur. The proceeds of each 'gate' were to be divided as follows: 50% to the clubs involved, and the dividing up of the other 50% among established charities such as the National Playing Fields Association, King George VI Memorial Fund and the

Central Council of Physical Recreation.

To be honest, at that time Celtic did not merit inclusion among 'the top clubs' but were invited solely on their drawing power. It was felt that the club would attract a large crowd to their tie and would be eliminated at that hurdle.

That first match was against Arsenal, the current English champions. The Parkhead outfit were given no chance of advancing but the critics – and the Celtic support in the 59,000 crowd at Hampden – were surprised by Celtic's display. The new signing, Neil Mochan from Middlesbrough, had given a stuttering forward line confidence and Bobby Collins scored direct from a corner kick, his cross ball deceiving the veteran Arsenal keeper George Swindin. Even more surprising was the manner in which Celtic dominated the encounter after that 21-minute goal; the English side rarely threatened a comeback and were fortunate to escape with a 1-0 defeat. Even Alec Rollo, at a time when full backs rarely ventured beyond the halfway line, was foiled by Swindin – as Celtic pressed for a second goal.

Manchester United had eliminated Rangers by 2-1 and qualified to face Celtic on the following Saturday. This match started off in brilliant sunshine, and Celtic's early form matched the weather. The 73,000 crowd roared in anticipation of goals as Celtic stormed into attack to be rewarded with a raking drive from Bertie Peacock after clever wing play from Charlie Tully. Early in the second half Tully again released Neil Mochan who raced in from the centre circle to slip the ball past Crompton. United fought back gamely and Jack Rowley netted with ten minutes

Mike Haughney with Coronation Cup

remaining. A sudden rain storm and a freshening wind added to Celtic's troubles in the last few minutes but they survived.

It was fated to be an all-Scottish final as Hibernian had also eliminated their two English opponents on the road to Hampden Park: Tottenham Hotspur by 2-1 after a replay, and Newcastle United – even with Ronnie Simpson in goal – 4-0. Their strength lay in one of the most famous forward lines in the entire history of Scottish football: Smith, Johnstone, Reilly, Turnbull and Ormond – and rightly they started as favourites.

Celtic, despite playing without the injured Charlie Tully, dominated the first half, gaining corner after corner and forcing Tommy Younger into desperate action time after time. He was beaten only once, and by a goal destined to enter the Celtic folklore. Neil Mochan gathered a pass from Tully's replacement, Willie Fernie – who himself had terrorised Hibernian's defenders – and advanced about fifteen yards into Hibernian's territory. He prepared for a right-foot shot from thirty-five yards and his rising drive left Younger, a Scotland international keeper, helpless.

A minute from halftime, in virtually their first real attack on Celtic's goal, Hibs sent Celtic a warning of what was to come. Gordon Smith raced down the right wing and his cross reached Lawrie Reilly whose header was diverted by an alert Bonnar.

The second half belonged almost entirely to Hibernian as 'the Famous Five' set about Celtic's goal for the equaliser. But they found themselves up against an inspired goalkeeper in Celtic's John Bonnar. The smallish keeper did almost everything possible in the longest forty-five minutes endured by a Celtic support: he clutched crosses and corners from Smith and Ormond, or punched them away, he twisted miraculously in mid-air to deflect headers from Reilly and Bobby Johnstone – who sportingly applauded his opponent after one such save. He made several point-blank saves and had to parry a fierce free kick from Eddie Turnbull and dive bravely at his feet to block the follow-up shot.

A goal had to come, but it came at the other end for Celtic. Willie Fernie broke away and his shot was scrambled off the line but fell to Jimmy Walsh who netted Celtic's second three minutes from the end.

It was a night for heroes and some Celtic players had their finest hour in the Coronation Cup final: John Bonnar, most obviously, but Bobby Evans was in magnificent form in all three ties while Jock Stein marshalled his defence throughout. John McPhail, restored to the side after long absences due to poor form and injuries, deserves particular mention as an emergency left half.

The results were as follows:
Celtic 1, Arsenal 0 (Hampden Park)
Hibernian 1, Tottenham Hotspur 1 (Ibrox Park)
Hibernian 2, Tottenham Hotspur 1 (Ibrox)
Manchester United 2, Rangers 1 (Hampden)
Newcastle United 4, Aberdeen 0 (Ibrox)

Celtic 2, Manchester United 1 (Hampden)
Hibernian 4, Newcastle United 0 (Ibrox)

Celtic 2, Hibernian 0 (Hampden)

The side fielded for the Coronation Cup final was:
Bonnar, Haughney, Rollo, Evans, Stein, McPhail, Collins, Walsh, Mochan, Peacock, Fernie.

COURT CASES

Archie Kyle played briefly with Celtic in 1904 on a Highland tour but joined Rangers on contract instead. After retirement he was involved in a betting scandal along with John Browning (another ex-Celt) and in March 1924 was found guilty and sentenced to sixty days' hard labour.

Willie Crilly was sentenced to four weeks' imprisonment at Dumbarton Sheriff

Court in May 1930 for the theft of gold coins worth £6 from his father-in-law. The motive was to clear gambling debt. Later, Crilley – accused of assaulting his wife – was admonished at Glasgow Sheriff Court and deported under the Aliens Restriction Act in November 1930.

Lou Macari claimed an amount of £431,000 'as damages against wrongful dismissal' as Celtic's manager at the Court of Session on 11 October 1994; in retaliation Celtic counterclaimed £727,000 because of the team's failure on the pitch which had led to loss of potential income.

Dick Beattie was sentenced to nine months imprisonment for his part in a match-fixing scandal in England.

After an Old Firm clash at Ibrox Park in 1987 four players were charged by the police and appeared at Govan Police Court. The players were Chris Woods, Terry Butcher and Graham Roberts of Rangers and Frank McAvennie of Celtic. The verdicts represented the full range of possibilities under Scots Law: Woods and Butcher were found 'Guilty', Roberts 'Not Proven' and McAvennie 'Not Guilty'.

El Hadji Diouf of Liverpool was involved in a spitting incident with a spectator at Celtic Park in the 2003 UEFA Cup tie. He had tumbled into the crowd and was helped to his feet by spectators, one of whom patted him on the head – a gesture which was misinterpreted by the Liverpool player. The Glasgow Sheriff Court fined Diouf £5,000 – despite his being represented by distinguished lawyer and Celtic fan Joe Beltrami – and UEFA gave him a two-match ban.

Jim Melrose, when playing for Shrewsbury Town in January 1988, was the victim of 'grievous bodily harm' when he was assaulted by Chris Kamara of Swindon Town. The former Celtic striker suffered a broken cheekbone as the players were leaving the pitch. Kamara was convicted and fined £1,200, and also had to pay £250 in compensation.

CRICKETERS

Some Celtic players have also enjoyed success in the summer sport:

Jim Welford: the Celtic full back from 1897 to 1899 played as a batsman for Durham and more importantly later for Warwickshire. He played in 13 first-class matches as an all-rounder with an average of 21.85 runs (including one century), and 2 wickets. He also picked up both English and Scottish Cup medals with Aston Villa and Celtic.

Davie Storrier: a left back for Celtic between 1898 and 1901, he captained Scotland against Ireland in 1899 and also played against Wales and England the same year. He played cricket for Arbroath and also Forfarshire.

Dave McLean: the man favoured to replace the aging Jimmy Quinn at Celtic Park and Celtic's centre forward in 1907 to 1909 also played cricket for Strathmore.

Shaun Maloney represented Scotland in an Under-13 match.

In the 1960s Celtic FC played East Kilbride CC in a 'friendly' cricket match.

Andy Goram, Rangers goalkeeper and so often Celtic's nemesis, was also an outstanding cricketer.

Barry Robson scored within seconds in his debut as substitute against Aberdeen in 2008

Tommy McInally, Celtic's jester in the 1920s, scored a hat-trick on his debut against Clydebank

Off to a good start

Bobby Collins made his debut in a 1949 win against Rangers

D

DATES

Significant dates in Celtic's history include the following:

6 November 1887: The meeting which agreed to found a football club was held on this date in St. Mary's Hall, Abercromby Street, Glasgow;

28 May 1888: The first Celtic team to be fielded defeated Rangers (Swifts) 5-2 at the first Celtic Park;

The club tried to clear up the confusion regarding the founding date of Celtic, as seen in this excerpt from the 1936/37 handbook:

> At the Annual Meeting of the Company held on 23rd June, 1936, the Chairman announced that the Board had decided to celebrate the Club's Jubilee in January, 1938. Although the Club was actually formed in September, 1887, it did not really function until January, 1888.

19 October 1957: Celtic defeated Rangers 7-1 in the League Cup final at Hampden Park;

10 March 1965: Jock Stein's arrival at Celtic Park as manager heralded a new start with a 6-0 win at Airdrie;

25 May 1967: Celtic became the first Scottish, British and Northern Europe club to win the European Cup by beating Inter Milan 2-1 in Lisbon;

4 March 1994: Fergus McCann took over at Celtic Park, and the club swung in a new direction;

8 February 2000: Celtic lost to Inverness Caledonian Thistle (3-1) in the Scottish Cup, a sensational result which forced John Barnes' departure and eventually Martin O'Neill's appointment.

DEBUTS

Roy Baines, an English goalkeeper signed as backup from Morton, replaced the injured Peter Latchford for the vital league fixture against Dundee United at Parkhead on 23 March 1977. He marked his debut with a a save from a penalty kick taken by Hamish McAlpine, United's keeper, when the score was 0-0 and Celtic went on to a 2-0 victory.

Pat Bonner, as an Irishman, chose a fitting day for his debut: St. Patrick's Day 1979 in a 2-1 victory over Motherwell at Celtic Park.

The Celtic team on the opening day of the 1948/49 season with Charlie Tully making his debut appearance. Back row: Evans, Boden, McAuley, Miller, Milne, Mallan; Front row: Weir, McPhail, Lavery, Tully, Paton.

Bobby Collins, a diminutive teenager, made his first Celtic appearance in the League Cup tie against Rangers at Celtic Park and helped Celtic to a 3-2 victory, the winning goal coming from Mike Haughney also a debutant that same day (13 August 1949).

George Connelly made his debut on a memorable occasion at East End Park against Dunfermline Athletic on 30 April 1968. Celtic had just ensured winning the championship and the Pars had lifted the Scottish Cup; a record crowd of 27,816 packed the ground to see Celtic win 2-1 with Connelly coming on as a substitute.

Sean Fallon – who would become a fixture at Celtic Park as a player, coach and assistant manager – made his first appearance for Celtic as a right back against Clyde at Shawfield in an end-of-season league fixture on 15 April 1950. Celtic and Clyde drew 2-2, but Sean marked the occasion with an own-goal.

Patsy Gallacher was underweight and undersized when he made his debut against St. Mirren at Celtic Park in a 3-1 win on 2 December 1911. Still a teenager, he won over the hearts of the supporters with a courageous display on a heavy pitch against some resolute defending.

William Goldie's goalkeeping debut in a league fixture against Airdrie at Broomfield was bizarre. On his way to the match as a supporter, Goldie was spotted at a bus stop and invited on to the Celtic coach. The chairman, Bob Kelly, was so impressed with the lad's fervour that he immediately changed the starting lineup to include him. Celtic lost 2-0 in Goldie's only appearance for the first team. (1 October 1960)

Henrik Larsson came on as a second-half substitute against Hibernian at Easter Road on 3 August 1997 and promptly gave the ball away to Chic Charnley for Hibs' winning goal (1-2).

Malcolm MacDonald, destined to be one of Celtic's most skilful and versatile players, made his debut against Partick Thistle on 30 April 1932 at Firhill Park in a league match. Played as a left winger on this occasion, he scored both goals in a 2-0 win.

Tommy McInally, Celtic's jester in the 1920s, made a great impression on his debut as he scored a hat-trick against Clydebank at Parkhead in a 3-1 win on 16 August 1919 – the first day of the season.

Billy McNeill, at eighteen years of age, was drafted into Celtic's side as centre half to replace the injured Bobby Evans for the League Cup tie against Clyde at Parkhead on 23 August 1958 and helped the side to a 2-0 win.

Richard Madden had a nightmare debut (and farewell appearance) in Celtic's goal against Kilmarnock at Rugby Park on 27 March 1963 as Killie won 6-0. He had better luck on his return home where he learned that he had won the football pools!

Neil Mochan made his Celtic debut against Queen's Park in the Charity Cup final at Hampden Park on 9 May 1953, scoring twice in a 3-1 victory. Astonishingly, his first four appearances for Celtic were at Hampden Park as he led Celtic to triumph in the Coronation Cup.

Frank Munro, signed for Celtic in an emergency, made a most unfortunate debut against St. Mirren in a league fixture at Celtic Park despite being made captain. He scored an own-goal in Celtic's 1-2 defeat on 15 October 1977.

Bobby Murdoch made his first appearance on the opening day of the 1962 season in a League Cup tie against Hearts at Parkhead and scored within seven minutes in a 3-1 win. He was only a teenager at the time.

Phil O'Donnell made a promising start to his Celtic career with both goals in a 2-1 win at Firhill against Partick Thistle on 10 September 1994. The club's most expensive signing (from Motherwell) up to that time, O'Donnell was plagued with injury woes throughout his ultimately disappointing seasons with Celtic.

Willie O'Neill was a last-minute choice for Celtic at left back for the Scottish Cup final replay against Dunfermline Athletic on 26 April 1961 when Jim Kennedy was rushed to hospital with appendicitis. He played well enough but Celtic went down to a surprise 0-2 defeat.

Willie Rennet made his debut in distressing circumstances. As a protest against recent refereeing decisions in Old Firm matches the Celtic support largely decided to boycott the fixture at Ibrox on 24 September 1949; Rennet replaced Charlie Tully, omitted from their lineup as a disciplinary measure. Predictably, Celtic lost 0-4.

Ronnie Simpson, a veteran goalkeeper signed from Hibernian as cover, was forced into action against Barcelona at the Nou Camp in the Inter-Cities' Fairs Cup on 18 November 1964 – but Celtic lost 1-3.

Jock Stein was a surprise signing from Llanelly for a modest fee of £1200 and was drafted into the first team only four days later against St. Mirren in a 2-1 win at Celtic Park on 8 December 1951. The former Albion Rovers pivot played well enough to retain his place until his retirement in 1956.

Alan Stubbs made his first appearance at Pittodrie against Aberdeen in a 2-2 draw on 10 August 1996 but he gave away a penalty kick and was simultaneously ordered off by referee Hugh Dallas).

Charlie Tully first played for Celtic in the opening League fixture of the 1948/49 season (14 August) against Morton before a crowd of 55,070. The match at Celtic Park ended as a 0-0 draw and, interestingly, future Celt Neil Mochan also made his debut that day for Morton at outside left.

Peter Wilson, a recently turned nineteen year old from Beith, made an unexpected appearance for Celtic against the formidable Motherwell side at Fir Park on 13 February 1924 at right half. It appears that the untried youngster was simply told that the Motherwell left-wing pair of Stevenson and Ferrier were 'quite useful'. The relatively innocent Wilson was unaware that the Motherwell duo were the most famous wing partnership in Scottish football. Celtic won 1-0.

GOALSCORING DEBUTS:

The idea for this entry was inspired by two articles which appeared in *The Celt* (a fanzine of interest and importance for football historians) in August 1988 and May 1995. Entitled 'Adrenalin Accolades', the articles were written by David Allison and 'U.U. Horningstoft'.

As some competitions such as the Glasgow Cup and the Charity Cup did once count as first-class football – and provided vast entertainment for huge crowds at Celtic Park, the late-lamented Cathkin, Hampden, Ibrox and Shawfield – such goals have been included in this chronological list.

Memorable scoring debuts include hat-tricks for Davie McLean in 1907, Tommy McInally in 1919, and David Prentice in 1929;

Gil Heron's first goal was a raging twenty yard shot past Morton's Jimmy Cowan, the Scotland international keeper in 1951, while Bobby Murdoch scored in only seven minutes against Hearts in 1962.

Jorge Cadete scored within a minute of coming on as a substitute against Aberdeen in 1996, while Chris Sutton marked his Old Firm debut against Rangers with a goal in the first minute in a 6-2 rout at Celtic Park on 27 August 2000.

Andy Walker and Billy Stark made their debuts on the same day (8 August 1987) and both scored in a 4-0 win over Morton at Cappielow.

Joe Craig provided a question for pub quizzes by scoring for Scotland without having kicked a single ball. Joe, a striker with Celtic, netted with a header with his first touch after coming on as a substitute against Wales in 1968.

Note: In some cases players have scored more than once; this information is included inside brackets in the list opposite and overleaf. The abbreviations are as follows: H (Home), A (Away), N (Neutral), Sl (Scottish League), SC (Scottish Cup), LC (League Cup) CC (Charity Cup), GC (Glasgow Cup), RL (Regional League, PD (Premier Division, PL (Premier League.

23 August 1890: Peter Dowds vs Hearts (5-0) A SL

14 May 1892: Joey Foran vs Leith Athletic (2-0) H SL

24 September 1892: James Davidson vs Rangers (2-2) A SL

5 November 1892: Mick Mulvey vs Hearts (5-0) A SL

16 March 1895: John Devlin vs Leith Athletic (4-0) H SL

30 March 1895: John Ferguson vs Leith Athletic (6-5) A SL

10 August 1895: Allan Martin vs Dundee (2-1) A SL

28 November 1896: Pat Gilhooly vs Hibernian (1-1) H SL

11 May 1897: Jack Reynolds vs Rangers (1-4) N CC

4 September 1897: Adam Henderson (2) vs Hibernian (4-1) H SL

4 December 1897: Peter Somers vs Third Lanark (4-0) H SL

20 August 1898: William McAuley vs Third Lanark (2-1) H SL

14 January 1899: Johnny Hodge (2) vs 6 th GRV (8-1) H SC

18 August 1900: Rab Findlay vs Morton (3-2) A SL

1 September 1900: John Gray Third Lanark (2-1) A SL

17 September 1900: Willie Loney vs Hearts (2-0) A SL

19 January 1901: Jimmy Quinn vs St. Mirren (4-3) A SL

19 May 1902: Davy Hamilton vs Hearts (3-1) H CC

15 November 1902: Paddy Murray vs Partick Thistle (4-1) H SL

22 November 1902: Jimmy McMenemy vs Port Glasgow (3-0) H SL

14 March 1903: John Clark vs Morton (2-0) A SL

15 August 1903: Alec Bennett vs Partick Thistle (2-1) H SL

20 August 1904: Finlay McLean vs Partick Thistle (2-0) A SL

25 August 1906: Bobby Templeton vs Kilmarnock (5-0) H SL

24 August 1907: Willie Kivlichan (2) vs Morton (3-2) H SL

2 November 1907: Davie McLean (3) vs Port Glasgow (5-0) H SL

22 April 1909: John Atkinson vs Morton (5-1) H SL

10 May 1911: Willie Nichol vs Rangers (1-2) N CC

15 August 1911: John Brown vs Airdrie (3-0) H SL

3 February 1912: Joe Clark vs Third Lanark (3-1) H SL

13 April 1912: Andrew Gibson vs Kilmarnock (2-0) H SL

31 August 1912: Alex Gray vs Kilmarnock (2-0) A SL

6 December 1913: Ebenezer Owers vs Third Lanark (3-0) H SL

8 April 1916: Joe O'Kane vs Falkirk (2-0) A SL

12 October 1918: Willie Brown vs Kilmarnock (1-1) A SL

16 August 1919: Tommy McInally (3) vs Clydebank (3-1) H SL

17 January 1920: Tully Craig (2) vs Kilmarnock (3-2) A SL

GOAL SCORING DEBUTS

13 March 1920: Archie Longmuir (2) vs Raith Rovers (5-0) H SL
23 September 1922: Jim F. Murphy vs Dundee (1-0) A SL
8 November 1924: Willie Fleming vs Kilmarnock (6-0) H SL
17 March 1926: Willie Malloy vs Dundee (2-1) A SL
9 March 1929: David Prentice (3) vs Raith Rovers (4-1) A SL
23 August 1930: Hugh Smith vs Hibernian (6-0) H SL
24 January 1931: Joe Cowan vs Aberdeen (1-1) A SL
26 August 1931: Jerry Solis vs Cowdenbeath (7-0) H SL
24 October 1931: Joe McGhee (2) vs Ayr United (4-2) H SL
30 April 1932: Malky MacDonald (2) vs Partick Thistle (2-0) A Sl
13 August 1932: Jimmy Cameron vs Aberdeen (3-0) H SL
30 August 1932: Charlie McGillivray vs Ayr United (4-1) H SL
22 October 1932: Johnny Crum vs Motherwell (4-1) H SL
7 April 1934: Frank Murphy vs Airdrie (4-2) A SL
11 August 1934: John McInally vs Kilmarnock (4-1) H SL
5 December 1936: Joe Carruth vs Falkirk (3-0) A SL
10 August 1940: George Gillan vs Hamilton Acad (2-2) H RL
31 August 1940: Morris Jones vs Albion Rovers (3-1) A RL
6 April 1942: Robert Fisher vs Partick Thistle (3-1) A RL
5 December 1942: Davie Duncan vs Motherwell (3-2) H RL
4 September 1943 Jackie Gallagher vs Dumbarton (1-4) H RL
18 September 1943 Gerry McAloon vs Hamilton Acad (1-0) H RL
7 October 1944 Jim McKay vs Rangers (2-3) N GC
15 September 1945 Dennis Hill vs Hamilton Acad (2-0) H RL
14 August 1946: Jack Cantwell (2) vs Clyde (2-2) A SL
22 March 1947: Frank Quinn vs Partick Thistle (2-0) H SL
11 October 1947: Jim McLaughlin vs Morton (3-2) H SL
15 November 1947: Frank Walsh vs Partick Thistle (5-3) A SL
3 April 1948: Dan Lavery vs Hibernian (2-4) A SL
30 October 1948: Leslie Johnston (2) vs Hibernian (2-1) A SL
13 August 1949: Mike Haughney vs Rangers (3-2) H LC
30 December 1950: John McAlindon (2) vs Hearts (2-2) H SL
18 August 1951: Gil Heron vs Morton (2-0) H LC
9 August 1952: John McDonald vs St. Mirren (1-0) A LC
1 November 1952: Jimmy Duncan vs St. Mirren (2-1) A SL
6 December 1952: Jim McIlroy vs Hibernian (1-1) A SL

9 May 1953: Neil Mochan (2) vs Queen's Park (3-1) A CC

18 December 1954: Jim Rowan vs Dundee (4-1) H SL

1 October 1955: Jim Sharkey vs Raith Rovers (2-0) H SL

16 November 1957: John Divers vs St. Mirren (2-2) H SL

8 August 1959: Tommy Mackle vs Raith Rovers (1-2) A LC

13 August 1960: John Hughes vs Third Lanark (2-0) H LC

11 August 1962: Bobby Murdoch vs Hearts (3-1) H LC

22 August 1967: Pat Mc Mahon (2) vs Partick Thistle (5-0) H GC

29 March 1969: Harry Hood vs St. Mirren (3-0) A SL

15 October 1969: Vic Davidson (2) vs Clyde (4-1) H GC

23 September 1970: Paul Wilson vs Dundee (5-1) H LC

27 November 1971: Dixie Deans vs Partick Thistle (5-1) A SL

16 November 1974: Ronnie Glavin vs Airdrie (6-0) H SL

15 April 1978: Mike Conroy vs Hibernian (1-4) A PD

23 January 1982: John Halpin vs Queen of South (4-0) H SC

1 September 1982: Jim Dobbin vs Arbroath (4-1) H LC

19 February 1985: Paul Chalmers vs Morton (4-0) H PD

8 August 1987: Billy Stark (2) vs Morton (4-0) A PD

8 August 1987: Andy Walker (2) vs Morton (4-0) A PD

14 November 1987: Joe Miller vs Dundee (5-0) H PD

17 August 1991: Gary Gillespie vs Falkirk (4-1) H PD

10 September 1994: Phil O'Donnell (2) vs Partick Thistle (2-1) A PD

11 January 1995: Pierre van Hooijdonk vs Hearts (1-1) H PD

19 August 1995: Andreas Thom vs Ayr United (3-0) A LC

1 April 1996: Jorge Cadete vs Aberdeen (5-0) H PD

9 August 1997: Regi Blinker vs Berwick Rangers (7-0) N LC

30 October 1999: Ian Wright vs Kilmarnock (5-1) H PL

30 July 2000: Chris Sutton vs Dundee United (2-1) A PL

5 September 2000: Allan Thompson vs Raith Rovers (4-0) H LC

16 December 2000: Ramon Vega (2) vs Aberdeen (6-0) H PL

25 April 2004: Aiden McGeady vs Hearts (1-1) A PL

29 July 2006: Jiri Jarosik vs Kilmarnock H Kilmarnock (4-1) H SPL

26 August 2006: Jan Vennegoor of Hesselink vs Hibernian (2-1) H PL

2 February 2008: Georgios Samaras vs Kilmarnock A 5-1

10 February 2008: Barry Robson vs Aberdeen A (5-1) PL

George Allan 1899 Died from tuberculosis Aged 24
Joe Baillie 1966 Drowned following car accident 37
Tom Barber 1925 Died from tuberculosis 37
Barney Battles 1905 Died from influenza 30
Jimmy Cameron 1935 Died from pneumonia 29
John Clark 1906 Died from enteric fever 25
Joe Coen 1941 Died in plane crash 29
Robert Craig 1918 Died in action, WWI 29
Joe Cullen 1905 Died from pneumonia
John Cunningham 1910 cause not known 37
John Divers 1910 cause not known 37
Peter Dowds 1895 Died from consumption 27
Johnny Doyle 1981 Died from electrocution 30
Willie Dunning 1902 Died from tuberculosis 37
Paddy Gallagher 1899 Died from inflammation 34
Pat Gilhooly 1907 Died from cancer 30
Willie Groves 1908 Died from tuberculosis 38
Peter Johnstone 1917 Died in action, WWI 28
Frank Kelly 1919 Died while in Forces after train accident 26
Allan Martin 1906 33
Joe McCulloch 1945 Died in action, WWII 26
Charles McEleny 1908 36
John McIlhatton 1954 33
Mick McKeown 1903 Died from asphyxiation 33
Donnie McLeod 1917 Died in action, WWI 35
John Millsopp 1952 Died from peritonitis 22
John Mulrooney 1914 complication from rheumatic condition 27
Phil O'Donnell 2007 Died from heart failure 36
L. R. Roose 1916 Died in action, WWI 38
Peter Scarff 1933 Died from tuberculosis 25
Peter Somers 1914 Died from infection after amputated leg 36
Bobby Templeton 1919 Died from heart attack 40
John Thomson 1931 Died in football accident 22
Bertie Thomson 1937 Died from heart failure 30
Donald Weir 1959 Died in mining accident 29
Jim Young 1922 Died in motor-bike accident 40

Willie Garner, a centre half signed from Aberdeen, played his first match – a League Cup tie against St. Mirren in 1981 and also scored an own-goal in a surprise 3-1 defeat at Celtic Park.

Barry Robson scored with literally his first kick of the ball when he fired in a free kick at Pittodrie on 8 March 2008. He had come on as a substitute 30 seconds earlier.

DEATHS

It is always hard to reconcile death and the young; it becomes even more difficult to accept the death of an athlete, invariably young and presumably in the best physical condition. The list opposite is of the names of Celtic or former Celtic players who died before reaching forty.

All deaths are sad but that of Brian McGrane is particularly poignant. A reserve-team full back of considerable promise, Brian was playing in a home match against Clydebank on 26 November 1977, but failed to appear for the second half. John Clark, Lisbon Lion and team coach, reported in the *Celtic View* (30 November 1977) of the 6-1 victory; 'We took the lead from a very good Brian McGrane goal, and added two more before halftime from Peter Mackie and Willie Temperley. Brian McGrane, who had been doing well playing in midfield, was suffering from a stomach pain and had to be replaced by Robert Ward at halftime.'

On 1 December Brian's condition worsened and he was admitted to the Western Infirmary where, despite an emergency operation to remove his enlarged spleen, he died from a cerebral haemorrhage on 4 December 1977. Leukemia was also diag-

nosed after tests at the hospital. Jock Stein said: 'We all find it hard to believe that a young man of only twenty is no longer with us, a young man with a promising football career and all life before him.'

On Wednesday 7 December 1977 the club was represented at the Requiem Mass and funeral by directors, management, backroom staff and players; on 10 December the players of Celtic and Partick Thistle wore black armbands during their Premier Division match at Celtic Park as a gesture of respect. His wife was expecting the couple's first child later that month.

DEFEATS (SEE ALSO HOME DEFEATS)

Celtic's heaviest defeats in major competitions are as follows:

Scottish League:
30 April 1937
Motherwell at Fir Park 0-8

Scottish Cup:
14 April 1928
Rangers at Hampden Park 0-4

4 April 1959
St. Mirren at Hampden Park 0-4

League Cup:
9 October 1948
Clyde at Celtic Park 3-6

30 August 1958
St. Mirren at Love Street 3-6

31 August 1955
Rangers at Celtic Park 0-4

Europe:
27 July 2005
Artmedia Bratislava in Slovakia 0-5

DELAYED STARTS

When Celtic and Clyde met in the 1888/89 Scottish Cup allegedly the Clyde team arrived late for the match; the visitors won by 1-0 but Celtic protested and won the re-match by 9-2. Clyde were so incensed that they refused to change in the dressing room and turned up already stripped for action.

In the 1980s Alex Ferguson used to claim that Celtic would often try to delay the start of Aberdeen matches at Parkhead 'because of long queues at the tunstiles'. Ferguson suspected it was a ruse to upset the concentration of his side.

When Celtic went to Blackburn Rovers in the 2002/03 UEFA Cup, the kick-off was delayed for almost fifteen minutes as police and stewards tried to sort out attempts to enter the ground with forged tickets.

The kick-off for the Celtic vs Barcelona match in September 2004 was delayed by thirty minutes, caused by a power failure which affected the newly installed electronic turnstiles.

DIRECTORS

Prior to becoming a Limited Liability Company in 1897, Celtic were run primarily by various committees, presided over by John Glass.

The first meeting of the new company, held on 17 June 1897, produced the following Board of Directors:

M. Dunbar, J. Glass, J. Grant, J. Kelly, J. McKillop, J. H. McLaughlin, J. O'Hara.

The following is a list of Celtic directors until 1994:

Michael Dunbar: 1897–1921

John Glass: 1897- 1906

James Grant: 1897–1914

James Kelly: 1897–1932

John McKillop: 1897–1914

John H. McLaughlin: 1897–1909

John O' Hara: 1897–1905

Tom Colgan: 1905–1939

Tom White: 1906–1947

John Shaughnessy: 1911–1952

John McKillop: 1921–1941

Robert Kelly: 1932–1971

Tom Devlin (Sr.): 1940–1941

Desmond White: 1947–1985

Tom Devlin (Jr.): 1949–1986

James Farrell: 1964–

Kevin Kelly: 1971–

John C. McGinn: 1981

Chris White: 1981–1994

Tom Grant: 1985–

Michael Kelly: 1990–1994

Brian Dempsey: May 1990–Oct 1990

David Smith: 1992–1994

In 1994 Celtic entered a new era under the leadership of Fergus McCann. Until then, the directors did take a relatively active part in the running of the football aspects of the club. With specialisation, re-organisation and the formation of new committees, it seems pointless to list all the directors since 1994. However, the current

The Directors in 1907 (Standing): Michael Dunbar, Willie Maley, Tom Colgan; (Seated): John McKillop, James Kelly, John McLaughlin, Tom White, James Grant

City Chambers reception: Willie Lyon with Charity Cup in 1938, Chairman Tom White on his left and Bob Kelly behind White. Manager Willie Maley stands hat in hand

Members of the Celtic board appear with leaders of different faiths in 2007 and with First Minister Jack McConnell in support of anti-sectarianism.

board with different responsibilities is:

John Reid, Peter Lawwell, Eric Riley, Dermot Desmond, Tom Allison, Brian McBride, Brian Wilson, Ian Livingstone, John Keane, Michael McDonald, Kevin Sweeney.

DISASTERS

The two most horrific stadium disasters occurred on opposite sides of the world.

In May 1964 Peru played Argentina in Lima in an Olympic qualifying decider, and the referee disallowed a last-minute 'equaliser' for Peru. A riot broke out, the police intervened with tear-gas, panic spread among the spectators and in their scramble for the exits – some of which were locked – three hundred and eighteen (318) people died.

In October 1982 at the Central Lenin Stadium in Moscow, Spartak were leading 1-0 against Haarlem (Holland) in a UEFA Cup tie. In the closing seconds as the crowds started to leave down icy and unlit steps, Spartak scored a second goal. Some spectators tried to turn back upon hearing the cheers but were met by the vast exodus seconds later as the match ended; a crush followed, some slipped on the ice and a massive pile-up ensued.

The incident went unreported in the Soviet Union for the next seven years but in 1989 *Sovietsky Sport*, the official government paper, put the death toll at 69. However newspapers outside the Soviet Union have estimated the fatalities as high as 340.

Those stadium disasters that have involved Celtic, directly or indirectly, include:

Ibrox Park 2 April 1902

Special provision was made to enlarge the capacity of the stadium for the lucrative international match between Scotland and England. Ibrox had been chosen in preference to Celtic Park, the only other valid contender for the staging of the bi-annual fixture. The work carried out was approved by the Dean of the Guild Court and the city magistrates – although the new terracing was little more than a flimsily supported wooden structure.

The gates were opened three hours before the kick-off and by the time the match started the terracing on the south-west was full to overflowing and more people were queuing to gain admittance; the gangways at the top of the terracing were completely congested. Ten minutes into the action disaster struck – allegedly when the crowd started to sway to get a better view of winger Bobby Templeton on the ball. The inadequate wood planking gave way and hundreds were plunged through a gaping hole. Panic spread among those closest to the scene; spectators spilt onto the pitch and caused a stoppage in the game lasting some twenty minutes.

Despite the horror of the situation, the decision was made to restart the game and it was played to a finish; no doubt the authorities feared that trouble might break out among spectators in other parts of the ground who were largely unaware of developments. The final statistics were chilling: twenty-six dead, and 587 injured badly enough to be compensated for their injuries.

The fixture was rescheduled a month later at Villa Park with the gate-receipts going to the Ibrox Disaster Fund but only 15,000 turned up to contribute a little more than £1,000 to the fund.

The SFA had chosen Ibrox for the 1892 fixture with England but Celtic Park was selected for all other occasions between 1894 and 1904 – with the exception of the ill-fated 1902 match. Revenue from these matches was important and Celtic were aggrieved at losing out to Rangers for 1902. The *Glasgow Observer* could not resist commenting: 'Celtic's splendidly equipped ground which has stood the test of previous record crowds' had been rejected and hinted that the Ibrox Park venue was unsafe, adding, 'Catastrophe, vaguely apprehended, spoken of last week in whispers as a possibility, has unfortunately taken place, and the International Football Association match at Ibrox Park has been marked by an appalling disaster.'

Ibrox Park 16 September 1961
At the end of the Rangers-Celtic league fixture two men stumbled and fell on the way out at Passageway 13 towards Copland Road. Their slip brought down other spectators pushing to get out of the ground. The surge of the crowd caused the central hand rail to collapse, as well as the outside fence. Two people were killed, and forty-six (46) were injured.

Ibrox Park 2 January 1971
The accepted myth is that some Rangers supporters leaving the ground, upon hearing that the home side had equalised in the last minute, had turned back to join in the celebration; they were met on the steps by the general exodus as the whistle sounded. That, however, is NOT what happened!

From eye-witness accounts it seems that the tragedy occurred more than five minutes after the match ended. This account – and one backed by several sources – is that as the crowd squeezed down Stairway 13, a boy waving a scarf fell

The Old Firm were brought closer together in 1971 following deaths of supporters at Ibrox

from the shoulders of the man carrying him and caused a human wave down the steep steps in a domino effect. One report described it: 'The crowd just caved in like a pack of cards as if all of them were falling into a huge hole.'

The outcome left sixty-six (66) dead, many of whom were youngsters – and a further 145 injured.

A Lord Provost's Fund was immediately set up to help the families of the dead and injured. Both clubs involved (Rangers and Celtic) made substantial donations to this fund, and a match was arranged for Hampden Park between an Old Firm Select and Scotland. Celtic and Rangers players and officials attended church funeral services; a Memorial Service was held at Glasgow Cathedral, and a Requiem Mass at St. Andrew's Roman Catholic Church.

In hindsight this was a disaster waiting

to happen. Over the previous decade there had been ominous signs: in 1961 as described above, in 1967 when eleven spectators were injured. and only two years earlier (on 2 January 1969) more than thirty had been injured when a metal hand rail gave way – and all of these incidents had taken place on or near Stairway 13. One nurse, rushing to the scene of the latest calamity in 1971, is said to have uttered the significant words: 'Not again!'

Rangers directors were severely reprimanded by the official inquiry which sat for fourteen days and was conducted by Sheriff Irvine Smith. Despite that, no action was taken against the club or any individuals subsequent to the disaster. The Wheatly Report led eventually to the Safety of Sports Grounds Act being introduced in 1975 – and saw stadium capacities reduced and facilities improved.

To be perfectly blunt such an event as happened at Ibrox could have occurred at any football ground in Scotland – although perhaps not on such a massive scale.

Tragically, it would require more catastrophe and greater loss of life before football spectators could feel safe in modern all-seater stadia.

DOCTORS

Dr. John Conway, a much-loved practitioner in Glasgow's East End, was a founding member of the club in 1887 and the club's first Honorary President.

Willie Kivlichan had a highly unusual 'part-time' career as an outside right in that his only two senior clubs in Scotland were Rangers and Celtic. On 1 January 1907 he scored the winning goal for Rangers against Celtic at Ibrox, but he joined the Parkhead club later that year; in 1908 he scored both Celtic goals in a 2-1 Scottish Cup victory at Ibrox against Rangers. He graduated as a doctor from Glasgow University in 1917 and became Celtic's team doctor in the 1920s, and attended John Thomson on the pitch at Ibrox on 5 September 1931 when the Celtic goalkeeper was fatally and accidentally injured.

John Atkinson, an amateur player and medical student, played only one match for Celtic (in April 1909) but he scored two goals in a 5-1 win over Morton at Celtic Park. He qualified as a doctor in 1910 and moved to the North East of England.

Hugh McFarlane, recently qualified as a doctor at Mearnskirk Hospital, played several times in the wartime season of 1941/42 on loan from Alloa Athletic

L.R. Roose, a Welsh internationalist goalkeeper, was invited to play for Celtic against Clyde in the Scottish Cup in 1910 and did so, but unfortunately Celtic lost by 3-1. He was reputed to have congratulated the scorer of Clyde's third goal. A genuine sportsman and also an amateur, he was a remarkable all-round personality; he won the Military Medal in World War 1, but was killed in action at the Somme. He was a qualified doctor.

John Fitzsimons joined Celtic in 1934 as an outside left but his appearances were restricted to five during his four years as a Celtic player because Frank Murphy was the regular winger. Fitzsimons proved more successful when he moved to Alloa Athletic; and did well throughout the wartime seasons with stints at Falkirk, Clyde, East Fife, Third Lanark, Partick Thistle, and Hamilton Academical. He graduated as a doctor in June 1940 and was appointed Celtic's club physician in 1953 – a post he held for many years. He was also the Scotland team doctor at the World Cup in Argentina in 1978, when Willie Johnstone was sent home in some disgrace for failing a drugs-test.

Celtic's manager in 1999/2000 – the venerable Jozef Venglos – held a Ph.D. for his work on Physical Education in Czechoslovakia.

Celtic's current chairman John Reid is also a PhD in History with a thesis on West Africa.

Michael Kelly, a Celtic director before Fergus McCann's takeover in 1994, earned a doctorate in Economics.

Henrik Larsson was honoured with a doctorate from Strathclyde University in 2005 'for his contribution to football and charity'.

Martin O'Neill was given an honorary doctorate from Queen's University in Belfast 'for services to sport' in 2005.

Billy McNeill was awarded an honorary doctorate from Glasgow University in March 2008 for his contribution to football and the community.

DOUBLES

For many years (until after World War II) the double of League Championship and the Scottish Cup within the same season was the Holy Grail of Scottish football.

Celtic have accomplished the feat in the following seasons: 1906/07, 1907/08, 1913/14, 1953/54, 1966/67, 1968/69, 1970/71, 1971/72, 1973/74, 1978/77, 1987/88, 2000/01, 2006/07. They became the first club to achieve this domestic double by beating Hearts 3-0 in the Cip final.

In 1908/09 Celtic were deprived of the opportunity to win three successive doubles when the Scottish Cup was withheld after a riot at Hampden Park following a drawn replay with Rangers.

DOUBLE FIGURES (GOALS)

On a number of occasions Celtic have reached double figures in goals scored in a single match.

Only two, however, have been scored in competitive fixtures: on 26 October 1895 Celtic defeated Dundee by 11-0 at Celtic Park, a result which still stands as a record for the top league division – partly explained by the fact that Dundee finished the match with only nine men. The other match was a League Cup tie against Hamilton Academical, won 10-0 on 11

Celtic's double-wiining side of 1953/54
Back row: Haughney, Fallon, Bonnar, Evans, Stein, Peacock
Front row: Collins, Fernie, Walsh, Tully, Mochan. Missing were Frank Meechan and John Higgins

September 1968 (with both Stevie Chalmers and Bobby Lennox scoring five times).

Until a few years after the end of World War II the Glasgow Cup competition was taken seriously by the participating clubs. In October 1888 (in only their third-ever fixture) Celtic defeated Shettleston by 11-2 and in September 1891 defeated Kelvinside Athletic by 11-1.

On other occasions in 'friendly matches' lop-sided scores have been rung up. A selection follows:

1899: Dumfries Hibernian 10-0;

1953: Bohemians (Dublin) 10-1;

1959: Girvan Amateurs 12-2;

1962: Throttur (Iceland) 10-1;

1966: Bermuda FA XI 10-1 and Hamilton Primo (Ontario) 11-0;

1972: St. Ouen (Jersey) 11-1;

1993: U.S. Carisolo (Italy) 12-0;

1996: Reunie Borculo (Netherlands) 16-0;

1997: F.C. Beatrix (Netherlands) 21-0.

The match in 1953 was styled as 'a benefit match for Willie Maley' but the proceeds went to the Grampian Sanatorium at Kingussie; the 1959 fixture at Girvan had been arranged for Celtic's Third team but, as matches had been postponed, Celtic fielded their first eleven; in 1996 the minor outfit were celebrating their ninetieth anniversary and welcomed Celtic by having them piped on to the pitch by a black Dutchman resplendent in green-and-white tartan; the 1997 game was Wim Jansen's debut as manager and ten different Celtic players scored with central defender Alan Stubbs getting a hat-trick.

DRYBROUGH CUP

A pre-season knock-out competition staged between 1971 and 1980, limited originally to the eight clubs who had scored most goals in the previous season's Scottish League First Division. The top four sides were seeded in the first round.

The competition was put on hold between 1974 and 1979 as the Scottish Premier Division was introduced in 1974. It re-emerged in 1979 with the four highest scorers in the Premier Division augmented by the two highest-scoring sides in the First and Second Divisions

Although Celtic appeared in six finals, they picked up the silverware only once – in 1974 when they beat Rangers on penalty-kicks after a 2-2 draw.

The tournament was sponsored by a brewery, but interest waned and the competition was axed after a crowd of only 7,000 attended the 1980 final between St. Mirren and Aberdeen.

Celtic's record was as follows:

1971:
Dumbarton H 5-2
St. Johnstone N 4-2
Aberdeen A 1-2

1972:
Dumbarton H 2-1
Aberdeen H 3-2
Hibernian N 3-5

1973:
Dunfermline Athletic H 6-1
Dundee H 4-0
Hibernian N 0-1

1974:

Airdrie A 4-2

Dundee A 2-1 (aet)

Rangers N 2-2 (aet) Celtic win on penalties

1979: Rangers N 1-3

1980: Ayr United H 0-1

DUBAI CUP

Dubai, located in the United Arab Emirates, was the surprising location for two matches between Celtic (the Scottish champions) and Liverpool (the English champions).

On 9 December 1986 Celtic faced Liverpool in Dubai's Al Wasl Stadium before a crowd estimated at 15,000 for the Dubai Super Cup. Owen Archdeacon put Celtic into the lead early in the second half, but Alan Hansen equalised near the end.

The game went to penalty-kicks and Liverpool, lifted by their narrow escape, triumphed 4-2 to take the trophy.

On 4 April 1989 Celtic, after their success in the preceding centenary season, again faced Liverpool this time at the Al Nasr Stadium. The contest again ended in a 1-1 draw with Mark McGhee scoring for Celtic and John Aldridge for Liverpool. This time Celtic won by 4-2 on penalty-kicks, the deciding spot kick taken by Billy Stark. The winning Celtic team was:

Bonner, Morris, Rogan, McCahill, McCarthy, Grant, Miller (Stark), P. McStay (Walker), Coyne, McGhee, Fulton.

The trophy had been re-named the Dubai Champions' Cup by then and, as the competition lapsed at that time, the gold cup remains in Celtic's permanent collection.

Cardinal O'Brien and the Moderator of the Church of Scotland attend an Old Firm match flanked by Celtic Chairman John Reid, First Minister Jack McConnell and representatives of other faiths

E

ECCLESIASTIC CONNECTIONS

For most Irish and Catholic immigrants life in Scotland was no easier after the Famines and economic hardships of their native land. They suffered discrimination and resentment as a result of their nationality and religion – as well as hostility from a workforce anxious about the effects of such mass immigration.

Celtic came into being as a direct consequence of the deprivation which was afflicting an entire community. The club was founded in 1887 (or 1888) by the efforts of leading members of that community in Glasgow and the west of Scotland. Its original purpose was to cash in on the mass appeal of football in order to raise money for charity and especially the Poor Children's Dinner Tables set up in several schools in the East End of Glasgow by the Marist Brothers, Walfrid and Dorotheus.

The club and its team became an instant success and a source of pride in a community desperately in need of such comfort. However, despite its origins and initial aim Celtic has never been an exclusive club. From the earliest days membership, as committee men and players, was not restricted to Irishmen or Catholics. Naturally, the majority of the membership – and its following – were both Irish and Catholic and this has led to some confusion and conflict within the larger community of a Scotland apparently unwelcoming to such incomers.

Today the club stands for inclusion, numbering among its directors, shareholders, players and supporters many of different faiths and backgrounds. It remains a matter of pride that the great Celtic side which won the European Cup in 1967 was managed by a traditionally Scottish non-Catholic and featured players of both religions. That was its greatest manifestation of its traditional tolerance.

Archbishop Eyre: the leading Roman Catholic churchman in Scotland – and incidentally an Englishman – was a Patron of the club from its earliest days. It is not known if he was interested in football but he approved of the charitable aims of Celtic's founders.

Brother Walfrid: the Marist Brother was the moral driving force behind the move to establish a new football club in the East End of Glasgow in order to raise funds for Catholic charities and especially the Poor Children's Dinner Table.

Brother Clare (James E. Handley) was the Headmaster of St. Mungo's Academy in Glasgow from 1944 until 1960. He was commissioned by the club to research and write *The Celtic Story*, published in 1960.

Archbishop Winning (1925 – 2001): a fanatical Celtic supporter, he was made a cardinal on the same day that Celtic lost to Raith Rovers in the 1994 League Cup final.

Archbishop Conti: Not a football fan, he was bemused at first with the interest in Celtic among his fellow students at Blairs College in Aberdeen.

On 11 March 2007 the Old Firm league match at Celtic Park was attended by Cardinal O'Brien and the Moderator of the General Assembly of the Church of Scotland, as well as representatives of other religions. The invitation to attend was in conjunction with efforts to eliminate sectarianism from Scottish football.

When Celtic went to Argentina in 1967 for the ill-fated World Club Championship, they were boosted by a travelling support of some 107. The party included six priests – and the Reverend Robert Jack, a Lutheran minister from Iceland (and a keen Celtic supporter).

Despite his name, Owen Archdeacon who played for Celtic in the 1980s unfortunately cannot be included in this list.

Celtic are not the only British club to be formed with some ecclesiastic connections:

1874: Aston Villa (developed from Villa Cross Wesleyan Chapel); Bolton Wanderers (developed originally from Christ Church Sunday School;

1875: Hibernian (founded by Canon Hannan in Edinburgh);

1879: Fulham (an offshoot of another Church Sunday School in Kensington);

1883: Stockport County (derived from Heaton Norris Rovers which was founded in a Congregational Chapel);

1885: Southampton (originating in St. Mary's Church).

ECLIPSE

On 24 January 1925 an eclipse of the sun took place but, more importantly, Celtic were playing Third Lanark at Cathkin in the Scottish Cup with more than 40,000 in the ground. Although the Hi-Hi scored first in 29 minutes, Celtic ran out comfortable winners by 5-1 with youngster Jimmy McGrory scoring four times. Patsy Gallacher netted the other.

The home side, not too sure of what would happen during an eclipse, provided the journalists with candles in the somewhat primitive press box.

ELIGIBILITY

In their first-ever league match (against Renton in 1890/91) Celtic fielded an ineligible player (a goalkeeper named James Bell) and were deducted four points for the offence.

In 1995 Celtic signed the Portuguese striker, Jorge Cadete from Sporting Lisbon. However, a delay occurred before he made his first appearance and Fergus McCann complained at length about this. Eventually his stand was vindicated and Jim Farry, the

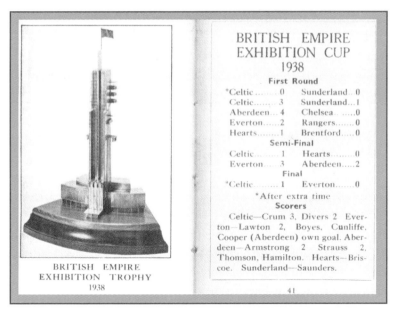

BRITISH EMPIRE
EXHIBITION CUP
1938

First Round

*Celtic	0	Sunderland	0
Celtic	3	Sunderland	1
Aberdeen	4	Chelsea	0
Everton	2	Rangers	0
Hearts	1	Brentford	0

Semi-Final

Celtic	1	Hearts	0
Everton	3	Aberdeen	2

Final

*Celtic	1	Everton	0

*After extra time

Scorers

Celtic—Crum 3, Divers 2 Everton—Lawton 2, Boyes, Cunliffe, Cooper (Aberdeen) own goal. Aberdeen—Armstrong 2 Strauss 2, Thomson, Hamilton. Hearts—Briscoe. Sunderland—Saunders.

41

BRITISH EMPIRE
EXHIBITION TROPHY
1938

Chief Executive of the SFA, was dismissed for gross misconduct in 1999 – almost three years after Celtic started the process.

THE EMPIRE EXHIBITION TROPHY (1938)

On Wednesday 17 November 1937 the plans for an Empirex football competition, to be run on knock-out lines, were announced. The competition, running from 25 May 1938 till 10 June 1938 would be in conjunction with the Empire Exhibition at Bellahouston Park in Glasgow and all the ties would take place at nearby Ibrox Park.

The Exhibition had been conceived by the Scottish Development Council in 1936 'to illustrate the progress of the British Empire at home and overseas', and as a shop-window to encourage new industry to come to Scotland at a time when the traditional ones (shipbuilding and heavy engineering) were seen to be in terminal decline. Glasgow Corporation hoped also

that a successful Exhibition would dispel the city's unsavoury image as depicted in such best-selling novels as *No Mean City*.

At the time of the announcement the Scottish clubs nominated to take part were Celtic, Rangers, Hearts and Aberdeen; the English sides put forward were Arsenal, Chelsea, Manchester City and Sunderland but in the months prior to the tournament Arsenal and Manchester City withdrew and their places were taken by Brentford, a surprisingly strong side in pre-war days, and a very powerful Everton.

Each club would nominate a squad of fourteen players, and each member would receive £5 per match; in addition every player would receive a miniature model of the tower which symbolised the Exhibition.

The opening match in the competition was between Celtic and Sunderland, and it finished as a 0-0 draw before 53,791 spectators on 25 May – but Celtic were lucky to survive the last fifteen minutes of extra-time against the English side which had improved after the interval. Willie Lyon at centre-half and Kennaway in goal deserved the praise for keeping Celtic's hopes alive; Celtic's forward-line had to be re-aligned in the closing stages, as both Delaney and Carruth had picked up injuries. Delaney went on to the left wing and his inside-right Carruth moved to the wing. In 1938 no substitutes were allowed in competitive matches.

The replay took place the next night – on Thursday 26 May – and Celtic had to make changes, Matt Lynch replacing Delaney and Malcolm MacDonald coming in for Carruth. The attendance (20,226) had been affected because of heavy rain throughout the day and evening; the playing surface was heavy and treacherous but Sunderland started brightly. Kennaway had to turn a magnificent shot from Raich Carter over the crossbar, and save at point-blank range from Burbank, but in 28 minutes Saunders gave Sunderland a deserved lead.

Celtic were stung into retaliation and Crum surprised the visitors' defence with a quick turn and shot for Celtic's equaliser in 38 minutes. Johnny Divers proved to be Celtic's hero early in the second half with two vital goals: the first came in 49 minutes when rapid-fire interpassing between MacDonald and Crum left Divers in the clear only ten yards out; and the second ten minutes later when he avoided the offside-trap before chipping the ball over Mapson, the Sunderland keeper and into the net off the far post.

Celtic: Kennaway, Hogg, Morrison, Geatons, Lyon, Paterson, Lynch, MacDonald, Crum, Divers, Murphy.

First Round Results
25 May Celtic 0, Sunderland 0
26 May Celtic 3, Sunderland 1
27 May Aberdeen 4, Chelsea 0
30 May Rangers 0, Everton 2
1 June Hearts 1, Brentford 0

For the semi-final Celtic lined up against Hearts, who had hung on to defeat Brentford by 1-0 although totally outplayed throughout. Hearts' strength lay in defence where they fielded four Scottish caps, but they had skill up-front with Tommy Walker and Andy Black at inside forward.

Hearts dominated the play for the first hour, but found Joe Kennaway in top form; his handling of the ball was immaculate and the Edinburgh side were becoming discouraged. After 65 minutes, Crum finished off a Celtic break from defence to score the only goal of a tense match. Hearts resumed their attacks but Kennaway – and the others in a resolute defence – refused to give in and the Celtic supporters among the crowd of 48,027 were vastly relieved to hear the whistle.

Celtic: Kennaway, Hogg, Morrison, Geatons, Lyon, Paterson, Lynch, MacDonald, Crum, Divers, Murphy.

Semi-Final Results
3 June Celtic 1, Hearts 0
6 June Everton 3, Aberdeen 2

Final
Celtic: Kennaway, Hogg, Morrison, Geatons, Lyon, Paterson, Delaney, MacDonald, Crum, Divers, Murphy.

Everton: Sagar, Cook, Greenhalgh, Mercer, Jones, Thomson, Geldard, Cunliffe, Lawton, Stevenson, Boyes.

Referee: Mr. T. Thomson (North'b'land)

A match which lived up to expectations! Before a crowd of 82,653 on 10 June 1938 both sides attempted to play attractive football throughout and, although the forward lines contained outstanding goalscorers, two well-organised defences remained in control.

Celtic's front men, famous for their swift interchanging, attacked in waves but Everton's defence, organised by the stolid Welsh internationalist Jones, remained cool and Joe Mercer was adept in switching the play into attack; Tommy Lawton, England's most feared centre-forward, was the chief danger to Celtic both on the ground and in the air and Lyon, Celtic's captain had to be steady and resolute. Once again Joe Kennaway came to Celtic's rescue with a brave dive at Lawton's feet to save a certain goal.

After 90 minutes of a cup-tie in which the play had swung from end to end, the final was to be decided in extra-time. Celtic, urged on by the majority in the crowd, dominated this period – helped considerably by the fact that Everton's Cunliffe had been injured and was limping on the wing. Early on, Jones had to scramble a shot from the goal-line with his keeper stranded.

After 7 minutes of extra time Johnny Crum, the diminutive successor to Jimmy McGrory, collected a neat flick from Divers, steadied himself and shot powerfully from 15 yards; Sagar got his hand to the ball but could not stop the shot.

Crum raced behind the goal to celebrate with an impromptu jig. In 1938 such expressions of joy were most uncommon – and Crum's 'antics' were recalled for years by a Celtic support for whom the capture

of this trophy had achieved mythic proportions. Perhaps not too surprisingly because this competition did deserve to rank as an unofficial 'British Championship'.

Final Result:
Celtic 1, Everton 0

The Exhibition was a considerable success, attracting an attendance of 12,882,548 during its six-month duration. This virtually was double that for the year-long Millennium Dome in London during 2000. Not only that, the Empire Exhibition was closed on Sundays, the Sabbath being very much observed throughout Scotland in those days.

(GREAT) ESCAPES

The Scottish Cup has been the competition for Celtic's most celebrated last-gasp heroics to avoid elimination:

Motherwell 2, Celtic 2: 11 April 1931
Celtic fall two goals behind to a classy Motherwell side in the Scottish Cup final at Hampden Park but fight back to earn a replay with two goals in the last seven minutes, the equaliser coming only seconds from the end and was a tragic own-goal by 'Well's captain, Craig.

Falkirk 2, Celtic 3: 21 February 1953
Before a record crowd at Brockville, Celtic are hesitant in defence and trail by two goals at halftime. Charlie Tully starts the revival with his famous twice-taken corner kick, Willie Fernie equalises and John McGrory scores the winner.

Elgin City 1, Celtic 2: 5 March 1960
Celtic fall behind to underdogs Elgin City at Boroughriggs Park but with only minutes

to go win through with goals from John Divers and Eric Smith.

Dunfermline Athletic 2, Celtic 3: 24 April 1965
Twice Celtic are behind to the Pars in this pulsating final before 108,800 at Hampden Park. Twice Bertie Auld equalises, before Billy McNeil's header in the 82nd minute wins the Cup.

Dundee United 1, Celtic 2: 18 May 1985
Kevin Gallacher, grandson of Celtic's Patsy, gives United the lead in this Scottish Cup final but Davie Provan equalises from a long-range free kick, and Frank McGarvey heads the winning goal near the end.

Celtic 2, Hearts 1: 9 April 1988
Celtic's centenary celebrations are endangered when Hearts take the lead early in the second half with a disputed goal in this Scottish Cup semi-final. Mark McGhee somehow scrapes his shot past everybody in a packed goalmouth to equalise with three minutes left, and Andy Walker smashes in the winner two minutes later after mishandling by Hearts' keeper Henry Smith.

Dundee United 1, Celtic 2: 14 May 1988
In the Scottish Cup final Frank McAvennie's late goals are enough to edge the Taysiders, who had scored early in the second half, and to give Celtic the coveted 'double' in their centenary season.

Celtic 2, Dundee United 1: 10 March 1996
The holders Celtic look doomed as they trail to a penalty goal, but Pierre van Hooijdonk heads in the equaliser with less than a minute to go, and Andreas Thom nets the winner after stealing the ball just after the kickoff.

Inverness Caledonian Thistle 1, Celtic 2: 25 February 2007
Celtic's bogey side look like inflicting a third Scottish Cup shock when they hold their lead until the 88th minute; Steven Pressley heads in the equaliser after a corner kick, and Kenny Miller breaks Inverness hearts with his injury-time winner.

Aberdeen 1, Celtic 1 10 March 2008
Aberdeen go ahead with twelve minutes left of this Scottish Cup tie. Artur Boruc saves Celtic from elimination with three magnificent saves in the last ten minutes. Jan Vennegoor of Hesselink slides in to score in the dying seconds. Unfortunately, the heroics were in vain as Celtic lost the replay at Parkhead.

However, perhaps the greatest escapes of all were in two league fixtures:

Dundee 2, Celtic 3: 17 April 1948
At Dens Park Celtic are down by 2-1 midway through the second half in the last league match of the season. A defeat would have involved Celtic in the ongoing relegation struggle but two late goals by Jock Weir (to complete his hat-trick) ease Celtic's worries;

Celtic 4, Rangers 2: 21 May 1979
The winners would be guaranteed the championship. Celtic's Johnny Doyle is ordered off and Rangers led by 2-1 with thirty-five minutes left. Although short-handed Celtic produce a heroic effort to score three times.

In 2007/08 with only 7 league games left, Celtic were 7 points behind Rangers with a game more played. They won all 7 games to take the title by 3 points on the last day of the season at Tannadice.

The Celtic bench rise in victory at the final whistle in the European Cup final in Lisbon on 25 May 1967

EUROPE

EUROPEAN CUP (RESULTS)

1966/67 (1):
28 September
Zurich H 2–0 Gemmell, McBride

5 October: Zurich A 3–0 Gemmell (2), Chalmers (5–0)

30 November
Nantes A 3–1 McBride, Lennox, Chalmers

7 December
Nantes H 3–1 Johnstone, Chalmers, Lennox (6–2)

1 March
Vojvodina A 0–1

8 March
Vojvodina H 2–0 Chalmers, McNeill (2-1)

12 April
Dukla H 3–1 Wallace (2), Johnstone
25 April: Dukla A 0–0 (3–1)

25 May
Inter Milan N 2–1 Gemmell, Chalmers

1967/68 (2)
20 September
Dynamo Kiev H 1-2 Lennox

4 October
Dynamo Kiev A 1-1 Lennox (2–3)

1968/69 (3)
18 September
St. Etienne A 0-2

2 October
St. Etienne H 4-0 Gemmell (p), Craig,
Chalmers, McBride (4–2)

13 November
Red Star Belgrade H 5-1 Johnstone (2),
Wallace, Murdoch, Lennox

27 November
Red Star Belgrade A 1-1 Wallace (6–2)

19 February 1969
AC Milan A 0-0

12 March
AC Milan A 0-1 (0–1)

1969/70 (4)
17 September
Basle A 0-0

1 October
Basle H 2-0 Hood, Gemmell (2–0)

12 November
Benfica H 3-0 Gemmell, Wallace, Hood

26 November
Benfica A 0-3 (3–3 aet, Celtic won on toss
of coin)

4 March 1970
Fiorentina H 3-0 Auld, Wallace, o.g.

18 March: Fiorentina A 0-1 (3–1)

1 April
Leeds United A 1-0 Connelly

15 April
Leeds United N 2-1 Hughes, Murdoch
(3–1)

6 May
Feyenoord N 1-2 (aet) Gemmell

1970/71 (5)
6 September
KPV Kokkola H 9-0 Hood (3), Wilson (2),
McNeill, Hughes, Davidson, Johnstone

30 September
KPV Kokkola A 5-0 Wallace (2),
Davidson, Callaghan, Lennox (14–0)

21 October
Waterford A 7-0 Wallace (3), Macari (2),
Murdoch (2)

4 November
Waterford H 3-2 Johnstone (2), Hughes
(10–2)

10 March
Ajax A 0-3

24 March
Ajax H 1-0 Johnstone (1–0)

1971/72 (6)
15 September
B1903 Copenhagen A 1-2 Macari

'How does this Rangers side
compare with the Lisbon Lions?
I have to be honest and say it
would be a draw but remember
that some of us are getting on
for sixty.'
Bertie Auld, when asked to
comment upon a successful run
in Europe for Rangers.

29 September
B1903 Copenhagen H 3-0 Wallace (2),
Callaghan (4–2)

20 October
Sliema Wanderers H 5-0 Hood (2),
Gemmell, Brogan, Macari

3 November
Sliema Wanderers A 2-1 Lennox, Hood
(7–1)

8 March
Ujpest Dozsa A 2-1 Macari, o.g.

22 March
Ujpest Dozsa H 1-1 Macari (3–2)

5 April
Inter Milan A 0-0

19 April
Inter Milan H 0-0 (0–0, Celtic lost on
penalties)

1972/73 (7)
13 September
Rosenborg H 2-1 Deans, Macari (played
at Hampden)

27 September
Rosenborg A 3-1 Hood, Dalglish, Macari
(5–2)

25 October
Ujpest Dozsa H 2-1 Dalglish (2)

> 'They can't shoot you when
> you're out there juking and
> jiving. I can't move; I'll be
> sitting there in that dugout!'
> Jock Stein to Jimmy
> Johnstone, after both had
> received death-threats prior
> to a European semi-final in
> Madrid.

8 November
Ujpest Dozsa A 0-3 (2–4)

1973/74 (8)
19 September
TPS Turku A 6-1 Callaghan (2), Connelly,
Johnstone, Hood, Deans

3 October
TPS Turku H 3-0 Johnstone (2), Deans
(9–1)

24 October
Vejle H 0-0

6 November
Veijle A 1-0 Lennox (1–0)

27 February
Basle A 2-3 Dalglish, Wilson

20 March
Basle H 4-2 (aet) Murray, Deans,
Callaghan, Dalglish (6–5)

10 April
Atletico Madrid H 0-0

24 April
Atletico Madrid A 0-2 (0–2)

1974/75 (9)
18 September
Olympiakos H 1-1 Wilson

2 October
Olympiakos A 0-2 (1–3)

1977/78 (10)
14 September
Jeunesse Esch H 5-0 Craig (2),
MacDonald, Wilson, McLaughlin

28 September
Jeunesse Esch A 6-1 Glavin (2),
Edvaldsson (2), Lennox, Craig (11–1)

19 October
SW Innsbruck H 2-1 Craig, Burns

2 November
SW Innsbruck A 0-3 (2–4)

1979/80 (11)
10 September
Partizan Tirana A 0-1

3 October Partizan Tirana H 4-1 Aitken (2), MacDonald, Davidson (4–2)

24 October
Dundalk H 3-2 MacDonald, McCluskey, Burns

7 November
Dundalk A 0-0 (3–2)

5 March
Real Madrid H 2-0 McCluskey, Doyle

19 March
Real Madrid A 0-3 (2–3)

1981/82 (12)
16 September
Juventus H 1-0 MacLeod

30 September
Juventus A 0-2 (1–2)

1982/83 (13)
15 September
Ajax H 2-2 Nicholas, McGarvey

29 September
Ajax A 2-1 Nicholas, McCluskey (4–3)

20 October
Real Sociedad A 0-2

3 November
Real Sociedad H 2-1 MacLeod (2) (2–3)

1986/87 (14)
17 September
Shamrock Rovers A 1-0 MacLeod

1 October
Shamrock Rovers H 2-0 Johnston (2) (3–0)

22 October
Dynamo Kiev H 1-1 Johnston

5 November
Dynamo Kiev A 1-3 McGhee (2–4)

1988/89 (15)
7 September 1988
Honved A 0-1

5 October Honved H 4-0 Walker, Stark, McAvennie, McGhee (4–1)

26 October
Werder Bremen H 0-1

8 November
Werder Bremen A 0-0 (0–1)

1998/99 (16)
22 July 1998
St. Patrick's Athletic H 0-0

29 July
St. Patrick's Athletic A 2-0 Larsson, Brattbakk (2–0)

12 August
Croatia Zagreb H 1-0 Jackson

26 August
Croatia Zagreb A 0-3 (1–3)

2001/02 (17)
8 August
Ajax A 3-1 Petta, Agathe, Sutton

22 August Ajax H 0-1 (3–2)

18 September
Juventus A 2-3 Petrov, Larsson (p)

25 September
Porto H 1-0 Larsson

10 October
Rosenborg H 1-0 Thompson

17 October
Porto A 0-3

23 October
Rosenborg A 0-2

31 October
Juventus H 4-3 Sutton (2), Valgaeren, Larsson (p)

2002/03 (18)
14 August
Basle 3-1 H Larsson, Sutton, Sylla

28 August
Basle 0-2 A (3–3)

2003/04 (19)
30 July
Kaunas 4-0 A Larsson, Sutton, Maloney, L Miller

6 August
Kaunas 1-0 H o.g. (5–0)

13 August
MTK Budapest 4-0 A Larsson, Sutton, Agathe, Petrov

27 August
MTK Budapest 1-0 H Sutton (5–1)

17 September
Bayern Munich 1-2 A Thompson

30 September
Lyon 2-0 H Sutton, L. Miller

21 October
Anderlecht 0-1 A

5 November
Anderlecht 3-1 H Larsson, Sutton, L. Miller

25 November
Bayern Munich 0-0 H

10 December
Lyon 2-3 A Sutton, Hartson

2004/05 (20)
14 September
Barcelona 1-3 H Sutton

29 September
AC Milan 1-3 A Varga

20 October
Shakhtar Donetsk 0-3 A

2 November
Shakhtar Donetsk 1-0 H Thompson

24 November
Barcelona 1-1 A Hartson

7 December
AC Milan 0-0 H

2005/06 (21)
27 July
Artmedia Bratislava A 0-5

2 August
Artmedia Bratislava H 4-0 McManus, Hartson, Thompson, Beattie (4–5)

2006/07 (22)
13 September
Manchester United 2-3 A Vennegoor of Hesselink, Nakamura

26 September
FC Copenhagen 1-0 H K. Miller (pen)

17 October
Benfica 3-0 H K. Miller (2), Pearson

1 November
Benfica 0-3 A

21 November
Manchester United 1-0 H Nakamura

6 December
FC Copenhagen 1-3 A Jarosik

20 February
AC Milan 0-0 H

7 March
AC Milan 0-1 (aet) A (0–1)

2007/08 (23)
15 August
Spartak Moscow 1-1 A Hartley

29 August
Spartak Moscow 1-1 H McDonald (aet,
2–2, Celtic win on penalties)

16 September
Shakthar Donetsk 0-2 A

3 October
AC Milan 2-1 H McManus, McDonald

24 October
Benfica 0-1 A

6 November
Benfica 1-0 H McGeady

28 November
Shakthar Donetsk 2-1 H Jarosik, Donati

4 December
AC Milan 0-1 A

20 February
Barcelona 2-3 H Vennegoor of Hesselink,
Robson

4 March
Barcelona 0-1 A (2–4)

EUROPEAN CUP-WINNERS' CUP
(RESULTS)

1963/64 (1)
17 September
Basle 5-1 A Hughes (3), Divers, Lennox

9 October
Basle 5-0 H Divers (2), Johnstone,
Murdoch, Chalmers (10–1)

4 December
Dinamo Zagreb 3-0 H Chalmers (2),
Hughes

11 December
Dinamo Zagreb 1-2 A Murdoch (4–2)

26 February
Slovan Bratislava 1-0 H Murdoch

4 March Slovan Bratislava 1-0 A Hughes
(2–0)

15 April
MTK Budapest 3-0 H Chalmers (2),
Johnstone

29 April MTK Budapest 0-4 A (3–4)

1965/66 (2)
29 September
Go Ahead Deventer 6-0 A Lennox (3),
Johnstone (2), Hughes

7 October Go Ahead Deventer 1-0 H
McBride (7–0)

3 November
AGF Aarhus 1-0 A McBride

17 November AGF Aarhus 2-0 H
McNeill, Johnstone (3–0)

12 January
Dinamo Kiev 3-0 H Murdoch (2),
Gemmell

26 January
Dinamo Kiev 1-1 A Gemmell (4–1)

14 April
Liverpool 1-0 H Lennox

19 April Liverpool 0-2 A (1–2)

1975/76 (3)
16 September
Valur 2-0 A Wilson, MacDonald

1 October
Valur 7-0 H Hood (2), Edvaldsson, Dalglish, P. McCluskey, Deans, Callaghan (9–0)

22 October
Boavista 0-0 A

5 November
Boavista 3-1 H Dalglish, Edvaldsson, Deans (3–1)

3 March 1976
Sachsenring Zwickau 1-1 H Dalglish

17 March
Sachsenring Zwickau 0-1 A (1–2)

1980/81 (4)
20 August
Diosgyoeri Miskolc 6-0 H McGarvey (3), McCluskey (2), Sullivan

3 September
Diosgyoeri Miskolc 1-2 A Nicholas (7–2)

17 September
Politecnika Timisoara 2-1 H Nicholas (2)

1 October
Politecnika Timisoara 0-1 A (2–2)

1984/85 (5)
19 September
Ghent 0-1 A

3 October
Ghent 3-0 H McGarvey (2), McStay (3–1)

24 October
Rapid Vienna 1-3 A McClair

7 November
Rapid Vienna 3-0 H (Match ordered to be replayed)

2 December Rapid Vienna 0-1 N (1–4)

1985/86 (6)
18 September
Atletico Madrid 1-1 A Johnston

2 October
Atletico Madrid 1-2 H Aitken (played behind closed doors) (2–3)

1989/90 (7)
12 September
Partizan Belgrade 1-2 A Galloway

27 September
Partizan Belgrade 5-4 H Dziekanowski (4), Walker (6–6)

1995/96 (8)
14 September
Dinamo Batumi 3-2 A Thom (2), Donnelly

28 September
Dinamo Batumi 4-0 H Thom (2), Donnelly, Walker (7–2)

19 October
Paris St. Germain 0-1 A

2 November Paris St. Germain 0-3 H (0–4)

INTER CITIES FAIRS CUP/ UEFA CUP (RESULTS)

1962/63 (1)
26 September 1962 Valencia 2-4 A Carroll, o.g.
24 October Valencia 2-2 H Crerand,o.g.

1964/65 (2)
23 September
Leixoes 1-1 A Murdoch

7 October
Leixoes 3-0 H Chalmers (2), Murdoch (4–1)

18 November
Barcelona 1-3 A Hughes

2 December
Barcelona 0-0 H (1–3)

1976/77 (3)
15 September
Wisla Krakow 2-2 H MacDonald, Dalglish

29 September
Wisla Krakow 0-2 A (2–4)

1983/84 (4)
14 September
Aarhus 1-0 H Aitken

28 September
Aarhus 4-1 A MacLeod, McGarvey,
Aitken, Provan (5–1)

19 October
Sporting Lisbon A 0-2

2 November
Sporting Lisbon H 5-0 Burns, McAdam,
McClair, MacLeod, McGarvey (5–2)

23 November
Nottingham Forest A 0-0

7 December
Nottingham Forest H 1-2 MacLeod (1–2)

1987/88 (5)
15 September
Borussia Dortmund 2-1 H Walker, Whyte

29 September
Borussia Dortmund 0-2 A (2–3)

1991/92 (6)
18 September
Germinal Ekeren 2-0 H Nicholas (2, pen)

1 October
Germinal Ekeren 1-1 A Galloway (3–1)

22 October
Neuchatel Xamax 1-5 A O'Neil

6 November
Neuchatel Xamax 1-0 H Miller (2–5)

1992/93 (7)
15 September
Cologne 0-2 A

30 September
Cologne 3-0 H McStay, Creaney, Collins
(3–2)

20 October
Borussia Dortmund 0-1 A

3 November
Borussia Dortmund 1-2 H Creaney (1–3)

1993/94 (8)
14 September
Young Boys Berne 0-0 A

29 September
Young Boys Berne 1-0 H o.g. (1–0)

20 October
Sporting Lisbon 1-0 H Creaney

3 November
Sporting Lisbon 0-2 A (1–2)

1996/97 (9)
8 August
Kosice 0-0 A

20 August
Kosice 1-0 H Cadete (1–0)

10 September
Hamburg 0-2 H

24 September
Hamburg 0-2 A (0–4)

1997/98 (10)
23 July
Inter Cable Tel 3-0 A Thom (p), Johnson,
Wieghorst

29 July
Inter Cable Tel 5-0 H Jackson, Thom (p),
Johnson, Hannah, Hay (8–0)

12 August
Tirol Innsbruck 1-2 A Stubbs

26 August
Tirol Innsbruck 6-3 H Donnelly (2),
Burley (2), Wieghorst, Thom (7–5)

16 September
Liverpool 2-2 H McNamara, Donnelly
(pen)

30 September
Liverpool 0-0 A (2–2)

1998/99 (11)
15 September
Vitoria Guimarses 2-1 A Larsson,
Donnelly

29 September
Vitoria Guimarses 2-1 H Stubbs, Larsson
(4–2)

24 October
FC Zurich 1-1 H Brattbakk (3–5)

3 November
FC Zurich 2-4 A Larsson, O'Donnell

1999/2000 (12)
12 August
Cwmbran Town 6-0 A Larsson (2),
Berkovic, Tebily, Viduka, Brattbakk

26 August
Cwmbran Town 4-0 H Brattbakk, Mjallby,
Johnson, Smith (10–0)

16 September
Hapoel Tel Aviv 2-0 H Larsson (2, pen)

30 September
Hapoel Tel Aviv 1-0 A Larsson (3–0)

21 October
Olympique Lyonnais 0-1 A

4 November
Olympique Lyonnais 0-1 H (0–2)

2000/01 (13)
12 August
Jeunesse Esch 4-0 A Moravcik (2),
Larsson, Petta

24 August
Jeunesse Esch 7-0 H Burchill (3),
Berkovic (2), Riseth, Petrov (11–0)

14 September
HJK Helsinki 2-0 H Larsson (2)

28 September
HJK Helsinki 1-2 A Sutton (3–2)

26 October
Bordeaux 1-1 A Larsson (p)

9 November
Bordeaux 1-2 H (aet) Moravcik (2–3)

2001/02 (14)
22 November
Valencia 0-1 A

6 December
Valencia 1-0 H Larsson (1–1, Celtic lost
on penalties)

2002/03 (15)
19 September
Suduva 8-1 H Larsson (3), Petrov, Sutton,
Hartson, Lambert, Valgaeren

3 October
Suduva 2-0 A Thompson, Fernandez (10–1)

31 October
Blackburn Rovers 1-0 H Larsson

14 November
Blackburn Rovers 2-0 A Larsson, Sutton
(3–0)

28 November
Celta Vigo 1-0 H Larsson

12 December
Celta Vigo 1-2 A Hartson (2–2, Celtic win on away goals)

20 February
Stuttgart 3-1 H Petrov, Lambert, Maloney

27 February
Stuttgart 2-3 A Sutton, Thompson (5–4)

13 March
Liverpool 1-1 H Larsson

20 March
Liverpool 2-0 A Thompson, Hartson (3–1)

10 April
Boavista 1-1 H Larsson

Celtic starting eleven line up before kick-off in the UEFA Cup Final 2003
Back: Balde, Mjallby, Sutton, Douglas, Agathe; Front: Petrov, Lennon, Valgaeren, Thompson, Larsson, Lambert

24 April
Boavista 1-0 Larsson (2–1)

21 May
Porto 2-3 N Larsson (2) aet

2003/04 (16)
26 February
Teplice 3-0 H Larsson (2), Sutton

3 March
Teplice 0-1 A (3–1)

11 March
Barcelona 1-0 H Thompson

25 March
Barcelona 0-0 A (1–0)

Celtic captain Neil Lennon shows his determination in a European tie

8 April
Villareal 1-1 H Larsson

14 April
Villareal 0-2 A (1–3)

EUROPEAN OPPOSITION

(By country)

Albania
Partizan Tirana EC 1979/80 4-1, 0-1

Austria
SW Innsbruck EC 1977/78 2-1, 0-3;
Rapid Vienna ECWC 1984/85 1-3, 0-1;
Tirol Innsbruck UEFA C 1997/98 6-3, 1-2

Belgium
KAA Gent ECWC 1984/85 3-0, 0-1;
Germinal Ekeren UEFA C 1991/92 2-0, 1-1
Anderlecht CL 2003/04 3-1,0-1

Croatia
Croatia Zagreb CL 1998/99 1-0, 0-3

Czechoslovakia
Slovan Bratislava 1963/64 ECWC 1-0, 1-0;
Dukla Prague 1966/67 EC 3-1, 1-1

Denmark
AGF Aarhus ECWC 1965/66 2-0,1-0,
UEFA C 1983/84 1-0, 4-1;
B1903 Copenhagen EC (*sic*) 1971/72 3-0, 1-2; CL 2006/07 1-0, 1-3
Vejle EC 1973/74 0-0, 1-0

Eire
Waterford EC 1970/71 3-2, 7-0;
Dundalk EC 1979/80 3-2, 0-0;
Shamrock Rovers EC 1986/87 2-0, 1-0;
St. Patrick's Athletic CL 1998/99 0-0,
2-0

England
Liverpool ECWC 1965/66 1-0, 0-2; UEFA
C 1997/98 2-2, 0-0; UEFA C 2003/03 1-1,
2-0;
Leeds United EC 1969/70 2-1, 1-0;
Nottingham Forest UEFA C 1983/84
1-2, 0-0
Blackburn Rovers UEFA C 2002/03 1-0,2-0
Manchester United CL 2006/07 1-0, 2-3

Finland
KPV Kokkola EC 1970/71 9-0, 5-0;
TPS Turku EC 1973/74 3-0, 6-1;
HJK Helsinki UEFA C 2000/01 2-0, 1-2

France
Nantes 1966/67 EC 3-1, 3-1;
St. Etienne 1968/69 EC 4-0, 0-2;
Paris St. Germain ECWC 1995/96 0-3, 0-1;
Olympique Lyonnais UEFA C 1999/2000
0-1, 0-1;
Bordeaux UEFA C 2000/01 1-2, 1-1;
Lyon CL 2003/04 2-0, 2-3

Germany
Borussia Dortmund UEFA C 1987/88
2-1, 0-2, UEFA C 1992/93 1-2, 0-1;
Werder Bremen EC 1988/89 0-1, 0-0;
Cologne UEFA C 1992/93 3-0, 0-2;
Hamburg UEFA C 1996/97 0-2, 0-2;
Sachsenring Zwickau ECWC 1975/76
1-1, 0-1

Georgia
Dynamo Batumi ECWC 1995/96 4-0, 3-2

Greece
Olympiakos EC 1974/75 1-1, 0-2

Holland
Go-Ahead Deventer ECWC 1965/66 1-0,
6-0;

Feyenoord EC 1969/70 Neutral 1-2 (aet);
Ajax EC 1970/71 1-0, 0-3; EC 1982/83
2-2, 2-1; CL 2001/02 0-1,3-1

Hungary
MTK Budapest ECWC 1963/64 3-0, 0-4;
Ujpest Dozsa EC 1971/72 1-1, 2-1,
EC 1972/73 2-1, 0-3;
Diosgyori Miskolc ECWC 1980/81 6-0, 1-2;
Honved EC 1988/89 4-0, 0-1

Iceland
Valur ECWC 1975/76 7-0, 2-0

Israel
Hapoel Tel Aviv UEFA C 1999/2000
2-0,1-0

Italy
Inter Milan 1966/67 EC Neutral 2-1,
1971/72 EC 0-0, 0-0;
AC Milan 1968/69 EC 0-1, 0-0;
CL 2004/05 0-0, 1-3; CL 2006/07 0-0,
0-1; CL 2007/08 2-1, 0-1
Fiorentina 1969/70 EC 3-0, 0-1;
Juventus EC 1981/82 1-0, 0-2; CL 2001/
02 4-3, 2-3

Lithuania
FC Suduva UEFA C 2002/03 8-1, 2-0;
FBK Kaunas CL 2003/04 4-0,1-0

Luxembourg
Jeunesse Esch EC 1977/78 5-0, 6-1;
UEFA C 2000/01 7-0, 4-0

Malta
Sliema Wanderers EC 1971/72 5-0, 2-1

Norway
Rosenborg EC 1972/73 2-1,3-1;
CL 2001/02 1-0, 0-2

Poland
Wisla Krakow UEFA C 1976/77 2-2, 0-2

Portugal
Leixoes 1964/65 ICFC 3-0, 1-1;
Benfica 1969/70 EC 3-0, 0-3; CL 2006/07
3-0, 3-0; CL 2007/08 1-0, 0-1;

Boavista ECWC 1975/76 3-0, 1-1;
Sporting Lisbon UEFA C 1983/84 5-0, 0-2;
UEFA C 1993/94 1-0, 0-2;
Vitoria Guimaraes UEFA C 1998/99
2-1,2-1;
Porto CL 2001/02 1-0, 0-3; UEFA C
2002/03 2-3

Russia
Spartak Moscow 2007/08 EC 1-1,1-1

Romania
Politechnica Timisoara ECWC 1980/81
2-1, 0-1

Slovakia
Kosice UEFA C 1996/97 1-0, 0-0;
FC Artmedia CL 2005/06 0-5, 4-0

Spain
Valencia 1962/63 ICFC 2-2, 2-4;
UEFA C 2001/02 1-0, 0-1;
Barcelona ICFC 1964/65 0-0, 1-3; UEFA
C 2003/04 1-0,0-0; CL 2004/05 1-3, 1-1;
CL 2007/08 2-3, 0-1;
Atletico Madrid EC 1973/74 0-0, 0-2;
ECWC 1985/86 1-2, 1-1;
Real Madrid EC 1979/80 2-0, 0-3;
Real Sociedad EC 1982/83 2-1, 0-2;
Celta Vigo UEFA C 2002/03 1-0, 1-2

Switzerland
Basle 1963/64 ECWC 5-0, 5-1; 1969/70
EC 2-0, 0-0; 1973/74 EC 4-2, 2-3;
2002/03 CL 3-1, 0-2
FC Zurich 1966/67 EC 2-0, 3-0; UEFA C
1998/99 1-1, 2-4
Neuchatel Xamax UEFA C 1991/92 1-0,
1-5
Young Boys Berne UEFA C 1993/94 1-0,
0-0

Ukraine
Shakhtar Donesk CL 2004/05 0-3, 1-0;
CL 2007/08 2-1, 0-2

USSR
Dinamo Kiev 1965/66 ECWC 3-0,1-1;
1967/68 EC 1-2, 1-1; EC 1986/97 1-1, 1-3

Wales
Inter Cabletel UEFA C 1997/98 5-0,
3-0;
Cwmbran Town UEFA C 1999/2000 4-0,
6-0

Yugoslavia
Dynamo Zagreb 1963/64 ECWC 3-0,
1-2;
Vojvodina Novi Sad 1966/67 EC 2-0,
0-1;
Red Star (Belgrade) 1968/69 EC 5-1,
1-1;
Partizan Belgrade ECWC 1989/90 5-4,
1-2

Abbreviations:
CL (Champions League),
EC (European Cup),
ECWC (European Cup-Winners' Cup),
ICFC (Inter Cities Fairs Cup),
UEFA C (UEFA Cup)

EXPERIENCE

Apparently most sides need a leaven of experience to get through the difficult matches. Here is one representative Celtic side (4-4-2) with considerable league experience, based on appearances:

Pat Bonner (483);
Alec McNair (584), Billy McNeill (486),
Roy Aitken (483), Danny McGrain (433 + 8);
Bobby Evans (385), Paul McStay (509),
Patsy Gallacher (432), Jimmy McMenemy (456);
Jimmy McGrory (378), Bobby Lennox (297 +50)

On the other hand, Celtic fielded a young side with six players making their debuts against Dundee United at Celtic Park on 21 May 2000 – and won 2-0.

What links Nicholas II, the last Tsar of Russia and Celtic?
Carl Gustav Faberge, the Tsar's imperial jeweller created the original
lavish and jewelled Faberge egg, a tradition carried on to this day by
his great granddaughter who made the above Faberge egg dedicated
to Jimmy Johnstone. Made from gold, silver, enamel and black gold,
it is displayed at Celtic Park.

F

FABERGE

Jimmy Johnstone became the first living person since the time of the tsars to be honoured with a Faberge Egg designed in his honour. 'Celtic's Greatest Ever Player' had his designed by the grand daughter of Carl Faberge himself.

FALKIRK

It must be recognised generally that Celtic are a bigger club than Falkirk. Accordingly, several players, having played for Celtic, have moved to Falkirk later on in their careers. The following might be included in this category: Jimmy Delaney, George Connelly, Patsy Gallacher, Willie Gallacher, and Jock Weir.

The Gallachers, father and son, must constitute a unique distinction in that they both played for Celtic and Falkirk.

Hugh Maxwell, the scorer of one of Celtic's quickest goals, moved in the other direction in 1964.

FANS FROM OTHER SPORTS

Celtic have attracted some famous fans, already distinguished in their own sport, such as Paul McGinlay, Padraig Harrington, Bob Torrance (golf), Scott Harrison (boxing), Kevin Little (speedway), James McLaren (rugby), and John Higgins (snooker).

FASTEST GOALS

Only in recent times, and helped by television evidence, can the time of the goal be judged accurately:

on 11 May 1965 at Hampden Park in the Glasgow Cup final against Queen's Park Bobby Lennox scored within ten seconds to help Celtic on the way to a 5-0 win;

on 21 November 1964 Hugh Maxwell, a recent signing from Falkirk, scored against his former club at Celtic Park in an estimated twelve seconds;

on 29 August 1962 Charlie Gallagher opened the scoring against Dundee at Celtic Park in a League Cup sectional match at a time estimated at fifteen seconds;

on 16 December 1950 John McPhail scored against East Fife at Celtic Park in just under ten seconds. That day on a snow-covered pitch Celtic won by 6-2 with McPhail and Bobby Collins each scoring a hat-trick;

on 18 February 1950 Jock Weir scored against Stirling Albion at Parkhead in fifteen seconds to help Celtic to a 2-1 win.

In Old Firm clashes Celtic have occasionally got off to a lightning-fast start:

on 10 April 1982 Danny Crainie started his debut against Rangers with a goal in the first minute to help Celtic to a 2-1 win at Parkhead;

on 3 September 1960 Steve Chalmers netted in the first minute in a League Cup tie but Celtic eventually lost 2-1;

on 17 September 1966 Celtic shocked Rangers with two goals inside the first four minutes through Bertie Auld and Bobby Murdoch and went on to coast to a 2-0 league win.

on 27 August 2000 at Parkhead Celtic raced to a 3-0 lead within the first eleven minutes with goals from Chris Sutton, Stiliyan Petrov and Paul Lambert to win in the end by 6-2;

on 7 December 2002 Chris Sutton scored at Ibrox against Rangers in 18 seconds, but Celtic eventually lost 3-2;

FIRES

A fire broke out in the Janefield Stand on 9 May 1904 and destroyed that stand and the original pavilion. Many valuable records and memorabilia were destroyed in the blaze. Another fire in 1929 also destroyed the pavilion and wiped out many valuable records. Among the charred remains were strips, 50 pairs of boots and club records. The four remaining home matches v Partick Thistle, Hibs, Queen's Park and Falkirk were switched to their opponents' grounds. Of Celtic's 38 league games 14 were played at Celtic Park and 24 away.

FIRST SEASON

In Celtic's first season as a football club (1888/89) most games played were exhibitions or 'friendlies'. The only competition available to all the clubs in Scotland was the Scottish Cup and Celtic astonished the football world by reaching the final in their very first season. In the final they came up against the formidable Third Lanark who beat them 2-1 in a re-match of a friendly staged a week earlier due to snow and bad weather.

The other local competitions in which Celtic competed were the Exhibition Cup, Glasgow Cup, Charity Cup and the North Eastern Cup which Celtic won by beating Cowlairs 6-1 on 11 May 1889 to pick up their first silverware.

Note that Celtic played against English clubs, amateur and professional and both home and away in friendly matches: Mitchell's St. George (Birmingham), Corinthians (London), Newcastle West End, Preston North End, Bolton Wanderers, and Burnley. They even found time to cross the Irish Sea in April to face Distillery (1-0) and United Belfast (5-2) on successive days.

1 August 1888 Abercorn N 1-1
   (Exhibition Cup)
4 August Hibernian H 3-2
11 August Airdrieonians A 6-0
18 August Clyde A 5-1
21 August Dumbarton N 3-1 (Exhib Cup)

22 August Third Lanark A 3-4

23 August Abercorn A 4-2

27 August Northern A 3-0

29 August Partick Thistle N 1-0 (Exhibition Cup)

1 September Shettleston H 5-1 (Scottish Cup)

3 September Whitefield A 5-1

6 September Cowlairs N 0-2 (Exhibition Cup)

8 September Dumbarton H 3-0

15 September Dumbarton A 2-1

22 September Cowlairs H 8-0 (Scottish Cup)

29 September Airdrieonians H 4-1

6 October Shettleston H 11-2 (Glasgow Cup)

13 October Albion Rovers H 4-1 (Scottish Cup)

15 October Dundee Harp A 7-1

20 October Hibernian A 3-0

27 October Rangers A 6-1 (Glasgow Cup)

3 November St. Bernards A 4-1 (Scottish Cup)

10 November Renton H 1-0

17 November Queen's Park H 0-2 (Glasgow Cup)

24 November Clyde H 0-1

1 December Port Glasgow Athletic A 4-2

8 December Clyde H 9-2 (Scottish Cup)

15 December East Stirlingshire A 2-1 (Scottish Cup)

22 December Vale of Leven A 2-1

29 December Clydesdale A 5-1 (North Eastern Cup)

31 December H 7-1

3 January 1889 Corinthians H 6-2

5 January Thistle A 2-1

12 January Dumbarton A 4-1 (Scottish Cup)

19 January Morton A 5-4

26 January Airdrieonians H 1-1

2 February Third Lanark N 0-3 (Scottish Cup) (played as friendly)

9 February Third Lanark N 1-2 (Scottish Cup)

16 February Corinthians A 1-3

23 February Clydesdale Harriers H 0-3

2 March Abercorn H 4-4

9 March Hibernian H 5-4

16 March Northern H 4-1 (North Eastern Cup)

23 March Newcastle West End A 4-3

30 March Third Lanark H 4-1

6 April Motherwell A 8-3

13 April Cowlairs A 1-0

19 April Bolton Wanderers A 0-2

20 April Burnley A 3-1

22 April Distillery A 1-0

23 April United Belfast A 5-2

4 May Renton N 2-5 (Charity Cup)

11 May Cowlairs N 6-1 (North Eastern Cup)

18 May Thistle A 2-0

23 May Bolton Wanderers H 5-1

25 May Preston North End H 2-1

FIXTURE CONGESTION

In April 1909 Celtic fulfilled ten league fixtures against St. Mirren, Third Lanark, Hearts, Hamilton Academical (2), Morton, Airdrie, Motherwell, Queen's Park and Hibernian. They won six of them, drew three and lost only one to win the league by a single point from Dundee. In addition to that they played Rangers twice in the Scottish Cup final on the tenth and seventeenth, drawing both before rioting caused the SFA to withhold the trophy.

On 15 April 1916 Celtic completed two Scottish League fixtures on the same day: Raith Rovers at Celtic Park (6-0) and Motherwell at Fir Park a couple of hours later (3-1). Several other clubs also played two matches that day but Celtic, the league champions, were the only one to win both. The rush was in order to complete the programme before the traditional ending date of 30 April.

In 1956/57 Celtic chose to play Partick Thistle on 9 September 1955 in a Glasgow Cup tie at Firhill, and on 10 September travelled to Brockville to face Falkirk in the opening league match of the season. They won the cup tie by 2-0, but lost the league match by 3-1, despite scoring first.

In 1967/68 Rangers withdrew from a Glasgow Cup tie against Celtic and cited 'a congestion of fixtures' as a reason. They might have had a case but they were criticised heavily for it. In the event, Hearts knocked them out of the Scottish Cup in a replay, Leeds United beat them in the Inter Cities Fairs Cup at Elland Road amid disgraceful scenes on the terracings, and Morton drew 3-3 with them at Cappielow to give Celtic the advantage in the run-in for the league championship. Ironically, on that same night (17 April 1968) Celtic went on to win the Glasgow Cup by beating Clyde 8-0 in the final at Hampden Park.

FLOODLIGHTS

Celtic's first experience with floodlights at Celtic Park came remarkably early – on Christmas Day, 1893. The lighting was supplied by sixteen arc lights, suspended from wires stretched as high as possible above the pitch. Near-neighbours Clyde provided the opposition for the friendly match, attended by 5,000 spectators on a wintry night. The experiment was barely successful: the light provided was shadowy and stoppages were inevitable when the ball struck the overhead wires.

A Scottish Cup tie against St. Bernard's on 13 January 1894 was won 8-1 by Celtic, but the Edinburgh side decided to protest because the ball had struck the wires several times. In view of the score the protest was disallowed by the SFA.

During the club's tour of North America in 1951 several matches were played under floodlights and the players were amused at having to apply a cork eye-shadow to avoid reflection from their cheekbones: 'We looked like raccoons.' (Charlie Tully)

It was not until 12 October 1959 when a modern floodlighting system was introduced to Celtic Park with the visit of Wolverhampton Wanderers, the then English Champions for a friendly match. It was a Monday evening and a crowd estimated at 45,000 turned up to see Mrs. Bob Kelly turn on the lights at 7.15 and to witness Wolves handle Celtic with some ease despite having to field several reserve players. The Midlands side, playing the offside game to perfection, won by 2-0 against a largely youthful and inexperienced Celtic eleven:

Fallon, MacKay, Mochan, Smith, Evans, Peacock, Chalmers, McVittie, Lochhead, Divers, Auld.

The *Daily Record's* principal football writer 'Waverley' commented: 'Against the cool, calculating, cohesive defence of Wolverhampton Wanderers, the Celtic attack were a bunch of mixed-up kids with fighting spirit about their sole possession.'

The floodlights themselves – a system called Drenchlite – were an outstanding success, installed by the Edinburgh firm of Miller & Stables Limited at a cost of approximately £40,000: '. . . not one inch of shadow on the park. About the only thing the spectators cannot see under the Celtic Park floodlights is the colour of the players' eyes.' (*Daily Record*)

However, the Celtic support were not exactly happy mainly because the cost of the floodlights had been paid, it was widely believed, through the sale of Bobby Collins to Everton (£23,500) and Willie Fernie to Middlesbrough (£17,000) both in 1958.

Celtic have also participated in memorable floodlit matches: on 20th October 1954 Clyde invited their neighbours to hansel their lights in a match billed as 'The Championship of the East End of Glasgow' and a large crowd turned up for the friendly match, won 3-2 by Celtic.

FOREIGNERS

Foreign players who have represented Celtic.

Albania: Rudi Vata
Australia: Mark Viduka, Dan Lavery,
    Scott McDonald
Belgium: Joos Valgaeren
Brazil: Rafael Scheidt, Junhino
Bulgaria: Stiliyan Petrov
Canada: Joe Kennaway
China: Du Wei
Czech Republic: Juri Jarosik
Denmark: Martin Wieghorst, Marc
    Rieper, Tommy Gravesen, Ulrik
    Laursen, Bent Martin

Lubomir (Lubo) Moravcik, – one of several hugely successful foreign players.

Eire: Patsy Gallacher, Charlie Gallagher, Sean Fallon, Pat Bonner, Peter Kavanagh, Aiden McGeady, Roy Keane, Tony Cascarino, Pierce O'Leary, Vince Ryan, Tommy Coyne, Mick McCarthy, Chris Morris, Eamon McMahon, Colin Healy, Cillian Sheridan, Liam Miller, Jim Goodwin

England: Alan Stubbs, Jim Welford, Lee Naylor, Peter Latchford, Paul Elliott, Tony Mowbray, Ebenezer Owers, Tony Warner, Chris Sutton, Stuart Slater, Lee Martin, Andy Payton, Martin Hayes, Jack Reynolds, Carl Muggleton, John McAlindon, Tommy Johnston, Ian Wright, Allan Thompson, Steve Guppy

France: Stephane Mahe, Didier Agathe

Germany: Andreas Thom, Andreas Hinkel

Greece: Georgos Samaras

Guinea: Bobo Balde

Holland: Regi Blinker, Bobby Petta, Jan Vennegoor of Hesselink, Pierre van Hooijdonk, Evander Sno

Iceland: Teddie Bjarnsson, Johannes Edvaldsson

Israel: Eyal Berkovic

India: Salim Bachi Khan

Italy: Paoli di Canio, Enrico Annoni, Rolando Ugolini

Ivory Coast: Olivier Tebily, Momo Sylla

Jamaica: Gil Heron

Japan: Shunsuke Nakamura, Koki Mizuno

New Zealand: Chris Killen

Northern Ireland: Neil Lennon, Allen McKnight, Charlie Tully, Bertie Peacock, Anton Rogan, Willie Cook, John Convery

Norway: Harald Brattbakk, Vidar Riseth, Geir Karlsen

Poland: Artur Boruc, Majiec Zurawski, Konrad Kapler, Dariusz Wdowczyk, Dariusz Dziekanowski

Portugal: Jorge Cadete

Russia: Dimitri Kharine

Slovakia: Stanislav Varga, Lubomir Moravcik

Spain: Javier Sanchez Broto, Davide Fernandez

Sweden: Henrik Larsson, Johan Mjallby, Magnus Hedman

Switzerland: Ramon Vega, Stephane Henchoz

Venezuela: Fernando de Ornales

Wales: L.R. Roose, John Hartson, Craig Bellamy

On 8 September 2001 Celtic started a match for the first time without a Scot in their line-up. The side that defeated Dunfermline Athletic 3-1 was:

Kharine (Russia), Tebily (Ivory Coast), Balde (Guinea), Valgearen (Belgium), Agathe (France), Lennon (Northern Ireland), Petrov (Bulgaria), Moravcik (Slovakia), Thompson (England), Sutton (England), Larsson (Sweden)

During the match Hartson (Wales), Healey (Republic of Ireland) came on as substitutes – and Crainey (Scotland) canme on in 69 minutes to preserve the Scottish link.

The *Daily Mail* (12 June 2001) noted:
Celtic, with the exception of Robert Douglas from Dundee, have not signed a first team squad player with a Scottish passport since November 1997 when Paul Lambert was repatriated from Dortmund.

FOREIGN MANAGERS

Celtic have had three Irish-born managers, although all would probably bridle at being considered 'foreigners': Willie Maley, Liam Brady and Martin O'Neill.

John Barnes, although winning representative honours with England, was born in Jamaica;

Wim Jansen, who played in two World Cup finals, was, of course, Dutch;

Dr. Josef Venglos was Slovakian.

FREQUENT OFFENDERS

Several Celtic players have had 'form' in the matter of being sent off .

Roy Aitken:
6 March 1978 vs. Kilmarnock
18 August 1979 vs. Rangers
13 September 1980 vs. Hearts
19 May 1984 vs. Aberdeen
20 September 1989 vs. Aberdeen

Tommy Burns:
29 February 1978 vs. Partick Thistle
13 December 1978 vs. Rangers
22 September 1979 vs. Aberdeen
9 September 1989 vs. St. Mirren

Peter Grant:
5 January 1991 vs. Hibernian
17 March vs. Rangers
1 October 1994 vs. Motherwell
20 March 1995 vs. Hearts
17 September 1996 vs. Hearts

Jimmy Johnstone:
13 November 1963 vs. Partick Thistle
1 January 1965 vs. Rangers

23 September 1967 vs. St. Johnstone
4 November 1967 vs. Racing Club
17 March 1973 vs. Aberdeen
25 August 1973 vs. Rangers

Mick McCarthy:
7 November 1987 vs. Hearts
5 March 1988 vs. Falkirk
11 March 1989 vs. Hearts

Willie Wallace:
2 December 1967 vs. Dundee United
6 September 1969 vs. Dunfermline Ath.
19 August 1970 vs. Clyde

FUNERALS

Barney Battles, a legendary Celtic full-back who played for the club between 1898 and 1904, died in February 1905 from the effects of influenza at the age of thirty. A funeral Mass was held at Sacred Heart, Bridgeton and some two thousand mourners followed the coffin to Dalbeth Cemetery. Crowds estimated at 40,000 lined the route to the graveyard.

Jimmy McGrory attended his father's funeral in the morning of 30 August 1924, and then turned out for Celtic in the afternoon at Falkirk, scoring one of the goals in a 2-1 win.

John Thomson died on the evening of 5 September 1931 after an accidental collision with a Rangers forward at Ibrox Park earlier that afternoon. His funeral was attended by representatives of almost every Scottish club, and was conducted by a family friend (John Howie) in Cardenden. Thousands of Celtic supporters made their way to the Fife village and some had to walk the distance from Glasgow to pay their respects to the goalkeeper.

A crowd, estimated at 10,000, assembled in Argyle Street in Glasgow for the funeral of Bertie Thomson on 20 September 1937. His gravestone reads 'Bertie of Celtic'.

The Celtic team attended the funeral of John Milsopp, a 21 year-old who had recently broken into the side, on 20 September 1952. Rangers were also considerably represented at the funeral. In the afternoon Celtic defeated Rangers by 2-1 in a league fixture at Celtic Park.

Sir Robert Kelly died on 20 April 1971 after a courageous battle against cancer. As Celtic's longtime chairman and a former president of the SFA and also the Scottish League, his funeral was attended by representatives of all Scottish football bodies and clubs.

Jock Stein, Celtic's most famous manager and former captain, died on 10 September 1985 while managing Scotland to a World Cup appearance virtually assured by a 1-1 draw with Wales. His sudden death from a heart attack at the stadium shocked the nation. He was cremated in Glasgow a few days later and every football fixture in Scotland held a minute's silence in tribute. It was a mark of his stature that the silence was impeccably observed throughout the country.

Jimmy Johnstone, after a brave struggle against Motor Neurone Disease, died on 13 March 2006. His funeral, a few days later, released an orgy of emotion as 'Celtic's Greatest Player' was laid to rest. The cortege passed along London Road and circled the frontage of the Main Stand at Celtic Park, an area which was crowded with thousands of Celtic followers who had gathered to pay a last homage to a gifted and archeytypal Celtic player.

The funeral of Tommy Burns on 20 May 2008 was held in St Mary's Church, Abercromby Street (the birthplace of the club). Apart from a packed church and hundreds more outside, an estimated 20,000 heard the Requiem Mass relayed over loudspeakers at Celtic Park.

(top) A street mural in Glasgow's east end photographed on the day of Jimmy Johnstone's funeral in March 2006; (bottom left) funeral order of service; (bottom right) Jinky holding the European Cup on the occasion of the final being played at Glasgow's Hampden Park between Real Madrid and Bayer Leverkusen in 2003

REQUIEM MASS
JIMMY JOHNSTONE

Tommy Gemmell, the only Celtic player ever to score in two European Cup finals

'No one ever mentions the goal that I scored against Feyenoord. When you are losers, no one wants to know; when you are winners, everybody wants to know.' Tommy Gemmell, commenting on his goalscoring in two European Cup finals.

G

GEMMELL'S GOALS

Tommy Gemmell has some rare distinctions as a Celtic player; to date he remains the only Celt to score in two European Cup finals, and also the only player to have scored for Celtic in Argentina (in the ill-fated series against Racing Club of Buenos Aires). He did not rely solely on penalty kicks or free kicks; in his 418 appearances for Celtic (between 1961 and 1971) he netted 64 times – an astonishing record for a full back.

GLASGOW CUP

The competition was introduced during the 1887/88 season at a time when interest in the new sport of football was booming but before the Scottish League was founded (1890). For most clubs in Scotland the Scottish Cup was the primary competition but an early exit meant that the remaining fixtures in a season would be friendly matches, usually against other 'also -rans'.

The first Glasgow Cup final was contested by Cambuslang and Rangers, Cambuslang running out 3-1 winners and sharing an excellent gate of £250. The powerful Queen's Park won the next two competitions by defeating Partick Thistle

8-0 in the 1888/89 final and Celtic by 3-2 in 1889/90. Celtic's first success in the Glasgow Cup came in 1891/92 with an impressive 4-0 win over Third Lanark.

Since its inception the following clubs have picked up the handsome trophy:

Rangers (43)
Celtic (30)
Partick Thistle (7)
Clyde (5)
Queen's Park (4)
Third Lanark (4)
Cambuslang (1).

Even during the two World Wars the competition continued annually without interruption. The Scottish Cup, on the other hand, was suspended between 1914 and 1918 and between 1940 and 1945.

With increased competition from the major tournaments and involvement in Europe the Glasgow Cup declined in importance. During the 1970s no competition was held during four separate seasons and in 1974/75, after Celtic and Rangers had drawn 2-2 in the final, no date could be found for a replay.

Starting in 1989/90 – after it became

obvious that clubs were fielding under-strength sides in the competition – it was decided to revamp the tournament. The Glasgow Cup was limited to the clubs' Under-18 sides, a wise step. Celtic won the first two revised Glasgow Cups in 1989/90 and 1990/91.

Throughout its venerable history the competition has thrown up memorable moments and finals. The largest margin of victory (eight goals) has been accomplished twice: by Queen's Park against Partick Thistle in 1888 and by Celtic against Clyde in 1968. In the latter competition Rangers had scratched earlier citing 'a congestion of fixtures' leaving the powerful Celtic side a free run through to the final against Clyde.

One of the largest crowds was the 87,000 who turned up to see Celtic defeat Third Lanark by 3-1 at Hampden Park in 1948, many attracted by Celtic's improved form inspired by the talented Charlie Tully.

In 1966 Celtic won the Glasgow Cup in most impressive style by registering 4-0 wins over Rangers, Queen's Park, and Partick Thistle. In the first round match at Ibrox Bobby Lennox scored three times before a crowd of 76,000.

The 1970 final saw Jock Stein field a side containing six recognised reserve players against a full-strength Rangers and win convincingly by 3-1.

'We climbed three mountains tonight, and then threw ourselves off the last one!' Billy McNeill, after 'winning' a thriller by 5-4 against Partizan Belgrade in 1989 but being eliminated on the away-goals rule.

GLASGOW LEAGUE

In the early days of organised football in Scotland there were a number of blank dates in the calendar as the combination of an early exit from the Scottish Cup, a meagre league programme and the difficulty of arranging profitable friendlies against attractive opposition could prove financially damaging for clubs.

The formation of the Glasgow League was an attempt to solve this problem, but it was hardly a success. Many clubs chose to field under-strength sides and trialists were tested under these 'match conditions'.

The first Glasgow League was in 1895/96 and featured only four teams: Celtic, Rangers, Queen's Park and Third Lanark. By the 1899/1900 season the league had expanded, changing its name to the Inter-City League in the process, and eventually included such as Hearts, Hibernian, Dundee and St. Mirren but the football public was not fooled and stayed away as witnessed by the crowd of only 3,000 who watched Celtic beat Rangers by 2-0 in 1902.

It remained active between 1895 and 1906 (although the competition was abandoned in 1903/04) and the following clubs can claim to have won it:

Third Lanark (3)
Celtic (2)
Rangers (2)
Hearts (2)
Queen's Park (1).

However, one fixture did attract considerable attention in 1904/05. Celtic and Rangers had finished level on points at the top of the Scottish League and a play-off game was arranged for Hampden Park with an English official in charge. The clubs agreed that this decider would also double up as the scheduled Glasgow League fixture. Celtic won by 2-1 to collect the championship, and also two meaningless points in the Glasgow League

GOAL AVERAGE

League championships are most often won outright on the number of points gained, whether it is three points for a win or two (as it was for so many years). However, this method breaks down when the challengers are level on points.

The very first league championship (1890/91) finished with Rangers and Dumbarton level on points; a play-off game ended in a 2-2 draw and the clubs were declared joint-winners.

In 1904/05 Celtic and Rangers ended up level on points but, fortunately for Celtic, goal average was not a deciding factor and Celtic won a play-off game 2-1 at Hampden Park, refereed by an English official, to start off a historic six league titles in a row.

The Scottish League eventually devised a stratagem for breaking such a deadlock – goal average.

It worked like this: the goals conceded were divided into the goals scored. For example, if a team scored 100 goals in a league campaign and conceded 25, its goal average would be 4.00 (but that would be inferior to a team which scored 80 and conceded 19, whose average would be 4.21).

Some championships were decided on the basis of goal average. In 1952/53 Rangers edged Hibernian on goal average by 2.05 to 1.82. On the day that Billy McNeill scored the winning goal against Dunfermline Athletic at Hampden Park (24 April 1965) Hearts played Kilmarnock at Tynecastle and lost by 2-0. This result meant that Kilmarnock were league champions by the narrowest of margins: a goal average of 1.879 compared to 1.837. When you consider that Hearts scored 90 goals and conceded 49 (compared to Kilmarnock's 63 against 33), it can be seen that the system was weighted in favour of defensive football.

GOAL DIFFERENCE

A much fairer method than goal average, goal difference was introduced in 1971. Simply, the Goals Against is subtracted from the Goals For to give a Plus or Minus total.

Celtic won the championship in 1985/86 on the last day of the season when they beat St. Mirren 5-0 at Paisley while Hearts lost 2-0 at Dundee. Celtic's goal difference was +29 and Hearts' +26. Actually, Celtic would have lost on Goal Average if that method had been still in operation.

Perhaps even more dramatically Celtic lost to Rangers despite winning 4-0 at Kilmarnock as Rangers defeated Dunfermline Athletic at Ibrox by 6-1 in 2002/03. The differences were +73 and +72. The television viewers saw a pivotal moment as Rangers scored at Ibrox within five seconds of Henrik Larsson's shot rebounding from a post at Rugby Park.

GOALKEEPERS

Forwards are graded on goals scored and games played; goalkeepers can perhaps be judged on 'shut-outs':

	Appearances	Shutouts	%
Pat Bonner:	642	255	(40%)
Charlie Shaw:	444	237	(53%)
'Joe' Kennaway:	295	83	(28%)
Davy Adams:	291	126	(43%)
Peter Latchford:	272	82	(30%)
Frank Haffey:	200	61	(30%)
John Thomson:	188	64	(34%)
Ronnie Simpson:	187	90	(48%)
John Fallon:	184	61	(33%)
John Bonnar:	180	49	(27%)
Willie Miller*:	123	29	(24%)
Evan Williams:	148	59	(40%)
Artur Boruc:	136	52	(38%)
Dan McArthur:	123	41	(33%)
Ally Hunter:	91	43	(47%)

*Most of Willie Miller's appearances were during World War II, which is considered 'unofficial'. These appearances are not listed here.

Good Days; Bad Days:

Tom Duff made nine appearances for Celtic in 1891/92 but his last game was a friendly against Dumbarton on New Year's Day, 1892. On that day, Celtic used goalnets at Parkhead for the first time but lost by 8-0. It is believed that some Celts, and particularly the goalkeeper, had been celebrating too much the night before.

Michael Dolan played only four competitive matches for Celtic but had a memorable career. On 12 December 1891 he was in goal in a 7-1 win over Clyde in the Glasgow Cup final and that was the first time goal nets were used in any Scottish final, making Dolan probably the first Celtic keeper officially to pick the ball out of the net! He was also the goalkeeper in Celtic's inaugural match against Rangers (Swifts) on 28 May 1888.

Tom Sinclair was borrowed from Rangers at the start of the 1906/07 season because of an injury to Davy Adams. The newcomer fitted in well, achieving shutouts in all his six league games – and two more in the Glasgow Cup. He won a winner's medal with Celtic, but was reportedly furious at conceding two goals against Third Lanark in the final – the only goals conceded in his nine-game run.

Davy Adams played in four Scottish Cup finals (seven, if you include replays) and was never on the losing side. This was during a long career from 1903 to 1912.

CELTIC LEGENDS

JOHN THOMSON

(left) Celtic goalkeeper Ronnie Simpson takes charge in the box in a match at Tannadice in the 1960s

(Above) a football card featuring Celtic goalkeeper John Thomson who suffered a fatal injury during play in 1931

'Sunny Jim' Young was an inspiration in Celtic's midfield for many seasons in the 1900s but he did not enjoy his one appearance in Celtic's goal on January 2nd 1909. Davy Adams, injured in the 3-1 win over Rangers the previous day, had to call off and Young took his place in goal. Celtic lost 3-1 to Kilmarnock at Rugby Park.

Charlie Shaw once had 13 shutouts in a row (10 in the League, 3 in the Cup) – between December 20th, 1913 to February 21st, 1914. In that same season (1913/14), between October 11th and December 6th he had already accomplished another run of 9 shutouts in a row. December 13th was his unlucky day because he gave up a goal in a 2-1 win over Raith Rovers at Starks Park; otherwise, he would have had 23 shutouts in a row.

L.R. Roose was a Welsh international goalkeeper and also an amateur. He was invited to play for Celtic against Clyde in the Scottish Cup and did so, but unfortunately lost by 3-1. A genuine sportsman, he was reputed to have congratulated the scorer of Clyde's third goal.

John Bonnar's greatest game for Celtic came in 1953 in the Coronation Cup final against Hibernian's 'Famous Five' forward line; the shortish goalkeeper defied that feared quintet time after time to help Celtic to a 2-0 victory. However, his worst moment came two years later in the same stadium when he fumbled a last-minute corner kick to allow Clyde an equaliser in the Scottish Cup final; Clyde won the replay 1-0.

Dick Madden made only one appearance for the club, but it was a 6-0 loss to Kilmarnock at Rugby Park in March 1963. When he returned home that night, he may have been cheered up with the news that he had won the football pools that day.

Tragedy

The saddest day for Celtic was September 5th, 1931 when John Thomson, a brilliant young goalkeeper, was injured at Ibrox Park in an accidental clash with Sam English of Rangers. He died later that night in Glasgow's Victoria Infirmary. Chic Geatons replaced him in goal for the last 40 minutes of the match which ended 0-0.

Jock Stein's Goalkeepers

Stein may well have been Celtic's greatest manager but, according to some of his critics (and players), he was not a good judge of goalkeepers. He was reported to have said once that, if he were to re-invent football, he would do it without any goalkeepers at all. What is certain, however, is that he used to work his goalkeepers ferociously hard on the training ground 'to keep them on their toes'.

His lengthy list of goalkeepers suggests that he did have a problem in deciding their worth:

John Fallon, Ronnie Simpson,
Bent Martin, Tom Lally,
Tom Livingstone, Jack Kennedy,
Bobby Wraith, Evan Williams,
Gordon Marshall, Denis Connaghan,
Ally Hunter, Peter Latchford,
Graham Barclay, Roy Baines,
and Pat Bonner.

Several of his signings were released without ever having played for the first team.

In 1998/99 Celtic used five goalkeepers on first-team duty: Jonathon Gould, Stuart Kerr, Andy McCondichie, Tony Warner, Barry Corr.

Opinions vary as to who was Celtic's best goalkeeper, as these lists from Celtic historians and pundits would suggest:

Pat Woods:
1. Willie Miller: Played in goal during worst period in club's history, performing brilliantly and bravely in adversity, the greatest test for a keeper.
2. Charlie Shaw: A model of consistency during a very lengthy period at Celtic Park after being signed from Queens Park Rangers.
3. Dan McArthur: Described by Willie Maley as Celtic's first top-notch keeper. A goalkeeper of unparalleled courage by all accounts.
4. Ronnie Simpson: The best Celtic goalkeeper in my lifetime and a man who brought a marvellous level of experience to the club with his twenty years in the game before he joined Celtic. He displayed a matchless awareness of the geometry of the penalty area.
5. John Thomson: Equipped to be the most outstanding Celtic keeper of them all, but his was a career tragically cut short. If goalkeepers mature late, I have to believe the best was yet to come of John Thomson.

Eugene MacBride:

1. Dan McArthur: Absolutely beloved of the supporters of his time. Incredibly brave – and had to be in those days. Often injured for the cause.
2. Charlie Shaw: A Celt, through and through. He was Celtic's captain as well, an unusual honour for a keeper. The crowds apparently could not stop 'howling' in appreciation of his shot-stopping.
3. Joe Kennaway: Joe filled a massive gap when it had to be done after John Thomson was killed.
4. Willie Miller: A neglected hero, but a truly magnificent goalkeeper adored by the fans during a dark period in the club's history.
5. Ronnie Simpson: A fairy-tale come true! After being rejected by Jock Stein at Hibernian, he became the backbone of the Lisbon Lions – and the best of all Stein's many keepers.

PS I couldn't pick one man over another in this list; so, I've put them into chronological order.

Patrick Reilly:

1. Willie Miller: Most definitely the best I've ever seen, a stylist. Playing in a poor Celtic side, he was the man to save us from humiliation on several occasions.
2. Ronnie Simpson: A capable keeper and as safe as houses. He had the gift of total concentration and could make the save even when called upon unexpectedly – as so often happens with Celtic keepers. My hands still sweat when I think of that moment in Lisbon when he backheeled the ball away from an Inter forward.

3. Pat Bonner: Celtic supporters took him for granted but, when he was called upon to perform on the world stage with Ireland, he certainly did not look out of place.
4. John Bonnar: Usually a very dependable goalkeeper, even if he was on the small side. Nobody could ever forget that display against Hibernian in the 1953 Coronation Cup final when he almost single-handedly defied one of the best Scottish forward lines of all time – but he played well on other occasions too.
5. Peter Latchford: He was called in by Jock Stein in an emergency and proved to be most reliable. He was a typical English goalkeeper, never flashy but steady and utterly dependable.

PS I have listed only the goalkeepers I saw personally; fortunately, I go back quite a long while as a Celtic supporter.

Peter Latchford makes a save at Hampden in a Scottish Cup final against Rangers

© snspix.com

GRANDSTANDS

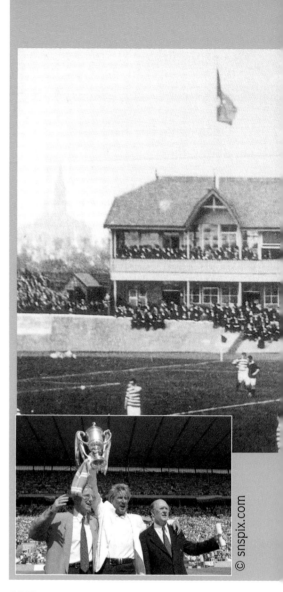

13 August 1892:

The new Celtic Park's first event is the Celtic Sports and the stand consists of a structure three-hundred-twenty feet long (320 ft) with fifteen rows of seats (15) and a detached pavilion at the north-west corner. This stand, with a capacity of 3,500, is parallel with Janefield Street, and plans are being made for a parallel structure on the London Road side of Celtic Park.

1898:

An ultra-modern stand is constructed on the London Road side, built and financed as a private concern by one of the directors (James Grant). It contains several features: a two-storey building, padded, tip-up seats, and 'large, sliding windows which could be shut when it rained'. The windows, however, have to be removed permanently when frequent condensation makes viewing difficult for the spectators.

May 1904:

The stand (and pavilion) on Janefield Street is completely destroyed by fire; the club decides to purchase the so-called Grant Stand to replace it.

10 August 1929:

After the demolition of the ageing Grant Stand, another new structure is built in its place in time for the opening game of the new season, a 2-1 victory over Hearts.

1971:

Massive renovations are carried out on the main stand: a dramatic new roof, supported by a steel girder 97.5 metres long and 5.3 metres thick, a press box with room and facilities for a hundred journalists. Seating replaces the enclosure in front of the previous stand, and capacity is 8,686.

1988:

The exterior and front entrance of the stand is re-developed extensively: a bright modern facade, a glass-fronted foyer and reception area, executive boxes, a restaurant and lounges.

8 August 1995:

The singer – and keen Celtic fan – Rod Stewart opens the new North Stand at Celtic Park, a massive structure that holds 26,000 spectators. The occasion was a pre-season friendly match against Newcastle United (1-1).

The old Pavilion at Celtic Park (left) and the Lisbon Lions stand in the impressive modern stadium, part of Fergus McCann's legacy to the club

(below) The main stand, renovated in 1988, provides a fitting backdrop for Tommy Burns, Rod Stewart and Fergus McCann to celebrate a Scottish Cup triumph

Willie Wallace scoring against Partick Thistle at Celtic Park in the 1960s. The photograph shows the famous pylon eventually demolished in 1994 to make way for the present stands at Celtic Park

Goalkeeper and captain Charlie Shaw poses with his team in front of the old Pavilion

Some footballers, because of their skill or personality, impose themselves upon an era. Celtic have been blessed with several such performers, and the following list (essentially subjective) is presented in a rough chronological order:

Alexander (Sandy) McMahon: He was the fulcrum of Celtic's earliest teams and the dynamo of the attack. Born in the rugby stronghold of Selkirk in the Scottish Borders around 1871, at 6 feet 1 inch tall he was well above the average height for the times and became a prominent forward (inside left) for Hibernian, but he was 'poached' by the new Celtic club in Glasgow.

His playing style could be described only as 'ungainly' with arms outspread like wings, head down, and shoulders stooped but he was highly effective and his awkward style and strong running from midfield upset defenders. Although celebrated as a dribbler, he knew how to finish and he was the first Celt to reach the mark of 100 goals in league matches; his partnership on the left wing with Johnny Campbell produced 290 goals for Celtic in all competitions. He was a famed header of the ball with excellent timing in the air and a high proportion of his goals came from his head. He was nicknamed 'The Duke' by schoolmaster Tom Maley, probably after the former President of France, the Duke de Mac-Mahon but it was more probably a tribute to his leadership on and off the field.

He left Celtic in 1903, after playing in 174 league matches and 43 Scottish Cup ties and as the scorer of 177 goals and having earned six 'caps' for Scotland.

James (Jimmy) Quinn: This 'rampaging tiger' of a centre forward was born in Croy in 1878, and was the first of the club's genuine superstars. Although originally fielded most often at outside-left, Jimmy Quinn was destined to be a centre-forward because of his sturdy, powerful frame and an appetite for the physical challenges prevalent in the Scottish game at that time. Later in his career, he added an element of guile and craft to his game which made him a most formidable opponent for any defender.

He was a 'never-give-up player', a feature of his game never more apparent than in the 1904 Scottish Cup final against Rangers when his side were two down after only twelve minutes. It was young Jimmy who led the onslaught against a veteran Rangers defence and who capped the fightback with a historic hat-trick.

The ultimate one-club man, Jimmy Quinn, despite frequent injuries, played for Celtic from 1900 until 1915. He was the recognised leader of Celtic's 'six-in-a-row' side, the spearhead of a famous forward line. He scored 187 league goals in his 273 appearances, and 29 goals from 58 outings in the Scottish Cup. In addition he scored 7 goals in his 11 appearances for Scotland before retiring to his native Croy where he died in 1945.

James (Jimmy) McMenemy: Rutherglen-born (1880) Jimmy McMenemy was the template of the crafty Scottish inside-forward. Jimmy Quinn may have charged the enemy and fired the bullets, but it was 'Napoleon' who loaded the gun for him and set up the target as well. His nickname suggested that he was the general of the team, most famously the side that won six

Jimmy McMenemy

all-time league appearances and seventh in the all-time goal-scoring list: 456 league appearances, 59 Scottish Cup appearances and 168 goals, in addition to 12 'caps' for Scotland and a further 5 goals.

Alexander (Alec) McNair: He was born in Bo'ness in 1883 and, after a season as an inside forward with Stenhousemuir, was transferred to Celtic where he was to remain for the next twenty-odd seasons. A complete footballer Alec – later to be nicknamed 'The Icicle' for his coolness under pressure – was utilised in a variety of positions starting off at outside-left on his debut against Queen's Park in 1904 but eventually became a fixture at right-back to become part of a litany which began 'Shaw, McNair and Dodds. . .'

championships in a row but he was more than that: a regular goalscorer himself as well as the playmaker his acceleration meant that no defence could rest easy and he was a durable character as his eighteen years at Celtic Park as a regular player would indicate. During that time he amassed an impressive collection of 11 Scottish League medals and 6 Scottish Cup ones.

In fact, after his surprise release from Celtic the veteran McMenemy master-minded Partick Thistle to their only only Scottish Cup triumph in 1921. Jimmy McMenemy returned to Celtic Park as the club's trainer in 1935 and had a consider-able effect on the side's excellent showing in the seasons immediately preceding World War II. 'Napoleon' stands sixth in

Despite domestic problems (his wife died in 1915 and Alec had to raise his family on his own in Larbert, as well as working a 12-hour day in essential war work), Alec McNair rarely missed a game for Celtic. He played in 12 league championship winning Celtic teams and won 5 Scottish Cup medals – and would have won more had the competition not been abandoned during the Great War (1914-1918).

After retiring from active playing Alec McNair embarked on a varied career: as manager of Dundee, as a stockbroker in Falkirk, and as an SFA referee inspector. He played 583 league matches for Celtic, and appeared in 56 Scottish Cup ties for the club. In addition he won 15 'caps' for Scotland. Not a great goalscorer, neverthe-less, he netted ten times for Celtic.

Patsy Gallacher

After mazy, meandering dribbling inside a packed penalty area he was felled near the goal line but, with the ball wedged between his feet, executed a backward roll into the net. Unsurprisingly, Dundee wilted after that and Celtic won 2-1. Sadly, Celtic's administration felt that his best days were over and allowed him to leave for Falkirk in 1926 – and Patsy staked a claim to be the Bairns' greatest player by playing for them until 1932.

He stands as eighth in the league appearance table, and third in the league goalscorers: 432 league appearances and 186 goals, 32 Scottish Cup ties and 6 goals. He was capped for both Northern Ireland (10) and the Republic (1).

Patrick (Patsy) Gallacher: Born in Ramelton in County Donegal in 1893, Patsy Gallacher must be considered as a candidate as 'The Greatest Celt of All Time'. His family migrated to Scotland and settled in Clydebank when Patsy was a youngster and he joined Celtic from the local junior club in 1911. Small and slight he looked frail but he was a bundle of trickery and energy – and he was also a thoughtful player, able to anticipate developments on the field and to react with lightning speed. Some of his tricks were simply audacious and, despite his size and physique, he could take care of himself against more physical opponents.

Some of his goals became legendary, none more so than Celtic's equaliser in the 1925 Scottish Cup final against Dundee.

James (Jimmy) McGrory: Resembling Jimmy Quinn in physique, the broad-shouldered McGrory went on to create all sorts of goal-scoring records for Celtic and, by the time he retired, he was out of sight as the club's all-time scorer. He was born in the Celtic stronghold of Garngad and struggled to make an early impact at Parkhead which resulted in a season's loan at Clydebank (1923).

On his recall he finished as the top-scoring Celt in twelve of his fifteen seasons at Celtic Park. Like Quinn before him he was played on the left wing before it was realised the havoc he could cause playing through the middle. A brave centre forward, he was famed for his ability to head goalwards crosses that were well within the range of defenders' boots and he was prolific – his eight goals against Dunfermline in a 9-0 win in 1928 attests to his pursuit of goals, as do fifty-five hat-tricks in his career. He exceeded fifty goals in a single season three times.

Despite his popularity with the support and his contribution to the only club he ever wanted to play for, Celtic shamefully attempted to sell him to Arsenal in 1928 – but Jimmy McGrory simply refused to budge. He retired as a player in 1938 to become manager of Kilmarnock and returned to Celtic Park as the club's manager in 1945. Unfortunately his career as a manager was not nearly as successful as his days as a player. He died in Glasgow in 1982 at the age of seventy-eight. He scored 396 goals in 378 league fixtures, 73 goals in 67 Scottish Cup ties, and 6 goals in his meagre 7 appearances for Scotland.

John Thomson: By the age of 22 John Thomson was recognised as the best goalkeeper in the country, and his early death ensured that he would be a legendary figure. Born in Kirkcaldy in 1909 John Thomson was signed for Celtic by a scout, the document being signed on the lid of a roadside fuse box in Gallatown just outside Kirkcaldy in 1926. Celtic had lacked a top-class goalkeeper since the departure of Charlie Shaw two years previously but the young Fifer was to fill that gap. He was as agile as a cat and his hands, strong but supple, made him a candidate for the perfect goalkeeper.

Referees gave little protection to keepers in the 1920s and 30s and men like John Thomson paid a heavy price in injuries. Thomson, as brave as he was skilful, suffered concussions, a broken jaw, a broken collar bone, broken and bruised ribs and the inevitable lost tooth. By 1931, just short of his 23rd birthday, and at the top of his form, he could have anticipated another ten years in football but the events of 5 September 1931 ended all the dreams.

In an attempt to save his goal at the feet of Rangers centre forward Sammy English his head crashed into the forward's knee and he had to be stretchered off the Ibrox pitch. He never regained consciousness and died in the Victoria Infirmary at 9.25pm that night.

His funeral released a river of emotion with 30,000 present at the small village of Cardenden and hundreds had walked all the way from Glasgow to Fife to attend and pay their respects. The journalist John Rafferty would sum up later his effect: 'He had no predecessor, no successor. He was unique.'

William (Billy) McNeill: Celtic's greatest age was in the late 1960s and the team leader of that magnificent side was the majestic 'Big Billy'. As Celtic's captain, the side's centre-half, and his manager's (Jock Stein) eyes and ears on the pitch, Billy McNeill looked the part. A commanding figure at 6 feet 1 inch, he had the military bearing of his soldier father and from his earliest days in a very young Celtic side he looked certain to be one player who would make it to the very top. The frustrations of being one of 'the Kelly Kids' during that unsuccessful period, hardened his determination to succeed and with the appointment of Jock Stein as manager that success was achieved.

McNeill's trademark header in the closing stages of the 1965 Scottish Cup final against Dunfermline Athletic ignited an era unimaginable previously. Powerful and totally dominant in the air he went on to become arguably the club's greatest-ever pivot. By the end of his playing days in 1975 he had a massive haul of medals: nine league championships, seven Scottish

Jimmy (Jinky) Johnstone voted by supporters as 'Celtic's Greatest Ever Player'

Cups, six League Cups, and one European Cup.

Bellshill-born, Billy McNeill has played in more Celtic matches than any other player: 486 in the league, 94 in the Scottish Cup, and 138 in the League Cup; in addition, 72 matches in European competition and 29 'caps' for Scotland. Although a defensive player, McNeill was always a threat at set-pieces as his 35 goals for Celtic might suggest and three of those goals came in Scottish Cup finals. Three more goals for Scotland might be included, as well as his header against Racing Club of Argentina in the 1967 World Club championship.

James (Jimmy) Johnstone: Born in Viewpark, Lanarkshire in 1944, Jimmy Johnstone ('Jinky' to his adoring fans) was voted as 'the Greatest-Ever Celt' in a poll among Celtic supporters. Several things helped him to attain that accolade: his West of Scotland appearance (a tiny figure with a mop of ginger curls), his style (a twisting-like-a-corkscrew dribbling), his courage (facing up to defenders who attempted to intimidate him with ferocious tackling) – and his faults.

He was the wee man, a born entertainer, and a player who could stand up for himself. His temper sometimes let him down as his record of dismassals would suggest. But for many Celtic supporters he was an alter ego on the pitch and they loved him. Essentially a winger, he was expected to be a provider of goals – and he was – but he could score – 130 times for Celtic. He left Celtic in 1975 on a free transfer, a sad ending to a tempestuous career and he would go on to play for a few other clubs but, like so many others, he has to be

Celtic captain Billy McNeill lifts the European Cup in May 1967

considered as 'Jimmy Johnstone of Celtic'.

After a long illness Jimmy died at his Viewpark home in 2006; an estimated 20,000 turned up at Celtic Park to pay their respects on the day of his funeral. Sir Alex Ferguson attended and when reminded that Manchester United had been interested in signing him as a youngster, mused: 'George Best, Bobby Charlton, Denis Law and Jimmy Johnstone. . . What a forward line that would have been!'

Kenneth (Kenny) Dalglish: When Celtic played against Rangers in the League Cup at Ibrox Park in August 1971, they were holding on to a 1-0 lead with twenty minutes left. . . and were awarded a penalty kick. Kenny Dalglish, with only a few first-team games under his belt at the age of 20, was invited to take it; he stopped only to tie his lace before slotting the ball home for a 2-0 victory. The legend had started.

Dalglish was the perfect modern player; he could dribble, he could pass, he could shoot and score. Allied to upper-body strength, he had quick feet, tremendous energy, and a desire to win. In addition he had what all great players possess – an awareness of what was going on everywhere on the pitch. His manager, when asked about his best position, could not provide a specific answer: 'Just give him a jersey with a number on it; he can play anywhere.'

A striker who would be the club's leading scorer, as a midfielder he supplied the ammunition for the other strikers. During his time at Celtic Park the club was in decline and it would be true to say that Kenny Dalglish, the captain, carried the team almost single-handedly. Accordingly, it was a shock and a bitter blow when he decided to move to Liverpool in 1977. His subsequent success in England and on the international stage was a testament to a player who unreservedly could be considered 'great'. For Celtic he made more than 200 appearances in the league championship, 56 in the League Cup, 30 in the Scottish Cup, and 27 in European competition. In those games (and with 7 appearances as a substitute) he scored an impressive 167 times. By his career's end he had made 102 appearances for Scotland and scored another 30 goals.

Henrik Larsson: Born in Helsingborg, Sweden in 1971, Henrik Larsson started his career with his home-town team before moving to the Netherlands and Feyenoord. In 1994 he was a member of the Swedish national side which won third-place in the World Cup but rather disappeared from view as he was used in a variety of positions and roles.

Celtic signed him from Feyenoord, at Wim Jansen's insistence, and the transfer fee was a bargain £650,000. He would go on to play for seven seasons at Celtic Park and, long before the end of that Scottish sojourn, he was recognised as a truly world-class player. He was similar to Kenny Dalglish in some ways: a will to win, physical strength and fitness, quickness of thought and the technique to execute his wishes. After those seven seasons, and one lasted only three months through a serious leg injury, he had become Celtic's third highest-ever goal-scorer – and the first player in sixty-five years to score more than fifty in a single season.

His nicknames suggest the awe in which he was held: 'The Magnificent Seven' and 'The King of Kings'. In 2004 he made a memorable and emotional departure from Celtic, loved and respected in equal measure. Like Dalglish before him, he was the team's outstanding personality and often had to drag the side up to his level, and never more so than with his heroic

© snspix.com

Kenny Dalglish

'Just give him a jersey, and never mind about the number.'
Jock Stein, when asked about Kenny Dalglish's best position.

single-handed efforts in the UEFA Cup final of 2003 when he scored both Celtic goals.

In 2006, after coming on as a substitute, he spearheaded Barcelona's comeback to defeat Arsenal in the European Cup final – and later on he was recruited by Manchester United to help them in their bid for the same trophy. Superbly fit, the veteran Henrik Larsson went back to where he started – and it is a conscious decision on his part – as a player with Helsingborg. He played 218 league games with Celtic, scoring 174 goals.

'GREATS'

On 8 September 2002 at a Gala Dinner in Glasgow's Clyde Auditorium the following Celtic personalities were honoured:

Jimmy Johnstone:
'Celtic's Greatest-Ever Player';

Billy McNeill:
'Celtic's Greatest-Ever Captain';

Jock Stein:
'Greatest-Ever Celt';

Henrik Larsson:
'Greatest-Ever Foreigner';

Celtic 7, Rangers 1:
'Greatest-Ever Old Firm Match'.

'Scoring two goals in a European final does not mean a thing, if you lose.'
Henrik Larsson, after the 2003 UEFA Cup final in Seville.

Celtic Greats (clockwise from top left)
Jimmy Johnstone starts another mazy dribble;
Sunday Mail cutting of Celtic's biggest winning margin in an Old Firm game;
Henrik Larsson scores again;
Jock Stein - a strong manager confronts troublemakers at Stirling;
captain Billy McNeil holds aloft the European Cup in Lisbon, 1967

Greats

'GERS WERE LUCKY
NOT TO LOSE TEN

CELTIC 7
RANGERS 1

Scorers—Celtic—
Wilson (24 mins.),
Mochan (44 and 74),
McPhail (53 and 81),
Fernie, pen. (89). Rangers
—Simpson (58).

What a Celtic joy day

AND but for the acrobatic Niven—and the wood round the Rangers' door—it might have been double figures:

Don't blame Celtic for "piling it on." They simply couldn't help themselves — so they had to help themselves, if you see what I mean.

This was a Rangers team with hardly one redeeming feature.

THE DEFENCE HAD A GAPING HOLE DOWN THE MIDDLE WIDE ENOUGH TO HAVE TAKEN THE GUARDS MASSED BANDS

McColl and Davis played with the very fear of death in their boots. I don't blame them.

Up front, the heavy-footed Simpson and Baird took too long to do too little.

Murray was simply brushed aside by Evans — and the wingers, from whom so much was expected, seemed content to appear more or less as mourners.

I don't know when I have seen a more disgraced exhibition from any Rangers team—especially one parading as League Champions and carrying Scottish hopes in the European Cup.

THEY HAVEN'T A SINGLE

Contempt

In the 15th minute, Bobby Collins hit a 35 yards "free" that came cracking off the crossbar with Niven, seeing it all the way apparently hypnotised.

Then Tully dribbled round Valentine and Caldow near the bye-line and crashed the ball against the near post off which it flew right across the goal and past the other post.

Right now, some Rangers defenders about like they were operating pneumatic drills.

At the other end, Boden and Hubbard raised the Ibrox hopes with an odd flying scurry—only to prove that Celtic were as tight in defence as they were free and open in attack.

Then Mochan forced a corner off Shearer. When it came over, it was weakly headed out. Wilson wheeled round and hooked it fiercely into the net.

Rangers' long-passing thrusts didn't bother evans. and Co much. And, in any case, it was kicking out a mile that equal Beattie was only likely to be beaten by a shot of the unsavable kind.

A corker

Right on the interval, Celtic nailed their victory down with a corker of a score.

An old-fashioned solid burst from Neily Mochan took the ball down-swing. He cut along the bye-line beating two defenders cleverly on the way, then slammed the ball into the net from an "impossible" angle.

That was the striking thing about Celtic. When one type of attack failed to register, they had the others to try another.

Rangers didn't have one forward who surprised he could have mastered Niehaus. Certainly neither winger ever threatened to do so.

This was the most valuable goal of the lot—coming just on the break. And before the taste of the half-time lemon had left their palate, Rangers were three down.

Collins hotted a long, high ball onto the goalmouth. No apparent danger. Till McPhail rose above Valentine, Niven, the lot—and nodded almost apologetically into the net.

Celtic were now looking a bit taken aback with the ease of their scores.

Rangers now had Murray limping on the left-wing with

EXCUSE IT'S NO USE BLAMING VALENTINE FOR EVERYTHING, AS SOME WERE DOING.

Mark that word "unadulterated." Celtic kept paying the ball anywhere else. The fun stemmed from confidence in themselves.

At the first smell of defeat, some throw met adulterated any skill they had with the physical desperation that signposts defeat.

There are limits to what the ball-going attack can accomplish, apart from a natural thrust from the mind of the spectator.

BUT THERE ARE NO LIMITS TO WHAT PURE FOOTBALL CAN ACHIEVE.

From the very start, it was obvious that Celtic had nothing in their mind but to play that ball — and, if possible, to be first to it.

Simpson at centre, and Hubbard partnering Scott.

And the only thing this proved was that Simpson was certainly more dangerous in the middle than anywhere else. For he threw himself into the air to bullet a great header past Beattie from a McColl cross. Rangers' wing-halves moved up to the attack. McColl hit the cross-bar with a "free." Then Baird was cautioned.

Penned in

The Light Blues kept Celtic penned in for a time while they weaved this way and that without finding another loophole than Mochan raced away and forced another corner.

The unsmiling Wilson headed it low for goal. Niven set on it and gummed it out to McPhail's feet for an easy fourth.

You can Rangers could thrash themselves to fury all around that Celtic goal area and bring out nothing but sweat—while Celtic could fly away, snake out the obvious short-cuts at the other end, and do the needful.

The truth was of course, that Celtic had a much better attack. And it was Celtic that took the knocks.

Eventually it got monotonous. Wilson, after some tricky smooth football, on the right side swept the ball away towards Mochan on the corner of the area. He smacked it and it bounded into the net.

CELTIC COULD DO IT SOLO, DUET, OR TRIO — OR INDEED

McPhail Sadts Valentine then puts the ball past Niven from a difficult angle for Celtic's sixth and his third goal.

QUINTET D' THEY FELT LIKE IT

Instance: the sixth. Beattie clears from hand to midfield where only McPhail and Valentine are located.

Billy wise in the air, ground, roses away half the length of the field, and pokes the ball past a bewildered Niven. The rout was almost complete.

In the dying moments, Fernie slammed a penalty-kick home for a header by Shearer on McPhail after the centre had again picked Valentine and was as a cert.

It's as difficult to pick out a star Celt as to pick out a star Ranger. Celtic had eleven Rangers none.

Only men I felt sorry for the Ibrox side were the Wing halves, who had so much of the commonplace around them.

Every Celtic player did well. none more so than the front-runners and Sean Fallon.

Fantastic

While Fernie was the most distinguished ball-worker afield some of his fantastic distribution run-al-speed leaving the very hardest of the 'Gers.

Evans was terrific, too, and with Peacock, completed the great hinge upon which the game flowed Celtic's way.

I must work out the grounds Billy McPhail for a display so centre-forward play, the ease which was as misleading as it was deadly.

(Celtic — Beattie; Donnelly, Fallon; Fernie, Evans, Peacock; Tully, Collins, McPhail, Wilson, Mochan.

RANGERS — Niven; Shearer, Caldow; McColl, Valentine, Davis; Scott, Simpson, Murray, Baird Hubbard.

Referee: J. Mowat (Burnside).

A PAISLEY ROAR

NOT for years have I heard a crowd roar like the one that rewarded Paisley Pirates at Paisley Arena on Friday night, when they came from behind to shatter Brighton Tigers 8-3. Never before has Paisley had a Pirates team that created so early into such an electrifying pace.

It was their first match in the British competition—and the new player-coach, Bill Sempol had a dream debut, scoring wonder equaliser (Pirates' first goal) a few hours after landing from the Canadian plane.

The pace, skill and tremendous fighting spirit of these Pirate will enable any opposition to h back teeth, No wonder the fan left the rink humming with anticipation.

GROUNDS

Celtic started their life as a football team with a friendly match against Rangers (Swifts) 28 May 1888 and won by 5-2 at their first, primitive ground at Dalmarnock Street. Their last match at this ground was on 1 June 1892, a 2-0 win over Rangers in the Charity Cup Final.

The new Celtic Park was opened on 13 August 1892 with the annual Celtic Sports, and the first home game was a 4-3 win over Renton a week later. Johnny Madden and McQuilkie of Renton spoiled the festivities by being ordered off.

The 'Greatest-Ever Celt' often had to support 'Celtic's Greatest-Ever Player' – here, Jock Stein accompanies Jimmy Johnstone to SFA Headquarters to face a disciplinary hearing

H

HALF-TIME RUCTIONS

What happens inside the dressing room is usually kept secret but occasionally reports of unrest leak out to journalists:

In 1945 during the replay of the Victory Cup semi-final against Rangers several Celtic players at halftime complained to their manager and trainer that they considered that the referee had been drinking before the match. Increasingly, his decisions had become erratic and the players were concerned about his apparent bias in favour of their opponents. Although Celtic officials contacted the SFA representatives inside Hampden Park, nothing was done and the match resumed with the same referee in nominal charge. Rangers won by 2-0 and, after a disputed penalty award to the Ibrox men, two Celtic players were ordered off; four spectators invaded the pitch in an attempt to attack the referee but were stopped by the police short of their target.

During a New Year's Day match at Ibrox Park Celtic's wing-half Pat Crerand disagreed with his coach's assessment of the situation and the pair came close to blows at half time. Celtic collapsed in the second half to lose 4-0. Crerand was put on the transfer list and never played for Celtic again, moving to Manchester United a few weeks later.

Lubomir Moravcik was called to the referee's room at St. Johnstone's McDairmid Park at the halftime interval on 13 May 2000 after a spectator had complained to the police about his gestures as he left the field at halftime. The referee Willie Young, ironically a lawyer in private life, after speaking to the police issued a red card to the bemused Celtic player.

During the Scottish Cup defeat by Inverness Caledonian Thistle at Celtic Park on 8 February 2000 a fracas took place inside the dressing room at halftime. One player, Mark Viduka, was unwilling to resume for the second half after a heated discussion with Celtic's back-room staff. Celtic lost the cup tie 3-1, and the manager John Barnes was fired the following day.

HALL OF FAME

On 22 September 2001 Celtic staged a dinner to induct the first twenty-five players into the Glasgow Celtic Hall of Fame.

In alphabetical order the players elected were:

Pat Bonner

Tom Boyd

Tommy Burns

Stevie Chalmers

John Clark

Bobby Collins

Dixie Deans

Sean Fallon

Patsy Gallacher

David Hay

Paul Lambert

Jimmy Johnstone

Joe McBride

Danny McGrain

Jimmy McGrory

Murdo MacLeod

Billy McNeill

Billy McPhail

Paul McStay

Neil Mochan

Lubo Moravcik

Ronnie Simpson

Johnny Thomson

Charlie Tully

Willie Wallace

It may have been a difficult task to pick only twenty-five players from Celtic's glittering array of talent but the omission of Bobby Evans, Bobby Murdoch and Tommy Gemmell is surprising.

Like most lists of great players preference is given to performers of more recent vintage to the neglect of star players from earlier times such as Jimmy Quinn, Sandy McMahon, Jimmy McMenemy and 'Sunny Jim' Young. No doubt this situation will be rectified in the future.

Of the players chosen, the totals in games played and goals scored are as follows:

McNeill (790 – 35)

McStay (677 – 72)

McGrain (663 – 2)

Bonner (641)

Johnstone (515 – 130)

Burns (508 – 82)

Gallacher (464 – 192)

McGrory (445 – 469)

Boyd (407 – 2)

Chalmers (407 – 231)

MacLeod (395 – 82)

Tully (319 – 43)

Collins (320 – 117)

Clark (314 – 2)

Lambert (274 – 19)

Mochan (268 – 109)

Fallon (256 – 13)

Wallace (232 – 134)

Hay (193 – 12)

Simpson (188)

Thomson (188)

Deans (183 – 123)

Moravcik (130 – 35)

McBride (94 – 86)

McPhail (57 – 40)

Hall of Fame members – Paul Lambert. Dixie Deans and Steve Chalmers

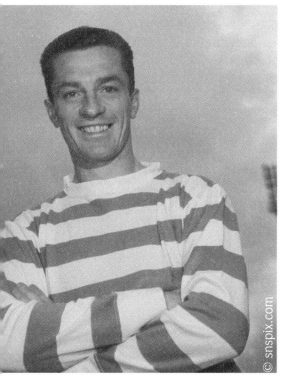

HAMILTON CUP

Not too many people recall that Celtic did win a trophy during the brief tenure of Lou Macari as manager in 1994. This was the Hamilton Cup, gained in a four-team tournament organised by local business-men as the highlight of a 'Scottish Week' in the Canadian city, situated twenty-five miles from Toronto.

Celtic won the opening match of the tourney, played on 22 May 1994 at Ivor Wynne Stadium, the home of the Hamilton Tiger Cats – an American-style football team. The pitch was an artificial one (Astroturf) and was possibly Celtic's first experience with this surface. However, they qualified for the final by edging Heart of Midlothian in a penalty shootout after the match ended 1-1. The game had been played in scorching heat, and at the pitch-level it reached temperatures close to 100°F.

Paul Byrne opened the scoring for Celtic in 75 minutes only three minutes after coming on as a substitute for Gary Gillespie. The shot was a fierce drive from nearly 30 yards and one which gained extra velocity from the surface. Hearts responded immediately and equalised only four minutes later. Carl Muggleton proved the hero for Celtic in the penalty shootout, saving two of Hearts' efforts. A feature of the match was the predictable reception given to Hearts' Maurice Johnston when he was introduced individually along with the other players in American-style to the 5,800 crowd, the vast majority of which were Celtic supporters. Celtic's team was:

Muggleton, Smith, Martin, MacKay, McNally, Gillespie, (Byrne), Holt, Falconer, Donnelly, Hay, Collins.

Aberdeen defeated Montreal Impact 2-0 in the other semi final to qualify to meet Celtic on 29 May at the same stadium. The crowd was marginally higher, estimated at just over 6,000 – and once more predominately Celtic supporters. They saw a final controlled by Celtic despite difficult conditions. The heat was again in the 90s but a strong wind helped the teams to cope with the high temperature. The wind and the fiery surface caused the ball to bounce erratically but one player unaffected was Paul Byrne who scored the only goal of the contest in 14 minutes. Barry Smith crossed from the right and both Falconer and Hay dummied the ball, allowing it to run to Byrne some 15 yards out and the young Irishman's fierce shot beat Burridge in Aberdeen's goal.

Stand-in captain Mark McNally lifted the trophy in place of John Collins, who had been recalled to Holland to play for Scotland; Collins himself was a replacement captain as Paul McStay had missed the tour because of injury. An interesting feature was the appearance of a former Celtic stalwart and captain in an Aberdeen jersey; Roy Aitken came on as a substitute in 65 minutes and played with his customary enthusiasm. Celtic:

Muggleton, McNally, (McQuilken), Gillespie (McLaughlin), MacKay, Smith, Byrne (Whittle), Holt, Gray, Martin, Falconer, Hay.

Aberdeen: Burridge, Wright, McLeish, G. Smith, Titus, Thomson, Grant, Kane, McKinnon (Aitken) Roddie (Mossavat), Booth.

HAMMERINGS

Celtic have inflicted a few heavy defeats on opposing teams:

Aberdeen: 8-0 (H) 30 January 1965
Airdrie: 9-0 (H) 26 October 1963
Albion Rovers: 7-0 (H) 16 December
   1893 (SC)
Alloa Athletic: 5-0 (A) 18 August 1982
   (LC) 5-0 (N) 2002 (SC)
Arbroath: 9-1 (A) 25 August 1993 (LC)
Ayr United: 7-0 (H) 3 November 1934
Berwick Rangers: 7-0 (N) 9 September
   1997 (LC)
Brechin City: 7-0 (H) 28 August 1985
   (LC)
Clyde: 9-1 (H) 25 December 1897;
   9-1; 4 September 1971
Cowdenbeath: 8-1 (A) 17 September
   1958 (LC)

Dumbarton: 8-0 (A) 23 August 1975 (LC)

Dundee: 11-0 (H) 26 October 1895

Dundee United: 7-0 (H) 1 March 1930

Dunfermline Athletic: 9-0 (H) 14 January 1928

East Fife: 9-1 (H) 10 January 1931

East Stirlingshire: 5-1 (A) 2 November 1963

Elgin City: 7-0 (H) 18 February 1967 (SC)

Falkirk: 7-0 (H) 6 January 1906;
7-0 (H) 5 October 1929;
8-1 (H) 21 September 2004 (LC)

Forfar Athletic: 5-0 (A) 21 February 1914 (SC)

Gretna: 3-0 (H) 29 December 2007

Hamilton Academical: 10-0 (H) 11 September 1968 (LC)

Heart of Midlothian: 6-0 (H) 20 April 1908; 6-0 (H) 1 April 1981

Hibernian: 6-0 (H) 23 August 1930;
6-0 (H) 1 May 1982;
6-0 (A) 15 October 1960

Inverness Caledonian Thistle*: 5-0 (H) 15 September 2007

Kilmarnock: 9-1 (H) 13 August 1938

Montrose: 7-1 (A) 4 February 1939 (SC)

Morton: 8-1 (H) 25 December 1965

Motherwell: 7-0 (A) 18 September 1982

Partick Thistle: 8-1 (H) 29 January 1969 (SC);
8-1 (H) 27 December 1969

Queen of South: 6-1 (H) 1 March 1952

Queen's Park: 6-0 (A) 10 March 1906;
6-0 (H) 23 October 1909

Raith Rovers: 8-1 (A) 15 September 1966

Rangers: 7-1 (N) 19 October 1957 (LC)

Ross County: 2-0 (H) 10 January 2004 (SC)

St. Johnstone: 6-0 (H) 23 October 1937

St. Mirren: 8-2 (H) 20 August 1966 (LC)

Stenhousemuir: 2-0 (H) 3 February 1937 (SC);

2-0 (A) 10 September 1975 (LC)

Stirling Albion: 8-0 (H) 6 November 2001 (LC)

Stranraer: 5-2 (H) 4 October 1973 (LC)

The abbreviations (SC) and (LC) stand for the Scottish Cup and the League Cup (in its many manifestations); the other results were achieved in regular league play.

Not too surprisingly many lop-sided scores are in cup-ties especially in the Scottish Cup – where there is a much greater chance of meeting non-league sides as in the following list. Some of these clubs are no longer active.

Abercorn: 6-0 (A) 29 Aug 1896 (SC)

Arthurlie: 7-0 (A) 8 January 1898 (SC)

Bathgate: 3-1 (H) 21 January 1928 (SC)

Bo'ness: 7-1 (H) 13 January 1900 (SC)

Burntisland Shipyard: 8-3 (A) 21 January 1939 (SC)

Cambuslang: 5-2 (H) 30 August 1890 (SC)

Carfin Shamrock: 3-1 (A) 4 October 1890 (SC)

Clydebank**: 6-0 (H) 17 December 1921;

Clydebank***6-0 (H) 29 October 1986

Cowlairs: 8-0 (H) 22 September 1888 (SC)

Dalbeattie Star: 6-0 (A) 29 January 1934 (SC)

Dumfries: 2-1 (A) 28 January 1905 (SC)

Duns: 4-0 (H) 10 February 1951 (SC)

> 'The best place to defend is in the other side's penalty box.'
> Jock Stein on attacking football

Eyemouth United: 4-0 (A) 24 January 1953 (SC)

5th KVR: 7-0 (H) 17 December 1892 (SC)

Forres Mechanics: 5-0 (A) 2 February 1957 (SC)

Gala Fairydean: 6-0 (H) 13 March 1963 (SC)

Galston: 1-0 (H) 11 February 1911 (SC)

Hurlford: 6-0 (H) 25 November 1893 (SC)

Inverness Caley: 6-0 (A) 18 January 1930 (SC)

Inverness Thistle: 6-0 (H) 16 February 1985 (SC)

Keith: 6-1 (A) 4 February 1928 (SC)

Kilmarnock Athletic: 3-0 (H) 19 December 1891 (SC)

Leith Athletic: 6-0 (H) 19 December 1931

Linthouse: 3-1 (H) 28 November 1892 (SC)

Lochgelly United: 3-0 (H) 11 February 1905 (SC)

Our Boys: 3-1 (A) 8 November 1890 (SC)

Meadowbank Thistle: 3-0 (H) 18 February 1985 (SC)

Nithsdale Wanderers: 5-0 (H) 12 February 1938 (SC)

Peebles Rovers: 4-0 (H) 25 January 1908 (SC)

Port Glasgow Athletic: 5-0 (H) 2 November 1907

Renton: 4-0 (A) 5 May 1892

Royal Albert: 2-0 (N) 13 December 1890 (SC)

St. Bernard's: 8-1 13 January 1894 (SC)

St. Johnstone: 6-0 (H) 23 October 1937

St. Mirren 8-2 (H) 20 August 1966 (LC)

Shettleston 5-1 (H) 1 September 1888 (SC)

6th GVR: 8-1 (A) 14 January 1899 (SC)

Solway Star: 2-0 (H) 21 February 1925 (SC)

Third Lanark: 7-0 (H) 19 November 1895; 5 January 1925

Thornliebank: 3-0 (H) 11 January 1902 (SC)

Vale of Leven: 9-1 (H) 5 May 1891

Wishaw Thistle: 6-2 (A) 18 October 1890 (SC)

* This club was an amalgamation of Inverness Caley and Inverness Thistle, both of whom also appear in the second list.

** This club folded in the early 1930s.

*** This club was founded in 1965

HAT-TRICKS

As in cricket, where 'a hat-trick' is defined as a bowler taking wickets with three consecutive deliveries, so football originally considered a hat-trick to consist of the same player scoring three consecutive goals. Nowadays, however, the feat is recognised as scoring three goals in a match.

Celtic's first hat-trick was scored in only their second official game – an 8-0 win over Cowlairs in the Scottish Cup on 22 September 1888 and the scorer was Mick Dunbar; the first hat-trick in the league came on 22 August 1890 with Peter Dowds netting three times in a 5-2 win over Cambuslang.

The record number of hat-tricks for the club is held, not too surprisingly, by Jimmy McGrory who scored three goals or more in a match on 55 occasions. McGrory also netted the most hat-tricks in a season with eight in 1926/27; remarkably, on those eight occasions he scored five goals three times, four goals four times and three goals only once.

In the following season (1927/28) he

scored hat-tricks in three successive matches, and in the last of these he scored eight times against Dunfermline Athletic on 14 January 1928.

Patsy Gallacher once scored consecutive hat-tricks – but four months apart. He netted three goals against Partick Thistle in the last fixture of the 1915/16 season, and scored four times against St. Mirren in the first game of the 1916/17 season.

Bobby Lennox could be considered as having surpassed Patsy's feat in 1971. He scored three times against Clyde in a 6-1 win in the last league game of 1970/71 on 1 May, and scored another hat-trick (also against Clyde) on the first day of the next season (1971/72). In between those fixtures Celtic appeared in the final of the Scottish Cup against Rangers and Lennox netted in a 1-1 draw on 8 May 1971.

Bobby Collins had the unusual distinction of scoring all three Celtic goals from the penalty spot against Aberdeen on 24 September 1953.

Mark Burchill recorded the fastest hat-trick in European competition history with three goals in under four minutes against Jeunesse d'Esch in the UEFA Cup tie on 24 August 2000.

HEART OF MIDLOTHIAN

Over the years a number of transfer deals have been worked out between these two founding members of the Scottish League.

Hearts to Celtic:
Barney Battles
Mike Galloway
Paul Hartley
Roy Kay
Alex King
Andy Lynch
Gordon Marshall
Tosh McKinlay
Steven Pressley
Davie Russell
Chris Shevlane
Willie Wallace.

Of these players Willie Wallace, one of the Lisbon Lions, was probably the most celebrated. His transfer cost £30,000 on 6 December 1966 and he proved a regular goalscorer. Andy Lynch, who doubled as a left winger or left back, scored a vital goal in the 1977 Scottish Cup final from a penalty kick against Rangers.

Celtic to Hearts:
Joe Carruth (loan)
John Colquhoun
Bert Fraser
Stephane Mahe
Roddie MacDonald
Willie McStay
Brian Whittaker

Willie McStay, after a Celtic career of some sixteen seasons, left Parkhead to join Hearts in 1923; John Colquhoun found himself as a Hearts player after a short spell at Celtic Park; Roddie MacDonald gave excellent service to the Tynecastle club as a central defender for six seasons between 1981 and 1987.

Some players turned out for both clubs during their careers, but did not move directly from one to the other. This list includes the following:

Jimmy Bone
Alfie Conn
Davie Duncan

Steve Fulton
Steve Hancock
Jimmy Hay
Tom Hynds
Mo Johnston
Jackie Jordan
George Livingstone
Charlie McGillivray
Harry Marshall
Martin Moran
Frank O'Donnell
Hugh O'Donnell
Robbie Sanderson.

HIBERNIAN

The Edinburgh club, founded by Canon Edward Hannon as an Irish and Catholic organisation in 1875, was the inspiration for Celtic – especially after winning the Scottish Cup in Glasgow in 1887. They were feted by the local Irish community before departing for Edinburgh and the idea of Celtic grew from that joyous occasion.

Hibernian opened the new club's first ground with a friendly match against Cowlairs on 8 May 1888, the proceeds going to Glasgow charities but relations with Celtic quickly foundered when the Glasgow club proceeded to poach several star players from Hibernian: Michael Dunbar, Paddy Gallagher, Johnny Coleman, Mike McKeown, Jimmy McLaren and Willie Groves.

In addition Hibernian could feel mightily aggrieved that Celtic also managed to land Renton's centre half James Kelly – recognised as Scotland's best defender – who had already turned out for them in a friendly against Hearts. Celtic claimed unconvincingly that the players had approached them first, and as 'amateurs' they were entitled to do so. In several subsequent fixtures between the clubs crowd trouble, especially in Edinburgh, broke out frequently.

Hibernian were so badly affected by the defection of the backbone of their side that they went into decline and disbanded; a year or so later they re-emerged but were no longer an exclusively Catholic or Irish club.

However, a remarkable number of players in addition to those above have joined Celtic from Hibernian over the years, a fact which might feed further resentment in Leith:

Didier Agathe
Jimmy Blessington
Tommy Bogan
Scott Brown
Gary Caldwell
John Collins
Johnny Divers
Darren Jackson
Charlie Kelly
Chris Killen
Ulrik Laursen
Willie McCallum
Sandy McMahon
James McLaughlin
Willie McGinnigle
Pat McGinlay
James McGhee
Allan Martin
Gordon Marshall
Derek Riordan
Pat Stanton
Ronnie Simpson

Some have suggested that Celtic's tribulations during the Eire flag controversy (when in 1952 Celtic were ordered to remove the tricolour by the SFA whose president then was Harry Swan of Hibernian) were an indication of the animosity that still lingered from the earliest days.

Perhaps the greatest coup was in persuading Sandy McMahon, born in Selkirk, to leave Hibernian to join Celtic. McMahon was probably the first genuine superstar in Scottish football. In later times Pat Stanton and John Collins proved to be valuable additions to Celtic. It could be considered that Didier Agathe, bought by Martin O'Neill for £50,000, was 'a steal'; if so, what about Ronnie Simpson, purchased for about £2,000?

Some players have made the return journey, from Hibernian to Celtic, and back to Hibernian: Johnny Divers, Pat McGinlay, Willie McGinnigle. John Collins, the recent Hibernian manager, might be included here; as might Pat Stanton, also a Hibernian manager.

Among other Hibernian managers with Celtic connections would be Bertie Auld, Murdo MacLeod and Tony Mowbray.

No doubt some residents of Leith still remember that Jock Stein left his post at Easter Road to become Celtic's manager in 1965.

Several Celts have moved on directly from Parkhead to Easter Road: Bertie Auld, Mike Conroy, Paddy Connolly, Eddie Gilfeather, John Hughes, John McCann, Joe McBride, John McNamee, Jackie McNamara, Allan Sneddon, Chris Shevlane.

Hibernian and Celtic have provided many entertaining clashes over the years but probably the most memorable for Celtic supporters would be the Coronation Cup final of 1953 when Johnny Bonnar defied the combined efforts of the best forward line in Scottish football, Hibernians 'Famous Five'. Perhaps older Hibs' fans might prefer the Scottish Cup final of 1902 when Hibernian defeated Celtic by 1-0 (at Celtic Park!)

JIMMY HOGAN

Celtic's first real coach in the modern sense of the role, Jimmy Hogan was brought to Celtic Park by chairman Bob Kelly in 1948 after the previous season's relegation scare. He tried to develop a football-playing, ball-holding style, and introduced some variation in the taking of free-kicks and the goalkeeper's use of the ball. He was far ahead of his time with British or Scottish players. He came to Parkhead at the age of sixty-five and with a tremendous reputation gained on the continent, having coached the Swiss teams Young Boys (Berne) and Lausanne and being largely responsible for the development of football in Austria, Hungary and Germany. He had returned to England to coach Fulham before going back to Austria where, under his tutelage, they reached the 1936 Olympic final.

He was invited by the Hungarian F.A. to attend the historic 6-3 defeat of England at Wembley in 1953; the German FA wrote to his son in 1974: 'Your father was the founder of modern football in this country.' An advocate of physical fitness, he died at the age of 91.

HOLLYWOOD CELTIC

In the blockbuster movie 'The Day After Tomorrow' scientists in a remote station somewhere in Scotland are seen watching a televised European Cup tie between Celtic and Manchester United. Unfortunately, from the scenes shown it appears that the English club are winning. In 2000 Ally McCoist of Rangers appeared as a Celtic player in 'A Shot at Glory'. Celtic's Didier Agathe played for Rangers in the film.

HOME DEFEATS

Celtic may have a fine record at Celtic Park but they have lost matches there, some heavily. The following list is of the heaviest defeats in the major competitions:

Scottish League:
    Hearts – 14 September 1895 0-5
Scottish Cup:
    Rangers – 28 February 1903 0-3
League Cup:
    Clyde – 9 October 1948 3-6
    Rangers – 31 August 1955 0-4
Europe:
    Paris St. Germain – 2 November 1995 0-3 (ECWC)

HONOURS

Several 'Celtic men' have been given individual honours largely for their contribution to football and society. Among them are the following:

Robert Kelly: Knighthood 1969
Jock Stein: CBE 1970
Billy McNeill: MBE 1974
Bobby Lennox: MBE 1981
Danny McGrain: MBE 1983
Paul McStay: MBE 1997

Ian Wright: MBE 1999
Tom Boyd: MBE 2003
Paul Elliott: MBE 2003
Henrik Larsson: MBE 2006

Both Martin O'Neill and Henrik Larsson have been awarded honorary doctorates from Scottish universities as has Billy McNeill.

Henrik Larsson also won the UEFA Golden Shoe for his goal-scoring heroics in 2000/01. Larsson received the award at the UEFA Gala in Monaco in August 2001 from President Lennart Johannson.

'HOOPS'

Among other football clubs worldwide who share – more or less – the same strip as Celtic are the following:

Buckie Thistle
Omonia Nicosia
Portland Timbers
Rapid Vienna
Shamrock Rovers
Sporting Lisbon
Yeovil Town

HUNS

A touchy problem in politically-correct days but. . .

During World War I Celtic, because of their domination of Scottish football, were often likened to the powerful German armies and described as 'Huns'. The term was not considered as an insult.

Also, a pupil under instruction with the Royal Flying Corps in the same World War was nicknamed 'a hun'.

I

INDIRECT FREE KICK GOALS

The rule was changed in 1992 so that goalkeepers were no longer allowed to touch the ball with their hands when it was deliberately kicked to them by a team-mate. An indirect free kick is awarded to the attacking team for an offence if decided by the referee. Like most clubs, Celtic have had little success with such awards mainly because of the number of players called upon inside the penalty area to defend the free kick. Only three instances of the successful conversion of such awards come to mind:

Pierre van Hooijdonk scored against Dundee United at Tannadice on 14 September 1995 following an indirect free kick awarded only six yards from the goal-line. His goal, a low shot which squeezed in under the feet of the defenders, helped Celtic to a 2-1 win.

In November 2004 in the Champions' League fixture against Shaktar Donesk Alan Thompson scored after an indirect free kick was awarded for the visitors' goalkeeper holding the ball for thirteen seconds. Petrov slipped the ball to him for the important goal.

Against Motherwell in the League Cup semi-final at Hampden Park on 1 February 2006 Celtic were awarded an indirect free kick inside the penalty area when Motherwell's goalkeeper had to save a pass back with his hands. With the score 1-1 and with only a few minutes left, Shaun Maloney fired in the winning goal when the ball was tapped to him.

INJURIES (SEE BREAKS)

Unfortunately, injuries are part of the game of football and Celtic have suffered their share:

On 5 September 1931 the Celtic goalkeeper John Thomson was carried off after an accidental collision with Rangers' Sam English in a league fixture at Ibrox Park, and died later that night in the Victoria Infirmary of his head injuries.

Jimmy Delaney, Celtic's star outside-right, suffered a broken arm in an incident with Atilio Becci, Arbroath's left-back at Celtic Park on 1 April 1939. The injury was so severe that the hospital surgeon considered amputation. Delaney was out of the game for almost two years but made a full recovery.

Henrik Larsson sustained a broken leg

Celtic and Scotland captain Roy Aitken

against Olympique Lyonnais in the UEFA Cup tie in France in November 1999. The injury was accidental and ironic in that Larsson suffered the break in attempting to tackle a Lyon defender. But the striker was out of action for six months, his absence contributing to the sacking of Celtic's manager before the end of the season.

John Kennedy, Celtic's young central defender, made his debut for Scotland against Romania at Hampden Park in March 2004. He was badly fouled by Ioan Ganea in the first half, a foul which caused horrendous damage to his knee. Up to the present time, Kennedy has been unable to regain his place in Celtic's first team, even after a number of operations in the United States.

INTERNATIONAL APPEARANCES
(SCOTLAND)

The concept of 'caps' for international appearances remains as a hint of the Public Schools origins of football. Back in 1873 the SFA introduced the idea for the Home Internationals; the FA followed suit in 1886.

Naturally, as one of the leading clubs in the country, Celtic are frequently called upon to provide members of the national side:

Roy Aitken: (52)
  Peru 1980;
  Belgium 1980, 1983, 1984, 1987, 1988;
  Wales 1980, 1984, 1986; England 1980, 1985, 1986, 1987, 1988, 1989;
  Poland 1980; Canada (2) 1983;
  Northern Ireland 1984;
  Iceland 1985;
  East Germany 1986;
  Australia (2) 1986;
  Israel 1986;
  Romania 1986;
  Denmark 1986;
  West Germany 1986;
  Uruguay 1986;
  Bulgaria (2) 1987;
  Eire (2) 1987;
  Luxembourg 1987, 1988;
  Brazil 1987;
  Hungary 1988;
  Saudi Arabia 1988;
  Malta 1988;
  Spain 1988;
  Colombia 1988;
  Norway 1989, 1990;
  Yugoslavia 1989, 1990;
  Italy 1989;
  Cyprus (2) 1989;

France 1989, 1990;
Chile 1989
(other international appearances
when with Newcastle United and St.
Mirren)

Bertie Auld: (3)
Hungary 1959;
Portugal 1959;
Wales 1960

Barney Battles: (3)
England 1901;
Northern Ireland 1901;
Wales 1901

Craig Beattie: (4)
Italy 2006, 2007
Norway 2006
Georgia 2007

John Bell: (5)
England 1899, 1900;
Wales 1899, 1900;
Northern Ireland 1899
(other international appearances
when with Dumbarton and Everton)

Alec Bennett: (3)
Wales 1904, 1908;
Northern Ireland 1907
(other international appearances
when with Rangers)

James Blessington: (4)
England 1894, 1896;
Northern Ireland 1894, 1896

Tom Boyd: (55)
Finland 1992, 1995, 1996, 1998;
Canada 1992;
Norway 1992, 1998;
CIS 1992;
Switzerland 1993, 1996;
Portugal 1993; Italy 1993, 1994;
Malta 1993, 1994, 1997;

© snspix.com

Bertie Auld, winner of too few Scotland caps, but a superb performer for Celtic in the 1960s

Holland 1994, 1996;
Austria 1994, 1997;
Germany 1993, 1999;
Estonia (2) 1993 (2), 1997, 1999;
Faroes 1995, (2) 1999;
Russia 1995;
San Marino 1995, 1996, 2001;
Greece 1996;
Serbia 1996, 1997;
Australia 1996, 2001;
Denmark 1996, 1998;
United States 1996, 1998;
Colombia 1996, 1998;
England 1996;
Latvia 1997, 1998, 2001;
Wales 1997;
Belarus 1997, 1998;
France 1998; Brazil 1998;
Morocco 1998;
Lithuania 1999;

Czech Republic (2) 1999;
Croatia 2001;
Belgium 2001, 2002;
Poland 2001
(other international appearances
when with Motherwell and Chelsea)

Jim Brogan: (4)
Wales 1971;
Northern Ireland 1971;
Portugal 1971;
England 1971

Scott Brown: (6)
France 2007
Ukraine 2007
South Africa 2007
Lithuania 2007
Italy 2007
Croatia 2008
(other international appearances
when with Hibernian)

John Browning: (1)
Wales 1914

Mark Burchill: (6)
Bosnia 2000;
Lithuania 2000;
England (2) 2000;
France 2000;
Holland 2000

Craig Burley: (16)
Belarus 1998;
Latvia 1998;
France 1998;
Colombia 1998;
United States 1998;
Brazil 1998;
Norway 1998;
Morocco 1998;
Faroes 1999;
Czech Republic 1999;
Bosnia (2) 2000;

Estonia 2000;
Lithuania 2000;
England (2) 2000
(other international appearances
when with Chelsea and Derby County)

Tommy Burns: (8)
Northern Ireland 1981,1983;
Holland 1982;
Wales 1982;
Belgium 1983;
Canada (2) 1983;
England 1988

Gary Caldwell: (6)
France 2006
Ukraine 2006
Austria 2007
South Africa 2007
Croatia 2008
Czech Republic (2008)
(other international appearances
when with Newcastle United and
Hibernian)

John Campbell: (12)
England 1893, 1898, 1900, 1901;
Northern Ireland 1893, 1898, 1900,
1901, 1902;
Wales 1901, 1902, 1903

Joe Cassidy: (4)
Wales 1921, 1924;
Northern Ireland 1921, 1923

Steve Chalmers: (5)
Wales 1965;
Finland 1965;
Portugal 1966;
Brazil 1966;
Northern Ireland 1967

John Clark: (4)
Brazil 1966;
Wales 1967;

Northern Ireland 1967;
USSR 1967

John Collins: (30)
Switzerland 1991, 1994, 1996;
Bulgaria 1991;
Northern Ireland 1992;
Finland 1992, 1995, 1996;
Portugal (2) 1993;
Malta 1993;
Germany 1993;
Estonia (2) 1993;
Holland (2) 1994, 1996;
Austria 1994; Faroes (2) 1995;
Russia 1995;
San Marino 1995, 1996;
Greece 1996;
Sweden 1996;
Australia 1996;
Denmark 1996;
United States 1996;
Colombia 1996;
England 1996
(other international appearances
when with Hibernian, Monaco and
Everton)

Bobby Collins: (22)
Wales 1951,1956, 1957, 1958;
Northern Ireland 1951, 1956, 1958;
Austria 1951, 1955;
Yugoslavia 1955, 1958;
Hungary 1955, 1958;
England 1957;
Spain (2) 1957;
Switzerland 1957, 1958;
West Germany 1957;
Poland 1958;
France 1958;
Paraguay 1958
(other international appearances
when with Everton and Leeds United)

© snspix.com

John Collins

George Connelly: (2)
Czechoslovakia 1974;
West Germany 1974

Jim Craig: (1)
Wales 1967

Joe Craig: (1)
Sweden 1977

Steve Crainey (4):
France 2002;
Nigeria 2002;
Denmark 2003;
Faroe Islands 2003
(other international appearances
when with Southampton)

Pat Crerand: (11)
Eire (2) 1961;
Czechoslovakia 1961, 1962 (2);
Northern Ireland 1962, 1963;
Wales 1962, 1963;
England 1962;
Uruguay 1962
(other international appearances
when with Manchester United)

Willie Cringan: (5)
Wales 1922, 1923;
England 1922, 1923;
Northern Ireland 1923

Johnny Crum: (2)
England 1936;
Northern Ireland 1939

Kenny Dalglish: (47)
Belgium 1972, 1974, 1975
Holland 1972
Denmark (2) 1973, (2) 1976
England (2) 1973, 1974, 1975, 1976, 1977
Wales 1973, 1975, (2) 1977
N Ireland 1973, 1974, 1975, 1976, 1977
Wales 1973, 1974
Switzerland 1973, 1976
Brazil 1973, 1974, 1977
Czechoslovakia (2) 1974, 1977
W Germany (2) 1974
Norway 1974
Zaire 1974
Yugoslavia 1974
E Germany 1975
Spain 1975
Sweden 1975, 1977
Portugal 1975
Romania 1975, 1976
Finland 1977
Chile 1977
Argentina 1977
(other international appearances when with Liverpool)

Dixie Deans: (2)
East Germany 1975;
Spain 1975

Jimmy Delaney: (9)
Wales 1936,1939;
Northern Ireland 1936, 1938, 1939;

Germany 1937;
England 1937;
Austria 1937;
Czechoslovakia 1937
(other international appearances when with Manchester United)

John Divers: (1)
Wales 1895

John Divers: (1)
Northern Ireland 1939

Joe Dodds: (3)
England 1914;
Wales 1914;
Northern Ireland 1914

Simon Donnelly: (10)
Wales 1997;
Malta 1997;
Latvia 1998;
France 1998;
Denmark 1998;
Finland 1998;
Colombia 1998;
United States 1998;
Estonia 1999;
Faroe Islands 1999

Rab Douglas: (17)
Nigeria 2002;
South Africa 2002;
Hong Kong 2002;
Denmark 2003;
Faroe Islands 2003, 2004;
Iceland 2003;
Portugal 2003;
New Zealand 2003;
Germany 2003;
Lithuania 2003;
Norway 2003;
Germany 2004;
Holland (2) 2004;
Wales 2004;

Italy 2005
(other international appearances
when with Leicester City)

Peter Dowds: (1)
Northern Ireland 1892

Dan Doyle: (8)
England 1892, 1894, 1895, 1897,
1898;
Wales 1893;
Northern Ireland 1895, 1898

Bobby Evans: (45)
England 1949, 1951, 1954, 1956,
1958, 1959, 1960;
Wales 1949, 1950, 1954, 1956, 1958,
1960;
Northern Ireland 1949, 1950, 1952,
1954, 1955, 1956, 1958, 1960;
France 1949, 1958;
Switzerland 1950, 1958;
Portugal 1950, 1955, 1959;
Austria 1951, 1955, 1956;
Sweden 1953; Norway 1954;
Finland 1954; Yugoslavia 1955, 1958;
Hungary 1955, 1958;
West Germany 1957, 1959;
Spain 1957;
Poland 1958, 1960;
Paraguay 1958;
Holland 1959
(other international appearances
when with Chelsea)

Willie Fernie: (12)
Finland 1954;
Austria 1954;
Uruguay 1954;
Wales 1955, 1957, 1958;
Yugoslavia 1957;
Northern Ireland 1955, 1957;
England 1957;
Switzerland 1958;

Paraguay 1958

Mike Galloway: (1)
Romania 1992

Tommy Gemmell: (18)
England 1966, 1967, 1968, 1969,
1970;
Wales 1967, 1969;
Northern Ireland 1967, 1968, 1969;
USSR 1967;
Denmark 1969;
Austria 1969;
West Germany 1969, 1970;
Cyprus 1969;
Eire 1970;
Belgium 1971

John Gilchrist: (1)
England 1922

Ronnie Glavin: (1)
Sweden 1977

Jonathon Gould: (2)
Lithuania 2000;
Australia 2000

Peter Grant: (2)
England 1989;
Chile 1989

Willie Groves: (2)
Northern Ireland 1889;
England 1890

Frank Haffey: (2)
England 1960, 1961

Paul Hartley: (8)
Georgia 2007
Italy 2007 (2)
Austria 2007
Faroes 2007
France 2007
Croatia 2008
Czech Republic 2008

Mike Haughney: (1)
 England 1954

David Hay: (27)
 Northern Ireland 1970, 1971, 1973, 1974;
 Wales 1970, 1971, 1973, 1974;
 England 1970, 1973, 1974;
 Denmark 1971;
 Belgium 1971, 1972, 1974;
 Poland 1971, 1972;
 Holland 1972;
 Norway 1974; Zaire 1974;
 Yugoslavia 1974
 Switzerland 1973;
 Brazil 1973, 1974;
 Czechoslovakia (2) 1974;
 West Germany 1974;

Jim Hay: (7)
 Northern Ireland 1905, 1909, 1910, 1911;
 Wales 1910;
 England 1910, 1911
 (other international appearances when with Newcastle United)

Bobby Hogg: (1)
 Czechoslovakia 1937

John Hughes: (8)
 Poland 1966;
 Spain 1966;
 Northern Ireland 1966;
 Italy (2) 1966;
 England 1968;
 Austria 1969;
 Eire 1970

Ally Hunter: (2)
 England 1973;
 Czechoslovakia 1974
 (other international appearances when with Kilmarnock)

Mo Johnston: (9)
 Iceland 1985;
 Spain (2) 1985;
 Wales 1985;
 East Germany 1986;
 Bulgaria 1987;
 Eire (2) 1987;
 Luxembourg 1987
 (other international appearances when with Watford, Nantes, and Rangers)

Jimmy Johnstone: (23)
 Wales 1965, 1967, 1968, 1974;
 Finland 1965;
 England 1966, 1970, 1971, 1972, 1974;
 USSR 1967;
 Austria 1969;
 West Germany 1969, 1970;
 Denmark 1971;
 Poland 1972;
 Belgium 1972, 1974;
 Holland 1972;
 Northern Ireland 1972;
 Norway 1974;
 East Germany 1975;
 Spain 1975

James Kelly: (7)
 England 1889, 1890, 1892, 1893;
 Northern Ireland 1893, 1896;
 Wales 1894
 (other international appearances when with Renton)

Joe Kennaway: (1)
 Austria 1934

Jim Kennedy: (6)
 Wales 1964, 1965;
 England 1964;
 West Germany 1964;
 Northern Ireland 1965;
 Finland 1965

John Kennedy: (1)
　　Romania 2004

Paul Lambert: (31)
　　Finland 1998; Colombia 1998;
　　United States 1998;
　　Brazil 1998;
　　Norway 1998, 2004;
　　Morocco 1998;
　　Lithuania 1999, 2000, 2003;
　　Czech Republic (2) 1999;
　　Germany 1999;
　　Faroe Islands 1999, 2003;
　　Bosnia 2000;
　　Holland 2000;
　　Eire 2000, 2003;
　　Belgium 2001, 2002;
　　San Marino 2001;
　　Croatia 2002;
　　France 2002;
　　Nigeria 2002;
　　Denmark 2003;
　　Iceland (2) 2003;
　　Poland 2003;
　　Germany 2003, 2004
　　(other international appearances
　　when with Motherwell, and Borussia
　　Dortmund)

Bobby Lennox: (10)
　　Northern Ireland 1967;
　　England 1967;
　　USSR 1967;
　　Wales 1968, 1970;
　　Luxembourg 1968;
　　Denmark 1969;
　　Austria 1969;
　　West Germany 1969;
　　Cyprus 1969

Willie Loney: (2)
　　Wales 1910;
　　Northern Ireland 1910

Dan McArthur: (3)
　　England 1895;
　　Northern Ireland 1895;
　　Wales 1899

Andy McAtee: (1)
　　Wales 1913

Frank McAvennie: (1)
　　Saudi Arabia 1988
　　(other international appearances
　　when with West Ham United)

Joe McBride: (2)
　　Wales 1967;
　　Northern Ireland 1967

Brian McClair: (4)
　　Luxembourg 1987;
　　Eire 1987;
　　England 1987;
　　Brazil 1987
　　(other international appearances
　　when with Manchester United)

Frank McGarvey: (5)
　　Uruguay 1984;
　　Belgium 1984;
　　East Germany 1984;
　　Northern Ireland 1984;
　　Wales 1984
　　(other international appearances
　　when with Liverpool)

Willie McGonagle: (6)
　　England 1933, 1934;
　　Austria 1934;
　　Northern Ireland 1934, 1935;
　　Wales 1935

Danny McGrain: (62)
　　Wales 1973, 1974, 1975, 1976, (2)
　　1977, 1980, (2) 1981;
　　Northern Ireland 1973, 1975, 1976,
　　1977, 1980, 1981, 1982;

England 1973, 1974, 1975, 1976, 1977, 1980, 1981;
Switzerland 1973, 1976;
Brazil 1973, 1974, 1977;
Czechoslovakia (2) 1974, 1977, 1978;
West Germany 1974;
Belgium 1974, 1980;
Norway 1974; Zaire 1974;
Yugoslavia 1974;
Spain 1975, 1982;
Sweden 1975, 1977, 1981, 1982;
Portugal 1975, 1980, 1981;
Romania 1975;
Denmark (2) 1976;
Finland 1977;
Chile 1977;
Argentina 1977;
East Germany 1978;
Poland 1980;
Hungary 1980;
Israel (2) 1981;
Holland 1982;
New Zealand 1982;
USSR 1982

Jimmy McGrory: (7)
Northern Ireland 1928, 1932, 1933, 1934;
England 1931, 1933;
Wales 1932

Tommy McInally: (2)
Northern Ireland 1926;
Wales 1927

Duncan MacKay: (14)
England 1959, 1960;
West Germany 1959;
Holland 1959;
Portugal 1959;
Poland 1960;
Austria 1960;
Hungary 1960;
Turkey 1960; Wales 1961;

Northern Ireland 1961, 1962;
Czechoslovakia 1962;
Uruguay 1962

Mick McKeown: (2)
Northern Ireland 1889;
England 1890

Tosh McKinlay: (22)
Greece 1996;
Finland 1996;
Denmark 1996;
Colombia 1996;
England 1996;
Switzerland 1996;
Austria (2) 1997;
Latvia 1997, 1998;
Sweden (2) 1997;
Estonia (2) 1997;
Wales 1997;
Malta 1997;
Belarus 1997, 1998;
France 1998;
United States 1998;
Brazil 1998;
Morocco 1998

Jimmy McLaren: (2)
England 1889, 1890
(other international appearances when with Hibernian)

Adam McLean: (4)
Wales 1926, 1927;
Northern Ireland 1926;
England 1927

Donnie McLeod: (4)
Northern Ireland 1905, 1906;
England 1906;
Wales 1906

Murdo MacLeod: (5)
England 1985, 1987;
Eire 1987;

Luxembourg 1987;
Brazil 1987
(other international appearances
when with Dortmund and Hibernian)

Sandy McMahon: (6)
England 1892, 1893, 1894;
Northern Ireland 1893, 1901;
Wales 1902

Stephen McManus (13)
Austria 2007
Faroes 2007
Georgia (2) 2007
Italy (2) 2007
South Africa 2007
Lithuania 2007
Ukraine (2) 2007
Croatia 2008
Czech Republic 2008

Jimmy McMenemy: (12)
Northern Ireland 1905, 1909, 1911,
1914, 1920;
England 1910, 1911, 1914;
Wales 1910, 1911, 1912, 1914

Jackie McNamara: (29)
Estonia 1997
Latvia 1997
Sweden 1997, 2005
Wales 1997, 2004
Colombia 1998
Denmark 1998
Morocco 1998
Norway 1998
USA 1998
Holland 2000, (2) 2004
San Marino 2001
Belgium 2002
France 2002
Germany 2003, 2004
Iceland 2003
Lithuania 2003, 2004

© snspix.com

Jackie McNamara

New Zealand 2003
Faroes 2004
Trinidad & Tobago 2004
Italy 2005
Moldova 2005
Slovenia 2005
Spain 2005
(other international appearances
when with Wolverhampton
Wanderers)

Alec McNair: (15)
Wales 1906, 1908, 1910, 1912, 1920;
Northern Ireland 1907, 1912, 1914,
1920;
England 1908, 1909, 1912, 1913,
1914, 1920

Billy McNeill: (29)
England 1961, 1962, 1964, 1965,
1968, 1969, 1972;
Eire (2) 1961, 1963;
Czechoslovakia 1961, 1962;
Northern Ireland 1962;
Uruguay 1962; Spain 1963, 1965;
Wales 1964, 1969, 1972;

West Germany 1964, 1970;
Finland 1965; Poland 1965, 1966;
Northern Ireland 1966, 1972;
USSR 1967;
Cyprus (2) 1969;

John McPhail: (5)
Wales 1950, 1951;
Northern Ireland 1951, 1954;
Austria 1951

Paul McStay: (76)
Uruguay 1984, 1986, 1988;
Belgium 1984, 1987;
East Germany 1984, 1986, 1990;
Northern Ireland 1984;
Wales 1984;
England 1984, 1987, 1988, 1989;
Yugoslavia 1985, 1989, 1990;
Iceland 1985;
Spain (2) 1985, 1988;
Wales 1985;
Australia 1986;
Israel 1986;
Bulgaria 1987, 1988, 1991;
Eire (2) 1987;
Luxembourg 1987, 1988;
Brazil 1987, 1990;
Hungary 1988;
Saudi Arabia 1988;
Colombia 1988;
Norway 1989, 1992;
Italy 1989, 1993, 1994;
Cyprus 1989;
Chile 1989;
France 1989, 1990;
Argentina 1990;
Egypt 1990;
Poland 1990;
Malta 1990;
Costa Rica 1990;
Sweden 1990;
Romania 1991;

USSR 1991;
San Marino 1992;
Finland 1992, 1995;
United States 1992;
Canada 1992;
CIS 1992;
Holland 1992, 1994;
Germany 1992;
Switzerland 1993;
Portugal 1993;
Estonia (2) 1993;
Faroe Islands 1995;
Russia 1995.

Willie McStay: (13)
Wales 1921, 1925, 1926, 1927, 1928;
Northern Ireland 1921, 1925, 1926, 1927, 1928;
England 1925, 1926, 1927

Lou Macari: (6)
Wales 1972,
England 1972,
Yugoslavia 1972,
Czechoslovakia 1972;
Brazil 1972;
Denmark 1973
(other international appearances when with Manchester United)

John Madden: (2)
Wales 1893, 1895

Willie Maley: (2)
England 1893;
Northern Ireland 1893

Shaun Maloney: (2)
Belarus 2006
USA 2006
(other international appearances when with Aston Villa)

David Marshall: (2)
Hungary 2005;
Sweden 2005

Gordon Marshall: (1)
United States 1992

Harry Marshall: (2)
Wales 1899;
Northern Ireland 1900

Peter Meechan: (1)
Northern Ireland 1896

Willie Miller: (6)
England 1947;
Wales 1947, 1948;
Belgium 1947;
Luxembourg 1947;
Northern Ireland 1948

Neil Mochan: (3)
Norway 1954;
Austria 1954;
Uruguay 1954

Bobby Murdoch: (12)
England 1966, 1969;
Wales 1966, 1969;
Italy (2) 1966;
Northern Ireland 1967, 1968, 1969;
West Germany 1969;
Cyprus 1969;
Austria 1970

Frank Murphy: (1)
Holland 1938

Charlie Napier: (3)
England 1932, 1935;
Wales 1935
(other international appearances
when with Derby County)

© snspix.com

Paul McStay was captain of Celtic and
Scotand - he won 76 caps for his country

Charlie Nicholas: (6)
1983 Switzerland;
Northern Ireland 1983;
England 1983;
Canada (3) 1983
(other international appearances
when with Arsenal and Aberdeen)

Brian O'Neill: (1)
Australia 1996
(other international appearances
when with Wolfsburg, Derby County
and Preston North End)

Willie Orr: (3)
   Northern Ireland 1900, 1903;
   Wales 1904

George Paterson: (1)
   Northern Ireland 1939

Steven Pearson: (5)
   Wales 2004
   Holland 2005
   Norway 2005
   Spain 2005
   Sweden 2005
   (others international appearances
   when with Motherwell and Derby
   County)

Davie Provan: (10)
   Belgium (2) 1980;
   Portugal 1980, 1982;
   Northern Ireland 1980, 1982;
   Israel 1981;
   Wales 1981;
   England 1981;
   Sweden 1982

Jimmy Quinn: (11)
   Northern Ireland 1905, 1906, 1908,
   1910;
   Wales 1906, 1910, 1912;
   England 1908, 1909, 1910, 1912

Barry Robson: (1)
   Czech Republic 2008

Davie Russell: (4)
   Wales 1897, 1901;
   Northern Ireland 1898, 1901

Peter Scarff: (1)
   Northern Ireland 1931

Ronnie Simpson: (5)
   England 1967, 1968;
   USSR 1967;
   Northern Ireland 1968;
   Austria 1969

Eric Smith: (2)
   Hungary 1959;
   Portugal 1959

Jamie Smith: (2)
   Austria 2003;
   Republic of Ireland 2003

Peter Somers: (4)
   England 1905;
   Northern Ireland 1905, 1907;
   Wales 1909

Dave Storrier: (3)
   England 1899;
   Wales 1899;
   Northern Ireland 1899

Alec Thomson: (3)
   England 1926;
   France 1932;
   Wales 1933

Bertie Thomson: (1)
   Wales 1931

John Thomson: (4)
   France 1930;
   England 1931;
   Wales 1931;
   Northern Ireland 1931

Andy Walker: (3)
   Colombia 1988;
   Finland 1995;
   France 1995

Willie Wallace: (4)
   England 1967, 1969 ;
   USSR 1967;
   Northern Ireland 1968
   (other international appearances
   when with Hearts)

Derek Whyte: (4)
   Belgium 1988;
   Luxembourg 1988;

Chile 1989;
United States 1992
(other international appearances
when with Middlesbrough and
Aberdeen)

Paul Wilson: (1)
Spain 1975

Peter Wilson: (4)
Northern Ireland 1926, 1931;
France 1931;
England 1933

'Sunny Jim' Young: (1)
Northern Ireland 1906

_____

SCOTLAND UNDER-21:

Roy Aitken (16), Marc Anthony (3),
Owen Archdeacon (1), Craig Beattie (7),
Mark Burchill (15), Tommy Burns (5),
Jim Casey (1), Ryan Conroy (1),
Stephen Crainey (7), Danny Crainie (1),
Gerry Creaney (11), Scott Cuthbert (5),
Simon Donnelly (11), Barry Elliot (2),
Steve Fulton (7), Mike Galloway (1),
Peter Grant (10), Stuart Gray* (7),
Gary Irvine (2/10), Paul Lawson (10),
Simon Lynch* (5/13),
John Paul McBride (2), Brian McClair (8),
George McCluskey (6), Frank McGarvey
(1/3), Michael McGlinchey (1),
Brian McLaughlin (1980) (8),
Mark McNally (2),
Jackie McNamara (5/12),
Tony McParland (1),
Jamie McQuilken (2), Paul McStay (5),
Shaun Maloney (21), David Marshall (10),
Joe Miller (4/7), Charlie Mulgrew (3/7),
Charlie Nicholas (5/6), Brian O'Neil (7),
Rocco Quinn (8), Mark Reid (2),
Barry Smith (5), Alan Sneddon (1),

Andy Walker (1), Ross Wallace (4),
Derek Whyte (9), Mark Wilson (2/19),

* Stuart Gray, born in Harrogate, had
Scottish qualifications, as did Simon Lynch,
although born in Montreal.

_____

SCOTLAND UNDER-23**:

Dick Beattie (3), John Colrain (1),
George Connelly (3), Pat Crerand (1),
Kenny Dalglish (4), David Hay (3),
John Hughes (4), Bobby Jeffrey (1),
Jimmy Johnstone (2), Lou Macari (2),
Duncan MacKay (4), Pat McCluskey (6),
Roddie MacDonald (1), Danny McGrain (2),
Billy McNeill (5), Bobby Murdoch (1),
Jimmy Walsh (1), Ian Young (1).

** This category was abandoned in 1976 and
was replaced by the Under-21s.

INTERNATIONAL 'CELTICS' (I)

Celtic, of course, are a Scottish club but with
distinctive Irish roots. Fortunately, this
'mix' has allowed the club to embrace a
form of sporting ecumenism as, from the
earliest days, the only criterion towards
acceptance as a Celtic player was the ability
to play football.

This section shows the diversity exhib-
ited in the recruitment of players and
managers; and with the recent influx of
non-Scottish players many reasonable sides
could be fielded from players with different
backgrounds

_____

BLACK CELTIC (4-4-2)

Warner,
Agathe, Balde, Elliott, Tebily/
Sylla, Sno, Blinker, Petta/
van Hooijdonk, Camara.
Manager: John Barnes

IRISH CELTIC (4-3-3)

Bonner,
Morris, McCarthy, Rogan, Fallon/
Keane, Lennon, Peacock/
Gallacher, Coyne, Tully.
Manager: Willie Maley

ENGLISH CELTIC (INCLUDING WALES) (4-4-2)

Latchford,
Welford, Lyon, Elliott, Naylor/
Bellamy, Sutton, Stubbs, Thompson/
Hartson, Payton.
Manager: Martin O'Neill (!)

EUROPEAN CELTIC (4-4-2)

Boruc,
Annoni, Riseth, Rieper, Mahe/
Wieghorst, Petrov, Graveson, Thom/
Zurawski, Larsson.
Manager: Josef Venglos

PROTESTANT CELTIC (4-3-3)

John Thomson,
Danny McGrain, Alec McNair, Willie
Lyon, Tommy Gemmell/
Bobby Evans, 'Sunny Jim' Young, Bertie
Peacock/
Bobby Collins, Henrik Larsson, Willie
Fernie.
Manager: Jock Stein

RED-HEADED CELTIC (4-4-2)

John Fallon,
Chris Shevlane, Bobby Evans, Jackie
McNamara Sr*, Frank Meechan/
Jimmy Johnstone, Tommy Burns,
Neil Lennon, Barry Robson/
Jimmy Walsh, John Hartson.
Manager: Gordon Strachan

SOUTHERN HEMISPHERE CELTIC (4-4-2)

Danny Milosevic [Australia]**/
Olivier Tebily [Ivory Coast], Bobo Balde
[Guinea], Rafael Scheidt [Brazil], Du Wei
[China]/
Didier Agathe [Reunion Island], Juninho
[Brazil], Shinsuke Nakamura [Japan]/
Momo Sylla [Ivory Coast], Mark Viduka
[Australia], Chris Killen [New Zealand].

'TRADES' CELTIC (4-4-2)

George Hunter/
Willie Cook, Lex Baillie, John Clark,
Joe Baillie/
Eric Smith, Willie Falconer, Tony
Shepherd/
Joe Miller, Stuart Slater, Willie Taylor.

* This player is included because of his
allegedly socialist views, which earned him
the nickname of 'Boris'.
** Milosevic came from Leeds early in Martin
O'Neill's tenure on a pay-per-play basis but
left claiming wages were too low.

INTERNATIONAL CELTICS (II)

Celtic have taken part in matches against
national sides:

23 February 1924
Irish Free State 0, Celtic 3. A record crowd
of 22,000 packed Dalymount Park in
Dublin to see the visitors win with some
ease thanks to goals from Joe Cassidy (2)
and Andy McAtee.

4 October 1933
Celtic 2, Chile-Peru Select 1. This unusual
match was played at Celtic Park before a
crowd of 10,000.

14 October 1967
Celtic Reserves 4, Great Britain Olympic XI 0. This match was played at Lesser Hampden, and shocked representatives of the Racing Club of Buenos Aires who attended.

13 July 1977
Singapore Select 0, Celtic 5. More than 45,000 spectators saw Alfie Conn (2), Tommy Burns, Bobby Lennox and Johannes Edvaldsson score the goals.

26 July 1977
Australia 2, Celtic 3. In the Sydney Sports Ground Johannes Edvaldsson (2) and Ronnie Glavin scored the goals that defeated the home side.

8 August 1979
Celtic 6 China 1. 18000 turned up to see the first Chinese team play in the UK. A Murdo MacLeod hat-trick, two from George McCluskey and one from Davie Provan gave Celtic a comfortable win though the biggest cheer of the night was for Xu Yonglai's 69th minute goal which made it 2-1.

INTERNATIONAL MATCHES

The financial acumen of the early directors or committee-men who ran the club was recognised in the choice of Celtic Park as the venue for Scotland matches.

In more recent times, with the renovation of Hampden Park (and its occasional use as a concert venue), Celtic Park is again being chosen to host Scotland international fixtures.

28 March 1891 vs. Ireland 2-1
25 March 1893 Ireland 6-1
7 April 1894 England 2-2
30 March 1895 Ireland 3-1
4 April 1896 England 2-1
2 April 1898 England 1-3
25 March 1899 Ireland 9-1
7 April 1900 England 4-1
23 February 1901 Ireland 11-0
21 March 1903 Ireland 0-2
9 April 1904 England 0-1
18 March 1905 Ireland 4-0
16 March 1907 Ireland 3-0
18 March 1911 Ireland 2-0
28 February 1913 Wales 0-0
13 March 1920 Ireland 3-0
4 March 1922 Ireland 2-1
1 March 1924 Ireland 2-0
22 February 1930 Ireland 3-1
16 September 1933 Ireland 1-2
2 April 1997 Austria 2-0
11 October 1997 Latvia 2-0
31 March 1999 Czechoslovakia 1-2
2 September 2006 Faroes 6-0

INTERNATIONAL OWN GOALS

Some Celts have been unlucky enough to score own-goals while playing for Scotland:

Tommy Gemmell: 10 May 1967 vs Russia;

Tom Boyd: 10 June 1998 vs Brazil;

David Marshall: 18 August 2004 vs Hungary.

Confusion in the Lazio penalty box following a Tully corner kick – John McPhail scored all four Celtic goals in the rout of the Italian side in this 1950 friendly. The backdrop is The Jungle. Previously referred to as The Hayshed, this huge covered enclosure was decribed as 'a large open-air barn whose corrugated-iron roof leaked badly on rainy days and on pleasant days dusted spectators below with flakes of rust'. Now replaced by the gigantic North Stand.

J/K/L

'JINKY'

This was the nickname bestowed upon Jimmy Johnstone, 'Celtic's Greatest-Ever Player', by his admirers. It was a recognition of his mastery of close-control dribbling which made him at times impossible to stop by fair means.

JUBILEES

Celtic celebrated the club's Golden Jubilee in 1937/38 by winning the League Championship and also the prestigious Empire Exhibition Trophy;

In the Centenary season 1987/88 Celtic accomplished the domestic double of Scottish League Championship and Scottish Cup.

THE JUNGLE

For many years Celtic Park was one of the few grounds in Scotland that possessed a large covered enclosure for standing-room patrons.

In its early years of its existence the structure was generally called 'The Hayshed' because of its appearance and strictly functional purpose. This covered enclosure replaced the burnt-out South Stand in 1929, and quickly became the habitat of the club's most enthusiastic and vocal supporters.

However, after World War II it was in a state of some decay overhead and underfoot and about this time the epithet 'The Jungle' began to be heard. The expression was probably coined by ex-servicemen returning from duty in the Far East mocking its primitive appearance – 'a large open-air barn whose corrugated-iron roof leaked badly on rainy days and on pleasant days dusted spectators below with flakes of rust'.

In 1966 it was replaced by a more modern structure, complete with concrete flooring – a contrast to 'the Jungle' which had still retained its earthen embankments edged with wooden steps. Other improvements took place over the years, but the location still deserved its fearsome reputation.

On 15 May 1993 – the last fixture of the 1993/94 season, a match won by 2-0 against Dundee – the Jungle made its last stand. By the next season's start 5,000 seats had been installed. In 1995 it was razed completely and replaced by the gigantic North Stand, the first step in the rebuilding and modernisation of Celtic Park.

KILMARNOCK

Kilmarnock and Celtic have had an interesting relationship over the years. For example, four former Celtic players have been appointed as managers of the Ayrshire club: Jimmy McGrory, Malcolm MacDonald, Willie Fernie and Tommy Burns.

Celtic have bought some outstanding players from Kilmarnock over the years most notably Davie Provan and Alistair Hunter.

It would be safe to say that players moving in the other direction (from Celtic to Kilmarnock) are star players who are reaching the end of their careers, or who were moved on by the club: Hugh Watson, Frank Welsh, Alex Wilson, Alec Rollo, Billy Stark, Bobby Templeton, Gordon Marshall, Matt Mair, James McPherson, Malcolm MacDonald, Dugald McCarrison, William Leitch, Robert Findlay and Tommy Burns.

Celtic have enjoyed an astonishing run of success against Kilmarnock in league matches at Celtic Park. Kilmarnock last won there on 10 December 1955.

LAW TROUBLE

John H. McLaughlin, Celtic's chairman and one of the leading lights in Scottish football, sued Frank Havelin, a Glasgow labourer, for damages for slander in 1896. Havelin, a Celtic shareholder, had objected to McLaughlin's comments about some committee men and McLaughlin apparently vindictively took him to court where the sheriff ruled in Havelin's favour.

Pat Gallagher was the cause of an unfortunate incident at Tynecastle on 27 August 1892 when in his second (and last) appearance for Celtic the outside right scored in the very first minute. Some Celtic officials (or committee men) seated on the balcony at the pavilion applauded the goal and were told to leave the premises; police were called in to evict them.

Jerry Reynolds was not the most astute of men but he was unfortunate on 11 February 1893 after a stormy match against Abercorn in Paisley. Crowd trouble – as well as violence on the field – had spoiled the occasion and one home fan who had invaded the pitch was punched by a Celtic player, most probably John Campbell. The spectator lost three teeth in the incident; he called the police into the matter and 'identified' Reynolds as the guilty party inside the dressing room.

John Campbell, one half of Celtic's famous left wing of McMahon and Campbell, was sued by his long-time companion Lizzie on 24 March 1898 in an early case of 'palimony'. The lady failed to prove her case of breach of promise on John's part but did win a financial settlement on the grounds of affiliation.

A bizarre series of events befell Willie

Cringan, Celtic's centre half in 1917/18. He had been on loan to Wishaw Thistle and Ayr United from Sunderland since 1915 and was working in the mines when he joined Celtic still on loan in 1917. At the time of his move he missed his regular shifts at the pit, and was arrested at least twice for 'desertion'. The matter was eventually cleared up, and Cringan later joined the Royal Field Artillery in 1918, afterwards returning to the pits.

John Browning played on Celtic's left wing between 1912 and 1919 two hundred and seventeen times and scored sixty-five goals, including two in the 1914 Scottish Cup final 4-1 win over Hibernian. In March 1924 he attempted to fix the outcome of a Lochgelly United vs Bo'ness United match – in collaboration with former Rangers player Archie Kyle. He was given a prison sentence (with hard labour) for his attempt.

Willie Orr played for ten seasons with Celtic making more than two hundred appearances, most of them at left half or left back and was the club's captain for the first two championships in the celebrated run of six successive titles between 1904 and 1910. Following his retirement as a player he was manager of Airdrie, Leicester City and Falkirk but his managerial career ended in disgrace with a *sine die* suspension in 1935. His offence was offering a bribe allegedly to an Ayr United player not to turn out for a vital match against Falkirk. The indefinite suspension was lifted in 1937.

James Foley made only six appearances in Celtic's goal between 1934 and 1936 but he will be remembered for an incident in a reserve match at Tynecastle on 28 November 1936. The Irishman was being jeered by the home support behind the goal, and kicked the ball angrily against the retaining wall. Several spectators invaded the pitch and one head-butted the Celtic keeper but it was the footballer who got arrested and charged with assault. The trial took place in Edinburgh in February 1937 and Foley was fined £2 (with the option of twenty days in jail).

Dick Beattie left Celtic in 1959 and went to England to join Portsmouth (and later Peterborough United) after five eventful years at Parkhead. In 1965 he pleaded guilty to two charges of taking a bribe in England and was jailed for nine months. His plea and subsequent conviction caused some in Scotland to re-evaluate his Celtic career and in particular an eccentric performance by the keeper in the Scottish Cup semi-final replay lost 3-1 to Kilmarnock in 1957.

Frank McAvennie was ordered off against Rangers at Ibrox on 17 October 1987 – along with Chris Woods and Terry Butcher of the home side. The police became involved and the three players were charged with 'conducting themselves in a disorderly manner and committing a breach of the peace'. They appeared in court in Govan along with Graham Roberts, also of Rangers. McAvennie was found Not Guilty, Woods and Butcher Guilty, and Roberts Not Proven.

Lou Macari raised an action against Celtic for £431,000 for 'damages against wrongful dismissal' in October 1994; Celtic's counterclaim was for £727,000 for the club's lack of success under their former manager. Macari lost and Celtic's claim was dismissed by Lady Cosgrove who described chairman Fergus McCann as 'devious'.

LEADING SCORERS
(SEASON-BY-SEASON)

Only league matches have been included in this season-by-season list of leading scorers for Celtic.

1890/91:	Peter Dowds (14)
1891/92:	Sandy McMahon (18)
1892/93:	John Campbell (12)
1893/94:	Sandy McMahon (16)
1894/95:	Johnny Madden (9)
1895/96:	Allan Martin (19)
1896/97:	Sandy McMahon (10)
1897/98:	George Allan (12)
1898/99:	Sandy McMahon (12)
1899/1900:	Pat Gilhooly (9).
1900/01:	John Campbell and Sandy McMahon (10)
1901/02:	John Campbell (8)
1902/03:	John Campbell (13)
1903/04:	Sam Gilligan (13)
1904/05:	Jimmy Quinn (19)
1905/06:	Jimmy Quinn (21)
1906/07:	Jimmy Quinn (29)
1907/08:	Jimmy Quinn (20)
1908/09:	Jimmy Quinn (23)
1909/10:	Jimmy Quinn (24)
1910/11:	Jimmy Quinn (14)
1911/12:	Jimmy Quinn and Jimmy McMenemy (8)
1912/13:	Jimmy Quinn (11)
1913/14:	Patsy Gallacher (21)
1914/15:	Jimmy McColl (25)
1915/16:	Jimmy McColl (34)
1916/17:	Jimmy McColl (24)
1917/18:	Patsy Gallacher (18)
1918/19:	Jimmy McColl (16)
1919/20:	Tommy McInally (30)
1920/21:	Tommy McInally (27)
1921/22:	Joe Cassidy ((18)
1922/23:	Joe Cassidy (22)

1923/24:	Joe Cassidy (25)
1924/25:	Jimmy McGrory (17)
1925/26:	Jimmy McGrory (35)
1926/27:	Jimmy McGrory (49)
1927/28:	Jimmy McGrory (47)
1928/29:	Jimmy McGrory (20)
1929/30:	Jimmy McGrory (32)
1930/31:	Jimmy McGrory (37)
1931/32:	Jimmy McGrory (28)
1932/33:	Jimmy McGrory (22)
1933/34:	Frank O'Donnell (22)
1934/35:	Jimmy McGrory (18)
1935/36:	Jimmy McGrory (50)
1936/37:	Jimmy McGrory (19)
1937/38:	John Crum (24)
1938/39:	John Divers (17).
1946/47:	Gerry McAloon (12)
1947/48:	Tommy McDonald (7)
1948/49:	Jackie Gallagher and Jock Weir (9)
1949/50:	John McPhail (13)
1950/51:	Bobby Collins (15)
1951/52:	Bobby Collins (12)
1952/53:	Bertie Peacock (8)
1953/54:	Neil Mochan (20)
1954/55:	Jimmy Walsh (19)
1955/56:	Neil Mochan (17)
1956/57:	Neil Mochan (11)
1957/58:	Sammy Wilson (23)
1958/59:	John Colrain (14)
1959/60:	Stevie Chalmers (14)
1960/61:	Stevie Chalmers (19)
1961/62:	John Divers (19)
1962/63:	Bobby Craig (13)
1963/64:	Stevie Chalmers (28)
1964/65:	John Hughes (22)
1965/66:	Joe McBride (31)
1966/67:	Stevie Chalmers (23)
1967/68:	Bobby Lennox (32)
1968/69:	Willie Wallace (18)
1969/70:	Willie Wallace (16)

1970/71:	Harry Hood (22)
1971/72:	Dixie Deans (19)
1972/73:	Kenny Dalglish (23)
1973/74:	Dixie Deans (24)
1974/75:	Kenny Dalglish (16)
1975/76:	Kenny Dalglish (24)
1976/77:	Ronnie Glavin (19)
1977/78:	Joannes Edvaldsson (10)
1978/79:	Andy Lynch and Tom McAdam (7)
1979/80:	George McCluskey (10)
1980/81:	Frank McGarvey (23)
1981/82:	George McCluskey (21)
1982/83:	Charlie Nicholas (29)
1983/84:	Brian McClair (23)
1984/85:	Brian McClair (19)
1985/86:	Brian McClair (22)
1986/87:	Brian McClair (35)
1987/88:	Andy Walker (26)
1988/89:	Mark McGhee (16)
1989/90:	Dariusz Dziekanowski (8)
1990/91:	Tommy Coyne (18)
1991/92:	Charlie Nicholas (21)
1992/93:	Andy Payton (13)
1993/94:	Pat McGinlay (10)
1994/95:	John Collins (8)
1995/96:	Pierre van Hooijdonk (26)
1996/97:	Jorge Cadete (25)
1997/98:	Henrik Larsson (16)
1998/99:	Henrik Larsson (29)
1999/2000:	Mark Viduka (25)
2000/01:	Henrik Larsson (35)
2001/2002:	Henrik Larsson (29)
2002/03:	Henrik Larsson (28)
2003/04:	Henrik Larsson (30)
2004/05:	John Hartson (25)
2005/06:	John Hartson (18)
2006/07:	Jan Vennegoor of Hesselink (13)
2007/08	Scott McDonald (25)

© snspix.com

Leading scorers Mark Viduka (1999/2000) and Scott McDonald (2007/08)

© snspix.com

LEAGUE FOOTBALL

The Scottish Football League came into existence in 1890, largely at the instigation of Celtic's John H. McLaughlin who recognised that football in Scotland required a structure and a regular schedule for the clubs. Up until then the only competition was the Scottish Cup and other less important competitions. A club, knocked out of the Scottish Cup (which started in September), had to rely on friendly matches to raise moneys to pay their nominally amateur players.

Celtic were one of the eleven clubs who formed that first league. Of those clubs only Celtic, Dumbarton, Hearts, Rangers and St. Mirren still survive – and only Celtic and Rangers have played every league match in the top flight of Scottish football.

Ironically, Celtic lost their very first league fixture (by 1-4 against Renton at Celtic Park). However, shortly afterwards Renton were disqualified from the competition for playing against a club suspended by the SFA and their playing records in the league were wiped out. Accordingly, Celtic's first official league match was a 5-0 victory over Hearts in Edinburgh on 23 August 1890.

Celtic have been champions on 42 occasions, and have seldom finished out of the top three places. The club holds the record of nine consecutive league titles in a row with Jock Stein as manager between 1965 and 1974 – an accomplishment later equalled by Rangers in the 1990s. The previous record of six consecutive championships was held by Celtic with Willie Maley as manager between 1904 and 1910.

Celtic historians are often eager to compare the merits of both Celtic league runs and the bare statistics point to a preeminence in Scottish football

1904 to 1910

P	W	D	L	For	Agst	Pts
192	136	33	23	444	153	305

1965 to 1974

P	W	D	L	For	Agst	Pts
306	235	45	26	868	258	515

The earlier side gained 79.43% of the available points; the later team 84.15%.

Biggest victories:
On 26 October 1895 Celtic defeated Dundee 11-0. This remains Celtic's largest victory in any competition, and it also stands as the largest win by any club over another in the top flight of Scottish League football. On that occasion Celtic's line-up was McArthur, Meechan, Doyle, Maley (W), Kelly, Battles, Blessington, Madden, Martin, McMahon, Ferguson. No accurate record exists of the actual goalscorers, but it is believed Celtic had another two goals disallowed – and that Dundee finished the match shorthanded, either through injury or ordering-off.

The biggest away win was a 9-1

> 'A bonus for beating East Fife! You must be joking!'
> Willie Maley, when a Celtic player asked about the benefits of winning the 1927 Scottish Cup final.

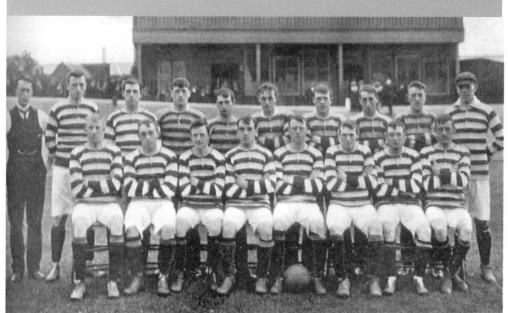

The players who carved out Celtic's first great era – they won the league championship six times in a row (1903-10). Goalkeeper Davie Adams was distinguished from outfield players only by his cap. (Back l to r) R Davis (trainer), Campbell, McLeod, Watson, Hamilton, McNair (A), Wilson, Garry, McCourt, Adams (Front) Young, Hay, Bennett, McMenemy, Loney, Quinn, Somers, McNair (W)

thrashing of Clyde at Barrowfield on Christmas Day 1897. The goals that day were scored by Allan (5), Russell (2), Campbell, and McMahon. Surprisingly, Celtic played the second half without an injured player, and George Allan scored four of his five goals after the interval.

Biggest Defeats:

On 14 September 1895 Celtic lost by 0-5 to Hearts, and this still remains the club's largest home defeat in league play.

On 30 Aprl 1937, only a few days after Celtic had won the Scottish Cup, Celtic travelled to Fir Park to complete the league schedule and they lost by 0-8 to Motherwell. This result remains the club's record defeat in all competitions.

League Deciders:

In 1904/05 Celtic and Rangers met in a play-off after the sides had finished level in points. The decider was played at Hampden Park on 6 May 1905, and was refereed by a referee imported from England for the occasion – a Mr. Kirkham

(Preston). Earlier in the season the Scottish Cup tie at Celtic Park had had to be abandoned because of crowd trouble caused by the ordering off of Celtic's Jimmy Quinn. Celtic won the play-off by 2-1 before a crowd estimated at just over 30,000. and the goals were scored by Hamilton and McMenemy. Celtic's side was Adams, Watson, Orr, McNair, Loney, Hay, Bennett, McMenemy, Quinn, Somers, Hamilton.

The Scottish League devised a system, aimed at avoiding the necessity of a play-off game to decide the championship and this was Goal Average. The method was to divide the Goals For by the Goals Against. Celtic still hold the record for the best goal-average in league history, a record established in 1913/14. They scored 81 goals and gave up only 14 in the 38 match schedule. The goal-average was 5.79 but it was scarcely needed as Celtic won the title by 6 points over Rangers.

In the 1970s the method was changed to Goal Difference. This is determined by subtracting the Goals Against from the Goals For. In the 1985/86 season Celtic won the championship over Hearts thanks to a superior Goal Difference (+29 as opposed to +26.) In the 2002/03 SPL season Rangers and Celtic entered the last weekend tied in points and close in goal difference. Rangers defeated Dunfermline Athletic at Ibrox by 6-1 and Celtic defeated Kilmarnock at Rugby Park by 4-0 to give Rangers the title by Goal Difference.

Obviously, Celtic have been frequent winners of the league championship but their lowest position came in 1947/48 when they finished in twelfth place (out of sixteen). In terms of the gap between games won (10) and games lost (15) this also represents Celtic's worst league performance.

LIMITED LIABILITY COMPANY

Celtic, founded with charity as its guiding principle in 1887, enjoyed tremendous early success as a football club and several members saw the opportunities that a change to a Limited Liability Company would provide as a source for charitable donations and also as a profitable investment. The schism between many of the original members was widening year by year, and the political in-fighting was bitterly contested. Eventually after ten years as a charitable trust, run by largely volunteer committees, the club became a Limited Liability Company in 1897.

The first meeting of the new company, held on 17 June 1897, produced the following Board of Directors: M. Dunbar, J. Glass, J. Grant, J. Kelly, J. McKillop, J.H. McLaughlin, J. O'Hara. Celtic was now a business and donations to charity, while never completely drying up, were secondary to financial gain.

Over the years the directorate became concentrated more and more on particular families, namely Kelly, White, and Grant.

With the enormous financial changes in the administration of football clubs coming in the 1980s, these families found themselves in a dilemma: unable to afford the running of a modern football club but unwilling to hand the club over to outsiders.

The end for Celtic as a Limited Liability Company came on 4 March 1994 when Fergus McCann took over.

LISBON LIONS

Almost every Celtic supporter can recite the team that won the European Cup by beating Inter Milan at the Estadio Nacional in Lisbon on 25 May 1967:

Simpson, Craig, Gemmell,
Murdoch, McNeill, Clark,
Johnstone, Wallace, Chalmers, Auld,
Lennox.

John Fallon as the back-up goalkeeper was the only possible substitute permitted; however, he was not used during the European campaign.

The very first appearance of that famous side was at Muirton Park against St. Johnstone on 14 January 1967, and Celtic won 4-0. The same line-up was fielded against Aberdeen on 19 April in a 0-0 draw at Celtic Park and Jock Stein persisted with it in the historic climax of the season which saw Celtic pick up the Scottish Cup, the League Championship and, of course, the European Cup.

The last time the same line-up was chosen was against Dynamo Kiev in the European Cup on 20 September 1967, but the result was a surprising 1-2 home defeat.

Contrary to a popular myth, the Lisbon Lions did not function as a unit against Clyde in the final league fixture of 1970/71. Ronnie Simpson, who had already retired after a shoulder injury, appeared only for the warm-up, his place being taken in the match by Evan Williams.

LOAN DEALS

Big clubs like Celtic can loan out players surplus to requirements at any given time to other clubs. Sometimes it is to get an expensive player off the pay-roll for a period, or to prepare a younger player for eventual permanent transfer; sometimes, however, it can be to give a younger player experience of regular first-team appearances.

In recent seasons frequently Celtic have loaned out players for the latter reason, and usually to the mutual benefit of players and clubs. At the 2006 January transfer window, for example, the following were placed on loan: Diarmuid O'Carroll (Ross County), James O'Brien (Dunfermline), Rocco Quinn (Kilmarnock), David Marshall (Norwich) and Paul Lawson (St. Mirren) while Gary Irvine returned from his loan spell at Ross County.

It is scarcely a new phenomenon as Celtic have often loaned out such players who developed into stars on their return to Celtic Park. A particularly busy period was in the 1920s when the club did not run a reserve side. Ayr United, who picked up Alec Thomson, John Thomson, and Peter Wilson in this manner, probably benefitted the most; previously they had had the services of Willie McStay between 1912 and 1916.

Other notable loan/transfers include Tom Maley (to St. Mirren in 1891), Barney Battles (on loan to Liverpool in 1895/96), Jimmy McMenemy (with East Stirling and Stenhousemuir in 1902/03), Joe Dodds (on loan to to Queen of South as player-manager in 1923), Jimmy McGrory (with Clydebank in 1924/25).

More recently Bertie Auld was loaned to Dumbarton for season 1955/56, and the troubled George Connelly to Falkirk in

1976; unsettled Jim Melrose went to Wolverhampton Wanderers in 1984, unlucky goalkeeper Ian Andrews went to Leeds United and later Southampton on loan after an unfortunate eight appearances for Celtic in 1988 while Lex Baillie went to Toronto Blizzard on loan in 1989/90; Gerry Britton tried his luck with Reading and Partick Thistle in 1991/92, as did Andy Walker with Newcastle United and Bolton in the same season.

The years of World War II (1939–1945) were particularly awkward for all clubs as soldier/footballers were moved round the country to military bases at relatively short notice. Celtic were among the few clubs who did not utilise the availability of such 'guest players' but several of their players were used by clubs throughout Scotland and England. Among them were Willie Corbett, Willie Buchan, John Divers, Hugh Dornan, Davie Duncan, Jackie Gallagher, Willie Lyon, Gerry McAloon, George Paterson and Johnny Paton.

Later, compulsory National Service affected such as Alec Boden who went on loan to Dumbarton 1945/46, and also to Forres Mechanics and Cowdenbeath.

Martin O'Neill in recent seasons utilised the system to obtain the services of such unsettled players as Craig Bellamy, Michael Gray and Henri Camara. The latter was a most interesting case as his transfer involved a payment of £1.5m in addition to meeting his wage demands; in the event of Celtic being willing to extend the loan period (and making the transfer permanent) a further cash sum, estimated at £5m, would be expected by his English club. However, Camara was plagued with injury problems, did not show his real form, and returned to England without sealing the transfer.

LOCAL HEROES

For many years Glasgow could boast of six teams in the top flight of Scottish football but 1958/59 marked the last such occasion for Celtic, Clyde, Partick Thistle, Queen's Park, Rangers and Third Lanark. Queen's Park were relegated at the end of that season, Third Lanark disappeared in 1967 and Clyde have since moved to Cumbernauld.

It has been claimed that the Celtic side that faced Inter Milan in the European Cup final of 1967 was a home-born and based side. Judge for yourself.

Ronnie Simpson: born in Glasgow, 1930
Jim Craig: born in Glasgow, 1943
Tommy Gemmell: born in Craigneuk, 1943
Bobby Murdoch: born in Bothwell, 1944
Billy McNeill: born in Bellshill, 1940
John Clark: born in Bellshill, 1941
Jimmy Johnstone: born in Viewpark, 1944
Willie Wallace: born in Kirkintilloch, 1940
Steve Chalmers: born in Glasgow, 1936
Bertie Auld: born in Maryhill, 1938
Bobby Lennox: born in Saltcoats, 1943.
John Fallon: born in Blantyre, 1940.
Jock Stein: born in Earnock, 1922.

M

MANAGERS (I)

Willie Maley was appointed secretary-manager in 1897 shortly after the formation of Celtic as a Limited Liability Company. He could be considered the first manager as most aspects of running the club had been left previously to various committees. In view of modern developments in football it is extremely unlikely that his tenure of almost forty-three years in charge will ever be challenged.

Willie Maley, (pictured below left) with the 1933 Celtic team, was boss of Celtic for a remarkable 43 years.
Back row: A. Thomson, Hogg, Kennaway, Napier, McGrory, McGonigle;
Front row: Crum, Geatons, J. McStay, Wilson, R. Thomson

Jozef Venglos

Wim Jansen

Willie Maley: 1897 to 1940
Jimmy McStay: 1940 to 1945
Jimmy McGrory: 1945 to 1965
Jock Stein: 1965 to 1978
Sean Fallon: 1975 to 1976 (acting
    as manager during Stein's recovery
    from car crash)
Billy McNeill: 1978 to 1983
David Hay: 1983 to 1987
Billy McNeill: 1987 to 1991
Liam Brady: 1991 to 1993
Lou Macari: 1993 to 1994
Tommy Burns: 1994 to 1997
Wim Jansen: 1997 to 1998
Jozef Venglos: 1998 to 1999
John Barnes: 1999 to 2000
Kenny Dalglish: 2000 (acted as
    manager after John Barnes' sacking
    in February)
Martin O'Neill: 2000 to 2004
Gordon Strachan: 2004 to present.

Billy McNeill

Liam Brady

Lou Macari

Most football men would consider that throughout their history so far Celtic have had three great managers, men who towered over their contemporaries: Willie Maley, Jock Stein and Martin O'Neill. Yet with the winning of the 2007/08 Championship Gordon Strachan joined Maley and Stein as the only managers to have led Celtic to three succesive titles.

Consider their accomplishments. In forty-two seasons Willie Maley's sides won fourteen Scottish Cups and fourteen league championships. It has been estimated that

Tommy Burns

Maley was in charge of Celtic as manager for 1,838 games.

Jock Stein: in twelve full seasons Celtic won eight Scottish Cups, and ten league championships as well as six League Cups and the European Cup.

Martin O'Neill: in his five seasons Celtic won three Scottish Cups, three league championships and two League Cups as well as reaching the UEFA Cup final in Seville.

Statistically Kenny Dalglish's short reign might be considered the best as he won the League Cup (beating Aberdeen in the final 2-0 at Hampden Park) during his four months in charge of Celtic.

MANAGERS (II)

A spell as a Celtic player – and thus experience with a great football club – can be described as a valuable contribution to a potential manager's CV as this list of ex-Celts indicates:

England:
John Bell: (Preston North End)
James Blessington: (Leicester Fosse)
Tommy Burns: (Reading)
Bobby Collins (Barnsley, Huddersfield Town, Hull City)
Willie Cook (Crewe Alexandria, Wigan Athletic)
Pat Crerand (Northampton Town)
Kenny Dalglish (Blackburn Rovers, Liverpool, Newcastle United)
Tommy Docherty (Aston Villa, Chelsea, Derby County, Manchester United, Preston North End, Queen's Park Rangers, Rotherham United, Wolverhampton Wanderers)

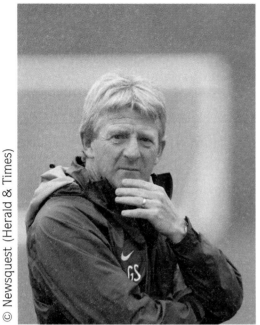

© Newsquest (Herald & Times)

Gordon Strachan

Martin O'Neill

© snspix.com

'If the manager is planning to buy new players, then he'll have to get the money out of his own pocket.'
Jack McGinn, to a reporter after hearing that David Hay was contemplating a move into the transfer market.

'Dally' Duncan (Blackburn Rovers,
Ipswich Town, Luton Town,
Manchester United)
John Gorman (Northampton Town,
Swindon Town, Wycombe Wanderers)
Peter Grant (Norwich)
Paul Lambert (Wycombe Wanderers)
Dugald Livingstone (Chesterfield,
Fulham, Newcastle United, Sheffield
Wednesday)
Lou Macari (Birmingham City,
Huddersfield Town, Stoke City,
Swindon Town, West Ham United)
Tom Maley (Bradford Park Avenue,
Manchester City)
Malcolm MacDonald (Brentford)
Mick McCarthy (Millwall, Sunderland,
Wolverhampton Wanderers)
James McGhee (Hearts)
Mark McGhee (Brighton & Hove Albion,
Leicester City, Millwall, Reading,
Wolverhampton Wanderers)
Billy McNeill (Aston Villa, Manchester
City)
Tony Mowbray (West Bromwich Albion)
David Moyes (Everton, Preston North
End)
Bobby Murdoch (Middlesbrough);
Willie Orr (Leicester City)
Peter O'Rourke (Bradford City, Bradford
Park Avenue, Walsall)
George Paterson (Yeovil Town)
Johnny Paton (Watford)
David Pratt (Clapton Orient, Notts
County, Port Vale)
Andy Ritchie (Barnsley, Oldham)
Jimmy Sirrell (Brentford, Notts County,
Sheffield United)
Jock Stein (Leeds United)
David Taylor (Carlisle United)

Scotland:
Roy Aitken (Aberdeen)
Bertie Auld (Dumbarton, Hamilton
Academical, Hibernian, Partick
Thistle)
Alec Bennett (Clydebank, Third Lanark)
Jim Bone (Airdrie, Arbroath, East Fife,
St. Mirren)
Gerry Britton (Partick Thistle, Stranraer)
Jim Brogan (Stirling Albion)
Tommy Burns (Kilmarnock)
John Clark (Cowdenbeath)
John Collins (Hibernian)
Frank Connor (Berwick Rangers,
Cowdenbeath, Raith Rovers)
Joe Craig (Cowdenbeath)
'Tully' Craig (Falkirk)
'Dally' Duncan (Cowdenbeath, Hamilton
Academical)
Bobby Evans (Third Lanark)
Sean Fallon (Dumbarton)
Willie Fernie (Kilmarnock)
Willie Garner (Alloa Athletic)
Tommy Gemmell (Albion Rovers,
Dundee)
Davie Hay (Dunfermline Athletic,
Livingston, Motherwell, St. Mirren)
James Hay (Ayr United, Clydebank)
Bobby Hogg (Alloa Athletic)
Harry Hood (Albion Rovers, Queen of
South)
John Hughes (Stranraer)
Mike Jackson (Queen of South)
Paul Lambert (Livingston)
George Livingstone (Clydebank,
Dumbarton)
Murdo MacLeod (Partick Thistle)
Frank McGarvey (Queen of South)
Danny McGrain (Arbroath)
Jimmy McGrory (Kilmarnock)
Jim McInally (Morton, East Stirling)
Alec McNair (Dundee)

John McNamee (Workington Town)
Billy McNeill (Aberdeen, Clyde)
Jimmy McStay (Alloa Athletic, Hamilton
    Academical)
Joe Miller (Clyde)
Tony Mowbray (Hibernian)
Steve Murray (Forfar Athletic, Montrose)
Willie Orr (Airdrie, Falkirk)
Peter O'Rourke (Dundee Hibernian)
George Paterson (Stirling Albion)
David Pratt (Hearts)
Davie Provan (Albion Rovers)
Andy Ritchie (Albion Rovers)
James Rowan (Clyde, East Stirling)
Ronnie Simpson (Hamilton Academical)
Eric Smith (Hamilton Academical,
    Morton)
Pat Stanton (Cowdenbeath, Dunfermline
    Athletic, Hibernian)
Billy Stark (Morton, Queen's Park, St.
    Johnstone)
Jock Stein (Dunfermline Athletic,
    Hibernian)
Dom Sullivan (Alloa Athletic, East
    Stirlingshire);
David Taylor (Dunfermline Athletic, St.
    Johnstone)
Willie Toner (Dumbarton)
Paddy Travers (Aberdeen, Clyde,
    Dumbarton)
Derek Whyte (Partick Thistle)
Peter Wilson (Dunfermline Athletic)
Sammy Wilson (Brora Rangers)

We might also include Roy Baines (Tranent
Juniors), John Brown (Lochgelly United),
John Hughes (SJFA), Alan Rough
(Glenafton Athletic), Evan Williams (Vale
of Leven).

ASSISTANT MANAGERS

1965 to 1976 Sean Fallon was assistant to
Jock Stein during this period. In 1975/76
he took charge while Stein was recovering
from the injuries sustained in a car crash;

1976 to 1978 Dave McParland was Jock
Stein's assistant;

1978 to 1983 John Clark was Billy
McNeill's assistant in this, McNeill's first
term in charge of Celtic;

1983 to 1986 Frank Connor assisted David
Hay and, after returning to the backroom
staff, acted as assistant manager and then
as caretaker manager in the wake of Liam
Brady's departure;

1987 to 1993 Tommy Craig was engaged
as first-team coach under David Hay, and
the position evolved into an assistant
managership role and in that capacity he
helped David Hay, Billy McNeill and Liam
Brady;

1993 Joe Jordan was appointed assistant
manager to Liam Brady in June 1993 but
he resigned the day after Brady's leaving
later in the same year;

1993 to 1994 Chic Bates was appointed as
assistant to Lou Macari during the latter's
short tenure as Celtic's manager;

1994 to 1997 Billy Stark assisted Tommy
Burns during his tenure as manager, and
took charge of the team for a few weeks in
1996/97 after Burns' departure;

1997 to 1998 Murdo MacLeod assisted
Wim Jansen during the Dutchman's one
season in charge;

2000 Tommy Burns returned as assistant
to Kenny Dalglish between February and

May after Dalglish assumed control after John Barnes' abrupt departure'.

2000 John Robertson, who had played alongside Martin O'Neill at Nottingham Forest, was appointed assistant manager shortly after O'Neill's arrival at Celtic Park.

MANCHESTER UNITED

The two clubs – the first Scottish and English clubs to win the European Cup – have had a long (and mainly friendly) relationship down the years as indicated by the number of Testimonial Matches between the sides played at either Celtic Park (CP) or Old Trafford (OT):

1972: Bobby Charlton OT
1976: Bobby Lennox/Jimmy Johnstone CP
1980: Danny McGrain CP
1984: Lou Macari OT
1987: Roy Aitken CP; Brian McClair OT
1990: Bryan Robson OT
1994: Mark Hughes OT
1995: Paul McStay CP
2001: Tom Boyd CP, Ryan Giggs OT
2006: Roy Keane OT

Several players have been stalwarts for both clubs: Tommy Bogan, Joe Cassidy, James Connachan, Pat Crerand, Jimmy Delaney, Scott Duncan, Billy Grassam, Roy Keane, Henrik Larsson, George Livingstone, Lou Macari, Brian McClair, Charles McGillivray, Lee Martin, Liam Miller, Tommy Morrison and perhaps surprisingly Bobby Charlton (who played for Celtic in another testimonial against Liverpool at Anfield).

On the managerial or coaching side the following might be cited: Tommy Docherty, Ashley Grimes, Joe Jordan, Lou Macari, Mick Martin.

MARIST BROTHERS

The Catholic teaching order, the Marist Brothers, was a key player in the founding of Celtic. Brother Walfrid, born as Andrew Kerins in Ballymote, County Sligo in 1840, taught in Glasgow's East End and was horrified at the social conditions that he saw among the mainly Irish parishioners. Brother Dorotheus was Walfrid's assistant and colleague, and a driving force behind the Poor Children's Dinner Table – a scheme to feed the hungry and destitute in the East End and especially among the young.

After becoming Headmaster of Sacred Heart School Walfrid was more than ever determined to raise money to alleviate that poverty. He saw that the newish craze for football could be utilised and was able to arrange exhibition games to raise funds. His efforts culminated in the founding of the Celtic Football Club following a public meeting held in St. Mary's Hall, Abercromby Street on 6 November 1887. He was transferred by the Order to London in 1892, and lived in Folkestone in his later years. He is buried in St. Joseph's College, Dumfries.

For a number of years – and especially until the club became a limited liability company in 1897 – Celtic made handsome contributions to local charities.

A statue of Brother Walfrid, erected just outside the main entrance at Celtic Park, was unveiled on 5 November 2005 to honour his memory and his contribution to the founding of Celtic.

MASCOTS

A mascot, defined as a person or thing designed to bring good luck, is usually personified nowadays by a youngster leading a team on to the field of play.

In addition, most clubs take out further insurance against fate by employing a grown-up in fancy dress to entertain the spectators before the kick-off; Celtic's current one is Hoopy, the Huddle Hound. Prior to Hoopy in the 1990s was Vinnie the Parrot who, resplendent in his brightly coloured plumage, would walk along the track adjacent to The Jungle and distribute sweets to the denizens.

Even before Vinnie, Celtic had another mascot: answered to Brian, had four legs, a constantly wagging tail . . . but he never appeared on match days! Brian was an Irish Wolfhound and he was presented to the club in January 1966 by Aer Lingus, Celtic's preferred airline for European matches. A retiring type, he stayed 'at the home of a Celtic official', generally believed to be Sean Fallon, the club's assistant manager.

One mascot however brought luck of a different sort. For the Scottish Cup semi-final at Ibrox in 1948 Celtic's goalkeeper Willie Miller was given a sparkling model of the Scottish Cup. He placed it inside his right hand post – only for Morton's inside forward (Murphy) to aim at it and strike it with a fierce shot for the only goal of the game in extra time.

MATCH REPORT NO. I

The *Glasgow Observer* (2 June 1888) carried this account of Celtic's very first appearance in Scottish football:

The Rangers kicked off against the wind, and at once made an incursion into Celtic territory. With some difficulty Dolan and the backs cleared their charge, and play was transferred to the other end. A mistake by Meikle gave the Celts a corner kick. Dunbar placed the ball in front of goal, and McCallum was enabled to head the first point of the game. The Rangers, from a pass by Sutter, equalised after ten minutes' play. Nicol was saving in grand style, and but for his clever goalkeeping the Celts must have increased their score on several occasions. A foul against the 'Light Blues' further enhanced the prospects of the home team. The ball was kept in dangerous proximity to Nicol's charge, and to avert what proved to be only a temporary and insufficient relief the Rangers were forced to concede a corner kick. Like the former, and placed by the same player, Kelly, who was playing a judicious game, headed the second goal for the home team a few minutes before half-time. The Rangers opened the second half with great vigour. The home defence, however, was not to be overcome. By short passing and keeping the ball low the Celts carried it to the other end, where Tom Maley was enabled to score another goal. In retaliation the Ibrox forwards were soon in front of their adversaries' upright, and a second goal was registered by Suter. Ultimately, Maley put on a fourth goal for the ground team. Through the instrumentality of McCallum the same player shortly after notched a fifth point. A sixth point was put through, but was disallowed owing to an infringement of the off-side rule. The whistle sounded with the ball hovering in front of Dolan.

CELTIC: Dolan (Drumpellier), Pearson (Cathkin Shamrock), McLaughlin (Govan Whitefield), W. Maley (Cathcart), Kelly (Renton), Murray (Cambuslang Hibs), McCallum (Renton), T. Maley (Cathcart), Madden (Dumbarton), Dunbar (Edinburgh Hibs), Gorevin (Govan Whitefield)

RANGERS: Nicol, McIntyre, Muir, McPherson, McFarlane, Meikle, Robb, McLaren, McKenzie, Suter, Wilson

REFEREE: Mr. McFadden (Edinburgh Hibs)

Some confusion remains about Celtic's scorers: from the report it is clear that 'Maley' scored three goals, but two Celtic players – Willie and Tom – were brothers. It is possible that Tom scored a hat-trick in Celtic's first game, and against Rangers!

MEDALS

Not surprisingly two members of Jock Stein's Lisbon Lions' squad vie for the honour of winning the most medals: Bobby Lennox and Billy McNeill.

Bobby Lennox picked up twenty-four winners' medals in major competitions; his haul included a European Cup medal, ten Scottish Championships, eight Scottish Cups and five League Cups.

Billy McNeill amassed twenty-three: a European Cup medal, nine Scottish Championships, seven Scottish Cups and six League Cups.

However, Bobby Lennox gained two of his medals while on the bench as a substitute in the 1972 and 1974 Scottish Cup finals.

Some former Celtic players have been members of Scottish and English F.A. Cup-winning sides:

Alec Brady: 1892 and 1896 (Sheffield Wednesday)

John Campbell: 1892, 1899, 1900 and 1897 (Aston Villa)

Jack Reynolds: 1892 and 1893 (West Bromwich Albion) and 1895, 1897 (Aston Villa)

Jim Welford: 1899 and 1895 (Aston Villa)

Willie Cook: 1931 and 1933 (Everton)

Hugh O'Donnell: 1933, and 1938 (Preston North End)

Jimmy Delaney: 1937 and 1948 (Manchester United)

Ronnie Simpson: 1967 and 1952, 1955 (Newcastle United)

Lou Macari: 1971, 1972 and 1977 (Manchester United)

Kenny Dalglish: 1972, 1974, 1975, 1977 and 1986 (Liverpool)

Brian McClair: 1985 and 1990 (Manchester United)

EUROPEAN CUP MEDALS

Most Celtic supporters can name the winning Lisbon Lions side but other Celtic players have gained winning European Cup medals:

John Fallon, as Ronnie Simpson's deputy throughout the 1966/67 run, was the only substitute allowed and he was granted a medal along with the other Lions

Pat Crerand won with Manchester United in 1968,

Kenny Dalglish won three times with Liverpool in 1978, 1981 and 1984,

Paul Lambert gained his with Borussia Dortmund when he was given the specific task of man-marking Zinedine Zidane,

Roy Keane, although he missed the actual final through suspension, gained a medal with Manchester United in 1999.

Henrik Larsson came off the bench for Barcelona and contributed to the two late goals that defeated Arsenal in the 2006 final.

MIDDLESBROUGH

Over the years Celtic and the North-Eastern English club have exchanged several players such as Tony Mowbray, Bobby Murdoch, Willie Fernie, Neil Mochan, Rolando Ugolini, 'Jean' McFarlane, Donnie McLeod, Jimmy Weir, Bob McFarlane, Joe Cassidy.

The legendary English international inside-forward Wilf Mannion was a particular target for Celtic in the late 1940s but Middlesbrough, despite several offers from Celtic, refused to part with their star.

MOTHERWELL

Celtic have done well in picking up goal-scoring forwards from Motherwell. Any list would include the following excellent buys: Joe McBride, Dixie Deans, Brian McClair, Andy Walker, and Scott McDonald. In return some Celtic strikers have moved on to Fir Park such as Tommy Coyne, Vic Davidson, Tom McAdam and Paul Wilson.

Fir Park has also been the scene of two major Celtic setbacks: in 1938 Motherwell inflicted upon the visitors their biggest-ever defeat, an 8-0 rout, and more recently (in 2005) Scott McDonald scored twice in the closing minutes to give Motherwell a 2-1 victory and deny Celtic the Scottish Premier League title.

MULTI-NATIONALS

Players move around from club to club, and some have interesting travellers' tales to relate:

Jimmy Delaney performed for Celtic, Manchester United, Aberdeen, Falkirk, Derry City, Cork Athletic and Elgin City. He won winners' cup medals with Celtic (1937), Manchester United (1948), Derry City of Northern Ireland (1954) – and came very close with Cork Athletic of Eire, when they lost by 3-2 in the 1956 final;

George Hazlett too was a well-travelled player turning out for Celtic (Scotland), Cardiff City (Wales), Millwall (England), and Belfast Celtic (Northern Ireland).

Rolando Ugolini was born in Italy and turned out for teams based in Scotland, England and Wales: Celtic, Dundee United, Middlesbrough, and Wrexham.

Raymond McStay – who never quite made it into Celtic's first eleven – played for three clubs in different countries in 1997: Hereford (England), Cardiff City (Wales) and East Stirling (Scotland).

Henrik Larsson could put four European Cup winners in his CV: Feyenoord, Celtic, Barcelona, and Manchester United.

In October 1961, Pye Records released *The Celtic Song*, written and sung by Glen Daly, and to the astonishment of the record company the disc became immediately popular and eventually reached worldwide sales of more than one million.

The song has retained its popularity with the Celtic support and even today, almost fifty years after its release, it remains a favourite anthem for Celtic supporters. Apparently, on the long walk on to the National Stadium in Lisbon for the European Cup final against Inter Milan, Bertie Auld started to sing this song and it was taken up by his team-mates – to the bewilderment of the Italian players.

When Celtic returned to Parkhead after winning the European Cup in Lisbon, the band which accompanied them round the track was The Coatbridge Accordion Band (founded in 1958) – and they later produced an LP (*Celtic Boys Hurrah!*) as a tribute to Celtic.

Thanks primarily to TV exposure on the great European nights, the anthem most readily identified with Celtic is *You'll Never Walk Alone* (from the musical *Carousel* by Rodgers and Hart. It was originally the anthem adopted by Liverpool supporters and it is believed that the close friendship between the clubs' managers, Jock Stein and Bill Shankly, led to Celtic adopting it also in the late 1960s. Several renditions at Celtic Park come to mind as one of the most moving sounds and spectacles in world football: in the wake of the Hillsborough Disaster, Celtic and Liverpool (playing their first match after the abandoned FA Cup semi final) participated in a testimonial match at Parkhead for the benefit of those killed and injured. More than 60,000 attended an emotional day, marked by a minute's silence and the singing of the classic by both sets of supporters.

In the UEFA Cup match between the same clubs in 2003 Gerry Marsden of Gerry and the Pacemakers' fame, led the combined singing at Celtic Park in another inspirational rendition before the kick-off.

Against Barcelona in the Champions' League match in 2004, on the day of the Madrid bombing, after the minute's silence the Celtic supporters were asked 'to sing in solidarity with the victims of Madrid.' They did so magnificently, the gesture being vastly appreciated by Barcelona's following; the coach, a clearly moved Frank Rijkaard, was seen applauding the home fans.

Some musicians are also on record as being keen followers of Celtic, including Jim Kerr (Simple Minds), Liam Gallagher (Oasis), Sharleen Spiteri (Texas), Bono (U2), Claire Grogan (Altered Images), Shane McGowan (The Pogues), and, of course, Rod Stewart.

Jimmy Johnstone died in March 2006 after a long and courageous battle against Motor Neurone Disease but, during his illness, Jimmy had recorded *Dirty Old Town* with Jim Kerr, the lead singer for Simple Minds. The duet, recorded in 2003, was re-released after his death, the royalties helping to raise funds for research into the disease.

'In September 1989, Celtic were beaten 2-1 in Belgrade in the UEFA Cup but returned with high hopes that this could be overturned. That game in Glasgow against Partizan turned out to be one of the most extraordinary in Celtic history, when the entire Celtic family experienced every football emotion – from confident apprehension, tension, frustration to despair – raw feelings that Celtic supporters are all too well acquainted with. The team was characteristically passionate and frenzied in attack, careless in defence. The dazzling, exhilarating display was ultimately futile for, although they won 5-4 on the night, they lost on the away-goals rule. It struck me as a vivid illustration of the facility in these parts, in these tribes, for shooting ourselves in the foot in sporting – and political

endeavours. It reminded me of stories about ancient Celtic and Viking 'berserkers', warriors who would work themselves into an aggressive frenzy on mead and magic mushrooms, plunging headlong into wild, often suicidal, attacks. My piano concerto, The Berserking, came about in response to this game and, I am proud to say, is the only concerto in the history of classical music to be inspired by the away-goals rule.'

The above words are written by James MacMillan, Scotland's best known classical composer who also drew attention to sectarianism throughout the country in a speech during the Edinburgh International Festival in 1999.

**Hail Hail, the Celts are Here
(The Celtic Song)
original version by Glen Daly**

Hail, Hail, the Celts are here
What the hell do we care,
What the hell do we care,
Hail, Hail, the Celts are here
What the hell do we care now. . .

For it's a grand old team to play for,
For it's a grand old team bedad,
When you know the history
It's enough to make your heart go sad.
God bless them.
We don't care if we win lose or draw,
Darn the hair we do care,
For we only know
That there's going to be a show,
And the Glasgow Celtic will be there.

**Hail Hail, the Celts are Here
(The Celtic Song)
arrangement by Derek Warfield**

Hail, Hail, the Celts are here
What the hell do we care,
What the hell do we care,
Hail, Hail, the Celts are here
What the hell do we care now. . .

For it's a grand old team to play for,
For it's a grand old team to see.
And if you know the history,
It's enough to make your heart go,
O-o-o-o.
We don't care what the animals say,
What the hell do we care,
For we only know,
That there's going to be a show,
And the Glasgow Celtic will be there.

To

THE GLASGOW CELTIC FOOTBALL CLUB

"The Fields of Athenry"

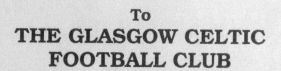

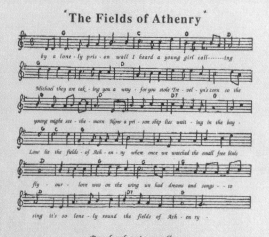

By a lonely prison wall
I heard a young man calling
Nothing matters Mary when your free,
Aginst the famine and the crown
I rebelled they ran me down
Now you must raise our child with dignity
Chorus :
By a lonely harbour wall
She watched the last star falling
As the prison ship sailed out aginst the sky
Sure she'llwait and hope and pray
For her love in Botany Bay
It's so lonely round the fields of Athenry
Chorus :

From Mary & Michael Melia
" The Fields of Athenry Gift Shop"

The Fields of Athenry – a song that
recalls the Irish roots of Celtic

© snspix.com

The manager (Tommy Burns), the fan (Rod Stewart)
and the owner (Fergus McCann) celebrate the 1995
Scottish Cup triumph

N

NAME OF CELTIC

Controversy still surrounds the name to be given the new club in 1887. Obviously, there would have to be Irish connotations – and some felt that such current names as 'Emerald', 'Emmet', 'Harp', 'Shamrock' would be appropriate, but most were in favour of the 'Glasgow Hibernian', in emulation of the Edinburgh side, recent winners of the Scottish Cup. It appears certain from contemporary accounts that Brother Walfrid preferred 'Celtic', and his wishes prevailed – a clear indication of the esteem in which he was held and his influence on the founding of the club.

Some people have claimed that Walfrid suggested the name – which embraces both Ireland and Scotland – as an early gesture of ecumenism. This appears to be fanciful as Walfrid's personal views have never been recorded.

Interestingly, when Michael Davitt officially opened the new Celtic Park in 1892, the Irish patriot referred to the club as 'Celtic', pronounced 'Keltic'; he was puzzled by the amusement among the crowd at his 'error'.

NAMES

Surely the longest name is that of the Dutch striker Jan Vennegoor of Hesselink, signed in 2006, and the shortest that of Joe Rae, a run-of-the-mill centre forward in the mid-1940s. Perhaps Roy Kay, who made five first-team appearances after being signed from Hearts in 1977, should be included. Others might suggest the Chinese player Du Wei, who played in the first half of a Scottish Cup defeat away to Clyde in January 2005.

The most unusual Celtic name among British-born players is Ebenezer Owers, an Englishman who made sixteen appearances as a centre forward in 1913 and who scored eleven goals. Other contenders include Tony Cascarino, Joseph Filippi, John Kurila, and L.R. Roose – a Welsh internationalist who played one Scottish Cup tie in 1910.

PALINDROMES

The best bet would be Bob Hannah an inside forward who made three appearances in 1975/76

Perhaps the most painful to recall would be Xamax of Switzerland who inflicted one of Celtic's heaviest defeats in Europe (1-5) in the UEFA Cup in 1992.

NICKNAMES

Reflecting their Irish roots, the most popular among the supporters is 'The Bhoys'. For many years, however, many referred to them as 'The Tims', while in recent times – as a tribute to one of the most famous strips in all football – some prefer 'The Hoops'.

During World War I, when Celtic were the dominant club in the country, some opposition fans referred to them as 'The Huns' – a clear reference to the much-feared German Army.

ASSUMED NAMES

Willie Maley turned out for Celtic under his mother's maiden name Montgomery for several matches in 1893/94 to avoid detection during the era of 'the paid amateur'.

Often, players on trial – most often with reserve sides – were listed as A. Junior, A.N. Other, or A. Trialist. Presumably, this was to avoid embarrassment for the player if he did not perform well and was not given another chance.

NEWSPAPER

The Celtic directors approved the proposal made by Jack McGinn that the club should publish its own newspaper. McGinn, a keen Celtic supporter who worked in the circulation department of Beaverbrook Papers, had come up with the idea in 1964 when he had become increasingly exasperated by the apparent lack of interest in Celtic by the major newspapers. Originally, he felt that the club newspaper should concentrate on snippets of information unappealing to regular newspapers such as free publicity for supporters' clubs and their events, background material about developments at Celtic Park, etc.

The proposal was accepted by the Board in March, 1965 and, according to most accounts, it was the first meeting attended by the new manager Jock Stein who promised McGinn that the first picture on its front page would be that of Celtic players with the Scottish Cup. Jack McGinn was granted a loan of £600 to finance the setting up of the paper, which was given the title of *The Celtic View*; this loan was to be repaid by the end of the financial year.

The first issue appeared on 11 August 1965 and, as promised, featured Celtic's Scottish-Cup winning team (after a dramatic 3-2 victory over Dunfermline Athletic). The effect of the dynamic Jock Stein on Celtic was to transform the struggling mid-table outfit into the most exciting team in Scotland – and perhaps Europe. This, of course, helped with the circulation figures of the club newspaper. During that first year the weekly sales averaged 26,000. On 11 May 1988 *The Celtic View* celebrated the appearance of its 1000th issue.

NON-LEAGUE OPPONENTS

Part of the romance of the Scottish Cup is to see non-league sides take on the richer, more established clubs. In the following list Celtic's opponents were non-league outfits at the time of the fixtures. Prior to August 1890 – when the Scottish League was founded – all clubs (including Celtic) were non-league. Games up to that point have not been included here.

1890/91
Carfin Shamrock 2-2 (H), 3-1 (A)
Wishaw Thistle 6-2 (A)
Dundee Our Boys 3-1 (A)
Royal Albert 2-0 (N)

1891/92
Kilmarnock Athletic 3-0 (H)
Cowlairs 4-1 (H)
Queen's Park 5-1 (N)

1892/93
Linthouse 3-1 (H)
5th Kirkcudbright Rifle Volunteers 7-0
    (H)
St. Bernards 5-0 (H)

1893/94
Hurlford 6-0 (H)
Albion Rovers 7-0 (H)

1894/95
Queen's Park* 4-1 (H)

1895/96
Queen's Park 2-4 (H);

1896/97
Arthurlie 2-4 (A)

1897/98
Arthurlie 7-0 (A)

1898/99
6th Galloway Rifle Volunteers 6-1 (A)
Queen's Park 2-1 (H)

1899/1900
Bo'ness 7-1 (H)
Queen's Park 4-3 (N)

1901/02
Thornliebank 3-0 (H)
Arbroath 3-2 (A)

1904/05
Dumfries 2-1 (A)
Lochgelly United 3-0 (H)

1905/06
Bo'ness 3-0 (H)

1907/08
Peebles Rovers 4-0 (H)

1910/11
Galston 1-0 (H)

1911/12
Dunfermline Athletic 1-0 (H)

1912/13
Albion Rovers 4-0 (H)
Peebles Rovers 3-0 (H)

1913/14
Forfar Athletic 5-0 (A)

1920/21
East Fife 3-1 (A)
Vale of Leven 3-0 (A)

1921/22
Montrose 4-0 (H)

1922/23
Lochgelly United 3-2 (A)
Hurlford 4-0 (H)

1924/25
Solway Star 2-0 (H)

1926/27
Brechin City 6-3 (A)

1929/30
Inverness Caledonian 6-0 (A)

1933/34
Dalbeattie Star 6-0 (A)

1937/38
Nithsdale Wanderers 5-0 (H)

1938/39
Buntisland Shipyard 8-3 (A)

1949/50
Brechin City 3-0 (A)

1950/51
Duns 4-0 (H)

1952/53
Eyemouth United 4-0 (A)

1956/57
Forres Mechanics 5-0 (A)

1959/60
Elgin City 2-1 (A)

1962/63
Gala Fairydean 6-0 (H)

1963/64
Eyemouth United 3-0 (H)

1966/67
Elgin City 7-0 (H)

1984/85
Inverness Thistle 6-0(H)

1995/96
Whitehill Welfare 3-0 (N)

* Queen's Park, although an established club, declined an invitation to join the Scottish League.

NORTH EASTERN CUP

This was the very first trophy won by Celtic, and earned Celtic a reputation as a cup team. The clubs eligible to compete were based in the north-east of Glasgow. However, the emergence of Celtic as an immediate power in Scottish football from the first season meant the demise of such local sides as Cowlairs and Northern.

Celtic won this trophy in their first season (1888/89) by beating Clydesdale (5-1), Northern (4-1) and Cowlairs (6-1) in the final at Clyde's ground on 11 May 1889. Celtic's first-ever cup-winning side was:

McLaughlin, Dowling, McKeown, Maley, Kelly, McLaren, H. Gallacher, Dowds, Groves, Coleman, Dunbar.

A year later Celtic retained the trophy by beating Northern (2-0) in the final again played at Clyde's ground, Barrowfield Park.

Further participation in such a local tournament did not appeal to the club which was making such an impact on the Scottish scene and Celtic made no more appearances in the competition.

NORWAY

Celtic have signed a few players from Norway such as Harald Brattbakk, Geir Karlsson and Vidar Riseth.

Karlsson, a goalkeeper, played for Rosenborg against Celtic in a European tie in the early 1970s and performed brilliantly. He was given a two-month trial period with Celtic and played twice for the reserves Already capped 13 times, by the end of his career he had gained thirty caps for Norway.

Brattbakk also played for Rosenborg and joined Celtic in 1997 and played as a striker for three seasons before returning to Norway (and Rosenborg). An intelligent player, he remained popular with the majority in Celtic's support despite a reputation for failing to convert chances. He was given a generous welcome on his appearance at Celtic Park with Rosenborg – but scored both their goals in Celtic's 0-2 defeat in the return match in Trondheim.

Riseth joined Celtic from the German club Linz in 1998 and was a hard-working midfielder and central defender for three years before being transferred to 1860 Munich. Another highly popular performer, he was nicknamed 'Psycho' by fans.

NUMBERS

Just prior to World War II (1939-1945) numbers were being introduced into British football but implementation was slowed down by wartime conditions. By 1950, however, every club in Scotland – with one notable exception – was identifying its players with numbers on the jersey.

The exception, of course, was Celtic, whose chairman, Bob Kelly, objected, claiming that 'they would ruin the most famous jerseys in football.' In 1960, though, Celtic did make an effort to comply with the trend when – in a friendly match against Sparta (Rotterdam) at Parkhead on May 14 – the numbers were displayed on the players' shorts.

On 6 August 1960 when Celtic played against Sedan in an ill-fated Anglo-Franco-Scottish Friendship Cup tie at Lens, they took the field – at the promoters' insistence – with yellow numbers, hard to distinguish against the green-and-white jerseys.

Since 1975 all European ties under UEFA rules have to be played with the numbers clearly visible on the back of the shirts – the starting eleven numbered from 1 to 11, and the substitutes from 12 to 16. Desmond White, the successor to Bob Kelly as chairman, objected unsuccessfully to the ruling and Celtic's first outing in the new jerseys with black numbers came on 5 November 1975 in the European Cup-Winners' Cup tie against Boavista at Celtic Park, a match won 3-1 by Celtic.

On 8 September 1973 for the opening home league fixture against Clyde, each Celtic player wore an '8' on his shorts to celebrate the eighth successive league championship won the previous season. Celtic celebrated in some style with a 5-0 victory over their neighbours.

For the League Cup final (CIS Cup) against Dunfermline Athletic on 19 March 2006 every Celtic player wore the number '7' in honour of Jimmy Johnstone who had died earlier that week

Old Firm turning points: (above) Scott McDonald equalises just before half time to revive Celtic's successful challenge for the 2007/08 League title

(below) Paul Lambert (no. 10) scoring a spectacular goal in the closing minutes of the January 1998 Old Firm derby to stop Rangers' bid for 10 league titles in a row

© snspix.com

O

O

A challenge! How many Celtic players' names end with an 'o'? To get you started – Juan Sanchez Broto, Paolo di Canio, Tony Cascarino, Juninho, Dan Munro, Frank Munro, Alec Rollo, Evander Sno, Koki Mizuno. . .

OFFSIDE

It may come as a surprise to some Celtic supporters but, in the club's very first match (a 5-2 win over Rangers in May 1888), a Celtic goal was disallowed for offside as a match report suggests: 'A sixth point (goal) was put through, but was disallowed owing to an infringement of the off-side rule.'

The interpretation of the offside rule has proved to be the most controversial and difficult to enforce consistently. A player is offside if he is in front of the ball when he has fewer than two defenders between him and the opponents' goal-line, and he is gaining an advantage by being in that position, or interfering with play.

The early legislation of football was derived from two sets of rules: the Sheffield F.A. and the London F.A. The main difference between the two was that Sheffield's required two defenders while London's favoured three. When the rules were formalised in 1877, the London interpretation was chosen. In the 1910/11 season in England some defenders became adept at trapping forwards in an offside position by moving upfield at appropriate times, and the sport was being distorted by the number of stoppages for offside.

The law was changed in 1925 when the original Sheffield ruling of only two defenders was accepted. However, highly trained defenders continued to trap careless forwards although there was a dramatic increase in goal-scoring. To counter this teams started to use a third-back system with the centre-half retreating further into defence as a stopper. Celtic, it should be noted, were most reluctant to employ such a solution and suffered during the 1930s as a consequence.

From 1990 onwards players were no longer considered as offside if they were adjudged level with the 'second defender' – a ruling which caused further difficulties for linesmen, now considered 'assistant referees'.

Celtic supporters feel a particular grievance with the offside law, and can recount various memorable 'injustices' arising from it:

25 February 1949: John McPhail headed an equaliser against Aberdeen in a Scottish Cup tie at Celtic Park but the referee disallowed it because Celtic's left-winger, Willie Rennett remote on the far touchline, was considered a yard offside.

19 April 1966: Bobby Lennox scored a late goal for Celtic against Liverpool in the European Cup-Winners' Cup tie at Anfield but the score was disallowed to the fury of the travelling Celtic support;

1 November 1967: A header by Raffo of Racing Club was netted from a suspiciously clear position several yards beyond the Celtic defence. However, the South American referee allowed the goal to stand and it marked a turning point in the World Club Championship.

27 January 1968: Celtic's Jim Brogan fired in a long-range shot past the Dunfermline goalkeeper in a Scottish Cup tie at Celtic Park but the goal was not allowed to stand because another Celtic player had strayed into an offside position (but not interfering with play).

2 January 1997: Jorge Cadete's equaliser against Rangers a few minutes from the end was disallowed on the evidence of a linesman's flag although TV footage showed he was not in an offside position.

No doubt many Celtic supporters could add to this representative list but the editors point out that views might be coloured by the results of the matches. Celtic lost all the games listed above. Perhaps those supporters might recall that the same linesman who caused Cadete's goal to be chalked off was equally at fault in not flagging Chris Sutton for offside when he scored in the opening minute of a 6-2 rout of Rangers on 27 August 2000.

THE OLD FIRM

Celtic and Rangers have been yoked together from the early days when they first started to dominate Scottish football both in a sporting and financial sense. On 15 April 1904, just before the forthcoming Scottish Cup final between the clubs, *The Scottish Referee* produced a cartoon with a disreputable tramp carrying a sandwich board with the words Patronise the Old Firm. This was the first reference which involved the particular expression and it was not intended to be complimentary.

OLD FIRM CUP FINALS
League Cup:
1957: Celtic 7, Rangers 1
1965: Celtic 1, Rangers 2
1966: Celtic 2, Rangers 1
1967: Celtic 1, Rangers 0
1971: Celtic 0, Rangers 1
1976: Celtic 0, Rangers 1
1978: Celtic 1, Rangers 2
1983: Celtic 2, Rangers 1
1984: Celtic 2, Rangers 3
1987: Celtic 1, Rangers 2
1991: Celtic 1, Rangers 2
2003: Celtic 1, Rangers 2

Scottish Cup:
1894: Celtic 1, Rangers 3
1899: Celtic 2, Rangers 0
1904: Celtic 3, Rangers 2
1909: Celtic 2, Rangers 2 and 1-1*
1928: Celtic 0, Rangers 4
1963: Celtic 0, Rangers 3 (after 1-1)
1966: Celtic 0, Rangers 1 (after 0-0)
1971: Celtic 2, Rangers 1 (after 1-1)
1973: Celtic 2, Rangers 3
1977: Celtic 1, Rangers 0
1980: Celtic 1, Rangers 0 (aet)
1989: Celtic 1, Rangers 0
1999: Celtic 0, Rangers 1
2002: Celtic 2, Rangers 3
* Cup withheld by SFA after riot

Celtic's 2-2 draw at Ibrox in May 1967 virtually guarantees the championship (Celtic players l to r) Lennox, Craig, Murdoch, Gemmell, McNeill and Wallace

OLDEST

Long-serving Alec McNair, a versatile performer who started his career with Celtic in 1904, played his last match for the club against Queen's Park in a 1-1 draw at Parkhead on 18 April 1925. He was forty-one years old (and 113 days) then.

Veteran goalkeeper Ronnie Simpson's last game for Celtic was the replay of a League Cup semi final against Ayr United at Hampden Park on 13 October 1969, won 2-1 by Celtic. Simpson thirty-nine years old (and two days) re-injured his shoulder in making a vital save minutes from the end. At the age of thirty six (and 186 days) he had become Scotland's oldest debutant when he was selected for the famous 3-2 win over England at Wembley in 1967.

Alec McNair, the oldest player ever to turn out for Celtic

OUR FOOTBALL BOYS—No. 8.

ALEC. McNAIR (Celtic). A household word in Glasgow. Plays right-back, stands 5 ft. 8 ins., weighs 11 st. 10 lbs., has lots of caps, and comes from Stenhousemuir.

ONE-GAME WONDERS

Celtic's roll-call of heroes and legends is apparently endless, but what about the lesser players? Especially those who pull on the famous Celtic jerseys only once – and then disappear. In reality most of them subsequently drop down to a more suitable level, either in a lower division or perhaps back to the juniors.

At least they can all say with pride; 'I played for Celtic once.'

Walter Arnott vs Third Lanark (H) 4-4 SL 23 February 1895

John Atkinson vs Morton (H) 5-1 SL 22 April 1909

Graham Barclay vs Clydebank (H) 4-1 SC 15 February 1975

James Barrie vs Airdrie (H) 1-2 SL 5 February 1930

John Blackwood vs Hearts H 0-2 SL 30 September 1899

John Blair vs Third Lanark (H) 0-0 SL 19 November 1910

Pat Breslin vs Dundee (H) 4-1 SL 7 January 1899

John Buckley vs Arbroath (H) 4-1 SLC 1 September 1982

Chic Cairney vs Raith Rovers (H) 2-2 SL 1 October 1949

James Carlin vs Dundee (H) 0-1 SL 20 February 1897

James Cassidy vs Leith Athletic (H) 2-0 SL 14 May 1892

James Coleman vs Shettleston (H) 5-1 SC 1 September 1888

John Convery vs Dundee United (H) 2-0 PL 21 May 2000

Barry Corr vs Hearts (A) 4-2 PL 14 April 1999

Joe Cowan vs Aberdeen (A) 1-1 SL 24 January 1931

Brian Coyne vs Clydebank (H) 5-2 PL 17 April 1978

Michael Craig vs Meadowbank Thistle (H) 3-0 SC 18 February 1995

Tommy Curley vs Hearts (A) 2-4 SL 26 September 1964

Michael Davitt vs Ayr United (H) 4-1 SL 26 March 1938

Pat Donlevy vs Hibernian (H) 1-2 SL 26 September 1898

Barry Elliot vs Aberdeen (H) 1-0 PL 2 November 1996

John Ferguson vs Leith Athletic (A) 6-5 SL 30 March 1895

Tom Fitzsimmons vs Rangers (A) 2-2 SL 24 September 1892

Bert Fraser vs Hibernian (H) 2-4 SL 3 April 1948

Willie Garden vs Cowdenbeath (A) 0-3 SL 14 March 1925

Lawrie Glancey vs Motherwell (H) 2-0 SL 15 March 1922

Willie Goldie vs Airdrie (A) 0-2 SL 1 October 1960

Jim Goodwin vs Dundee United (H) 2-0 PL 21 May 2000

John Gorman vs Hamilton Academical (A) 4-2 SLC 25 September 1968

Phil Gormley vs Aberdeen (H) 1-0 SL 10 January 1948

Steve Hancock vs Sliema Wanderers (A) 2-1 EC 3 November 1971

Joe Haverty vs St. Mirren (H) 4-1 SL 17 October 1964

Peter Jack vs Rangers (A) 1-1 SL 23 March 1895

Paddy Kelly vs Dundee United (H) 3-0 PL 10 May 1997

John Kennedy vs Raith Rovers (H) 4-0 SLC 22 September 1965

Peter Lamb vs St. Mirren (A) 1-0 SL 31 August 1946

Dick Madden vs Kilmarnock (A) 0-6 SL 27 March 1963

John McArdle vs Dunfermline Athletic (H) 2-1 SL 2 April 1927

Eddie McCann vs Renton (A) 2-0 SL 25 March 1893

Ryan McCann vs Dundee United (H) 2-0 PL 21 May 2000

Frank McCarron vs Hibernian (H) 2-0 SL 6 April 1963

John McCluskey vs Jeunesse Esch (A) 6-1 EC 28 September 1977

Brian McColligan vs Dundee United (H) 2-0 PL 21 May 2000

Andy McCondichie vs Dundee (H) 6-1 PL 7 November 1998

Benny McCready vs Aberdeen (A) 1-0 SL 22 April 1957

Danny McDowall vs Dundee (A) 1-3 SL 20 January 1951

Dan McGarvey vs Dumbarton (H) 4-2 SLSD 6 December 1941

Willie McGinnigle vs Third Lanark (H) 3-1 SL 30 September 1918

Tommy McGonagle vs Airdrie (A) 1-1 SL 9 April 1932

Alec McGregor vs Falkirk (A) 0-1 SL 28 February 1914

Johnny McIlhatton vs Hamilton Acad. (A) 0-1 SLSD 23 November 1940

Arthur McInally vs Motherwell (A) 4-3 SL 15 December 1917

George McLaughlin vs Partick Thistle (H) 1-2 SL 1 September 1923

Eamon McMahon vs Queen of South (H) 1-1 SL 16 October 1954

Peter McManus vs St. Bernard's (A) 0-3 SL 16 September 1895

James McPherson vs Carfin Shamrock (A) 3-1 SC 4 October 1890

Hugh Mills vs Dunfermline Athletic (A) 0-1 SL 14 December 1935

Frank Mitchell vs Clyde (H) 0-0 GC 28 September 1912

Ronnie Mitchell vs Hearts (A) 0-1 SL 3 January 1948

Sandy Morrison vs Hibernian (A) 1-0 SL 8 May 1907

Willie Morrison vs Raith Rovers (A) 0-1 SL 12 January 1952

David Nelson vs Clyde (A) 1-2 SLSD 3 January 1942

John O'Brien vs Leith Athletic (A) 6-5 SL 30 March 1895

Felix O'Neill vs St. Mirren (A) 1-1 SL 18 March 1911

John O'Neill vs Partick Thistle (H) 0-0 SL 9 November 1994

Roy Paton vs Clyde (H) 1-1 SC 18 February 1959

L.R. Roose vs Clyde (A) 1-3 SC 12 March 1910

Andrew Ross vs St. Bernard's (A) 3-2 SL 29 October 1898

Robert Scott vs Rangers (H) 3-0 SL 29 April 1893

Hugh Shaw vs St. Mirren (A) 3-2 SL 17 February 1906

Danny Shea vs Clyde (H) 2-0 SL 2 January 1919

Paul Shields vs Aberdeen (H) 5-1 PL 6 May 2000

Tom Stewart vs St. Mirren (A) 0-0 SL 5 January 1918

James Thom vs Hearts (A) 0-4 SL 16 February 1895

Danny Thomas vs Third Lanark (H) 4-4 SL 23 February 1895

Billy Thomson vs Leith Athletic (H) 4-0 SL 16 March 1895

Paddy Trodden vs Dundee (H) 2-1 SL 4 May 1895

Du Wei vs Clyde (A) 1-2 SC 8 January 2006

Bobby Wraith vs Hamilton Academical (A) 4-2 SLC 25 September 1968

John Wylie vs Hearts (A) 3-5 SLSD 13 February 1943

James Young vs Hearts (H) 3-0 SL 9 February 1918

ONE-OFF COMPETITIONS

Throughout its history football has provided a number of unique competitions devised to commemorate a particular event. The winners are allowed to keep the trophy for ever. Celtic have an astonishingly successful record in such tournaments:

GLASGOW EXHIBITION TROPHY (1901 & 1902)

In 1901 Celtic, along with the other seven top clubs in Scotland, competed for this handsome trophy. Celtic advanced to the final by disposing of the two Edinburgh sides: Hibernian (1-0) and Hearts (2-1). In that final, Celtic lost to Rangers by 3-1 at the University Recreation Grounds on 9 September 1901. The match became rough and ill-disciplined in the closing stages, and the atmosphere was described as 'ugly'.

Rangers were delighted with the trophy, so much so that they insured it for £100 – a massive amount in those days.

However, the Ibrox Disaster of 1902, in which twenty-five spectators were killed – forced Rangers to put the trophy up for competition again in order to raise funds for the victims. Rangers and Celtic, Sunderland and Everton – the champions and runners-up of Scotland and England competed for the trophy.

Celtic crushed Sunderland, the English champions, by 5-1 at Celtic Park on 30 April 1902 while Rangers defeated Everton by 3-2 at the same venue on 3 June.

The Old Firm met in the final at Cathkin Park, the ground of Third Lanark, on 17 June 1902. Rangers started as the betting favourites but Celtic surprised them with the choice of a young Jimmy Quinn at centre forward, a switch from his usual position on the left wing. Quinn, destined to become a Celtic legend, was unstoppable with his bustling style which upset the Rangers defence. At the end of ninety minutes the score was tied 2-2 with Quinn getting both goals for Celtic. Only two minutes remained in the extra time when Quinn headed in Celtic's winner in a 3-2 upset.

Rangers were taken aback when Celtic felt they had a right to retain the trophy, the Ibrox club expecting it to be returned after the competition. Celtic displayed it proudly as part of the permanent collection and resisted several Rangers overtures to have it returned to Ibrox – or put up for competition yet again.

Celtic: McPherson, Davidson, Battles, Loney, Marshall, Orr, Crawford, Campbell, Quinn, McDermott, Hamilton.

EMPIRE EXHIBITION TROPHY (1938) (SEE ENTRY UNDER EMPIRE EXHIBITION TROPHY)

Celtic won this virtual British Championship with one of the club's greatest sides.

V. E. CUP (1945)

To celebrate the successful conclusion to the war in 1945 the Glasgow Cup Committee hastily organised a competition for the Victory-in-Europe Cup, the proceeds to go to charity. Rangers and Celtic were invited to take part, but Rangers declined because of other commitments, and Queen's Park substituted for them at very short notice.

The match was held at Hampden Park with 31,000 in attendance on 9 May 1945 and Celtic won the contest and the trophy by 1 goal and 3 corners to 1 goal and two corners. Their goal was scored by Johnny Paton, and Celtic's winning side was:

Miller, Hogg, P. McDonald, Lynch, Mallan, McPhail, Paton, M. MacDonald, Gallagher, Evans, McLaughlin.

St. Mungo Cup (1951)

One of Glasgow Corporation's contributions to the Festival of Britain in the summer of 1951 was the staging of the St. Mungo Cup, named in honour of the city's patron saint. It began appropriately enough on Glasgow Fair Saturday and the eight ties involving the 'A' Division sides attracted a total of 172,000.

Celtic, relatively match-fit after a tour of the United States, defeated Hearts at Celtic Park by 2-1 before a crowd of 51,000 while Rangers lost by 2-1 to Aberdeen at Pittodrie. In the second round the venues were neutral grounds and Celtic had to come from behind twice to earn a 4-4 draw with Clyde at Firhill, the home of Partick Thistle with 29,000 in attendance. The replay was won very convincingly by Celtic by 4-1 with the Eire full back Sean Fallon introduced as a make-shift centre forward. Fallon upset the Clyde defenders with his robust play and scored two of the goals.

The semi final against Raith Rovers was held at Hampden Park and Celtic won easily enough by 3-1 with new signing Jimmy Walsh, a recruit from Bo'ness United, scoring all three Celtic goals.

The final against Aberdeen was held on 1 August 1951 and 81,000 enjoyed a thrilling match. Aberdeen made the better start and scored in fourteen minutes, when Celtic's youthful goalkeeper George

Hunter was injured in attempting to save Yorston's shot. He had to leave the pitch to be replaced by Bobby Evans for ten minutes while he was treated for a head wound. Aberdeen went further ahead in thirty-five minutes against the run of play, when Bogan, a wartime Celt, scored a spectacular goal in a breakaway. Sean Fallon scrambled home a corner kick taken by Tully only a minute before the interval. Aberdeen were furious because Tully had engineered the corner kick by taking a throw-in and pitching the ball at the back of a retreating Aberdeen defender.

Celtic came out fighting for the second half and Tully, delighted with his first-half gambit, was producing his best form and tormenting Aberdeen's right flank. Within ten minutes Fallon equalised, and Walsh – who had scored in every round – netted the winner after yet another twisting run down the left from Tully.

Celtic: Hunter, Haughney, Rollo, Evans, Mallan, Baillie, Collins, Walsh, Fallon, Peacock, Tully.

Some time afterwards it was revealed that the ornate trophy was a second-hand one, having been the prize in a yachting competition in 1894. Celtic's chairman, Bob Kelly, and Glasgow's Lord Provost, Victor Warren, quarreled in public over the matter with an exchange of letters in the *Glasgow Herald*.

Coronation Cup (1953)
(See entry for Coronation Cup)

To celebrate the coronation of Queen Elizabeth in 1953 a football competition involving the top sides in Scotland and England was held in football-mad Glasgow.

ORDERED OFF
(SEE ENTRY UNDER 'FREQUENT OFFENDERS')

The highest number of Celtic players dismissed by a referee is four – during the deciding match to determine the destination of the Inter-Continental Cup, better known as 'the World Club Championship', in the Centenario Stadium in Montevideo in 1967. In chronological order the referee – a Dr. Osorio from Paraguay – ordered off Bobby Lennox, Jimmy Johnstone, John Hughes and Bertie Auld. The last named simply refused to leave the field. Two Racing Club (Buenos Aires) were also dismissed: Basile and Rulli. Racing Club won 1-0.

On several occasions Celtic have been left short-handed in matches against Rangers. On 1 January 1943 Malcolm MacDonald and Matt Lynch were ordered off at Ibrox Park for protesting refereeing decisions, and it came as no surprise that Celtic lost by 8-1 to their great rivals.

On 8 June 1946 George Paterson and Jimmy Mallan were dismissed in the Victory Cup semi-final replay at Hampden Park after complaining about a penalty-kick award to Rangers – who won by 2-0.

On 20 November 2004 Alan Thompson and Chris Sutton were ordered off in a league fixture at Ibrox Park, won 2-0 by Rangers.

On 20 August 2005 Alan Thompson and Neil Lennon were dismissed by the referee as Celtic went down to a 3-1 defeat by Rangers, again at Ibrox Park.

Multiple ordering-offs have taken place in other Old Firm clashes:

Chris Woods and Terry Butcher of

Another potential flashpoint in an Old Firm match. Here, Bobby Murdoch eyeballs Rangers striker Alex Ferguson in the opening minute of the 1969 Scottish Cup final

Rangers and Frank McAvennie of Celtic were ordered off at Ibrox Park on 17 October 1987.

In a Scottish Cup tie at Celtic Park on 17 March 1991, won 2-0 by Celtic, four players were sent off: Peter Grant (Celtic), Terry Hurlock, Mark Walters, and Mark Hately (Rangers).

On 2 May 1999 three players were dismissed by the referee in a bad-tempered clash at Celtic Park: Celtic's Stephane Mahe and Vidar Riseth and Rod Wallace (Rangers).

In major cup finals several Celtic players have been ordered off:

Roy Aitken in the Scottish Cup final against Aberdeen (1-2) on 19 May 1984;

Chris Sutton, brought to Celtic from Chelsea by Martin O'Neill for £6 million was an intelligent yet aggressive contributor, ordered off against Rangers, Motherwell and Kilmarnock

'Mo' Johnston in the League Cup final against Rangers (1-2) on 26 October 1986;

Chris Sutton in the League Cup final against Kilmarnock (3-0) on 18 March 2001;

Neil Lennon against Rangers (1-2) in the League Cup final on 16 March 2003;

Bobo Balde in the UEFA Cup final against Porto (2-3) at Seville on 21 May 2003.

Occasionally, the ordering-off of a Celtic player has inspired the remaining ten to greater efforts. On 21 May 1979 at Celtic Park Johnny Doyle was ordered off in fifty-five minutes in the championship decider against Rangers. Celtic, although playing for thirty-five minutes a man short – and down by 2-1 – fought back to win 4-2 and gain the league title.

On 18 August 1979 Roy Aitken was ordered off in the first half against Rangers at Ibrox Park but Celtic, despite falling two goals behind, scored twice in the last six minutes to salvage a 2-2 draw.

ORDERED OFF WHILE ON INTERNATIONAL DUTY

Bertie Auld vs Holland May 1959

Pat Crerand vs Czechoslovakia (0-4) May 1960

Tommy Gemmell vs West Germany (2-3) October 1968

Craig Burley vs Morocco (0-3) June 1998

Morten Wieghorst vs South Africa June 1998; vs Italy September 1999

ORIGINS

Celtic owed its founding to the hardships borne by the mainly Irish inhabitants of the East End of Glasgow. Many of these unfortunates were descended from those who had fled Ireland in the aftermath of the Irish Potato Famine of the mid nineteenth century. Having arrived in Scotland, and settling principally in the West Coast, they had found life hard and were victims of religious intolerance and job discrimination. The result was often unemployment and appalling slum conditions in Glasgow's poorest districts.

Brother Walfrid of the Marists determined to alleviate some of the hardship by instituting the Poor Children's Dinner Table, an attempt to provide basic nutrition for the children of the East End. When he attended a reception to celebrate Edinburgh Hibernian's winning of the Scottish Cup in 1887, he thought that a similarly Irish football club in Glasgow could be the means of raising money for that and other charities.

Brother Walfrid was assisted by John H. McLaughlin and John Glass in establishing such an organisation. McLaughlin, a publican, and Glass, a building contractor, were primarily responsible for arousing the interest and cooperation of the Irish (and Catholic) community.

The founding meeting was held at St. Mary's Hall, Abercromby Street and that meeting agreed that a club should be established, that its name should be Celtic, and that a committee arrange to rent premises for a football club.

The ground was rented and prepared for football and only six months later Celtic was ready to play its first game – against a team representing Rangers and essentially their reserve side known as the Swifts. Celtic won by 5-2, with Neil McCallum (Renton) scoring the first goal.

(Above and opposite) Details from the Brother Walfrid statue at Celtic Park

OTHER SPORTS

Celtic Park has hosted sporting events other than football:

Baseball:
On 28 September 1918 two baseball teams representing the United States Forces played an exhibition game on the ground; a crowd of about 12,000 (with gate receipts of £500) turned up to watch.

Boxing:
Several boxing cards have been staged at Celtic Park. Benny Lynch fought (and lost to) Jim Warnock of Belfast in a non-title bout over fifteen rounds – a crowd of 20,000 attended.

More than 15,000 watched as Billy Thomson (England) defeated Harry Hughes (Motherwell) in a British and European lightweight title fight. The same bill featured Jake Kilrain (Bellshill) against Willie Whyte (Glasgow) and Peter Keenan (Glasgow) against Raoul Degryse (Belgium).

On 24 March 1917 Jimmy Wilde (World Flyweight Champion) boxed an exhibition against Sid Shields at the stadium.

At least two World Heavyweight champions have dropped in to Celtic Park as guests of the club: 'Gentleman Jim' Corbett and Mohammed Ali.

Celtic Sports:

Celtic used to stage an annual sports meeting in August just before the start of the football season, and it was a popular event for almost forty years (from 1890 to 1920s). The first meet at Celtic's original (and inadequate) ground attracted an enthusiastic crowd of 6,000 who saw among other things James Kelly, the team's captain, win the 220 yards and listened to the band of the Lancashire Fusiliers Regiment who provided musical entertainment throughout.

The building of the new Celtic Park saw the Celtic Sports expand into one of the premier athletic meetings in the calendar, and crowds of up to 40,000 attended to watch some luminaries such as future Olympic champion Eric Liddell perform. However, unemployment in the heavy industries in Scotland led to a decline in attendance, and the club struggled to keep the event alive until its demise in the late 1920s.

Cycling:

The World Cycling Championships were held over a few days at Celtic Park in August 1897, and to stage it Celtic expanded the ground by constructing a banked cycle-track. The financial risk was worth it as almost 50,000 attended the events.

Hurling:

An 'international' took place between representatives of Ireland (Kilkenny) and Scotland (a Select) on 21 June 1913. The event was organised by the Gaelic Athletic Association but failed to attract a large crowd – although the expenses were met.

Rugby League:

On 3 February 1909 England played Australia at Celtic Park before a crowd estimated at only 3,000 (because of heavy rain). The result was a 17-17 draw with the Australians fighting back in the last ten minutes.

Special Olympics:

The 1990 European Special Olympic Games were held at the ground and were opened before 32,000 by the Duke of Edinburgh on 21 July 1990.

Speedway:

On 28 April 1928 a crowd of 5,000 turned up to witness what is believed to be the first organised speedway meeting staged in Britain under the auspices of Dirt Track Speedways. A few other similar events were staged in the next week or so, but interest soon waned. The 80th anniversary was commemorated on 29th April 2008 with a photo call at Celtic Park by the city's speedway team, the Glasgow Tigers.

OWN-GOAL BONUSES

Three opposition players have shared the unfortunate distinction of scoring own-goals for Celtic in Scottish Cup finals:

Hugh Robertson (East Fife) netted Celtic's first goal, an equaliser, in Celtic's 3-1 victory at Hampden in 1927;

Alan Craig (Motherwell) headed a cross from Celtic's right wing into his own net in the last minute of the 1931 final to give Celtic an undeserved 2-2 draw;

Willie Young (Aberdeen) was unlucky enough to divert Neil Mochan's cross-shot from the right wing past his goalkeeper in 1954 to set Celtic on the way to a 2-1 win.

On 21 May 1979 Celtic staged a remarkable comeback to defeat Rangers by 4-2 at Parkehad and to win the league championship. Colin Jackson, Rangers' central defender, contributed an 'own goal' and admitted later that he was relieved when Murdo MacLeod scored Celtic's fourth goal in injury time because it deflected unwelcome attention from his lapse.

'One half of Glasgow just don't like you; the other half thinks it owns you.'
Tommy Burns, on being an Old Firm player.

Youngster Aiden McGeady broke into Celtic's first team in season 2004/05 scoring on his debut against Hearts.

He won the Scottish Football Writers' Player of the Year Award in 2007/08.

P

PARADISE

For many years the popular nickname for Celtic Park was 'Paradise'. The origin of the appellation remains doubtful, with two conflicting accounts:

The first is attributed to a journalist who overheard a spectator describing the move from the club's first ground adjoining Janefield Cemetery to the present site in 1892 as 'like leaving the graveyard to enter Paradise'.

The second, and perhaps the more likely explanation, took place at the club's AGM in May 1892 when the honorary secretary John H. McLaughlin described the new ground as 'a desert that would become a Garden of Eden' and another committee member responded by asking if the players 'would dream of Paradise when flitting on its sward?'

Certainly, Celtic Park did become known as 'Paradise' and reference is made in several poems:

By devious ways where the exile strays,
In many a land afar,
Their fancy flies to the Paradise,
No matter where they are.

and also

But, to my partial Celtic eyes,
There's no more lovely sight:
A sunny day on the Paradise,
Ten jerseys, green-and-white.

PASSING BACK

For many years goalkeepers were allowed to handle the ball inside their penalty area with impunity. However, this led to accusations of time-wasting. A case-study of the 1990 World Cup indicated that in some matches goalkeepers held the ball for as long as eight minutes in the course of a ninety-minute contest.

In 1992 the laws were changed so that the goalkeeper was to be treated like an outfield player when dealing with a passback. A later amendment prohibited a keeper from handling a throw-in.

No doubt the changes in the laws have contributed to a speed-up in play, as well as some unplanned entertainment in watching goalkeepers having to deal with awkward situations with the ball at their feet. However, some Celtic goalkeepers did fancy themselves as outfield players and used practice games to prove their point – notably Willie Miller and Ronnie Simpson.

Indeed, Simpson caused a few Celtic hearts to flutter when he ventured out of goal in the European Cup final in 1967 and tricked an Inter Milan forward with a cute back-heel!

Celtic's rearguard of Charlie Shaw, and his full-backs Alec McNair and Joe Dodds virtually perfected the art of using the keeper as a safety-valve during the seasons from 1913 to the early 1920s. It must have been a major irritation to opponents and their supporters.

PATTER

Many examples of wit attributed to footballers are apocryphal; they should have been said but probably weren't. Some stories circulate for years and are credited to different personalities. In this list the examples cited for Celtic players do have a hint of truth.

Tommy McInally, after being ordered off with the words, 'To the pavilion!' is said to have responded: 'No, ref. I've been to the Pavilion this week; can you not send me to the Empire instead?' (The Empire and Pavilion were well-known Glasgow theatres.)

Tommy Docherty, later a Scotland player, manager, TV pundit and after-dinner speaker, is given credit for several memorable sayings and they are almost certainly true. After his experiences with Scotland in the 1954 World Cup in Switzerland he commented: 'The team got back to Scotland before the postcards.' Asked his opinion about club directors, he felt that the best board would consist of only three: ' Two already dead, and the other in a hospice and comatose.'

Neil Mochan, commenting on the fact that the thirteen Scottish players had to supply their own club training kit for that same World Cup: 'We looked like licorice allsorts.'

Willie Maley, upon being asked by a customer in his Bank Restaurant if he remembered the time that Motherwell beat Celtic 8-0 in 1937, retorted: 'How could I forget when bastards like you remind me all the time?'

Charlie Tully, a genuine wit, is credited with several *bon mots*. When playing for Northern Ireland against England at Windsor Park, shortly after the kick-off he chatted with his marker Alf Ramsay, a most serious full-back and later England's manager: 'Do you enjoy playing for your country, Alf? Good, make the most of today because, when I'm finished with you, they'll never pick you again!' (For the record, Tully scored both Northern Ireland's goals in a 2-2 draw; one of them was direct from a corner kick.)

Joe McBride remembers telling a veteran Rangers centre-half after he had nutmegged him and when the pivot had threatened to break his leg if he ever repeated it: 'You'll have to catch me first!'

Numerous Celtic players, while being given treatment for a shot driven into their 'private parts', have advised the trainer: 'Don't massage them; count them!' (Told by Lisbon Lion Jim Craig.)

Bertie Auld, a youngster at the time, was being treated for a knock to the head by Celtic's trainer Willie Johnstone. Despite the time-honoured and universal remedy of ice-cold water poured down his neck, Bertie remained groggy. The trainer then asked him how many fingers he was holding up, Auld replied: 'Where's your bloody hand?'

One un-named Celtic defender was taken aback when he asked his Hearts opponent about why he was so overweight. The striker replied: 'Well, every time I sleep with your wife, she insists I stay for a cup of tea and a chocolate biscuit!' (Again contributed by Jim Craig).

In reality, unlike the more leisurely sport of cricket, footballers on the pitch have only rare opportunities to engage in banter with opponents.

ST. PATRICK'S DAY

March 17th should be a great day for the Irish, but sometimes it wasn't – at least in 1894.

1894 Leith Athletic A SL 0-5
1917 Airdrie A SL 2-1 McAtee, Gallacher
1923 Dundee H SL 2-1 W. McStay (2, 1p)
1926 Dundee A SL 2-1 McGrory, Malloy
1928 Hearts H SL 2-1 McGrory (2)
1934 Hibernian A SL 2-1 McGrory, H. O'Donnell
1937 Motherwell H SC 4-4 Crum (2), Buchan, Lyon (p)
1951 St. Mirren H SL 2-1 Weir, Collins (p)
1954 Airdrie A SL 6-0 Mochan (3), Fallon, Higgins, Fernie
1956 Dundee H SL 1-0 Collins
1957 Ayr United H SL 4-0 Byrne (2), Haughney, Collins
1962 Airdrie A SL 0-1
1973 Aberdeen H SC 0-0
1979 Motherwell H SL 2-1 Lennox (2)
1990 Dunfermline Athletic A SC 0-0
1991 Rangers H SC 2-0 Creaney, Wdowczyk
1992 Motherwell H PL 4-1 Nicholas, McStay, Creaney, Miller
1996 Rangers A PL 1-1 Hughes

PATRONS

Following the inaugural meeting of the club in 1887 a list of patrons was published:

The following subscriptions have already been received, viz.:

His Grace the Archbishop 20s.
Very Revd. Canon Carmichael 20s.
Revd. F. J. Hughes 20s.
Revd. A. Beyaert 20s.
Revd. A Vanderhyde 20s
Dr. John Conway 20s.
Mr. John Higney 20s.
Mr. James Doyle 20s.
Mr. Arthur McHugh 20s.
Mr. Thos. McCormick 20s.
Mr. Henry Aylmer 20s.
Mr. Michael Aylmer 20s.
Mr. George Hughes 20s.
Mr. Daniel Hughes 20s.
Mr. James Quillan 20s.
Mr. James McQuillan 20s.
Mr. James McConnell 20s.
Mr. John McGallegley 20s.
Mr. John Clancey 20s.
Mr. Francis Henry 20s.
Mr. John Conway 20s.
Mr. James Conway 20s.
Mr. E. Williamson 20s.
Mr. Andrew Bryan 20s.
Mr. Jos. A. Foy 20s.
Mrs. Flynn 20s.
The Granite House 10s 6d
Mr. John Brown 10s 6d
Mr. John Brien 10s 6d

Mr. Hugh Darroch 10s 6d
Mr. P. Donegan 10s 6d
Mr. Hugh Swan 10s 6d
Mr. Patrick Gaffney 10s 6d
Mr. James Hughes 10s 6d
Mr. James McCann 10s 6d
Mr. P. McCulloch 10s 6d
Mr. Owen Aylmer 10s 6d
Mr. Louis Mackenzie 10s 6d
Mr. John Blair 10s
Mr. Edward Mooney 10s
Mr. Charles Stewart 10s
Mr. William Stewart 10s
A Friend 10s
A Friend 10s
Mr. Young 10s

A word of explanation about the currency might be in order. There were twenty shillings in a pound, and twelve pence in a shilling. Therefore, all those who contributed 20s handed over £1; those who contributed 10s handed over 50p. Some subscribed 10s 6d (or ten shillings and sixpence); this was half a guinea and generally considered a more aristocratic way of evaluating money. It should be remembered that £1 in 1887 could purchase a great deal more than nowadays.

PENALTIES

Celtic, despite rumours to the contrary, have been awarded their share of penalty kicks. The following list shows the total of successful conversions by players in the League Championship, Scottish Cup, League Cup and European competition. It does not record the misses, nor does it include goals scored in penalty shoot-outs:

31 Tommy Gemmell

28 Willie McStay

26 Charlie Napier

25 Henrik Larsson

24 Mike Haughney

22 Bobby Collins, Charlie Nicholas

16 Joe Dodds, George Paterson

15 Bobby Murdoch

14 Jimmy Delaney, Willie Orr

13 Andy Lynch

12 Bobby Lennox

11 Bertie Auld, Ronnie Glavin, Willie Lyon, John McPhail, Neil Mochan

10 Brian McClair, Andy Walker

Other notables include Kenny Dalglish (8), Paolo di Canio (4), Paul McStay (3), Billy McNeill (1)

The idea of a penalty kick for an offence close to goal was put forward by William McCrum, a businessman and goalkeeper of Milford Co. Antrim and forwarded to the Irish Football Association. That organisation proposed its adoption to the International Board and it was enshrined in the laws of the game for the 1891/92 season.

Celtic's first penalty was granted at Cappielow against Morton but Neillie McCallum's shot was too straight and was saved by the home team's keeper. Officially Celtic's first successful penalty was netted by Dan Doyle against Dumbarton on 21 December 1895. This is not intended to imply that it took four years for Celtic to be awarded a penalty kick. It was not the custom of press reports at that time to mention if a goal had been scored from the spot.

Jimmy Hay was the first Celt to score from two penalty kicks in a match (1907/08), and numerous players have also achieved that in later seasons. Bobby Collins went one better when he scored from the spot three times against Aberdeen in a 3-0 win at Celtic Park in September 1953.

Penalties awarded in cup finals increase the pressure on the player delegated to take the kick, but only one Celtic player has missed from the spot in a Scottish Cup final: Chris Sutton in Celtic's 1-0 win over Dunfermline Athletic in 2005. Successful conversions have been made by Willie Orr in 1907 (3-0 vs Hearts), Harry Hood in 1971 (2-1 vs Rangers), George Connelly in 1973 (2-3 vs Rangers), Pat McCluskey in 1975 (3-1 vs Airdrie), Andy Lynch in 1977 (1-0 vs Rangers), and Henrik Larsson in 2001 (3-0 vs Hibernian).

The greatest number of penalties scored by Celtic in a single season is 16 (in 1966/67) when Joe McBride netted 9 and Tommy Gemmell 7. During that season McBride scored from the spot in five successive League Cup ties and Gemmell scored in four successive league fixtures.

The greatest number scored by one player in a season is 13 (by Charlie Nicholas in 1982/83).

Up to the present no Celtic goalkeeper has scored from the penalty spot although Frank Haffey came closest. With Celtic leading Airdrie by 9-0 in 1963/64 the crowd chanted for Haffey to take a penalty kick awarded late on. The goalkeeper hit the ball well, but his shot was saved by Roddy McKenzie.

PLAYER OF THE YEAR

Celtic have been well represented in these awards presented for outstanding play:

Scottish Football Writers' Player of the Year

1965: Billy McNeill

1967: Ronnie Simpson

1969: Bobby Murdoch

1973: George Connelly

1977: Danny McGrain

1983: Charlie Nicholas

1987: Brian McClair

1988: Paul McStay

1998: Craig Burley

1999: Henrik Larsson

2002: Paul Lambert

2004: Jackie McNamara

2005: John Hartson

2007: Shunsuke Nakamura

2008: Aiden McGeady

Scottish PFA Player of the Year

1980: Davie Provan

1983: Charlie Nicholas

1987: Brian McClair

1988: Paul McStay

1991: Paul Elliott

1997: Paolo di Canio

1998: Jackie McNamara

1999: Henrik Larsson

2000: Mark Viduka

2001: Henrik Larsson

2004: Chris Sutton

2005: John Hartson (jointly with
Fernando Ricksen)

2006: Shaun Maloney

2007: Shunsuke Nakamura

2008: Aiden McGeady

Scottish PFA Young Player of the Year

1982: Charlie Nicholas

1993: Paul McStay

2006: Shaun Maloney

2008: Aiden McGeady

**English Football Writers'
Player of the Year**

1965: Bobby Collins (Leeds United)

1979: Kenny Dalglish (Liverpool)

1983: Kenny Dalglish (Liverpool)

1988: John Barnes (Liverpool)

1990: John Barnes (Liverpool)

1991: Gordon Strachan (Leeds United)

2000: Roy Keane (Manchester United)

In 1998 and again in 2004 Henrik Larsson was voted Sweden's Player of the Year by the joint vote of the Swedish FA and the daily tabloid *Aftonbladet*. Magnus Hedman received the award in 2000.

In 2003 Stiliyan Petrov was voted Bulgaria's Player of the Year, and Morten Wieghorst was Denmark's Player of the Year. In 2001 Pierre van Hooijdonk was Player of the Year in the Netherlands.

PLAYS

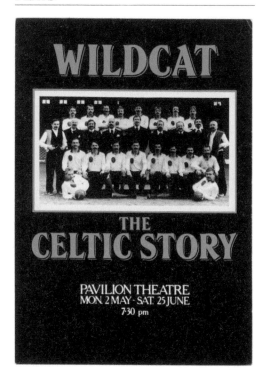

As well as inspiring a large number of books (and poetry), Celtic have been the subject of several stage plays:

Celtic FC commissioned a play to celebrate its centenary and the Wildcat Theatre Group performed *The Celtic Story* which opened at the Pavilion Theatre in Glasgow on 30 April 1988. Directed by David MacLennan, who wrote it with Dave Anderson, the highly professional production played to packed houses till 25 June.

The Lions of Lisbon was produced to celebrate the twenty-fifth anniversary of the European Cup triumph. The play, written by Willy Maley and Ian Auld (Bertie's brother), and directed by Libby McArthur, was presented by the Penny Mob Theatre Company in the Tron Theatre (and later at other venues) from 23 April to 14 June 1992

A Young Lad Named John Thomson, written by David Potter, was an entry in the Scottish Drama Association Festival of 1996 at the Buckhaven Theatre in Fife. It was presented by the Auld Kirk Players of Kirkcaldy.

At the present time Tony Roper is engaged in writing a play about the memorable events of the UEFA Cup final in Seville between Celtic and Porto in 2003.

POETRY

To Jimmy Johnstone

Wee juking, jiving, jinking Jimmy,
What endless joys yer antics gie me;
Ye twist and shuffle, shake and shimmy
Wi' feline grace,
Defenders sprachle oot behin' ye
A' ower the place.

O laddie wi' the twinkling feet,
Ye mak' defenders girn and greet;
Ye waltz aroon through rain and sleet Or
sunshine bricht. I sit and squirm here on
my seat Wi' sheer delicht.

Wee, teasing, tantalising chiel,
O shades o' Morton, James and Steel;
Wi' rasping shot and cute back heel
Or deadly flicks.
For like trump cairds in ony deal
Ye'er fu' o' tricks.

In fitba' books ye'll write yer name,
Wee weaving wizard o' the game;
Yer photo in the hall o' Fame
Will surely hing.
And Celtic fans will make the claim
Ye're soccer's king.

Henry McCracken

The Question

By devious ways where the exile strays,
In many a land afar,
Their fancy flies to the Paradise,
No matter where they are.
The Green and White, like a beacon light,
Upon their path has shone –
The question slips from Celtic lips,
'How did the Bhoys get on?'

Tho' seas divide we think with pride
Of the team we left behind;
We are faithful still, through good and ill
We bear the Celts in mind.
So memory clings in their wanderings
To lighten an exile's load –
The tramp of feet down Janefield Street
Or a vision of London Road.

Far across the surf we can see the turf
That came from the shamrock shore,
The team tripping out, the welcoming shout
We heard in days of yore.
We read with zest of Britain's best
And the mighty deeds they've done;
One thought in view when the mail comes through –
'Have the dear old Celtic won?'

From *Glasgow Observer*
(23 January 1926)
and composed by J.C.

Fireworks

up cumzthi wee man
beats three men
slingzowra crackir

an Lennux
aw yi wahntia seenim
coolizza queue cumbir

bump

rightnthi riggin
poastij stamp
a rockit

that wuzzit
that wuzthi end

finisht

Yon Night

yonwuz sum night
thi Leeds gemmit Hamdin
a hunnirn thurty four thousan
aw singin
yilnivir wok alone

wee burdnma wurk then
nutsnur a wuz
but she wuzny intristid
yi no thi wey

well there wuzza stonnin
ana wuz thaht happy
ana wuz thaht fed up
hoffa mi wuz greetnaboot Celtic
anhoffa mi wuz greetnaboot hur

big wain thata wuz
a kin laffitit noo

Crack

cuts inty thi box
croass cumzthi centre hoff
a right big animull

crack

doon goes Dalgleesh
ref waves play on
nay penahlti

so McNeill complainzty im
oot cumzthi book

tipicl
wan mair upfurthi luj

Three poems by Tom Leonard

223

POLAND

Celtic Reserves played a Polish Army XI at Parkhead on 5 October 1940. Celtic's side included Desmond White (ex QP), Joe McLaughlin, Pat McAuley and Johnny Divers. Celtic won 2-1.

Polish players who have appeared for Celtic include Artur Boruc, Majiec Zurawski, Konrad Kapler, Dariusz Wdowczyk, Dariusz Dziekanowski.

Celtic have faced Polish opposition in Europe only once – against Wisla Krakow in the 1976/77 UEFA Cup. The first match at Celtic Park was drawn 2-2, but the Poles won by 2-0 in Krakow. It is popularly believed that the Cardinal Archbishop of Krakow – who later became Pope John Paul II attended this match.

POLITICS

During the early years the principal political preoccupation of most of the club's members was the question of Home Rule for Ireland. It should be stressed that all of the organisations to which these members, directors, players and followers alike, belonged were perfectly legal and law-abiding in a manner similar to the Scottish Nationalist Party of present times

In 1892 Celtic won all the trophies available to them: the Scottish Cup, the Glasgow Cup and the Charity Cup. One member of a Celtic committee, Ned McGinn, was so delighted at the feat that he – allegedly – sent a telegram to the Vatican: WE'VE WON THE THREE CUPS, YOUR HOLINESS. Apparently, he was so incensed at not receiving a reply that it was with some difficulty that the other members of his Home Government branch of the Irish National League were able to persuade him from moving a vote of censure on the Pope.

John Glass, who might be considered the principal figure in the club's early days, was an outstanding member of various nationalist (Irish) circles: a member of the Catholic Union, the founder of the O'Connell Branch of the Irish National Foresters, and treasurer of the Home Government Branch of the United Irish League. Although he was a founding father of Celtic and the club's president from its inception until the change to a limited liability company in 1897 and a director until his death in 1906 – his obituary appeared in the political rather than the sports pages.

William McKillop, another prominent member of a Celtic committee, after starting off as a licensed grocer expanded into restaurants, including the Grosvenor in Glasgow, was also an MP, representing North Sligo for eight years and being elected for South Armagh the year before his death in 1908.

In the early 1900s the club was represented conspicuously, although informally, at various public functions related to Irish politics by several players and directors: Barney Battles, John Campbell, Sandy McMahon, and William McKillop, James Grant, Tom Colgan and James Kelly.

In June 1910 Willie Maley, Celtic's secretary-manager, spoke to the members of the United Irish League in Partick. The *Glasgow Observer* reported: 'Although the Maley family are best known by reason of their football fame, the various members

of it have always taken a keen interest in politics. Mr. Tom Maley is a constant figure on the Nationalist platforms, and Mr. Alex Maley took a prominent part some years ago in the affairs of the Pollokshaws branch of the United Irish League, while Father Charles O'Malley* of Ayr has never suffered his political sympathies to be secreted on the shady side of the bushel.'

Irish politicians took an interest in Celtic: Michael Davitt, at one time a Fenian and the founder of the National Land League, visited Celtic Park several times in his role as 'a patron of the club' to be greeted rapturously. In March 1892 he laid the first sod at the new Celtic Park, a piece of turf specially transported from Donegal and containing some shamrocks; T.D. Sullivan, an MP and composer of the anthem 'God Save Ireland' was welcomed to Celtic Park in 1892, and returned the hospitality extended to him by making a speech and singing some verses of his song to an appreciative gathering of committee men and players.

In recent times, Dr. Michael Kelly a former Lord Provost of Glasgow served some years as a Celtic director while several other former Lord Provosts have been regular visitors to Celtic Park.

The club's present Chairman, Dr. John Reid, was a Labour MP and also a cabinet minister in the government of Tony Blair; similarly, Brian Wilson, another current director, was a longtime Labour MP and spokesman for Scottish Affairs, Trade and Industry. The present Speaker of the House of Commons, Michael Martin MP is believed to be a keen Celtic supporter. Rather surprisingly, Tony Blair, while a pupil at Fettes in Edinburgh claimed to be 'the only Celtic supporter in the school'.

Billy McNeill was a candidate for the Scottish Parliament in 2003. Representing the Scottish Senior Citizens' Unity Party, he was unsuccessful in his bid to be an MSP.

* Charles O'Malley preferred to retain the Irish form of his name, unlike his brothers Tom and Willie Maley who adopted the Anglified version.

PREMIER LEAGUE SCORERS

Since the Premier League started in 1975/76 several Celtic players have reached 'the ton' by scoring more than a hundred goals. Not all of their goals, however, were scored for Celtic: Tommy Coyne, Maurice Johnston, Henrik Larsson, Brian McClair, Frank McGarvey, Charlie Nicholas. . .

PRESENTING. . .

Several luminaries have made a brief appearance on the pitch at Celtic Park for a variety of reasons.

Michael Davitt, the Irish patriot, performed the ceremonial opening of the first Celtic Park in 1892 by planting shamrocks in the centre spot.

Sgt. Willie Angus, VC, was paraded round the track at a game in 1917 to encourage spectators to enlist for the final push to end World War I.

Sean Connery was photographed with the team before a match in the late 1960s. He was believed to be a Celtic supporter at the time.

Billy Connelly opened the new Celtic

Park just before a friendly match with Newcastle United in 1995.

John Higgins, recently crowned World Snooker Champion, was presented to the crowd at halftime on the day that Celtic defeated St. Johnstone to win the league championship.

PRESS BOX

Celtic established the idea of a press-box for journalists with an admittedly primitive structure at their ground in 1894.

Celtic's Charlie Nicholas, a prolific goalscorer, reached over 100 goals in the Premier League before his transfer to Arsenal. He is shown here in action against Jim Bett of Aberdeen

PROFESSIONALISM

The two most important turning points in the history of Scottish football were the founding of the Scottish League in 1890 and the recognition of professionalism in 1893. The two landmarks were closely linked.

Scottish football was officially amateur but almost every club paid its players in one form or another – with the notable exception of Queen's Park which remained admirably amateur. The only fixtures available to clubs were in the Scottish Cup, financially hazardous at best, or in 'friendly matches'.

Clubs with an outlay in hidden wages to players required a fixture list and the Scottish League came into existence in 1890 to meet that need.

There were eleven original members but only five still survive within its framework: Celtic, Dumbarton, Heart of Midlothian, Rangers and St. Mirren. Of those clubs only Celtic and Rangers have fulfilled every league fixture at the top level since 1890.

Professionalism was inevitable after the formation of the league. John H. McLaughlin, a Celtic committee man from its earliest days and later (after 1897) a director, was one of the most forward-looking legislators in the developing Scottish game. He was a prime mover in establishing the league and in having professionalism recognised.

PROGRAMMES

Prior to World War II there were sporadic appearances of Celtic programmes. These were produced independently of the club and could not be described as 'official'. The earliest known one of this genre was for a Celtic vs Hearts league match on 10 August 1929.

On New Year's Day 1946 'the first issue of our official programme' was on sale. It was one of two issued in that style – the other for a Southern League Cup tie vs Clyde on 2 March 1946. Almost a year passed before another programme was produced for the league match against Clyde (14 December 1946). Among the comments was 'the club is pleased to issue our first official programme since the war and it will be published for every home Saturday game'. It was an eight-page production with little reading content and a white cover 'adorned' with a photograph of a player, and it was to remain the format for the next twenty-three years until 1969 when it took on a more modern appearance.

Advances in print technology led to improvements in the Celtic match-day programme – although it has to be admitted that it has seldom been rated very highly among collectors. Partly, this may have been due to the fact that some of the material expected in a programme might have already featured in the club's newspaper, *The Celtic View*.

However, Celtic's early European programmes are regarded highly by those in the know. The cover may have been stark but it was effective with the visitors' badge featured prominently – a departure from the norm for domestic fixtures.

The contrast between the amateurish programmes of the 1940s and those of the present could not be more striking: the original price was 2d going up to 3d on 11 September 1948 (for its eight pages) and remained the same until April 1969. Programmes at present cost £2.50 (for sixty-eight pages); programmes for the Champions' League matches may cost £4.00 but their format and excellent content, print and photographics make them much sought-after. www.celticprogrammesonline.com is the website that lists in detail Celtic programmes for both home and away fixtures.

Programme covers shown on these pages and overleaf are reproduced by kind permission of the Frank Glencross Collection

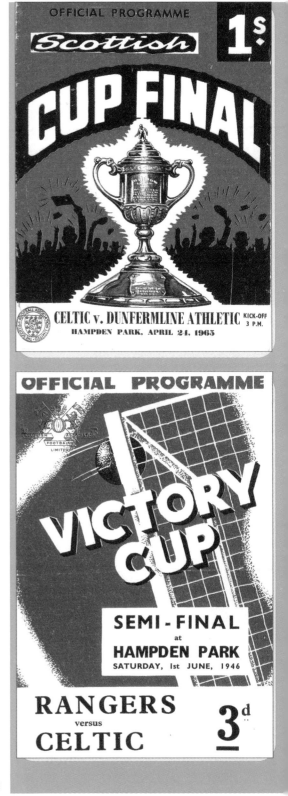

CELTIC
Official Programme

"They never die who live in the hearts
of those they leave behind"

LEAGUE CUP
Saturday, 11th Sept., 1948
Kick-off 3 p.m.

Celtic v **Hibs**

No. 4   PRICE 3d.

All proceeds from sale of this Programme will be devoted to Charity

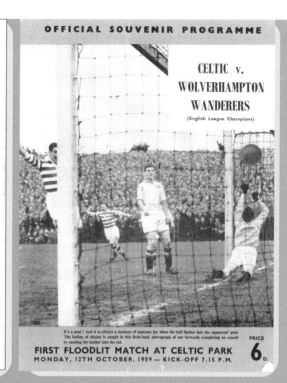

CELTIC v.
WOLVERHAMPTON
WANDERERS
(English League Champions)

It's a goal! And it is always a moment of supreme joy when the ball flashes into the opponents' goal.
The feeling of elation is caught in this flash-back photograph of our forwards completing an assault
by sending the leather into the net.

FIRST FLOODLIT MATCH AT CELTIC PARK
MONDAY, 12TH OCTOBER, 1959 — KICK-OFF 7.15 P.M.

PRICE **6**d.

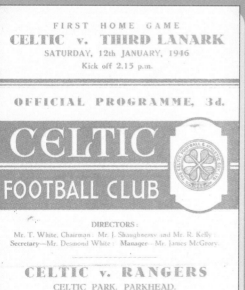

FIRST HOME GAME
CELTIC v. THIRD LANARK
SATURDAY, 12th JANUARY, 1946
Kick off 2.15 p.m.

OFFICIAL PROGRAMME, 3d.

CELTIC
FOOTBALL CLUB

DIRECTORS:
Mr. T. White, Chairman: Mr. J. Shaughnessy and Mr. R. Kelly:
Secretary—Mr. Desmond White: Manager—Mr. James McGrory.

CELTIC v. RANGERS
CELTIC PARK, PARKHEAD.
NEW YEAR'S DAY (1st JANUARY, 1946).
Kick off 2 p.m.

SATURDAY, 2nd FEBRUARY, 1946
CELTIC v. HIBERNIAN
CELTIC PARK, PARKHEAD
Kick off 2.15 p.m.

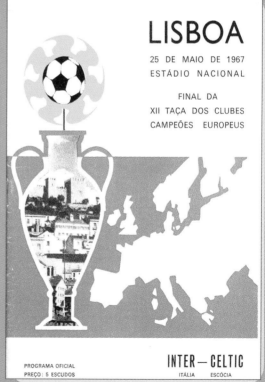

LISBOA
25 DE MAIO DE 1967
ESTÁDIO NACIONAL

FINAL DA
XII TAÇA DOS CLUBES
CAMPEÕES EUROPEUS

PROGRAMA OFICIAL
PREÇO: 5 ESCUDOS

INTER — CELTIC
ITÁLIA   ESCÓCIA

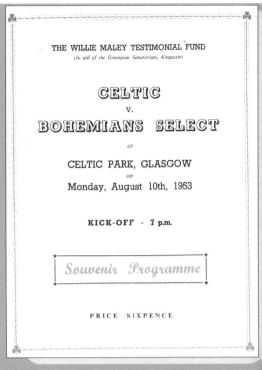

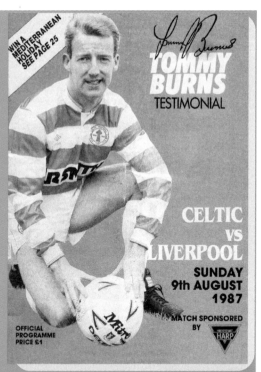

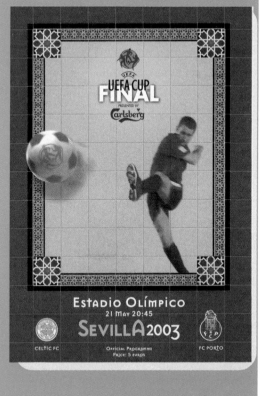

In the early seasons of organised football, protests against results were quite common. The objections were wide-ranging: adverse weather conditions, professional players, refereeing decisions and, most commonly, irregularities in the signing of players. It should be noted that protests remained common in the Junior game until after the end of World War II.

8 December 1888: Celtic – in their first season – defeated Clyde by 9-2 at Celtic Park in a Scottish Cup tie. A week previously Clyde had won the tie 1-0 but Celtic had protested on the grounds that Clyde's late arrival at the ground made visibility almost impossible in the closing stages. In the wake of Celtic's upheld protest Clyde refused to strip in the home pavilion and turned up for the fixture already prepared for action.

13 December 1890: Celtic defeated Royal Albert by 2-0 at Ibrox Park in the semi-final of the Scottish Cup. Previously, Celtic had defeated the Larkhall side 2-0 but the match had been cut short when Royal Albert's supporters invaded the pitch, causing the referee to blow for time a few minutes early.

15 December 1894/95: After a Scottish Cup tie in Edinburgh which Hibernian won 2-0 Celtic lodged a protest against Hibs' players Bobby Neil and Mick Murray. The protest was upheld and on 29 December Celtic reversed the scoreline with second-half goals by John Divers and Dan Doyle.

In an unsuccessful sequel Hibernian then protested: they claimed that Doyle's goal had been scored following the award of

Celtic's Dan Doyle, the subject of an 1894 protest from Hibernian

an indirect free-kick (and that there had been no deflection) and that Celtic's full back Charlie McEleny had been ineligible.

In those early days the clubs might agree in private prior to taking the field when playing conditions were totally unacceptable. Such matches were then played as 'friendlies' although the paying public were not informed.

This happened in several Scottish Cup finals, admittedly scheduled then for mid-winter, and it was a major cause of the riot which ensued at the end of the Old Firm cup final of 1909, the crowd thinking in part that both clubs had 'agreed' to stage another lucrative replay.

PUBS

Celtic were frequently criticised in the early days for the number of publicans associated with the club. In fact, the first directorate was described with some accuracy as consisting of 'six publicans and one Glass'.

The 'glass' in question was John Glass whose occupation was a contractor in the building trade.

It was not too surprising; some occupations and professions were effectively closed to the largely Irish and Catholic community that supported Celtic. Owning or managing a public house was the best route to financial comfort for some.

Players too were attracted to the idea, but with varying degrees of success. This has been a recurring motif throughout Celtic's (and football's) history. The following is a chronological list (partial) of Celtic stalwarts who owned, managed, or were connected with public houses:

Willie Groves: 29 Taylor St. Townhead (1890)

James Kelly: Blantyre

John H. McLaughlin: Hamilton

John Campbell: The Villa Bar 322 London Road (1907)

Sandy McMahon: The Duke's Bar 209 Great Eastern Road (1907)

Mick Dunbar: 72 Gallowgate (1910)

Dan Doyle: whisky bondsman

Davy Adams: Dunipace

Jimmy McMenemy: 209 Great Eastern Road (1910)

Donny McLeod: Lord Byron Hotel, Middlesbrough

Patsy Gallacher: Fulbar Street, Renfrew (1921)

Willie Maley: The Bank Restaurant, Queen Street

Willie McStay: Blackwood Arms, Kirkmuirhill (1930s)

Willie Miller: Willie Miller's Bar, McAslin Street and 100 Taylor Street (1951)

John McPhail: John McPhail's Bar, 208 Stevenson Street (1952)

Charlie Tully: Charlie Tully's Bar, 247 Cumberland Street and 97 Florence Street (1954)

Eric Smith: The Tartan Bar, Comelypark Street (1959)

Johnny Bonnar: Club Bar 588 Gallowgate (1974-79); The Londoner, London Road (1981-89); Spur Bar 296 Polmadie Road (1979 – 2000)

Paddy Crerand: The Jolly Friar, Altrincham

Jim Brogan: Wintergills, Great Western Road (1990s); Victoria Bar Victoria Road

Andy Lynch: Riverside Tavern, Gorbals (1980s); The Old Barns, London Road (1990)

John Fallon: Central Bar, Blantyre

Dixie Deans: Rhinestone Tavern, Baillieston (1990s); Star and Garter, Garscube Road (with Evan Williams)

Harry Hood: Angels Hotel, Uddingston (1980s to present); Sherwood Manor Hotel, Fallside Uddingston

Andy Ritchie: Vogue Bar, Rutherglen (2002 to present)

Bobby Murdoch: Sportsman's Bar, Rutherglen (1990s)

Jimmy Johnstone: The Double J, Hamilton (1960s to 1970s)

Bobby Lennox: Bobby's Bar, Saltcoats (1970s to 1990s)

John Hughes: The Great Bear Pub (1972); Springfield Tavern (2002)

Billy McNeill: Billy McNeill's Bar & Lounge, Torrisdale Street (1994)

Frank McAvennie: Macca's Bar & Lounge, Gallowgate

Tommy Gemmell: Commercial Hotel, Errol

Jock Stein: Off Licence, Springfield Road (1970)

Billy McNeill & Joe McBride: Milnrow Hotels – The Torran Yard, Irvine; The Strathaven Hotel; The Fenwick Hotel; The Barn Yard, Coatbridge

Joe McBride: The Wee Mill, Shawfield

Alfie Conn: The Captain's Rest, Maryhill Road

Evan Williams: Alexandria (1973)

Dom Sullivan: The Railway Hotel, Denny (with Tom Grant)

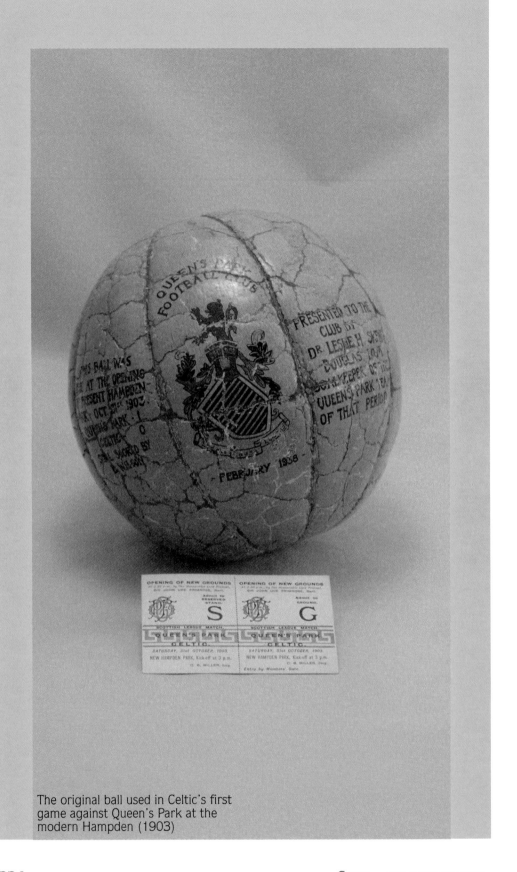

The original ball used in Celtic's first
game against Queen's Park at the
modern Hampden (1903)

Q

QUEEN'S PARK

In Celtic's first decade the most dedicated rivals were the amateur side Queen's Park. It was a rivalry based on two different philosophies: Queen's Park were vehemently opposed to the legalisation of professionalism while Celtic were its greatest advocates.

Many of their fixtures ended up in violence on and off the pitch but, after a while, some sort of peace was established and respect achieved. In fact, relations between the clubs have been very cordial, perhaps due to the fact that Celtic appeared reluctant to 'poach' any promising players from 'the Spiders' – as the skimpy list at the bottom of this column indicates.

When Queen's Park were in financial difficulties in the 1970s, and needed help in financing repairs and renovations to Hampden Park, Celtic gifted them the sum of £10,000.

Queen's Park still remain the club with the best record in the Scottish Cup outside of the Old Firm with ten triumphs – the last in 1893.

Celtic's QP Brigade includes:

Willie Black (1904/05)

John Buckley (1978 – 83)

Robert Campbell (1905/06)

Simon Donnelly (1993-99)

Jackie Jordan (1946/47)

Willie Lyon (1935-44)

Paul McLaughlin (1989-91)

Ian McWilliams (1977/78)

John O'Neill (1993-95)

Mark Smith (1986/87)

Willie Toner (1948-51)

Some others started at Queen's Park and eventually ended up at Celtic Park, such as Billy McPhail (Clyde) and Ronnie Simpson (Hibernian).

Celtic's former chairman Desmond White played for Queen's Park pre-World War II and was in goal for the Spiders when Jimmy McGrory scored his last goal for Celtic in 1937.

Celtic's record in the Scottish Cup against Queen's Park reads:

1889/90 Sep 14 H 1-2 Dowds

1891/92 Apr 9 N 5-1 Campbell (2), McMahon (2), o.g.

1892/93 Mar 11 N 1-2 Blessington

1894/95 Nov 24 H 4-1 Campbell (3), Divers

1895/96 Jan 18 H 2-4 Blessington, Doyle

1898/99 Feb 25 H 2-1 McMahon (2)

1899/1900 Apr 14 N 4-3 Divers (2), McMahon, Bell

1927/28 Mar 24 N 2-1 McGrory, McLean

1964/65 Feb 20 A 1-0 Lennox

1966/67 Mar 11 H 5-3 Wallace, Murdoch, Chalmers, Lennox, Gemmell (pen)

1985/86 Feb 15 H 2-1 McClair, Aitken

QUIZ BALL

Celtic took part in this popular TV prog-ramme three times in the late 1960s and early 70s, and valiantly upheld the reput-ation of Scottish education.

They succeeded in winning the trophy twice. The silverware remains in a display case inside Celtic Park.

Each club was allowed one 'guest' and in Celtic's case this was John Cairney, the distinguished actor and passionate Celtic supporter. The programme was taped in Manchester in thirty-minute segments and the questions were graded in order of difficulty: 4, 3, 2, 1... The '4' consisted of 'four easy questions' but all had to be answered correctly. Jim Craig, a university graduate, felt that the best method was to

go for the hardest 'Route One Question' – a strategy he employed with great success. He remembers one question: 'What is Big Bertha?' and, despite suggestions from his team-mates that it referred to Tommy Gemmell's shooting power, he answered correctly that it was a gun. Jim Craig also remembers that Willie Wallace was miffed that the judge did not agree with him that 'A Garry Owen' is a racing tipster in the *Daily Record*.

In the first 'season' (1967/68) the club was represented by this quartet: James Farrell, Billy McNeill, Willie Wallace, John Cairney. James Farrell, a lawyer, was also a Celtic director.

Unfortunately they lost 5-4 to Notting-ham Forest in the quiz equivalent of 'after extra time'.

A vital substitution (and perhaps extra training) paved the way for a triumph the following year. Jim Craig replaced his father-in-law James Farrell in the line-up and Celtic won the trophy by defeating, successively, Sunderland (3-0), West Brom-wich Albion – the holders (2-1), and Hearts (3-1).

In 1970/71 the same team was fielded and won against Manchester City (5-0), Aberdeen (4-3), and Everton (7-5) to retain the trophy.

At the risk of sounding nationalistic, we should point out that in 1969/70 and 1970/71 Celtic's stiffest competition came from Hearts and Aberdeen.

Perhaps Scottish education could derive some credit from that.

R

RADIO (AND TELEVISION)

In 1927 the Scottish Cup final between Celtic and East Fife was broadcast live over radio, the first such broadcast of a football match in Scotland. In 1955 the Scottish Cup final between Clyde and Celtic was telecast, the first such telecast in Scotland.

REFEREES

It has been suggested frequently that English referees should be imported for Old Firm matches. The idea is not new and, in fact, several English officials have taken charge of Rangers vs Celtic clashes in the past:

Mr. Kirkham (Preston) refereed the league play-off match in 1904 when the clubs finished the season level on points. Celtic won the decider, played at Hampden Park, by 2-1. The Old Firm match at Celtic Park was also refereed by an Englishman who abandoned the game because of crowd trouble and ill-discipline on the pitch.

Mr. Lewis (Blackburn) was the first English official to take an important match in Scotland when he was in charge of Celtic vs Queen's Park in the Charity Cup on 10 September 1904.

The 1904/05 season was an eventful one for referees. On 22 October, while refereeing a Scottish League match at Cathkin between Celtic and Third Lanark, Mr. Hamilton was struck in the face by a clearance from 'Sunny Jim' Young and lost five teeth. After some protests from Thirds, because of a previous decision, the linesman (Mr. Millar) was eventually accepted by the home side. Celtic won by 2-1.

The use of neutral linesmen was compulsory after 2 January 1911. Prior to that the clubs each had one linesman and disputes often arose out of their conduct and decision-making objectivity.

On 26 December 1901 the friendly match between Celtic and Bohemians in Dublin was refereed by a Mr. Farrell (IRA); it should be pointed out that IRA stood for the Irish Referees' Association.

In a Scottish Premier fixture at Ibrox Park between Rangers and Celtic the Assistant Referees were named Shearer and Davis; perhaps not too surprisingly Rangers won 3-0.

Players have to be registered with the SFA in order to play for clubs. On several highly controversial occasions Celtic have run into trouble with red tape:

Paddy Buckley was a highly sought after Junior in the late 1940s and generally considered to be Celtic's property – as the Parkhead club were virtually paying his wages until he joined them. Unfortunately, Buckley signed also for St. Johnstone and appeared to be on the books of two senior clubs simultaneously. The SFA ruled in favour of St. Johnstone despite Celtic's stronger case.

Bobby Collins was being chased by both Celtic and Everton in 1945 and travelled to Liverpool to look things over with his father. Nobody from Everton turned up to greet them on their visit and they returned home without signing. Celtic did sign him but Everton protested to the SFA. The matter took several weeks to resolve but Everton eventually withdrew and Celtic were free to sign him. Ironically, the player was transferred to Everton ten years later for some £25,000.

Jorge Cadete – the delay in getting the Portuguese striker registered cost the SFA's Jim Farry his job. The paperwork had been held up for no apparent reason and Fergus McCann stubbornly refused to accept this delay.

'A circus act!' Jock Stein, on penalty shoot-outs.

Brothers
Brogan: Frank (1960-74) and Jim (1962-75)
Devlin: James (1890-95) and John (1895)
Dolan: Frank (1890-94) and Mick (1888)
Lyon: Willie (1935-44) and Tom (1939)
Maley: Tom (1888-91) and Willie (1888-97)
Marshall: Gordon (1992-98) and Scott (1999)
McCluskey: George (1973-83) and John (1976-79)
McPhail: John (1941-56) and Billy (1956-58)
McStay: Willie (1912-1929) and Jimmy (1920-34)
McStay: Willie (1979-87) and Paul (1981-97)
Nelson: David and John (1897)
O'Donnell: Frank (1930-35) and Hugh (1932-35)

Fathers and Sons
Chalmers: Stevie (1959-71) and Paul (1979-86)
Conroy: Mike (1953-60) and Mike (1978-82)
Divers: Johnny (1932-45) and John (1956 66)
Gallacher: Patsy (1911-1926) and Willie (1937-49)
Kelly: Jimmy (1888-97) and Frank (1918)
Marshall: Gordon (1971-72) and Gordon (1992-98) and Scott Marshall (1999)
McMenemy: Jimmy (1902-1920) and John (1925-28)
McNamara: Jackie (1972-76) and Jackie (1995-2004)
Paton: Johnny (1919) and John (1942-49)

Grandfather and Grandson
Quinn; Jimmy (1901-15) and Jimmy (1964-75)

Uncles and Nephews
Patsy Gallacher (1911-26) and John Divers (1932-45)

'Jean' McFarlane (1919-29) and Willie Fagan (1934-36)

John McKnight (1920s) and Sam Hemple (1952-54)

Andy McAtee (1910-25) and Tony McAtee (1942-43

John Madden (1889-97) and Willie Malloy (1925-28)

Hugh Watson (1901-05) and James Price (1918-21)

Dr. John Fitzsimons was succeeded as Celtic's doctor by his nephew Dr. Jack Mulhearn,

RELEGATION

Up to the present time three clubs (Aberdeen, Celtic, and Rangers) have never been relegated from the top flight in Scotland since the measure was introduced at the start of the 1921/22 season. And Inverness Caledonian Thistle, a newcomer to the highest division since 2004, also have a legitimate claim.

Celtic have been involved in only one serious brush with the spectre of relegation. That came in 1947/48 when the club continued its downward spiral started throughout World War II.

The climax was Celtic's last league fixture on 17 April 1948 against fourth-placed Dundee at Dens Park – a ground where Celtic had lost 4-1 earlier in the season in the League Cup. To avoid any risk of relegation Celtic had to win or risk being overtaken by clubs with matches in hand.

Celtic: Miller, Hogg, Mallan, Evans, Corbett, McAuley, Weir, McPhail, Lavery, W. Gallacher, Paton

Celtic had made some important changes for this critical match: Bobby Evans – for the first time – was selected to start at right half, and Bobby Hogg, the veteran full back, was restored to add experience; Jock Weir, a recent signing from Blackburn Rovers, was switched to outside-right and John McPhail returned at inside right after injury. Celtic found themselves down 2-1 after sixty minutes' play, but rallied to win with a goal two minutes from the end as Jock Weir completed his hat-trick.

Some confusion has arisen over this match: it was claimed later that the Dundee players had been promised a large bonus for beating Celtic and, in direct contra-diction to this, that they had eased up in the closing stages to allow Celtic to recover. It is extremely unlikely that any club in Scotland would wish Celtic to be relegated; the financial implications alone would weigh heavily against that thinking.

In the end Celtic's rivals at the foot of the table did not gain sufficient points to overtake them, the standings ending:

	P	W	D	L	F	A	Pts
Celtic	30	10	5	15	41	56	25
Queen / South	30	10	5	15	49	74	25
Morton	30	9	6	15	47	43	24
Airdrie	30	7	7	16	40	78	21
Queen's Park	30	9	2	19	45	75	20

'I don't want to give them one thin dime!'
Fergus McCann, starting off financial negotiations with the members of the former Board.

Celtic, record holders of the Scottish Cup, have been involved in numerous replays down the years. Between 1889/90 and 1950/51 Celtic did not lose a replay in the competition; the record was snapped in 1951/52 by Third Lanark's 2-1 win after extra time at Cathkin .

Replays could have been for different reasons other than draws: abandoned games because of weather or crowd trouble, protests, or the first 'cup tie' being played as a friendly.

Aberdeen
1911/12 2-0 H (2-2)
1972/73 1-0 A (0-0)
1978/79 1-2 H (1-1)
1986/87 1-0 N (0-0, 2-2)
2007/08 0-1 H (1-1)

Airdrie
1954/55 2-0 N (2-2)
1970/71 2-0 N (3-3)
1976/77 5-0 H (1-1)

Albion Rovers
1932/33 3-1 H (1-1)

Ayr United
1976/77 3-1 A (1-1)

Carfin Shamrock
1890/91 3-1 H (2-2)

Clyde
1908/09 2-0 H (0-0)
1913/14 2-0 H (0-0)
1954/55 0-1 N (1-1)
1958/59 4-3 A (1-1)
1966/67 2-0 N (0-0)
1968/69 3-0 H (0-0)

1992/93   1-0 H (0-0)

Dundee
1903/04 5-0 H (1-1, 0-0)
1972/73 3-0 N (0-0)
1984/85 2-1 H (1-1)

Dundee United
1980/81 0-3 N (0-0)

Dunfermline Athletic
1960/61 0-2 N (0-0)
1970/71 1-0 A (1-1)
1989/90 3-0 H (0-0)
2000/01 4-1 H (2-2)

East Fife
1950/51 4-2 H (2-2)

Falkirk
1996/97 0-1 N (1-1)

Hamilton Academical
1910/11 N 2-0 (0-0)

Hearts
1901/02 2-1 H (1-1)
1932/33 2-1 N (0-0)
1938/39 H 2-1 (2-2)
1965/66   H 3-1 H (3-3)
1971/72 A 1-0 (1-1)

Hibernian
1906/07 3-0 H (0-0, 0-0)
1913/14 4-1 N (0-0)
1960/61 1-0 A (1-1)
1987/88 1-0 A (0-0)
1994/95 3-0 N (0-0)
1996/97 2-0 H (1-1)

Kilmarnock
1954/55 1-0 H (1-1)
1956/57 1-3 N (1-1)
1977/78 0-1 A (1-1)

Morton
1906/07 2-1 H (0-0, 1-1)

Motherwell
1928/29 2-1 A (0-0)
1930/31 4-2 N (2-2)
1936/37 2-1 A (4-4)
1953/54 3-1 N (2-2)
1964/65 3-0 N (2-2)
1973/74 1-0 A (2-2)
1984/85 3-0 N (1-1)
1990/91 2-4 N (0-0)

Partick Thistle
1934/35 3-1 A (1-1)
1968/69 8-1 H (3-3)

Queen's Park
1889/90 1-2 A (0-0)

Queen of the South
1926/27 4-1 H (0-0)

Rangers
1899/1900 4-0 H (2-2)
1908/09 1-1 N (2-2)
1956/57 2-0 A (4-4)
1959/60 1-4 N (1-1)
1962/63 0-3 N (1-1)
1965/66 0-1 N (0-0)
1970/71 2-1 N (1-1)

St. Mirren
1902/03 4-0 H (0-0, 1-1)
1924/25 1-0 N (0-0, 1-1)
1959/60 5-2 H (4-4, 1-1)
1979/80 3-2 A (1-1)

Stenhousemuir
1936/37 2-0 H (1-1)

Stirling Albion
1952/53 3-0 H (1-1)

Third Lanark
1888/89 1-2 N (0-3)
1949/50 4-1 H (1-1)
1951/52 1-2 A (0-0)
1961/62 4-0 N (4-4)

Celtic's record in League Cup replays is impeccable, having won all six replays or deciders:

31 October 1956 Partick Thistle N 3-0 (0-0)
18 October 1965 Hibernian N 4-0 (2-2)
13 October 1969 Ayr United N 2-1 (3-3)
7 October 1970 Dumbarton N 4-3 (0-0)
20 November 1972 Dundee N 4-1
   (After 0-1, 3-2)
29 October 1973 Motherwell H 3-2 (After
   0-1, 3-2)

In recent seasons the practice, of course, is for the tie to be decided on the night with extra time and then penalties as the decisive factor.

RESERVE TEAM

Celtic's reserve side, known initially as the Crusaders, sprang to prominence with the same impact as the senior side.

In 1890/91 they reached the final of the Second Eleven Cup and en route demolished Battlefield 10-0, Northern 9-0, St. Johnstone 12-1, Royal Albert 6-0, Morton 4-3 and Hearts 4-2. When St. Mirren took the lead early on in the final, it seemed that the bubble had burst but Celtic went on to win 13-1. Despite that impressive cup run, none of the players fully established himself as a first-team regular, rather surprisingly in that the same reserve side had played and defeated several first-elevens: Aberdeen (4-2), Ayr Parkhouse (9-0), Alloa (4-0) and Mauchline (5-0).

The chances of youngsters breaking through from the reserves into the first team were reduced when the club withdrew from the same competition in 1893/94 'in connection with the unfair treatment received in the semi-final tie with Hearts'. Whether it was justified – or merely sulking – Celtic chose to operate for many years without a back-up squad. Any criticism could be countered on the grounds that fielding a reserve side brought no financial return – an argument that was accepted while the first stringers were successful.

When the Alliance League was set up in 1919 Celtic entered a side, and one which attracted decent crowds (3,000 for a fixture against Ayr). It would be considered imperative nowadays to run a reserve side (or more than one) in order to develop fresh talent but Celtic made a fatal mistake in the 1920s by deciding to scrap their reserve side – on the grounds of economy.

On 11 April 1922 Celtic announced the folding of their Alliance League XI starting in August. By 1923 the second eleven had been disbanded, reportedly to allow the entry of newly formed Dundee Hibs (later to become Dundee United) into formal competition. Some players were later farmed out to other clubs (such as John Thomson to Ayr United and Jimmy McGrory to Kilmarnock).

The overall decision was disastrous as it handed the initiative in Scottish football to Rangers for more than a decade, as a threadbare squad of Celtic regulars played throughout complete seasons even though scarcely fit by the end. James Kelly, Celtic's first captain but now a director, lost some credibility when he insisted that Celtic 'reserves' would be better watching first-team fixtures and learning from that rather than playing in a reserve league.

Celtic did rejoin the Alliance League on 8 August 1930 and improvement was noted almost immediately in first-team performances throughout the 1930s with the annexation of the League Championship, the Scottish Cup and the prestigious Empire Exhibition Trophy of 1938. This improvement was due to such players as Malky MacDonald, Johnny Crum and John Divers building up an understanding while youngsters in that reserve side. In 1933 Celtic lost a Second Eleven cup final to Rangers in a replay – and more than 30,000 were in attendance. The next season's league championship was won with Willie Dunn scoring 45 goals. Success had returned: the Second Eleven Cup was won in 1935 and again in 1936, while the championship came to Parkhead in 1936/37 and 1937/38. In this latter season the side had to complete its last twelve fixtures inside three weeks.

Occasionally Celtic featured unusual players, partly as an inducement for curious spectators. One such was the Indian 'internationalist' Salim Bachi Khan who played barefoot although with feet wrapped heavily in bandages. His ball control and passing delighted the crowds and in particular his compatriots in the front row of the stand.

During World War II travel restrictions

A Celtic reserve side of the early 1930s. Can you spot Malcolm MacDonald, Jimmy Delaney and Johnny Crum?

meant that clubs were confined to their own locale and Celtic played in the Glasgow and District section but, after the war, competition resumed on a national basis. In 1948/49 the Scottish League set up a 'C' Division which consisted of reserve sides and included hitherto non-league clubs such as Leith and Berwick. This Division was split geographically along the traditional Highland Line and Celtic volunteered to play in the North East, possibly because they had sent teams to that location in pre-war days.

If the purpose of a reserve side was to win trophies, Celtic were singularly unsuccessful; however, they did achieve slightly more success in having back-up players in case of injury to first-team men.

It was not until the end of the 1950s that the reserve side returned to trophy-winning ways and this was primarily due to the man in charge of the side – Jock Stein. Under his guidance and inspiration – and assisted by such stalwarts as Sean

Fallon and Alec Boden – young players learned to turn their talents into titles. In the two-leg final of 1958 Celtic thrashed Rangers 8-2 on aggregate. A year later the youngsters embarked on an unbeaten run of sixteen matches starting in January to pip Rangers for the league championship – and four out of five league campaigns ended in triumph. Perhaps the so-called 'Kelly Kids' should have been called 'Stein's Starlets'.

In 1965/66, when Jock Stein was in over-all charge at Celtic Park, the reserve side managed the league and cup double – and featured several Brazilian players on extended trials, an innovation which pulled in five-figure crowds. During this season midfielder Jim Brogan scored eight times (and all from penalty kicks).

In 1967/68 striker Jimmy Quinn evoked memories of his grandfather with four hat-tricks and the role of top scorer, and a very young Kenny Dalglish made his debut.

In 1968/69 Celtic reserves won the League Cup but only after a scare in the sectional play; after a slip-up they had to beat Partick Thistle by a large score in their last sectional match and they did – by 12-0 – to qualify for the knock-out stages. In the final they defeated Aberdeen 4-0.

The 1970s was a time of emerging talent, an assembly-line of almost ready-made players for the first team: Danny McGrain, George Connelly, Kenny Dalglish, Lou Macari, Paul Wilson. . . all of whom went on to win international honours. The league was won comfortably, the side scoring 108 goals in the 1970/71 campaign (including a 7-1 win against Rangers). In the Reserve Cup the final was an Old Firm double-legged affair and Celtic won convincingly by 4-1 at Celtic Park and 6-1 at Ibrox where Kenny Dalglish scored three times. During the season the team travelled to Carlisle and took on their senior side – and won 5-2!

As an indication of how seriously Jock Stein took regular appearances for his younger players, Celtic asked to participate in the Scottish League Second Division but permission was refused.

In 1974 the reserves again won the Cup but not without anxiety: in the semi-final at Ibrox Celtic were down 4-0 at half-time, but fought back to salvage a 4-4 draw. Tommy Burns started to make his mark during that season.

In 1974/75 two Celtic players scored hat-tricks against Rangers in a 6-1 win: Jimmy Bone and Dixie Deans were the marksmen. Andy Lynch played in that match, observed how goal-scoring was done, and in the return fixture later in the season scored all four goals for Celtic in a 4-3 win

The Premier Reserve League was introduced in 1975/76 – and Celtic suffered some heavy defeats. The emphasis was not on establishing a strong second-eleven but on producing a player ready to take his place in the first team. On 8 May 1975 Celtic Reserves fulfilled two fixtures more than 147 miles apart; one squad was despatched to Ayr in the morning, and an entirely different group travelled to Aberdeen – the fixture at Ayr was won, the one at Aberdeen lost.

The new coach Frank Connor was the driving force behind a revival in the early 1980s. After a defeat to Aberdeen on 24 November 1979 the next loss sustained was not until 15 February 1982 with the League Cup won twice and youngsters such as Charlie Nicholas and Paul McStay breaking through.

In the 1980s re-organisation was the order of the day in the administration of reserve football; a Premier section and East-West sections were run but only sometimes in conjunction. At times Celtic used their youth teams, and even the 'West' description was highly misleading as Celtic had to travel to Dunfermline for fixtures. In 1983/84 both Jim Melrose and Paul Chalmers were to record hat-tricks in wins over Rangers; the double was achieved in 1984/85 with young Chalmers leading the way with 36 goals and Peter Latchford's twenty shut-outs helping considerably.

However, the names mentioned in the

last paragraph reveal the problem inherent in reserve team football: Melrose and Chalmers, despite their performances at that level, never fulfilled that promise in the first team – while Latchford was an experienced player turning out for the reserves to keep his eye in and to help the youngsters. Increasingly, the practice was for wealthier clubs to purchase ready-made players from other sides rather than to wait for them to develop within their own system. Charlie Nicholas and Paul McStay (like Dalglish and Macari before them) had little need of a lengthy apprenticeship within reserve-team football.

The 1990s again saw much reorganisation as it went from the Premier Reserve League to an Under-21 League (with the proviso that over-age players could be used). The reasons lay in changes within Scottish football. More and more foreign-born players were appearing in Scotland, squads were becoming larger, and the season longer. Senior players could be given a game or two in the reserves to try out after injuries – or if they required time to establish themselves to the peculiarities of the Scottish game. Throughout these seasons the Celtic Reserve side featured appearances by more than forty players in a single campaign; even the great Henrik Larsson made three appearances (and scored three times).

This trend has continued into the new century and Celtic have had unprecedented success. From 2001/02 they embarked on a run of seven consecutive league titles. While the primary object of a reserve side is to be the last stage in the conveyor belt towards the first team. it is satisfying to win trophies as well.

RESERVE COMPETITIONS
(WITH HONOURS)

Scottish Combination (1896/9) (1);
Scottish Alliance (1919-22 and 1930-38) (4);
Scottish Reserve League (1938/39);
Glasgow & District Reserve League (1942-45);
Scottish League C Division (1949-55);
Scottish Reserve League (1955-75) (8);
Premier Reserve League (1975 to date) (11);
Scottish Reserve League West (1980-83) and 1988/89) (3);
Scottish Reserve League Cup (12);
Second Eleven Cup (8).

RESTAURANTS

While many figures associated with Celtic owned or managed public houses, a few aspired to more up-market restaurants.

The Grosvenor, one of Glasgow's finest, was the location of Celtic's Golden Anniversary on 15 June 1938. It had been owned by John and William McKillop, Celtic shareholders and directors from the earliest days.

The Bank Restaurant was owned and operated by Willie Maley and Celtic business was often conducted there: signings and transfers, team meetings, meals and celebrations.

During the 1950s Ferrari's in West Nile Street was a favourite venue for many Celtic functions.

RIOTS

Two Old Firm Scottish Cup finals have resulted in 'riots' following the whistle.

In 1909 a replayed final ended in a draw and most of the crowd and some of the players assumed that extra time would be played but the rules of the competition expressly forbade that. The crowd of more than 60,000 were incensed to learn of this and staged a massive disturbance; they invaded the pitch, tore down the goals, set fire to the turnstiles and fought with both police and firemen. Surprisingly, the rival fans of both Celtic and Rangers were united in their anger against the authorities. The SFA withheld the trophy that season; and both Rangers and Celtic were fined and ordered to pay compensation to Queen's Park for the damage inflicted on Hampden Park.

In 1980 Celtic defeated Rangers 1-0 after extra time in a sportingly-contested cup final. At the end of the match several Celtic followers rushed on to the pitch to congratulate the winners and to celebrate. Rangers' fans invaded the pitch to stop this celebration and a full-scale riot broke out. The consequences were that both clubs were fined for the conduct of their supporters and the authorities imposed bans on drinking at or near football grounds.

RUNS

Celtic were undefeated in the Scottish League beween 20 November 1915 and 14 April 1917, an astonishing run of sixty-two matches. It began with a 2-0 win over Kilmarnock at Celtic Park on 13 November 1915 and ended with a 2-0 defeat by the same Kilmarnock also at Celtic Park.

The complete record is as follows:

P	W	D	L	F	A	Pts
62	49	13	0	162	26	111

Celtic won the Scottish League in 6 successive season from 1904/05 to 1909/10. They exceeded this with 9 consecutive titles form 1965/66 to 1973/74.

In 2007/08 Celtic won all five of their league fixtures after 'the split' – the first time any team has accomplished this, and so pipped Rangers for the title.

And talking of runs, as part of their pre-season training in the 1950s Celtic, on one occasion, ran up Ben Lomond.

Another run of success?
Bobby Evans, Sean Fallon, Bobby Collins and Hugh Fletcher on their way to the top of Ben Lomond

S

SAINTS

At one time the most common route to professional football in Scotland was via an apprenticeship in the junior ranks. Traditionally, some junior clubs were used as 'nurseries' for the seniors. Two such clubs come to mind when thinking of Celtic: St Roch's and St Anthony's.

St Roch's was a late developer in that it did not come into existence until 1920 but it made a meteoric start, the Garngad outfit winning the League, the Consolation Cup and the Victory Cup in its first season. In 1921 they achieved the pinnacle of the Junior game through winning the Scottish Cup by beating Kilwinning Rangers in the final. The star of the side was their youthful inside-right, a certain James Edward McGrory. Had they done nothing else throughout their existence, St. Roch's would have deserved eternal gratitude for unearthing and nurturing the greatest goalscorer in Celtic's history.

Other St Roch's players who went on to join Celtic include Joe Baillie, Frank and Jim Brogan, John Fitzsimons, John McMenemy, Frank Murphy, Peter Shevlin

(Opposite) Scottish Cup joy – Billy McNeill and his team celebrate the 1965 triumph

and Jackie Watters, all of whom gave sterling service at Celtic Park.

St Anthony's, whose original Moore Park was located only a stone's throw from Ibrox Park, has been a prolific farm club for Celtic. Consider some of the players who have left the Govan club and found fame at Parkhead: Hugh Brown, Mike Conroy Sr, Billy Craig, Bobby Evans, Willie Gallacher, John Gilchrist, Hugh Hilley, Matt Lynch, Malcolm MacDonald, Pat McEvoy, Jimmy McColl, Tommy McInally, Willie O'Neill. . .

Perhaps, their most memorable connection with Celtic is the fact that the Parkhead club so admired their strip back in 1902 that they appropriated the famous 'Hoops' for themselves.

SCORING (AND SAVING) STREAKS

Several Celtic players have embarked on impressive goal-scoring streaks:

Mark Viduka scored in ten successive league matches between 27 November and 5 March in season 1999/2000, netting eleven goals with three from the penalty spot;

Brian McClair scored in seven successive league fixtures in 1986/87 between 21 March and 2 May, scoring ten goals.

Harry Hood scored in six successive league matches in 1970/71 between 6 February and 27 March, netting nine goals in the process.

Bobby Lennox came to life in the closing stages of the 1967/68 season with a streak of scoring in twelve successive league matches. He started it with one goal against Kilmarnock on 2 March and ended it with two at Dunfermline on 30 April. During the run he netted twenty times.

Joe McBride netted goals in seven successive league fixtures in 1965/66 between 27 October and 11 December.

Tom Sinclair (on loan from Rangers) during a Parkhead goalkeeping crisis achieved six shutouts in his six league appearances for Celtic in 1906/07.

Carl Muggleton equalled that record in 1993/94 by posting six consecutive shutouts in league fixtures.

> 'Let the Cup go where it will as long as we reach the final.'
> Tom White 3 March 1928

SCOTTISH CUP

SCOTTISH CUP HAT-TRICKS

Record Scottish Cup holders (34 triumphs), Celtic have never won the competition three seasons in a row. In 1901 they were defeated 4-3 by Hearts at Ibrox Park to deny the Parkhead men the honour; in 1909 the Scottish Cup was withheld after a riot at Hampden Park had marred the conclusion of an Old Firm replay.

Gordon Strachan, Celtic's manager, went one better with three consecutive Scottish Cups with Aberdeen in 1982, 1983, and 1984.

SCOTTISH CUP OPPONENTS (TO END OF 2007/08)

Aberdeen
1907/08 Mar 21 A 1-0 McMenemy
1909/10 Feb 19 H 2-1 Quinn,
    McMenemy
1910/11 Mar 11 H 1-0 Quinn
1911/12 Mar 9 H 2-0 Travers (2)
1925/26 Mar 20 N 2-1 McGrory, McInally
1930/31 Feb 28 H 4-0 R Thomson (3),
    McGrory
1934/35 Mar 9 A 1-3 McGrory
1936/37 Apr 24 N 2-1 Crum, Buchan
1949/50 Feb 25 H 0-1
1950/51 Mar 10 H 3-0 J McPhail (2),
    Tully
1953/54 April 24 N 2-1 Fallon, o.g.
1966/67 Apr 29 N 2-0 Wallace (2)
1969/70 Apr 11 N 1-3 Lennox
1972/73 Mar 17 H 0-0
    Mar 21 A 1-0 McNeill
1978/79 Mar 10 A 1-1 Doyle
    Mar 14 H 1-2 Lennox
1981/82 Feb 13 A 0-1
1982/83 Apr 16 N 0-1

1983/84 May 19 N 1-2 P McStay
1986/87 Feb 1 A 2-2 McClair, McInally
  Feb 4 H 0-0
  Feb 9 N 1-0 McClair
1989/90 May 12 N 0-0 (Celtic lost 9-8 on
  penalties)
2001/02 Feb 25 A 2-0 Hartson, Petrov
2007/08 Mar 9 A 1-1;
  Mar18 H 0-1

P	W	D	L	F	A
28	13	6	9	34	25

Airdrie

1908/09 Feb 20 H 3-1 McMenemy (2),
  Hamilton
1954/55 Mar 26 N 2-2 Fernie, Walsh
  Apr 4 N 2-0 McPhail (2)
1955/56 Mar 3 H 2-1 Collins, Tully
1957/58 Feb 1 A 4-3 Byrne (2), Collins,
  Fernie
1960/61 Apr 1 N 4-0 Hughes (2),
  Chalmers, Fernie
1963/64 Feb 16 H 4-1 Chalmers, Hughes,
  Johnstone, Murdoch (pen)
1970/71 Apr 3 N 3-3 Hood (2),
  Johnstone
  Apr 7 N 2-0 Hood, Johnstone
1976/77 Jan 29 A 1-1 Doyle
  Feb 2 H 5-0 Craig (4), Glavin
1994/95 May 27 N 1-0 van Hooijdonk
1998/99 Jan 23 H 3-1 Larsson,
  O'Donnell, o.g.

P	W	D	L	F	A
14	11	3	0	39	14

Albion Rovers

1888/89 Dec 13 H 4-1 Groves, Dunbar, T
  Maley, Gallagher
1893/94 Dec 16 H 7-0 Cassidy (4),
  Madden (2), Blessington
1932/33 Mar 4 A 1-1 Napier
  Mar 8 H 3-1 Napier (2, pen), A
  Thomson

1936/37 Feb 13 A 5-2 McGrory (2),
  Buchan (2), Delaney
1958/59 Jan 31 H 4-0 Wilson (2),
  Jackson, o.g.

P	W	D	L	F	A
7	6	1	0	29	5

Alloa Athletic

1924/25 Feb 7 H 2-1 McGrory (2)
1927/28 Feb 18 H 2-0 McGrory, Connolly
1954/55 Feb 5 A 4-2 Walsh (2), Peacock,
  Haughney (pen)
2001/02 A 5-0 Balde, Wieghorst,
  Maloney, Petta, Sylla

P	W	D	L	F	A
4	4	0	0	13	3

Arbroath

1901/02 Jan 25 A 3-2 Campbell, Orr,
  Marshall
1912/13 Feb 8 H 4-0 Johnstone (2),
  Gallacher, Brown
1928/29 Feb 16 H 4-1 McGrory (4)
1929/30 Feb 1 H 5-0 McGrory(2),
  A Thomson, R Thomson, Scarff
1966/67 Jan 28 H 4-0
  Murdoch,Gemmell, Chalmers, Auld

P	W	D	L	F	A
5	5	0	0	20	3

Arthurlie

1896/97 Jan 9 A 2-4 Ferguson, McIlvenny
1897/98 Jan 8 A 7-0 McMahon (2),
  Henderson (2), Allan, Goldie.
  Campbell
1928/29 Jan 19 H 5-1 McGrory (3),
  Connolly, J McStay

P	W	D	L	F	A
3	2	1	0	14	5

Ayr United

1933/34 Feb 3 A 3-2 F O'Donnell,
  McGonagle, H O'Donnell

1955/56 Feb 18 A 3-0 Collins (2), Mochan

1976/77 Feb 27 H 1-1 Glavin

   Mar 2 A 3-1 Glavin (pen), Doyle,
   Aitken

2001/02 Mar 23 N 3-0 Thomson (2),
   Larsson

P	W	D	L	F	A
5	4	0	1	13	4

Bathgate

1927/28 Jan 21 H 3-1 McGrory, McLean,
   McInally

Berwick Rangers

1935/36 Jan 25 A (Berwick withdrew
   before fixture)

1978/79 Feb 26 H 3-0 Lynch, Burns, o.g.

1980/81 Jan 24 A 2-0 Nicholas, Burns

1983/84 Jan 28 A 4-0 McClair (2),
   McGarvey, Melrose

P	W	D	L	F	A
3	3	0	0	9	0

Bo'ness

1899/1900 Jan 13 H 7-1 Somers (2),
   McMahon (2), Divers, Bell, Orr

1905/06 Feb 10 H 3-0 McMenemy,
   Loney, Quinn

1926/27 Mar 5 A 5-2 McGrory (2),
   Thomson, McInally, McLean

P	W	D	L	F	A
3	3	0	0	15	3

Brechin City

1926/27 Feb 5 A 6-3 McGrory (4),
   McLean, A. Thomson

1949/50 Jan 28 A 3-0 Weir (2), McPhail

P	W	D	L	F	A
2	2	0	0	9	3

Burntisland Shipyard

1938/39 Jan 21 A 8-3 Crum (3),
   MacDonald (2), Watters, Delaney,
   Murphy (pen)

Carfin Shamrock

1890/91 Sept 27 H 2-2 Madden (2)

   Oct 4 A 3-1 Groves, Dowds, o.g.

P	W	D	L	F	A
2	1	1	0	5	3

Clyde

1888/89 Dec 8 H 9-2 Groves (4), T Maley
   (3), McLaren (2)

1906/07 Feb 2 H 2-1 Bennett, Hamilton

1908/09 Mar 20 H 0-0

   Mar 27 H 2-0 Quinn, Somers

1909/10 Mar 12 A 1-3 Kivlichan

1910/11 Feb 25 H 1-0 McMenemy

1911/12 Apr 6 N 2-0 Gallacher,
   McMenemy

1913/14 Feb 7 A 0-0

   Feb 10 H 2-0 Gallacher (2)

1936/37 Apr 3 N 2-0 McGrory, o.g.

1954/55 Apr 23 N 1-1 Walsh

   Apr 27 N 0-1

1955/56 Mar 24 N 2-1 Sharkey,
   Haughney (pen)

1957/58 Mar 1 H 0-2

1958/59 Feb 18 H 1-1 McVittie

   Feb 23 A 4-3 Wilson (2), McVittie,
   Auld (after extra time)

1966/67 Apr 1 N 0-0

   Apr 5 N 2-0 Lennox, Auld

1968/69 Feb 12 A 0-0

   Feb 24 H 3-0 Murdoch, Chalmers,
   Hughes

1992/93 Jan 9 A 0-0

   Jan 20 H 1-0 Coyne

2005/06 Jan 8 A 1-2 Zurawski

P	W	D	L	F	A
24	13	7	4	41	17

Clydebank

1973/74 Jan 27 H 6-1 Deans (3), Lennox
  (2), Davidson
1974/75 Feb 15 H 4-1 Dalglish (2),
  McNamara, MacDonald
1982/83 Jan 28 A 3-0 Nicholas (2),
  McCluskey
1988/89 Feb 18 H 4-1 Burns (2),
  McAvennie, Stark
1989/90 Apr 14 N 2-0 Walker (2)
1996/97 Jan 26 A 5-0 Cadete (2), Van
  Hooijdonk, MacKay, di Canio (pen)

P	W	D	L	F	A
6	6	0	0	24	3

Cowdenbeath

1947/48 Feb 7 H 3-0 McPhail (2), W
  Gallacher
1961/62 Dec 13 H 5-1 Chalmers (2),
  Jackson, Hughes, Divers

P	W	D	L	F	A
2	2	0	0	8	1

Cowlairs

1888/89 Sept 22 H 8-0 M. Dunbar(3),
  McCallum (2), T. Maley, Kelly, Groves
1891/92 Jan 23 H 4-1 Brady (2),
  Madden, McMahon

P	W	D	L	F	A
2	2	0	0	12	1

Dalbeattie Star

1933/34 Jan 20 A 6-0 Crum (4), F
  O'Donnell (2)

Dumbarton

1888/89 Jan 12 A 4-1 Groves (3),
  McCallum
1890/91 Dec 20 A 0-3
1909/10 Jan 22 A 2-1 Loney, McMenemy
1925/26 Mar 6 H 6-1 McGrory (2),
  McLean (2), A Thomson, W McStay
  (pen)

1974/75 Mar 8 A 2-1 Glavin, Wilson
1988/89 Jan 28 H 2-0 Walker, Burns

P	W	D	L	F	A
7	6	0	1	20	7

Dumfries

1904/05 Jan 28 A 2-1 Quinn, Bennett

Dundee

1894/95 Jan 19 A 0-1
1900/01 Feb 16 A 1-0 Findlay
1903/04 Feb 20 H 1-1 Hamilton
  Feb 27 A 0-0
  Mar 5 H 5-0 McMenemy (2), Bennett,
  Quinn, Muir
1905/06 Jan 27 A 2-1 Somers, o.g.
1919/20 Feb 7 A 3-1 McLean, McInally,
  Cringan
1924/25 April 11 N 2-1 Gallacher.
  McGrory
1926/27 Feb 19 A 4-2 Connolly, McLean,
  W. McStay (pen), McGrory
1946/47 Jan 25 A 1-2 McAloon
1965/66 Feb 23 A 2-0 Chalmers, McBride
1969/70 Mar 14 N 2-1 Macari, Lennox
1971/72 Feb 26 H 4-0 Lennox (2),
  Dalglish, Deans
1972/73 Apr 7 N 0-0
  Apr 11 N 3-0 Johnstone (2),Dalglish
1973/74 Apr 3 N 1-0 Johnstone
!974/75 Apr 2 N 1-0 Glavin
1976/77 Apr 6 N 2-0 Craig (2)
1977/78 Feb 6 H 7-1 McCluskey(3),
  McAdam (2), Burns, MacDonald
1984/85 Mar 9 A 1-1 Johnston
  Mar 13 H 2-1 McGarvey, Johnston

P	W	D	L	F	A
21	15	4	2	44	13

Dundee United

1930/31 Feb 4 A 3-1 Scarff (2), Napier
1948/49 Jan 22 A 3-4 J Gallacher (2), Tully
1969/70 Feb 7 H 4-0 Hughes (2), Macari, Wallace
1973/74 May 4 N 3-0 Hood, Murray, Deans
1980/81 Apr 11 N 0-0
    Apr 15 N 2-3 Nicholas (2, pen)
1984/85 May 18 N 2-1 Provan, McGarvey
1987/88 May 14 N 2-1 McAvennie (2)
1991/92 Feb 11 H 2-1 Creaney, Coyne
1995/96 Mar 10 H 2-1 van Hooijdonk, Thom
1998/99 Apr 10 N 2-0 Blinker, Viduka
2000/01 Apr 15 N 3-1 McNamara, Larsson (2, pen)

P	W	D	L	F	A
14	11	1	2	32	16

Dunfermline Athletic

1911/12 Jan 27 H 1-0 Brown
1932/33 Jan 21 A 7-1 McGrory (2), H O'Donnell (3), R Thomson
1960/61 Apr 1 N 0-0
    Apr 26 N 0-2
1964/65 Apr 24 N 3-2 Auld (2), McNeill
1965/66 Mar 26 N 2-0 Auld, Chalmers
1967/68 Jan 27 H 0-2
1970/71 Feb 13 H 1-1 Wallace
    Feb 17 A 1-0 Hood
1982/83 Feb 19 H 3-0 McGarvey (2), McCluskey
1989/90 Mar 17 A 0-0
    Mar 24 H 3-0 McStay, Coyne, Miller
1997/98 Feb 16 A 2-1 Mahe, Brattbakk
1998/99 Feb 13 H 4-0 Larsson (3), Brattbakk
2000/01 Feb 17 A 2-2 Larsson (2)
    Mar 7 H 4-1 Larsson (2, pen), Vega (2)

P	W	D	L	F	A
20	14	4	2	42	14

Duns

1950/51 Feb 10 H 4-0 J Weir (2), D Weir, Peacock

East Fife

1920/21 Feb 19 A 3-1 McInally (2), Gallacher
1922/23 Feb 10 H 2-1 Cassidy
1926/27 Apr 16 N 3-1 McLean, Connolly, o.g.
1930/31 Jan 17 A 2-1 Scarff, Napier
1936/37 Feb 27 A 3-0 McGrory (2), Buchan
1950/51 Jan 27 A 2-2 J Weir, Collins
    Jan 31 H 4-2 McPhail (2), Peacock, Collins
1972/73 Feb 3 H 4-1 Deans (2), Dalglish (2)
1983/84 Feb 18 A 6-0 Burns (2), McGarvey, Colquhoun, McClair, MacLeod

P	W	D	L	F	A
9	8	1	0	29	9

East Stirlingshire

1888/89 Dec 15 A 2-1 McCallum (2)
1911/12 Feb 10 H 3-0 Quinn (2), Travers
1928/29 Feb 2 H 3-0 McGrory (2), J McStay
1980/81 Mar 8 H 2-0 Conroy, MacLeod

P	W	D	L	F	A
4	4	0	0	10	1

Elgin City

1959/60 Mar 5 A 2-1 Divers, Smith
1966/67 Feb 18 H 7-0 Lennox (3), Wallace (2), Hughes, Chalmers

P	W	D	L	F	A
2	2	0	0	9	1

Eyemouth United
1952/53 Jan 24 A 4-0 McGrory (4)
1963/64 Jan 11 H 3-0 Chalmers (2),
  Gallagher

P	W	D	L	F	A
2	2	0	0	7	0

Falkirk
1926/27 Mar 26 N 1-0 McLean
1931/32 Jan 16 H 3-2 Napier (2),
  R Thomson
1932/33 Feb 4 H 2-0 McGrory (2)
1933/34 Feb 17 H 3-1 F O'Donnell (2),
  McGrory
1952/53 Feb 21 A 3-2 Tully, McGrory,
  Fernie
1953/54 Feb 17 A 2-1 Fernie, Higgins
1960/61 Jan 28 A 3-1 Peacock (2 pens),
  Auld
1962/63 Jan 28 A 2-0 Hughes, Gallagher
1992/93 Feb 6 A 0-2
1996/97 Apr 12 N 1-1 Johnson
  Apr 23 N 0-1

P	W	D	L	F	A
11	8	1	2	20	11

Fifth (5th) Kirkcudbright RV
1892/93 Dec 17 H 7-0 Madden (5),
  Campbell, Blessington

Forfar Athletic
1913/14 Feb 21 A 5-0 McColl (3), Dodds
  (pen), McMenemy
1989/90 Jan 20 A 2-1 Morris (pen),
  Dziekanowski
1990/91 Jan 26 A 2-0 Wdowczyk, Coyne

P	W	D	L	F	A
3	3	0	0	9	1

Forres Mechanics
1956/57 Feb 2 A 5-0 W McPhail (3),
  Higgins, Mochan

Gala Fairydean
1962/63 Mar 13 H 6-0 Murdoch (3),
  Hughes (2), Divers

Galston
1910/11 Feb 11 H 1-0 Quinn

Hamilton Academical
1910/11 Apr 8 N 0-0
  Apr 15 N 2-0 Quinn, McAteer
1921/22 Feb 25 H 1-3 Dodds
1925/26 Feb 6 H 4-0 A Thomson,
  McLean, McInally, McGrory
1953/54 Mar 13 A 2-1 Fernie, Haughney
  (pen)
1954/55 Mar 5 H 2-1 Collins, Fernie
1984/85 Jan 30 A 2-1 McGarvey (2)

P	W	D	L	F	A
7	5	1	1	13	6

Heart of Midlothian
1900/01 Apr 6 N 3-4 McOustra, Quinn,
  McMahon
1901/02 Feb 15 A 1-1 Quinn
  Feb 22 H 2-1 McMahon (2)
1905/06 Feb 24 H 1-2 McMenemy
1906/07 Apr 30 N 3-0 Young, Somers,
  Orr (pen)
1911/12 Mar 30 N 3-0 McMenemy (2),
  Brown
1912/13 Mar 8 H 0-1
1920/21 Mar 5 H 1-2 Gallacher
1925/26 Feb 20 A 4-0 McInally (2),
  McGrory, Connolly
1932/33 Mar 18 N 0-0
  Mar 22 N 2-1 McGrory, A Thomson
1938/39 Feb 18 A 2-2 Delaney,
  MacDonald
  Feb 22 H 2-1 Divers (2)
1950/51 Feb 24 A 2-1 J Weir, McPhail
1955/56 Apr 21 N 1-3 Haughney
1961/62 Feb 17 A 4-3 Divers (2),
  Chalmers, Crerand (pen)

1962/63 Mar 6 H 3-1 Murdoch,
McNamee, Hughes
1965/66 Mar 5 A 3-3 Chalmers, McBride,
Auld
Mar 9 H 3-1 Chalmers, Johnstone,
Murdoch
1971/72 Mar 18 H 1-1 Deans
Mar 27 A 1-0 Macari
1982/83 Mar 12 H 4-1 Nicholas (2),
MacLeod, McGarvey
1986/87 Feb 21 A 0-1
1987/88 Apr 9 N 2-1 McGhee, Walker
1988/89 Mar 18 H 2-1 McGhee, Aitken
(pen)
2000/01 Mar 11 H 1-0 Larsson

P	W	D	L	F	A
28	17	5	6	56	33

Hibernian
1894/95 Dec 29 A 2-0 Campbell, Divers
1901/02 Apr 26 H 0-1
1906/07 Mar 30 H 0-0
Apr 6 A 0-0
Apr 13 H 3-0 Somers, Quinn,
McMenemy
1913/14 Apr 1 N 0-0
Apr 16 N 4-1 McColl (2), Browning (2)
1922/23 Mar 31 N 1-0 Cassidy
1960/61 Mar 11 H 1-1 Chalmers
Mar 15 A 1-0 Clark
1974/75 Jan 25 A 2-0 Deans, Murray
1979/80 Apr 12 N 5-0 Lennox, Provan,
Doyle, McAdam, MacLeod
1985/86 Mar 8 A 3-4 McClair (2, pen),
McGhee
1987/88 Feb 21 H 0-0
Feb 24 A 1-0 Stark
1988/89 Apr 16 N 3-1 McCarthy,
McGhee, Walker
1994/95 Apr 7 N 0-0
Apr 11 N 3-1 Falconer, Collins,
O'Donnell

1996/97 Feb 17 A 1-1 O'Donnell
Feb 26 H 2-0 O'Donnell, di Canio
2000/01 May 26 N 3-0 Larsson (2, pen),
McNamara

P	W	D	L	F	A
22	13	7	2	41	11

Hurlford
1893/94 Nov 25 H 6-0 Campbell (2),
Blessington (2), Cassidy, McMahon
1922/23 Jan 27 H 4-0 Cassidy (4)

P	W	D	L	F	A
2	2	0	0	10	0

Inverness Caley
1929/30 Jan 18 A 6-0 McGrory (3),
Wilson, Connolly, Napier

Inverness Caledonian Thistle
1999/2000 Feb 8 H 1-3 Burchill
2002/03 Mar 23 A 0-1
2006/07 Feb 25 A 2-1 Pressley, Miller

P	W	D	L	F	A
3	1	0	2	3	5

Inverness Thistle
1984/85 Feb 16 H 6-0 P McStay (3),
Johnston, McGarvey, MacLeod

Keith
1927/28 Feb 4 A 6-1 McGrory (3),
McInally (3)

Kilmarnock
1899/1900 Feb 17 A 4-0 McMahon, Bell,
Divers, Gilhooly
1900/01 Feb 9 H 6-0 Campbell (2),
Findlay, McMahon, Divers, McOustra
1923/24 Jan 26 A 0-2
1925/26 Jan 23 A 5-0 Thomson (2),
McLean, McInally, McGrory
1930/31 Mar 14 A 3-0 Napier, Hughes,
McGrory

1937/38 Mar 5 H 1-2 MacDonald
1954/55 Feb 19 A 1-1 Smith
    Feb 23 H 1-0 Walsh
1956/57 Mar 23 N 1-1 Higgins
    Mar 27 N 1-3 Collins
1964/65 Mar 6 H 3-2 Lennox, Auld,
    Hughes
1971/72 Apr 12 N 3-1 Deans (2), Macari
1977/78 Feb 27 H 1-1 MacDonald
    Mar 6 A 0-1
1994/95 Mar 10 H 1-0 Collins (pen)
    (Played at Hampden)
2001/02 Jan 26 A 2-0 Larsson, o.g.

P	W	D	L	F	A
18	10	3	5	38	16

Kilmarnock Athletic
1891/92 Dec 19 H 3-0 Brady (2), Dowds

Leith Athletic
1908/09 Jan 23 A 4-2 Quinn (3), Hay

Linthouse
1892/93 Nov 28 H 3-1 McMahon (2),
    Madden

Livingston
2003/04 Apr 11 N 3-1 Sutton (2), Larsson
2006/07 Feb 4 A 4-1 Riordan (2), O'Dea,
Venegoor of Hesselink

P	W	D	L	F	A
2	2	0	0	7	2

Lochgelly United
1904/05 Feb 11 H 3-0 Somers, Quinn,
    Orr (pen)
1922/23 Jan 13 A 3-2 Cassidy (3)

P	W	D	L	F	A
2	2	0	0	6	2

Meadowbank Thistle
1994/95 Feb 18 H 3-0 van Hooijdonk (2),
    Falconer

Montrose
1921/22 Jan 28 H 4-0 McFarlane (2),
    McInally, McLean
1934/35 Jan 26 H 4-1 F. O'Donnell (2),
    Paterson (pen), Buchan
1938/39 Feb 4 A 7-1 Crum (3), Divers (2),
    Delaney, MacDonald
1947/48 Mar 6 H 4-0 McPhail (2),
    D. Weir, Paton
1960/61 Feb 11 H 6-0 Hughes (2),
    Chalmers (2), Byrne, og
1978/79 Jan 31 A 4-2 McCluskey (3),
    Lynch
1991/92 Jan 22 H 6-0 Creaney (3), Coyne
    (3)

P	W	D	L	F	A
7	7	0	0	35	4

Morton
1906/07 Feb 9 A 0-0
    Feb 16 H 1-1 McMenemy
    Feb 23 H 2-1 McMenemy, Hay
1930/31 Feb 14 A 4-1 McGrory (3),
    Napier
1947/48 Mar 27 N 0-1
1955/56 Feb 4 A 2-0 Tully, Collins
1961/62 Jan 27 A 3-1 Carroll, Divers,
    Jackson
1963/64 Jan 25 A 3-1 Hughes, Gallagher,
    Johnstone
1968/69 Mar 22 N 4-1 Chalmers,
    McNeill, Wallace, Johnstone
1991/92 Mar 3 H 3-0 Creaney (2), Collins
1997/98 Jan 24 H 2-0 Brattbakk, Jackson
1998/99 Mar 8 A 3-0 Viduka (2), Larsson

P	W	D	L	F	A
13	10	2	1	29	7

Motherwell

1913/14 Mar 7 A 3-1 Gallacher, McColl,
  McAtee
1922/23 Mar 10 N 2-0 Cassidy, McAtee
1927/28 Mar 3 A 2-0 McGrory, Doyle
1928/29 Mar 6 H 0-0
  Mar 13 A 2-1 McGrory, Connolly
1930/31 Apr 11 N 2-2 McGrory, o.g.
  Apr 15 N 4-2 McGrory (2),
  R Thomson (2)
1931/32 Feb 13 A 0-2
1932/33 Apr 15 N 1-0 McGrory
1936/37 Mar 17 H 4-4 Crum (2), Buchan,
  Lyon (pen)
  Mar 24 A 2-1 McGrory, Buchan
1938/39 Mar 4 A 1-3 Delaney
1947/48 Feb 21 H 1-0 Paton
1950/51 Apr 21 N 1-0 McPhail
1953/54 Mar 27 N 2-2 Mochan, Fallon
  Apr 5 N 3-1 Fernie, Mochan, o.g.
1964/65 Mar 27 N 2-2 Lennox, Auld
  (pen)
  Mar 31 N 3-0 Lennox, Chalmers,
  Hughes
1972/73 Feb 24 A 4-0 Deans (2), Dalglish,
  Lennox
1973/74 Mar 10 H 2-2 Hood (2)
  Mar 13 A 1-0 Deans
1975/75 Jan 24 A 2-3 Dalglish, Lynch
1983/84 Mar 17 A 6-0 McClair (2), Reid,
  Burns, McGarvey, MacLeod
1984/85 Apr 13 N 1-1 Burns
  Apr 17 N 3-0 Johnston, Aitken
1990/91 Apr 3 N 0-0
  Apr 9 N 2-4 Rogan, o.g.

P	W	D	L	F	A
28	15	8	5	56	32

Nithsdale Wanderers

1937/38 Feb 12 H 5-0 Murphy (3),
  Carruth (2)

Our Boys

1890/91 Nov 8 A 3-1 Crossan (2),
  Campbell

Partick Thistle

1904/05 Feb 25 H 3-0 Somers, Bennett,
  Orr (pen)
1919/20 Feb 21 H 2-0 McInally, McStay
1932/33 Feb 18 H 2-1 McGrory,
  R Thomson
1934/35 Feb 9 H 1-1 H O'Donnell
  Feb 13 A 3-1 H O'Donnell (2),
  McGrory
1959/60 Mar 12 H 2-0 Smith, Colrain
1968/69 Jan 25 A 3-3 Hughes, Wallace,
  Murdoch
  Jan 29 H 8-1 Callaghan (2), Lennox,
  Hughes, Gemmell, Johnstone,
  McNeill, Wallace
1987/88 Mar 12 A 3-0 Walker, Burns,
  Stark

P	W	D	L	F	A
9	7	2	0	27	7

Peebles Rovers

1907/08 Jan 25 H 4-0 Kivlichan (2),
  Hamilton, Somers
1912/13 Feb 22 H 3-0 McMenemy (2),
  Quinn

P	W	D	L	F	A
2	2	0	0	7	0

Port Glasgow Athletic

1898/99 Mar 11 H 4-2 Bell (2),
  McMahon, Divers
1899/1900 Jan 27 A 5-1 Campbell (2),
  Gilhooly (2), McMahon
1902/03 Feb 21 H 2-0 Campbell,
  McDermott
1908/09 Feb 6 H 4-0 Hay (2), Quinn,
  Hamilton

P	W	D	L	F	A
4	4	0	0	15	3

Queen's Park

1889/90 Sep 14 H 1-2 Dowds
1891/92 Apr 9 N 5-1 Campbell (2),
    McMahon (2), o.g.
1892/93 Mar 11 N 1-2 Blessington
1894/95 Nov 24 H 4-1 Campbell (3),
    Divers
1895/96 Jan 18 H 2-4 Blessington, Doyle
1898/99 Feb 25 H 2-1 McMahon (2)
1899/1900 Apr 14 N 4-3 Divers (2),
    McMahon, Bell
1927/28 Mar 24 N 2-1 McGrory, McLean
1964/65 Feb 20 A 1-0 Lennox
1966/67 Mar 11 H 5-3 Wallace, Murdoch,
    Chalmers, Lennox, Gemmell (pen)
1985/86 Feb 15 H 2-1 McClair, Aitken

P	W	D	L	F	A
12	8	1	3	29	19

Queen of the South

1926/27 Jan 22 A 0-0
    Jan 26 H 4-1 McGrory (2), McLean, A
    Thomson
1970/71 Jan 23 H 5-1 Hood (2), Wallace,
    Callaghan, McNeill
1976/77 Mar 13 H 5-1 Glavin (3, 2 pens),
    Craig, Dalglish
1981/82 Jan 23 H 4-0 McGarvey,
    McGrain, Halpin, G McCluskey (pen)

P	W	D	L	F	A
5	4	1	0	18	3

Raith Rovers

1907/08 Feb 22 A 3-0 McMenemy (2),
    Kivlichan
1922/23 Feb 24 H 1-0 McLean
1950/51 Mar 31 N 3-2 J. Weir, McPhail,
    Tully
1960/61 Feb 25 A 4-1 Hughes, Chalmers,
    Fernie, o.g.
1962/63 Apr 13 N 5-2 Mackay (2 pens),
    Chalmers, Divers, F Brogan

1970/71 Mar 6 H 7-1 Lennox (3),
    Davidson, Wallace, Callaghan,
    Gemmell (pen)
1979/80 Jan 26 H 2-1 Lennox, Doyle
1995/96 Feb 17 H 2-0 Donnelly, Thom

P	W	D	L	F	A
8	8	0	0	27	7

Rangers

1890/91 Sep 6 H 1-0 Groves
1891/92 Feb 6 H 5-3 Brady (2),
    Cunningham, McMahon, McCallum
1983/94 Feb 17 N 1-3 W Maley
1898/99 Apr 22 N 2-0 McMahon, Hodge
1899/1900 Feb 24 A 2-2 Campbell, Bell
    Mar 10 H 4-0 McMahon (2), Hodge,
    Bell
1900/01 Jan 12 H 1-0 o.g.
1902/03 Feb 28 H 0-3
1903/04 Apr 16 N 3-2 Quinn (3)
1904/05 Mar 25 H 0-2
1906/07 Mar 9 A 3-0 Hamilton, Hay,
    Somers
1907/08 Feb 8 A 2-1 Kivlichan (2)
1908/09 Apr 10 N 2-2 Quinn, Munro
    Apr 17 N 1-1 Quinn
1919/20 Mar 6 A 0-1
1924/25 Mar 21 N 5-0 McGrory (2),
    McLean (2), A Thomson
1927/28 Apr 14 N 0-4
1952/53 Mar 14 A 0-2
1956/57 Feb 16 H 4-4 W McPhail,
    Higgins, Collins, Fernie
    Feb 20 A 2-0 Higgins, Mochan
1958/59 Feb 28 H 2-1 Divers, McVittie
1959/60 Apr 2 N 1-1 Chalmers
    Apr 6 N 1-4 Mochan
1962/63 May 4 N 1-1 Murdoch
    May 15 N 0-3
1963/64 Mar 7 A 0-2
1965/66 Apr 23 N 0-0
    Apr 27 N 0-1

1968/69 Apr 26 N 4-0 McNeill, Lennox,
Connelly, Chalmers
1969/70 Feb 21 H 3-1 Lennox, Hay,
Johnstone
1970/71 May 8 N 1-1 Lennox
May 12 N 2-1 Macari, Hood (pen)
1972/73 May 5 N 2-3 Dalglish, Connelly
(pen)
1976/77 May 7 N 1-0 Lynch (pen)
1979/80 May 10 N 1-0 McCluskey
1988/89 May 20 N 1-0 Miller
1989/90 Feb 24 H 1-0 Coyne
1990/91 Mar 17 H 2-0 Creaney,
Wdowczyk
1991/92 Mar 31 N 0-1
1995/96 Apr 7 N 1-2 van Hooijdonk
1996/97 Mar 3 H 2-0 MacKay, di Canio
(pen)
1997/98 H 1-2 Burley
1998/99 N 0-1
2001/02 May 4 N 2-3 Hartson, Balde

P	W	D	L	F	A
46	22	8	16	70	59

Royal Albert
1890/91 Dec 13 N 2-0 Campbell, Crossan
(First match abandoned)

St. Bernard's
1888/89 Nov 3 A 4-1 Groves (2),
McCallum, T Maley
1892/93 Feb 4 H 5-0 Madden (2),
Blessington (2), McMahon
1893/94 Jan 13 H 8-1 McMahon (4),
Madden (2), Cassidy, W Maley
1898/99 Feb 4 H 3-0 McMahon, Hodge,
Campbell
1903/04 Feb 13 A 4-0 McMenemy (2),
Orr (2)

P	W	D	L	F	A
5	5	0	0	24	2

St. Johnstone
1931/32 Jan 30 A 4-2 Napier (3), A
Thomson
1935/36 Feb 8 H 1-2 Buchan
1968/69 Mar 1 H 3-2 Chalmers, Hughes,
Lennox
1985/86 Jan 25 H 2-0 Grant, Johnston

P	W	D	L	F	A
6	5	0	1	15	7

St. Mirren
1891/92 Nov 28 A 4-2 Madden,
McMahon, W Maley, o.g.
1900/01 Mar 23 H 1-0 Campbell
1901/02 Mar 22 A 3-2 Livingston,
McDermott, Campbell
1902/03 Jan 24 H 0- 0
Jan 31 A 1-1 McDermott
Feb 14 4-0 Campbell, Murray,
McMahon, Watson
1910/11 Jan 28 H 2-0 McMenemy, Hastie
1924/25 Mar 7 A 0-0
Mar 10 H 1-1 McGrory
Mar 16 N 1-0 McGrory
1925/26 Apr 10 N 0-2
1929/30 Feb 15 H 1-3 A Thomson
1933/34 Mar 3 A 0-2
1956/57 Mar 2 H 2-1 Higgins, Peacock
1958/59 Apr 4 N 0-4
1959/60 Feb 13 A 1-1 Byrne
Feb 24 H 4-4 Mochan (2), Divers (2)
Feb 29 H 5-2 Mochan (5)
1961/62 Mar 31 N 1-3 Byrne
1962/63 Mar 30 A 1-0 F Brogan
1964/65 Feb 6 A 3-0 Lennox (2),
Chalmers
1979/80 Feb 16 H 1-1 MacLeod
Feb 20 A 3-2 Doyle (2), Lennox (pen)
1983/84 Apr 14 N 2-1 McClair, P McStay
1990/91 Feb 26 H 3-0 Miller, Creaney,
o.g.
1994/95 Jan 28 H 2-0 Falconer, van
Hooijdonk

P	W	D	L	F	A
28	16	7	5	54	33

Shettleston
1888/89 Sept 1 H 5-1 Untraced

Sixth (6th) GRV
1898/99 Jan 14 A 8-1 McMahon (3),
    Hodge (2), King, Divers, Campbell

Solway Star
1924/25 Feb 21 H 2-0 McGrory, A
    Thomson

Stenhousemuir
1935/36 Jan 30 A 1-1 McGrory
    Feb 3 H 2-0 McGrory (2)

P	W	D	L	F	A
2	1	1	0	3	1

Stirling Albion
1952/53 Feb 7 A 1-1 McGrory
    Feb 11 H 3-0 McGrory (2), Peacock
1953/54 Feb 27 A 4-3 Mochan (2),
    Higgins, Haughney (pen)
1958/59 Mar 16 A 3-1 Divers, Wilson,
    Lochhead
1973/74 Feb 17 H 6-1 Hood (2),
    Murray (2), Dalglish, Wilson
1980/81 Feb 14 H 3-0 McGarvey,
    McCluskey, Burns
1957/58 Feb 15 H 7-2 Smith (2), Wilson
    (2), Byrne (2), Mochan
2007/08 Jan 12 H 3-0 Vennegoor of
    Hesselink, McDonald, Nakamura

P	W	D	L	F	A
8	7	1	0	30	8

Stranraer
1965/66 Feb 5 H 4-0 Gallagher,
    Murdoch, Lennox, McBride
1987/88 Jan 30 H 1-0 McAvennie
2000/01 Jan 28 A 4-1 Valgaeren,
    McNamara, Moravcik, o.g.

P	W	D	L	F	A
3	3	0	0	9	1

Third Lanark
1888/89 Feb 9 N 1-2 McCallum
1892/93 Jan 21 H 5-1 McMahon (3),
    Towie (2)
1893/94 Feb 3 A 5-3 McMahon (3),
    Blessington, Cassidy
1897/98 Jan 21 A 2-3 Campbell, King
1903/04 Mar 19 H 2-1 Quinn, Muir
1909/10 Feb 12 H 3-1 Quinn (3)
1913/14 Mar 28 A 2-0 McAtee, Owers
1921/22 Feb 11 A 1-0 McLean
1924/25 Jan 24 A 5-1 McGrory (4),
    Gallacher
1937/38 Jan 22 A 2-1 Crum (2)
1949/50 Feb 15 A 1-1 Weir
    Feb 20 H 4-1 J McPhail (3), Tully
1951/52 Jan 30 H 0-0
    Feb 4 A 1-2 Rollo (after extra time)
1961/62 Mar 10 H 4-4 Chalmers (2),
    Hughes, F Brogan
    Mar 14 A 4-0 Hughes (2), Chalmers,
    Byrne (played at Hampden)

P	W	D	L	F	A
16	10	3	3	42	21

Thornliebank
1901/02 Jan 11 H 3-0 Livingston(2),
    Campbell (pen)

Vale of Leven
1920/21 Feb 5 A 3-0 Cassidy (2), McLean

Wishaw Thistle
1890/91 Oct 18 A 6-2 Madden (2),
    Dowds, Campbell, Untraced

GRAND TOTAL:

P	W	D	L	F	A
512	359	71	82	1126	463

1892: Celtic 5, Queen's Park 1 Ibrox Park
(1st) 9 April
Celtic: Cullen, Reynolds, Doyle, W.
Maley, Kelly, Gallacher, McCallum,
Brady, Dowds, McMahon, Campbell.
Scorers: Campbell (2), McMahon (2),
o.g.

1899: Celtic 2, Rangers 0 Hampden Park
22 April
Celtic: McArthur, Welford, Storrier,
Battles, Marshall, King, Hodge,
Campbell, Divers, McMahon, Bell.
Scorers: McMahon, Hodge

1900: Celtic 4, Queen's Park 3 Ibrox Park
(1st)
Celtic: McArthur, Storrier, Battles,
Russell, Marshall, Orr, Hodge,
Campbell, Divers, McMahon, Bell.
Scorers: Divers (2), McMahon, Bell

1904: Celtic 3, Rangers 2 Hampden Park
Celtic: Adams, McLeod, Orr, Young,
Loney, Hay, Muir, McMenemy, Quinn,
Somers, Hamilton.
Scorer: Quinn (3)

1907: Celtic 3, Hearts 0 Hampden Park
Celtic: Adams, McLeod, Orr, Young,
McNair, Hay, Bennett, McMenemy,
Quinn, Somers, Templeton.
Scorers; Somers (2), Orr (pen)

1908: Celtic 5, St. Mirren 1 Hampden Pk
Celtic: Adams, McNair, Weir, Young,
Loney, Hay, Bennett, McMenemy,
Quinn, Somers, Hamilton.
Scorers: Bennett (2), Quinn, Somers,
Hamilton

1911: Celtic 2, Hamilton Academical 0
Ibrox Park (after 0-0 first game)
Celtic: Adams, McNair, Hay, Young,
McAteer, Dodds, McAtee, McMenemy,
Quinn, Kivlichan, Hamilton.
Scorers: Quinn, McAteer

1912: Celtic 2, Clyde 0 Ibrox Park
Celtic: Mulrooney, McNair,
Dodds,Young, Loney, Johnstone,
McAtee, Gallacher, Quinn,
McMenemy, Brown.
Scorers: McMenemy, Gallacher

1914: Celtic 4, Hibernian 1 Ibrox Park
(after 0-0 first game)
Celtic: Shaw, McNair, Dodds,Young,
Johnstone, McMaster, McAtee,
Gallacher, McColl, McMenemy,
Browning.
Scorers: McColl (2), Browning (2)

1923: Celtic 1, Hibernian 0 Hampden
Park
Celtic: Shaw, McNair, W. McStay, J.
McStay, Cringan, McFarlane, McAtee,
Gallacher, Cassidy, McLean, Connolly.
Scorer: Cassidy

1925: Celtic 2, Dundee 1 Hampden Park
75,317
Celtic: Shevlin, W. McStay, Hilley,
Wilson, J. McStay, McFarlane,
Connolly, Gallacher, McGrory, A.
Thomson, McLean.
Scorers: Gallacher, McGrory

1927: Celtic 3, East Fife 1 Hampden Park
79,500
Celtic: J. Thomson, W. McStay, Hilley,
Wilson, J. McStay, McFarlane,
Connolly, A. Thomson, McInally,
John McMenemy, McLean.
Scorers: McLean, Connolly, o.g.

1931: Celtic 4, Motherwell 2 Hampden
Park 98,579 (after 2-2 first game)
Celtic: J. Thomson, Cook,
McGonagle, Wilson, J. McStay,
Geatons, R. Thomson, A. Thomson,
McGrory, Scarff, Napier.
Scorers: McGrory (2), R. Thomson (2)

1933: Celtic 1, Motherwell 0 Hampden Park 102,339
Celtic: Kennaway, Hogg, McGonagle, Wilson, J. McStay, Geatons, R. Thomson, A. Thomson, McGrory, Napier, H. O'Donnell.
Scorer: McGrory

1937: Celtic 2, Aberdeen 1 Hampden Park 146,433 or 147,365
Celtic: Kennaway, Hogg, Morrison, Geatons, Lyon, Paterson,Delaney, Buchan, McGrory, Crum, Murphy.
Scorers: Crum, Buchan

1951: Celtic 1, Motherwell 0 Hampden Park 133,331
Celtic: Hunter, Fallon, Rollo, Evans, Boden, Baillie, Weir, Collins, J. McPhail, Peacock, Tully
Scorer: J. McPhail

1954: Celtic 2, Aberdeen 1 Hampden Park 130,060
Celtic: Bonnar, Haughney, Meechan, Evans, Stein, Peacock, Higgins, Fernie, Fallon, Tully, Mochan.
Scorers: Fallon, o.g.

1965: Celtic 3, Dunfermline 2 Hampden Park 108,806
Celtic: Fallon, Young, Gemmell, Murdoch, McNeill, Clark, Chalmers, Gallagher, Hughes, Lennox, Auld.
Scorers: Auld (2), McNeill

1967: Celtic 2, Aberdeen 0 Hampden Park 127,117
Celtic: Simpson, Craig, Gemmell, Murdoch, McNeill, Clark, Johnstone, Wallace, Chalmers, Auld, Lennox.
Scorer: Wallace (2)

1969: Celtic 4, Rangers 0 Hampden Park 132,870
Celtic: Fallon, Craig, Gemmell, Murdoch, McNeill, Brogan (Clark), Connelly, Chalmers, Wallace, Lennox, Auld.
Scorers: McNeill, Lennox, Connelly, Chalmers

1971: Celtic 2, Rangers 1 Hampden Park 103,332 (after 1-1 first game)
Celtic: Williams, Craig, Brogan, Connelly, McNeill, Hay, Johnstone, Macari, Hood (Wallace), Callaghan, Lennox.
Scorers: Macari, Hood (pen)

1972: Celtic 6, Hibernian 1 Hampden Park 106,102
Celtic: Williams, Craig, Brogan, Murdoch, McNeill, Connelly, Johnstone, Deans, Macari, Dalglish, Callaghan.
Scorers: Deans (3), Macari (2), McNeill

1974: Celtic 3, Dundee United 0 Hampden Park 75,959
Celtic: Connaghan, McGrain (Callaghan), Brogan, Murray, McNeill, P. McCluskey, Johnstone, Hood, Deans, Hay, Dalglish.
Scorers: Hood, Murray, Deans

1975: Celtic 3, Airdrie 1 Hampden Park 75,457
Celtic: Latchford, McGrain, Lynch, Murray, McNeill, P. McCluskey, Hood, Glavin, Dalglish, Lennox, Wilson.
Scorers: Wilson (2), P. McCluskey (pen)

1977: Celtic 1, Rangers 0 Hampden Park 54,252
Celtic: Latchford, McGrain, Lynch, Stanton, McDonald, Aitken, Dalglish, Edvaldsson, Craig, Wilson, Conn.
Scorer: Lynch (pen)

1980: Celtic 1, Rangers 0 (aet) Hampden
Park 70,303
Celtic: Latchford, Sneddon, McGrain,
Aitken, Conroy, MacLeod, Provan,
Doyle (Lennox), McCluskey, Burns,
McGarvey (Davidson).
Scorer: McCluskey

1985: Celtic 2, Dundee United 1
Hampden Park 60,346
Celtic: Bonner, W. McStay, McGrain,
Aitken, McAdam, MacLeod, Provan, P.
McStay (O'Leary), Johnston, Burns
(McClair), McGarvey.
Scorers: Provan, McGarvey

1988: Celtic 2, Dundee United 1
Hampden Park 74,000
Celtic: McKnight, Morris, Rogan,
Aitken, McCarthy, Whyte (Stark),
Miller, McStay, McAvennie, Walker
(McGhee), Burns.
Scorers: McAvennie (2)

1989: Celtic 1, Rangers 0 Hampden Park
72,000
Celtic: Bonner, Morris, Rogan, Aitken,
McCarthy, Whyte, Grant, McStay,
Miller, Burns, McGhee.
Scorer: Miller

1995: Celtic 1, Airdrieonians 0 Hampden
Park
Celtic: Bonner, Boyd, McKinlay, Vata,
McNally, Grant, McLaughlin,
McStay,van Hooijdonk (Falconer),
Donnelly (O'Donnell), Collins.
Scorer: van Hooijdonk

2001: Celtic 3, Hibernian 0 Hampden
Park
Celtic: Douglas, Mjallby, Valgaeren,
Vega, Thompson, Agathe, Lennon,
Lambert, Moravcik (McNamara),
Larsson, Sutton (Johnston)
Scorers: Larsson (2, pen), McNamara

2004: Celtic 3, Dunfermline Athletic 1
Hampden Park
Celtic: Marshall, McNamara, Varga,
Balde, Thompson, Petrov, Lennon,
Agathe, Pearson (Wallace), Larsson,
Sutton
Scorers: Larsson (2), Petrov

2005: Celtic 1, Dundee United 0
Hampden Park
Celtic: Douglas, Agathe, Varga, Balde,
McNamara, Petrov, Lennon,
Thompson (McGeady), Sutton,
Hartson (Valgaeren), Bellamy
Scorer: Thompson

2007: Celtic 1, Dunfermline Athletic 0
Hampden Park
Celtic: Boruc, Perrier-Doumbe,
Pressley, McManus, Naylor,
Nakamura, Lennon (Caldwell),
Hartley, McGeady, Miller (Beattie),
Vennegoor of Hesselink
Scorer: Perrier-Doumbe

SCOTTISH CUP LOSING FINALS:

1889: Celtic 1, Third Lanark 2 Hampden
Park (2nd)
1893: Celtic 1, Queen's Park 2 Ibrox Park
1894: Celtic 1, Rangers 3 Hampden Park
1928: Celtic 0, Rangers 4 Hampden Park
118,115
1955: Celtic 0, Clyde 1 Hampden Park
68,831 (after 1-1 first game)
1956: Celtic 1, Hearts 3 Hampden Park
132,840
1961: Celtic 0, Dunfermline 2 Hampden
Park 87,866 (after 0-0 first game)
1963: Celtic 0, Rangers 3 Hampden Park
120,273 (after 1-1 first game)
1966: Celtic 0, Rangers 1 Hampden Park
96,862 (after 0-0 first game)

1970: Celtic 1, Aberdeen 3 Hampden
  Park 108,434
1973: Celtic 2, Rangers 3 Hampden Park
  122,714
1984: Celtic 1, Aberdeen 2 (aet)
  Hampden Park 58,900
1990: Celtic 0, Aberdeen 0 (aet)
  Aberdeen won 9-8 on penalties
  Hampden Park 60,493
1999: Celtic 0, Rangers 1 Hampden Park
2002 Celtic 2, Rangers 3 Hampden Park

SCOTTISH CUP GOALSCORING

Only three players have scored hat-tricks in Scottish Cup finals. Two were Celtic players; Jimmy Quinn in a 3-2 win over Rangers in 1904, and Dixie Deans in a 6-1 rout of Hibernian in 1972.

Two Celtic players have netted five goals in Scottish Cup ties: John Madden on 17 December 1892 against 5th Kirkcudbright Rifle Volunteers at Celtic Park; and Neil Mochan in a 5-2 win over St. Mirren in a replayed tie at Celtic Park on 29 February 1960.

Four Celtic players have scored four goals in an away Scottish Cup tie: Jimmy McGrory against Third Lanark on 24 January 1925, Jimmy McGrory against Brechin City on 5 February 1927, Johnny Crum against Dalbeattie Star on 30 January 1934, and John McGrory against Eyemouth United on 24 January 1953.

SCOTTISH CUP PENALTY KICKS

In regular play or extra time in Scottish Cup finals only one Celtic player (Chris Sutton) has missed a penalty kick. Sutton's lapse came when he lost his footing against Dundee United and skied the ball over the bar in the closing minutes. Successful kicks were taken by the following:

Willie Orr who opened the scoring against Hearts in the 1907 final, calmly converting a controversial award in the 55th minute to start Celtic off on a 3-0 win;

Harry Hood scored from the spot against Rangers in the 1971 replay after Jimmy Johnstone had been fouled in 25 minutes;

George Connelly equalised in 54 minutes against Rangers in 1973 but the Ibrox men recovered to win 3-2;

Pat McCluskey scored Celtic's third goal from the spot in a 3-1 win over Airdrieonians in 1975;

Andy Lynch kept his nerve to convert a penalty kick awarded controversially by Mr. R. Valentine in 21 minutes and protested furiously by Rangers players in 1977 as Celtic went on to win by 1-0.

In 2001 shortly after the interval Henrik Larsson scored Celtic's second goal from the penalty spot against Hibernian in a 3-0 win.

SCOTTISH LEAGUE CUP

In 1939, at the start of World War II, the SFA decided to dispense with the Scottish Cup for the duration of hostilities and James Bowie, Rangers' chairman, suggested the League Cup as an alternative.

The competition – inaugurated as the Southern League Cup in 1941 – had an interesting format: clubs were drawn, cup-tie style out of a hat, but into mini-leagues of four clubs, and each would play the others home and away; each section would be decided on points, or goal-average, and the winners would advance to a knock-out stage. This meant that the participating clubs would be guaranteed six matches, an important financial consideration in the 1940s and a format that was retained in the post-war period when crowds, starved of football, packed the grounds.

Celtic's history in the competition has been a mixed one.

It was surprisingly poor initially considering the club's reputation as cup-fighters. There may have been some excuse throughout the wartime seasons but afterwards it was a clear indication of Celtic's chronic unreadiness for the schedule, as the competition was usually staged in the earlier part of the season. Noted for physical fitness, Celtic were too often astonishingly slow to gain match readiness and suffered accordingly. Another reason was that the luck of the draw frequently decreed they would be in the same section as a very strong Rangers side, famed for its Iron Curtain defence.

Celtic had to wait until 1956/57 before winning the trophy – a feat already accomplished by Rangers, East Fife, Motherwell, Dundee, Hearts, and Aberdeen. After a replay against Partick Thistle, Celtic won 3-0. Celtic had been drawn in a formidable section which included Rangers, Aberdeen and East Fife, and for the first time edged out the Ibrox club in the sectional play.

One year later, on October 19, 1957, the Old Firm met in the final at Hampden Park before a crowd of 82,293. It was surely the most astonishing result in the tourn-

ament's history – a resounding 7-1 triumph for Celtic – an event which has entered the folklore of the club and its supporters.

CELTIC LEAGUE-CUP WINNERS

1956/57
Celtic 0, Partick Thistle 0 (aet) (58,973)
Celtic 3, Partick Thistle 0 (31,126)
Celtic: Beattie, Haughney, Fallon, Evans, Jack, Peacock, Tully, Collins, McPhail, Fernie, Mochan.
Scorers: McPhail (2), Mochan

1957/58
Celtic 7, Rangers 1 (82,293)
Celtic: Beattie, Donnelly, Fallon, Fernie, Evans, Peacock, Tully, Collins, McPhail, Wilson, Mochan.
Scorers: McPhail (3), Mochan (2), Wilson, Fernie (pen).

1965/66
Celtic 2, Rangers 1 (107,609)
Celtic: Simpson, Young, Gemmell, Murdoch, McNeill, Clark, Johnstone, Gallagher, McBride, Lennox, Hughes
Scorer: Hughes (2 pens)

1966/67
Celtic 1, Rangers 0 (94,532)
Celtic: Simpson, Gemmell, O'Neill, Murdoch, McNeill, Clark, Johnstone, Lennox, McBride, Auld, Hughes (Chalmers).
Scorer: Lennox

1967/68
Celtic 5, Dundee 3 (66,660)
Celtic: Simpson, Craig, Gemmell, Murdoch, McNeill, Clark, Chalmers, Lennox, Wallace, Auld (O'Neill), Hughes.
Scorers: Chalmers (2), Lennox, Hughes, Wallace

1968/69
Celtic 6, Hibernian 2 (72,240)
Celtic: Fallon, Craig, Gemmell (Clark), Murdoch, McNeill, Brogan, Johnstone, Wallace, Chalmers, Auld, Lennox.
Scorers: Lennox (3), Craig, Auld, Wallace

1969/70
Celtic 1, St. Johnstone 0 (73,067)
Celtic: Fallon, Craig, Hay, Murdoch, McNeill, Brogan, Callaghan, Hood, Hughes, Chalmers (Johnstone), Auld.
Scorer: Auld

1974/75
Celtic 6, Hibernian 3 (53,848)
Celtic: Hunter, McGrain, Brogan, Murray, McNeill, McCluskey, Johnstone, Dalglish, Deans, Hood, Wilson.
Scorers: Deans (3), Johnstone, Murray, Wilson

1982/83
Celtic 2, Rangers 1 (55,372)
Celtic: Bonner, McGrain, Sinclair, Aitken, McAdam, MacLeod, Provan, McStay (Reid), McGarvey, Burns, Nicholas.
Scorers: Nicholas, MacLeod.

1997/98
Celtic 3, Dundee United 0 (49,305) (Ibrox)
Celtic: Gould, Boyd, Mahe (Annoni), McNamara, Rieper, Stubbs, Larsson, Burley,Thom (Lambert), (Donnelly), Wieghorst, Blinker.
Scorers: Rieper, Larsson, Burley

1999/2000
Celtic 2, Aberdeen 0 (50,073)
Celtic: Gould, Boyd, Riseth, Mjallby, Mahe, McNamara, Wieghorst, Petrov, Moravcik, Johnston, Viduka.
Scorers: Riseth, Johnston

2000/01
Celtic 3, Kilmarnock 0 (48,830)
Celtic: Gould, Mjallby, Vega, Valgaeren, Petta (Crainey), Moravcik, Lennon, Lambert, Healy, Sutton, Larsson.
Scorer: Larsson (3)

2005/06
Celtic 3, Dunfermline Athletic 0 (50,090)
Celtic: Boruc, Telfer, Balde, McManus, Wallace, Nakamura, Keane (Dublin), Lennon, Maloney, Zurawski, Petrov.
Scorers: Zurawski, Maloney, Dublin.

LEAGUE CUP SCORING FEATS:

Steve Chalmers scored five times against East Fife at Parkhead on 16 September 1964, Celtic's 6-0 win cancelling a 0-2 loss in the first leg;

Bobby Lennox scored five goals against Partick Thistle at Firhill on 31 August 1968 in a 6-1 win;

Steve Chalmers and Bobby Lennox each scored five goals in a 10-0 rout against Hamilton Academical at Celtic Park on 11 September 1968;

Sammy Wilson scored four goals against Cowdenbeath at Central Park on 17 September 1958 in an 8-1 victory;

Joe McBride netted four against St. Mirren at Celtic Park on 20 August 1966, as did Willie Wallace in a 4-0 win over Partick Thistle on 17 August 1968;

Charlie Nicholas scored four times against Dunfermline Athletic at East End Park in a 7-1 win on 28 August 1982;

Shaun Maloney also scored four times against Stirling Albion on 6 November 2001;

Joe McBride and John Hughes scored hat-tricks against Raith Rovers in another 8-1 win at Starks Park in 1965, as did Frank McAvennie and Andy Payton in a 9-1 win over Arbroath at Gayfield on 25 August 1993;

Four Celtic players have scored hat-tricks in League Cup finals:
Billy McPhail (1957),
Bobby Lennox 1969),
Dixie Deans (1974),
Henrik Larsson (2001)

LEAGUE CUP OPPONENTS

Aberdeen:
1948/49
Aug 17 A 5-4 Haughney (3), Collins, J. McPhail
Aug 31 H 1-3 Haughney

1953/54
Aug 8 H 0-1
Aug 22 A 2-5 Walsh, Mochan

1956/57
Aug 11 A 2-1 Fernie, Higgins
Aug 25 H 3-2 Collins, Tully, Fernie

1967/68
Aug 19 H 3-1 Lennox, Gemmell (p), Auld
Sep 2 A 5-1 McMahon, Johnstone, Auld, Craig, Gemmell (pen)

1969/70
Sep 10 A 0-0
Sep 24 H 2-1 Lennox, Wallace

1972/73
Nov 27 N 3-2 Hood, Johnstone, Callaghan

1973/74
Oct 31 A 3-2 Dalglish (2), McCluskey
Dec 21 H 0-0

1975/76
Aug 9 H 1-0 Dalglish
Aug 27 A 2-0 Lennox, Ritchie

1976/77
6 Nov N 1-2 Dalglish (pen)

1979/80
Oct 31 A 2-3 Edvaldsson, Provan
Nov 24 H 0-1

1983/84
Feb 28, A 0-0
Mar 10, H 1-0 Reid (pen)

1986/87
Sep 3 A 1-1 Johnston (Celtic win on penalties)

1987/88
Sep 1 A 0-1

1989/90
Sep 20 N 0-1

1992/93
Sep 23 N 0-1

1994/95
Oct 26 N 1-0 O'Neil

1999/2000
Mar 19, 00 N 2-0 Riseth, Johnson

P	W	D	L	F	A
26	13	4	9	40	33

Airdrie:
1951/52
15 Aug A 1-1 Peacock
29 Aug H 2-0 Walsh, Heron

1953/54
    15 Aug A 1-2 Walsh (pen)
    29 Aug H 2-0 Walsh, J McPhail

1957/58
    10 Aug H 3-2 B McPhail, Mochan,
    Peacock
    24 Aug A 2-1 Smith, Fernie

1958/59
    13 Aug H 3-3 Auld, Conway, Collins
    27 Aug A 2-1 Peacock, Conway

1959/60
    15 Aug A 2-4 Carroll, o.g.
    29 Aug H 2-2 Divers, Auld (pen)

1966/67
    17 Oct N 2-0 Murdoch, McBride

1969/70
    9 Aug H 6-1 Hughes (2), Wallace,
    Connelly, Hood, Gemmell
    23 Aug A 3-0 Wallace, Lennox,
    McNeill

1974/75
    9 Oct N 1-0 Murray

1983/84
    31 Aug A 6-1 McGarvey, MacLeod
    (pen), Provan, Whittaker, McStay, o.g.
    9 Nov H 0-0

1984/85
    29 Aug A 4-0 Burns, McInally, Grant,
    McClair

1986/87
    20 Aug H 2-0 McClair (2)

1991/92
    3 Sep A 0-0 (lost on penalties)

1993/94
    31 Aug H 1-0 McAvennie

1998/99
    19 Aug A 0-1

P	W	D	L	F	A
20	12	5	3	43	19

Albion Rovers:
1976/77
    22 Oct A 1-0 Callaghan
    6 Nov H 5-0 Dalglish (3, pen), Doyle
    (2)

P	W	D	L	F	A
2	2	0	0	6	0

Alloa Athletic:
1982/83
    18 Aug A 5-0 McCluskey, McGrain,
    McStay, Burns, Reid (pen)
    25 Aug H 4-1 Nicholas, MacLeod,
    Aitken, Burns

1996/97
    4 Oct N 5-1 Cadete (3), Thom, van
    Hooijdonk (pen)

P	W	D	L	F	A
3	3	0	0	14	2

Arbroath:
1972/73
    19 Aug A 5-0 Dalglish (2), Deans (2),
    Murdoch (pen)
    8 Aug N 3-3 Hood, Dalglish, o.g.

1973/74
    11 Aug H 2-1 Lennox, Lynch
    29 Aug A 3-1 Dalglish, Lennox,
    Wilson

1976/77
    21 Aug A 5-0 Dalglish, Glavin,
    McGrain, Wilson, Edvaldsson
    28 Aug H 2-1 Doyle, Wilson

1982/83

21 Aug A 3-0 McCluskey, Nicholas, Crainie

1 Sep H 4-1 MacLeod, McCluskey, Nicholas, Dobbin

1993/94

25 Aug A 9-1 McAvennie (3), Payton (3), Nicholas, McGinlay, McNally

P	W	D	L	F	A
9	8	1	0	36	8

Ayr United:

1967/68

13 Sep H 6-2 Lennox (2), Johnstone (2), Murdoch, McMahon

27 Sep A 2-0 Brogan, Wallace

1969/70

8 Oct N 3-3 Hughes, Auld, Gemmell (pen) (aet)

13 Oct N 2-1 Hood, Chalmers

1971/72

21 Aug A 3-0 Hughes, Hay, Dalglish

30 Aug H 4-1 Lennox, Macari, Dalglish, Hay

1974/75

14 Aug A 2-3 Murray, Connelly

21 Aug H 5-2 Johnstone (2), Wilson (2), Lennox

1988/89

17 Aug H 4-1 Walker (2), McAvennie, Burns

1990/91

22 Aug H 4-0 Elliott (2), Djiekanovski (2)

1994/95

16 Aug A 1-0 Grant

1995/96

19 Aug A 3-0 Thom, van Hooijdonk, Collins (pen)

1999/2000

13 Oct A 4-0 Viduka, Blinker, Mjallby, Petta

P	W	D	L	F	A
13	11	1	1	43	13

Berwick Rangers:

1997/98 9 Aug N 7-0 Donnelly (2), Jackson, Larsson, Blinker, Wieghorst, Thom

Brechin City:

1983/84

24 Aug A 1-0 Melrose

27 Aug H 0-0

1985/86

28 Aug H 7-0 Johnston (2), McStay, McInally, Provan, Burns, Aitken (pen)

P	W	D	L	F	A
3	2	1	0	8	0

Clyde:

1948/49

18 Sep A 2-0 J. Gallagher, W. Gallacher

9 Oct H 3-6 J. Gallagher (3)

1956/57

6 Oct N 2-0 B McPhail (2)

1957/58

28 Sep N 4-2 Wilson, B McPhail, Collins, Fernie

1958/59

9 Aug A 4-1 Tully, Collins, Wilson, Auld

23 Aug H 2-0 Wilson, Auld

1966/67
17 Aug H 6-0 McBride (3, pen),
Lennox, Auld, Chalmers
31 Aug A 3-1 McBride (2, pen),
Gemmell

1968/69
9 Oct N 1-0 Connelly

1970/71
12 Aug H 5-3 Lennox (3), Johnstone (2)
19 Aug A 2-0 Gemmell (2 pens)

1996/97
14 Aug A 3-1 Cadete (2), Thom

P	W	D	L	F	A
12	11	0	1	37	14

Clydebank:
1971/72
8 Oct A 5-0 Macari (2), Hood,
Callaghan, Wallace
22 Oct H 6-2 Hood (3), Macari (2),
o.g.

P	W	D	L	F	A
2	2	0	0	11	2

Cowdenbeath:
1958/59
10 Oct H 2-0 Collins, Auld
17 Oct A 8-1 Wilson (4), Colrain (2),
Auld, o.g.

P	W	D	L	F	A
2	2	0	0	10	1

Dumbarton:
1970/71
7 Oct N 0-0 (aet)
12 Oct N 4-3 Lennox (2), Wallace,
Macari (aet)

1975/76
16 Aug H 3-1 Edvaldsson, Wilson,
Lennox
23 Aug A 8-0 Hood (2), Dalglish (2),
Wilson (2), McGrain, Callaghan

1977/78
18 Aug H 18 Aug H 3-0 Dalglish (2 pens), Doyle
25 Aug A 3-3 Wilson, MacDonald,
Doyle

1986/87
28 Aug H 3-0 Johnston (2), McStay

1987/88
26 Aug A 5-1 Stark (2), Walker, Burns,
McGhee

1989/90
15 Aug A 3-0 McStay, Dziekanowski,
Burns

P	W	D	L	F	A
9	7	2	0	32	8

Dundee:
1947/48
16 Aug H 1-1 Paton
6 Sep A 1-4 Bogan

1954/55
18 Aug A 1-3 Mochan
1 Sep H 0-1

1962/63
15 Aug A 0-1
29 Aug H 3-0 Hughes (2), Gallagher

1965/66
21 Aug H 0-2
4 Sep A 3-1 Divers, Hughes, McBride

1967/68
28 Oct N 5-3 Chalmers (2), Hughes,
Lennox, Wallace

1970/71
9 Sep A 2-2 Johnstone (2)
23 Sep H 5-1 Macari (2), Hughes, Hood, Wilson

1972/73
11 Oct A 0-1
1 Nov H 3-2 Macari (2), Lennox (aet)
20 Nov N 4-1 Deans (2), Hood, Dalglish

1973/74
15 Dec N 0-1

1978/79
16 Aug H 3-1 McAdam (2), Glavin
23 Aug A 3-0 Doyle (2), Conn

1992/93
19 Aug H 1-0 Payton

1994/95
31 Aug A 2-1 Collins, Walker

1999/2000
1 Dec H 1-0 Wieghorst

2007/08
26 Sep A 2-1 McDonald, Vennegoor of Hesselink

P	W	D	L	F	A
21	12	2	7	40	27

Dundee United:

1962/63
18 Aug H 4-0 Hughes (2), Gallagher, Crerand (pen)
1 Sep A 0-0

1965/66
14 Aug A 1-2 Auld
28 Aug H 3-0 Chalmers, McBride, Young (pen)

1967/68
12 Aug H 1-0 Johnstone
26 Aug A 1-0 Lennox

1970/71
15 Aug H 2-2 Callaghan, Lennox
26 Aug A 2-2 Hay, Macari

1974/75
17 Aug H 1-0 McNamara
24 Aug A 1-0 Wilson

1976/77
14 Aug A 1-0 Dalglish
1 Sep H 1-1 MacDonald

1978/79
30 Aug A 3-2 Lynch, MacDonald, Conroy
2 Sep H 1-0 Glavin (pen)

1980/81
12 Dec A 1-1 Nicholas
19 Dec H 0-3

1982/83
27 Oct H 2-0 McGarvey, Nicholas (pen)
10 Nov A 1-2 Nicholas

1984/85
4 Sep A 1-2 McInally

1988/89
31 Sep A 0-2

1990/91
25 Sep N 2-0 Creaney, McStay

1994/95
21 Sep H 1-0 Collins

1997/98
30 Nov N 3-0 Rieper, Larsson, Burley

P	W	D	L	F	A
24	14	5	5	36	19

Dunfermline Athletic:

1956/57
12 Sep H 6-0 Mochan (2), B McPhail (2), Collins, o.g.
15 Sep A 0-3

1966/67
14 Sep H 6-3 Auld (2), McNeill, Hughes, Johnstone, McBride (pen)
21 Sep A 3-1 Chalmers (2), McNeill

1982/83
14 Aug H 6-0 McCluskey (2), Provan (2), McGarvey, Reid (pen)
28 Aug A 7-1 Nicholas (4, pen), McCluskey, Burns, o.g.

1984/85
22 Aug A 3-2 McClair (2), McInally

1997/98 14 Oct N 1-0 Burley

2005/06 19 Mar N 3-0 Zurawski, Maloney, Dublin

P	W	D	L	F	A
9	8	0	1	35	10

East Fife:

1950/51
12 Aug H 2-0 Peacock, J McPhail
26 Aug A 1-1 J McPhail

1953/54
12 Aug A 1-1 Peacock
26 Aug H 0-1

1956/57
18 Aug H 2-1 Fernie, B McPhail
1 Sep A 1-0 B McPhail

1957/58
14 Aug A 4-1 B McPhail (3), Collins
28 Aug H 6-1 B McPhail (2), Wilson (2), Auld, Collins

1964/65
9 Sep A 0-2
16 Sep H 6-0 Chalmers (5), Kennedy

1972/73
16 Aug H 1-1 Dalglish
23 Aug A 3-2 Dalglish (2), Lennox

P	W	D	L	F	A
12	7	3	2	27	11

Falkirk:

1954/55
14 Aug H 3-0 Fallon (2), Higgins
28 Aug A 2-2 Fernie, Haughney (pen)

1955/56
20 Aug H 5-1 Collins (2), Tully, Fernie, Mochan
3 Sep A 1-1 Mochan

1973/74
15 Aug A 2-0 Hay, Lennox (pen)
22 Aug H 2-1 Lennox (2, pen)

1979/80
29 Aug A 2-1 McCluskey, Provan
1 Sep H 4-1 Conroy (2), Lennox, Doyle

2004/05
21 Sep H 8-1 Wallace (3), Balde, Sylla, McManus, Lambert, McGeady

2005/06
21 Sep H 2-1 Hartson Zurawski

2006/07
7 Nov H 1-1 Zurawski (lost on penalties)

P	W	D	L	F	A
11	8	3	0	32	10

Forfar Athletic:

1951/52
15 Sep H 4-1 Peacock, Collins, Baillie, Walsh
19 Sep A 1-1 Peacock

1987/88
19 Aug H 3-1 Walker (2), Stark

P	W	D	L	F	A
3	2	1	0	8	3

Hamilton Academical:

1946/47
   5 Oct A 2-2 Kiernan (2)
   26 Oct H 3-1 Kiernan (2), Rae

1968/69
   11 Sep H 10-0 Chalmers (5), Lennox (5)
   25 Sep A 4-2 McBride (2), McMahon, Clark

1974/75
   11 Sep H 2-0 Hood (2)
   25 Sep A 4-2 Deans, McNamara, Lennox, Callaghan (pen)

1980/81
   22 Sep A 3-1 Doyle, Nicholas, Burns
   24 Sep H 4-1 McGarvey (2), Nicholas, Burns

1988/89 24 Aug H 7-2 Walker (2), McAvennie (2),Stark, Burns, Archdeacon

1990/91
   29 Aug A 1-0 Dziekanowski

P	W	D	L	F	A
10	9	1	0	40	11

Hearts:

1954/55
   21 Aug H 1-2 Higgins
   4 Sep A 2-3 Tully, Collins

1962/63
   11 Aug H 3-1 Murdoch, Gallagher, Hughes
   25 Aug A 2-3 Murdoch, Hughes

1964/65
   12 Aug A 3-0 Murdoch (2, pen), Chalmers
   26 Aug H 6-1 Murdoch (3, 2pens), Gallagher (2), Kennedy

1966/67
   13 Aug A 2-0 McBride (2, pen)
   27 Aug H 3-0 McBride (2, pen), Chalmers

1970/71
   8 Aug A 2-1 Hughes, Johnstone
   22 Aug H 4-2 Hughes (2), Macari, Connelly

1975/76
   13 Aug A 0-2
   20 Aug H 3-1 Glavin, Lynch, Edvaldsson

1976/77
   25 Oct N 2-1 Dalglish (2, pen)

1977/78
   1 Mar N 2-0 Craig, McCluskey

1989/90
   30 Sep A 2-2 Dziekanowski, Walker (Celtic won on penalties)

1992/93
   26 Aug A 2-1 Payton, Creaney

1996/97
   17 Sep A 0-1

2000/01
   1 Nov A 5-2 McNamara, Healy, Smith, Moravcik, Crainey (aet)

2007/08
   31 Oct H 0-2

P	W	D	L	F	A
18	12	0	6	42	23

Hibernian:

1946/47
   21 Sep A 2-4 Bogan, W. Gallacher
   12 Oct H 1-1 McAloon

1948/49
   11 Sep H 1-0 Weir
   2 Oct A 2-4 J. Gallagher (2)

1952/53
16 Aug H 1-0 J. McPhail
30 Aug A 0-3

1957/58
17 Aug A 1-3 Collins
31 Aug H 2-0 Wilson, B. McPhail

1961/62
19 Aug A 2-2 Hughes, Chalmers
3 Sep H 2-1 Divers (2)

1965/66
4 Oct N 2-2 McBride, Lennox (aet)
18 Oct N 4-0 McBride, Hughes,
Lennox, Murdoch

1968/69
5 Apr 69 N 6-2 Lennox (3), Wallace,
Auld, Craig

1972/73
9 Dec N 1-2 Dalglish

1974/75
26 0ct N 6-3 Deans (3), Johnstone,
Wilson, Murray

1981/82
15 Aug H 4-1 MacLeod (2), Nicholas
(2)
26 Aug A 4-1 McGarvey (2), Sullivan,
MacLeod

1983/84
7 Sep H 5-1 Reid (2, pen), Melrose,
McGarvey, McStay
26 Oct A 0-0

1985/86
4 Sep A 4-4 Johnston (2), Provan,
Aitken (Celtic lost on penalties)

2003/04
18 Dec A 1-2 Varga

P	W	D	L	F	A
21	10	5	6	51	36

Inverness Caledonian Thistle

2002/03
23 Oct H 4-2 Hartson (2), Thompson,
Maloney

Kilmarnock:
1963/64
14 Aug A 0-0
28 Aug H 2-0 Divers, Gallagher

1964/65
15 Aug H 4-1 Gallagher (2),
Chalmers, Johnstone
29 Aug A 0-2

1983/84
5 Oct H 1-1 MacLeod (pen)
30 Nov A 1-0 Melrose

1999/2000
16 Feb 2000 N 1-0 Moravcik

2000/01
18 Mar N 3-0 Larsson (3)

P	W	D	L	F	A
8	5	2	1	12	4

Livingston:
2001/02
19 Dec A 2-0 Balde, Hartson

Montrose:
1978/79
8 Nov A 1-1 Lynch (pen)
15 Nov H 3-1 McAdam, Edvaldsson,
Lynch (pen)

P	W	D	L	F	A
2	1	1	0	4	2

Morton:
1951/52
18 Aug H 2-0 Evans, Heron
1 Sep A 0-2

1964/65

29 Sep N 2-0 Lennox, Gallagher

1967/68

11 Oct N 7-1 Hughes (2), Craig (2), Johnstone, Wallace, Lennox

1968/69

14 Aug H 4-1 Wallace, Hughes, Murdoch, Gemmell (pen)
28 Aug A 3-0 Wallace, Lennox, Hughes

1971/72

18 Aug A 1-0 Lennox
25 Aug H 0-1

1991/92

21 Aug A 4-2 Nicholas (2), Creaney (2)

P	W	D	L	F	A
9	7	0	2	23	7

Motherwell:

1950/51

16 Sep H 1-4 J. McPhail
20 Sep A 1-0 J. McPhail

1965/66

18 Aug H 1-0 Divers
1 Sep A 3-2 Lennox (2), Hughes (pen)

1973/74

12 Sep A 2-1 Hood, Murray
10 Oct H 0-1 (aet)
29 Oct H 3-2 Murray, Deans, Johnstone

1974/75

10 Aug H 2-1 Dalglish, Wilson
28 Aug A 2-2 Dalglish (2)

1977/78

31 Aug H 0-0
3 Sep A 4-2 Wilson, Burns, Craig, o.g.

1978/79

4 Oct H 0-1
11 Oct A 4-1 McAdam (2), Lennox, Aitken

1986/87

23 Sep N 2-2 McClair, Aitken (aet, Celtic win on penalties)

1997/98

10 Sep H 1-0 Larsson

2005/06

1 Feb N 2-1 Zurawski, Maloney

P	W	D	L	F	A
16	10	3	3	28	10

Partick Thistle:

1952/53

13 Aug H 2-5 Tully, McDonald
27 Aug A 1-0 Peacock

1956/57

27 Oct N 0-0
31 Oct N 3-0 B McPhail (2), Collins

1958/59

1 Oct N 1-2 Conway

1959/60

12 Aug H 1-2 Mochan (pen)
26 Aug A 2-0 Jackson (2)

1960/61

17 Aug A 1-1 Carroll
31 Aug H 1-2 Hughes

1961/62

12 Aug A 3-2 Jackson (2), Hughes
26 Aug H 3-2 Hughes (2), Carroll

1964/65

8 Aug H 0-0
22 Aug A 5-1 Chalmers (3), Gallagher, Johnstone

1968/69
    17 Aug H 4-0 Wallace (4)
    31 Aug A 6-1 Lennox (5), o.g.

1971/72
    23 Oct N 1-4 Dalglish

1975/76
    6 Oct N 1-0 Edvaldsson

1980/81
    8 Oct A 1-0 Nicholas (pen)
    20 Oct H 2-1 Burns, MacDonald (aet)

1982/83
    8 Sep H 4-0 Provan, Nicholas,
    MacLeod, McGarvey
    22 Sep A 3-0 Nicholas (2), MacLeod

2002/03 6 Nov H 1-1 Lambert (aet,
    Celtic win on penalties)

2003/04 4 Dec A 2-0 Beattie, Smith

P	W	D	L	F	A
23	14	4	5	45	24

Queen of South:
1955/56
    13 Aug H 4-2 Mochan, Walsh, Collins,
    Fernie
    17 Aug A 2-0 Walsh, o.g.

1963/64
    17 Aug H 1-1 F. Brogan
    31 Aug A 3-2 Chalmers (2), Gallagher

1985/86
    21 Aug A 4-1 Johnston (2), McClair,
    McInally

1989/90
    22 Aug H 2-0 Grant, Dziekanowski

1990/91
    5 Sep H 2-1 Dziekanowski, Miller

P	W	D	L	F	A
7	6	1	0	18	7

Raith Rovers:
1950/51
    19 Aug H 2-1 J McPhail (2)
    2 Sep A 2-2 Collins, Peacock

1959/60
    8 Aug A 1-2 Mackle
    22 Aug H 1-0 o.g.

1965/66
    15 Sep A 8-1 McBride (3), Hughes (3,
    pen), Lennox, Johnstone
    22 Sep H 4-0 Auld (2), Murdoch,
    Chalmers

1969/70
    16 Aug H 5-0 Wallace (2), Hood,
    McNeill, Hughes
    27 Aug A 5-2 Chalmers (2), Hood (2),
    Brogan

1991/92
    27 Aug H 3-1 Miller, Creaney, Fulton

1994/95
    19 Oct N 2-2 Walker, Nicholas (aet,
    Celtic lost on penalties)

1995/96
    31 Aug H 2-1 van Hooijdonk,
    Donnelly (aet)

2001/02
    5 Sep H 4-0 Johnson (2), Sutton,
    Thompson (pen)

P	W	D	L	F	A
12	9	2	1	39	12

Rangers:
1947/48
    9 Aug A 0-2
    1 Sep H 2-0 J. Gallagher, Paton

1948/49
    25 Sep H 3-1 J. Gallagher,
    W. Gallacher, J. Weir

16 Oct A 1-2 J McPhail (pen)

1949/50
13 Aug H 3-2 J McPhail (2, pen),
Haughney
27 Aug A 0-2

1951/52
13 Oct N 0-3

1955/56
27 Aug A 4-1 Smith (2), J McPhail,
Mochan
31 Aug H 0-4

1956/57
15 Aug H 2-1 Collins, Tully
29 Aug A 0-0

1957/58
19 Oct N 7-1 B McPhail (3),
Mochan (2), Wilson, Fernie (pen)

1960/61
20 Aug A 3-2 Carroll, Divers, Hughes
3 Sep H 1-2 Chalmers

1963/64
10 Aug H 0-3
24 Aug A 0-3

1964/65
24 Oct N 1-2 Johnstone

1965/66
23 Oct N 2-1 Hughes (2 pens)

1966/67
29 Oct N 1-0 Lennox

1967/68
16 Aug A 1-1 Gemmell (pen)
30 Aug H 3-1 Wallace, Murdoch,
Lennox

1968/69
10 Aug A 2-0 Wallace (2)
24 Aug H 1-0 Wallace

1969/70
13 Aug A 1-2 Hood
20 Aug H 1-0 Gemmell

1970/71
24 Oct N 0-1

1971/72
14 Aug A 2-0 Johnstone, Dalglish (pen)
28 Aug H 3-0 Dalglish, Callaghan,
Lennox

1973/74
18 Aug A 2-1 Lennox, Hood
25 Aug H 1-3 Lennox
5 Dec N 3-1 Hood (3)

1975/76
25 Oct N 0-1

1977/78
18 Mar 1978 N 1-2 Edvaldsson (aet)

1978/79
13 Dec N 2-3 Doyle, McAdam (aet)

1982/83
4 Dec N 2-1 Nicholas, MacLeod

1983/84
25 Mar 1984 N 2-3 McClair, Reid
(pen) (aet)

1986/87
26 Oct N 1-2 McClair

1990/91
28 Oct N 1-2 Elliott (aet)

1993/94
22 Sep A 0-1

1995/96
19 Sep H 0-1

2000/01
7 Feb 2001 N 3-1 Larsson (2, pen),
Sutton

2001/02

    5 Feb 2002 N 1-2 Balde (aet)

2002/03

    16 Mar N 1-2 Larsson

2004/05

    10 Nov A 1-2 Hartson

2005/06

    9 Nov 05 H 2-0 Maloney, o.g.

P	W	D	L	F	A
45	20	2	23	67	65

St. Johnstone:

1961/62

    16 Aug H 0-1

    30 Aug A 0-2

1969/70

    25 Oct N 1-0 Auld

1981/82

    12 Aug A 0-2

    19 Aug H 4-1 Provan (2), McGarvey, Nicholas

1997/98

    19 Aug A 1-0 Donnelly (pen) (aet)

P	W	D	L	F	A
6	3	0	3	6	6

St. Mirren:

1949/50

    17 Aug A 0-1

    3 Sep H 4-1 Haughney, Tully, J McPhail, McAuley

1952/53

    9 Aug A 1-0 McDonald

    25 Aug H 3-1 J McPhail, Peacock, Fernie

1958/59

    16 Aug H 3-0 Collins, Conway, Tully

    30 Aug A 3-6 Collins (2 pens), Auld

1966/67

    20 Aug H 8-2 McBride (4, pen), Lennox (2), Auld, Chalmers

    3 Sep A 1-0 Murdoch

1971/72

    6 Oct N 3-0 Hay, Hood, Lennox

1977/78

    9 Nov A 3-1 Craig (2), Edvaldsson

    16 Nov H 2-0 Wilson, Doyle

1981/82

    8 Aug H 1-3 McGarvey

    22 Aug A 5-1 McCluskey (3), MacLeod (2)

2006/07

9 Sep H 2-0 Beattie, Zurawski

P	W	D	L	F	A
14	11	0	3	39	16

Stenhousmuir

1975/76

    10 Sep A 2-0 Lennox, Dalglish

    24 Sep H 1-0 Lynch

P	W	D	L	F	A
2	2	0	0	3	0

Stirling Albion:

1972/73

    12 Aug A 3-0 Macari (2), Dalglish

    26 Aug H 3-0 Dalglish, Deans, Murdoch (pen)

1977/78

    5 Oct A 2-1 Doyle, Aitken

    26 Oct H 1-1 o.g.

1979/80

    26 Sep A 2-1 McAdam, Doyle

    10 Oct H 2-0 Doyle, MacLeod (pen)

1980/81

    27 Aug A 0-1

31 Aug H 6-1 Burns (2), Nicholas (2), Sullivan, Provan (aet)

1992/93
12 Aug N 3-0 3-0 Creaney (2), Coyne

1993/94
10 Aug A 2-0 McGinlay, McAvennie

2001/02
6 Nov H 8-0 Maloney (4), Hartson (2), Tebily, Healy

P	W	D	L	F	A
11	9	1	1	32	5

Stranraer:
1972/73
20 Sep A 2-1 Davidson, Lennox
4 Oct H 5-2 Lennox (2), Deans, Davidson, Murdoch (pen)

P	W	D	L	F	A
2	2	0	0	7	3

Third Lanark:
1946/47
28 Sep H 0-0
19 Oct N 3-2 Kiernan (2, pen), Bogan

1947/48
23 Aug H 3-1 J. Gallagher (2), R. Quinn
13 Sep N 2-3 Gallagher, o.g.

1950/51
16 Aug A 2-1 Collins, Fernie
30 Aug H 3-1 J McPhail (2 pens), Collins

1951/52
11 Aug H 1-1 Fallon
25 Aug A 1-0 Walsh

1957/58
11 Sep H 6-1 B McPhail (2), Collins (2), Wilson, Auld

14 Sep A 3-0 Collins, B McPhail, Wilson

1960/61
13 Aug H 2-0 Hughes, Mochan
27 Aug A 3-1 Hughes (2), Divers

P	W	D	L	F	A
12	9	2	1	29	11

GRAND TOTAL:

P	W	D	L	F	A
402	266	52	84	956	434

Celtic have never met the following clubs in the competition to date:

Airdrie United

East Stirling

Elgin City

Gretna

Peterhead

Queen's Park

Ross County

SCOTLAND'S CAPTAINS

The following (in chronological order) have captained Scotland while they were Celtic players:

Jimmy McLaren

James Kelly

Dan Doyle

David Storrier

Harry Marshall

Johnny Campbell

Jimmy Hay

Alec McNair

Willie Cringan

Willie McStay

'Peter' McGonagle

Bobby Evans

Billy McNeill

Kenny Dalglish

Danny McGrain

Roy Aitken

Paul McStay

Tom Boyd

Paul Lambert

Stephen McManus.

SEASONS IN THE SUN

Some Celtic strikers have enjoyed exceptional league campaigns, some more than once:

Jimmy McGrory: 1935/36 – 50 goals; 1926/27 – 49; 1927/28 – 47;

Henrik Larsson: 2003/04 – 35; 2001/02 – 30;

Brian McClair: 1986/87 – 35;

Jimmy McColl: 1915/16 – 35;

Bobby Lennox: 1967/67 – 32;

Joe McBride: 1965/66 – 31 (despite playing only half of the season)

'SELTIC'

An often-asked question is answered in this letter to *The Celt* fanzine (August 1997):

> When the club was founded the words 'Celt' and 'Celtic' would have been pronounced with a soft 'c', in accordance with the almost invariable rule that 'c' is soft when followed by 'e' or 'i'. The First World War scholars were maintaining that the initial consonant should be hard, and for many years the Oxford Dictionary gave the alternative spellings 'Kelt' and 'Keltic'. The new pronunciation caught on, but not the new spelling. A Celtic bronze axe or 'celt' still retains the soft 'c'.

Now you know.

SHAMROCKS

Michael Davitt, an Irish patriot and founder of the National Land League, was invited more than once to Celtic Park and was given rapturous welcomes by the spectators. In March 1892 he laid the first sod at the new ground – a bit of Donegal turf with shamrocks. Shortly afterwards the actual turf was stolen, an action which provoked an outbreak of poetry condemning the unknown thief:

> Again I say, May Heaven blight
>   that envious, soulless knave;
> May all his sunshine be like night
>   and the sod rest heavy on his grave.

John Thomson, Celtic's outstanding young goalkeeper, died in Glasgow's Victoria Infirmary several hours after he sustained head injuries in an accidental clash with Rangers' centre forward Sam English on 5 September 1931. A memorial inside Celtic Park remains to this day and it features a shamrock motif.

In the 1950s and 60s a frequently used change strip was the reverse of Hibernians: a white jersey with green sleeves and a large shamrock on the breast. It is a strip remembered with affection.

The Shamrock could claim to be Celtic's first fanzine. It was produced in the early

1960s by the Shamrock Celtic Supporters' Club (Edinburgh), was sold by vendors outside Celtic Park for sixpence (2.5p). It was frowned upon by the club for its sentiments: bitterly anti-Board, ferociously anti-Rangers and SFA, and with sympathies for the IRA.

SHARING THE GOALS

Sometimes, in a high-scoring game, several players share the scoring. The following are the authenticated matches in which six (or more) players have scored:

13 August 1938 Kilmarnock H SL 9-1 (Delaney (2), Divers (2), Lyon (p), Crum (p), Geatons, MacDonald, Murphy);

29 January 1969 Partick Thistle H SC 8-1 (Callaghan (2), Lennox, Hughes, Gemmell, Johnstone, McNeill, Wallace);

16 September 1970 Kokkola H EC 9-0 (Hood (3), Wilson (2), Hughes, McNeill, Johnstone, Davidson);

4 September 1971 Clyde H SL 9-1 (Lennox (3), Macari (2), McNeill, Callaghan, Murdoch, Dalglish);

1 October 1975 Valur Reykjavik H ECWC 7-0 (Hood (2), Edvaldsson, Dalglish, McCluskey P., Deans, Callaghan);

28 August 1985 Brechin City H LC 7-0 (Johnstone (2), Aitken (p), McInally, Burns, McStay P., Provan);

9 August 1997 Berwick Rangers N LC 7-0 (Donnelly (2), Wieghorst, Larsson, Jackson, Thom, Blinker);

11 December 1999 Aberdeen A SPL 6-0 (Viduka, Moravcik, Mahe, Lambert, Blinker, Wright);*

19 September 2002 FK Suduva H UEFAC 8-1 (Larsson (3), Valgaeren, Petrov, Sutton, Lambert, Hartson);*

*In these games Celtic's goals were scored by players born in six different countries.

SHOCKS

A league match provides an upset; a cup tie a shock. Celtic have always been a power in Scottish football and, accordingly, all the shocks listed below were defeats for Celtic.

9 January 1897
Arthurlie 4, Celtic 2
Celtic's defeat ranks as one of the shocks thrown up by the Scottish Cup as short-handed Celtic never get to grips with the pitch and their opponents. A year later Celtic crush Arthurlie 7-0 on the same ground;

23 October 1971
Celtic 1, Partick Thistle 4
Heavily-favoured Celtic are swept aside by a rampant Thistle in the first half of the League Cup final;

27 November 1994
Celtic 2, Raith Rovers 2
Celtic lose on penalty kicks after extra time to lower-division Rovers in the League Cup final;

23 April 1997
Celtic 0, Falkirk 1
On a rain-swept Ibrox Park, Falkirk hang on gallantly to win this Scottish Cup semi-final replay;

8 February 2000
Celtic 1, Inverness Caledonian Thistle 3
The underdogs fully merit their 3-1 win as Celtic are disorganised on and off the pitch;

23 March 2003
Inverness Caledonian Thistle 1, Celtic 0
Only days after eliminating Liverpool
from the UEFA Cup Celtic crash to
Inverness Caledonian Thistle again;

8 January 2006
Clyde 2, Celtic 1
Part-time Clyde spoil Roy Keane's Celtic
debut, and should have won by more in
this Scottish Cup tie.

SHORTEST LEAGUE SEASON

Surely the shortest league campaign of all
was that of 1939/40 – a schedule curtailed
by Britain's entry into World War II on 3
September 1939.

This was the season which never
finished, at least not in its original format.

The first traditional trial match took
place on 4 August 1939 and consisted of
the Hoops versus the Greens. It attracted
a crowd of almost 10,000 to see these sides:

Hoops: Kennaway, Hogg, Kelly, Geatons,
Lyon, Paterson, Anderson, Watters,
Crum, Ouchterlonie, Birrell.

Greens: Trialist, Davitt, Doyle, Lynch,
Thomson, McLaughlin, Campbell,
Shields, Carruth, Miller, Kelly.

The second trial was held on 7 August
and the Hoops, with a stronger lineup
(Kennaway, Hogg, Morrison, Geatons,
Lyon, Paterson, Anderson, MacDonald,
Crum, Divers, Murphy) ran out winners by
6-0.

The opening league fixture was at
Pittodrie on 12 August 1939, a venue where
Celtic had last won back in 1925. After

Johnny Crum had equalised Aberdeen
scored two second-half goals to win
comfortably by 3-1. Press reports indicated
that 'Celtic were not the force of old and
appeared to be ill-balanced.' This was
surprising because, with the exception of
Anderson for Delaney, this was the Celtic
side which had won the Empire Exhibition
Trophy in 1938.

A week later Matt Lynch came in for
Oliver Anderson on the right wing, and
Celtic defeated Hearts 2-0 at Celtic Park.
Surprisingly, the return league fixture
against Aberdeen was scheduled for 23
August and Aberdeen again won by 3-1,
with Celtic fielding an unchanged side. On
26 August Celtic travelled to Cowdenbeath
and Lynch moved to his more regular right-
half berth and Anderson returned on the
right wing. Celtic were coasting with a two-
goal lead until Cowdenbeath scored in 85
minutes to provide a nervous conclusion
to the match.

For this match Celtic introduced
Johnny Kelly (Arthurlie) at inside right.
Kelly was a highly promising Junior but his
Celtic career was short. He was transferred
to Morton during the war and eventually
moved south to Barnsley where he became
a legendary winger – in fact, he earned
international recognition for Scotland –
and turned out for Celtic in an Old Crocks
charity match in 1969 at the age of 48!

The day after Hitler's armies invaded
Poland, Celtic played Clyde at Parkhead
and, amid a funereal atmosphere, ran out
1-0 winners. Hugh (Teddy) O'Neill came
in at centre-half and another John Kelly
made his debut at left back; the latter was
the captain of Scotland's Junior side.

Only twenty-four hours later (on 3 September 1939) Britain declared war on Germany and on 5 September all mass entertainment – including league football – was suspended. The government fear was that gatherings of large crowds could provide targets for the Luftwaffe.

Later in the month football resumed in Scotland on a regional basis and, with most players being eligible for service in the armed forces, the war-time seasons were considered 'unofficial'.

Celtic's complete record in this campaign consisted of five (5) league games;

12 August 1939 Aberdeen A 1-3 Crum

19 August Hearts H 2-0 Lyon, Divers

23 August Aberdeen H 1-3 Murphy (pen)

26 August Cowdenbeath A 2-1 Lynch, Crum

2 September Clyde H 1-0 Divers

Ever-presents throughout the campaign were Joe Kennaway, Bobby Hogg, Chic Geatons, Johnny Crum, John Divers, Frank Murphy.

SHUT OUTS

Charlie Shaw (1913/14–1924/25) leads the way with 227 shutouts. As he played in 421 matches his percentage is impressive. Shaw holds the record for consecutive shutouts by a Celtic goalkeeper. Between 20 December 1913 and 21 February 1914 he recorded thirteen. Earlier in the same season he had played nine successive league matches without conceding a goal (from 29 September 1913 to 13 December). In fact, between 20 September 1913 and 18 April 1914, Celtic with Charlie Shaw as keeper, played 36 matches in the League and Scottish Cup and gave up only six goals, losing only one of those fixtures.

Davy Adams' record (1903/04–1911/12) was also impressive with 105 shutouts from 247 appearances.

Of modern goalkeepers Pat Bonner comes closest to Shaw with 172.

An honourable mention should go to Tom Sinclair (on loan from Rangers!) who achieved six consecutive league shutouts in 1906/07 in his six appearances for Celtic – a 100% record. Carl Muggleton (1993/94) matched this run with six consecutive shutouts within his twelve-appearance Celtic career.

Leaders:

Charlie Shaw: 227

Pat Bonner: 172

Davie Adams: 100

Joe Kennaway: 75

John Thomson: 57

Ronnie Simpson: 54

Artur Boruc: 52

Peter Latchford: 50

SNOW

In Celtic's first season (1888-1889) the major competition was the Scottish Cup and the new club astonished everybody by fighting its way through to the final in which they faced the redoubtable Third Lanark. The match was scheduled for Ibrox Park on 2 February 1889 but the conditions underfoot and overhead were deplorable; the pitch was bone-hard and icy, and a snow storm broke out an hour before the kickoff. Both sides agreed that the match would be unofficial and played as a friendly match. However, the spectators who had paid a high admission charge were not informed and assumed that Third Lanark had won the Cup Final by a 3-0 margin. The match was 'replayed' on 9 February and this time Thirds won 2-1. The first match went down in history as 'the Snow Final'.

Astonishingly, history almost repeated itself in February 1950 when the same clubs were due to meet at Cathkin Park in the Scottish Cup. Snow had been falling for at least an hour before the kickoff, but the decision was made – after some 19,000 had been admitted to the ground – that the match would be conducted as a friendly. Several hundred spectators walked on to the pitch to stop the game after one minute's farcical play. Only after the crowd started to throw snowballs at the old Cathkin pavilion was it announced that refunds would be offered – but at Celtic Park in midweek. For the record, Celtic (and Third Lanark) had to pay out more than the original takings at the turnstiles.

The first leg of the European Cup semi-final at the San Siro against Inter Milan on 5th April 1972 was played to a 0-0 draw in a snowstorm.

SOUTH AMERICAN OPPOSITION

Celtic faced a touring Chile-Peru Select on 4 October 1933 at Celtic Park and an estimated 10,000 spectators turned up to see the unusual visitors.

Celtic: Wallace, Hogg, Morrison, Wilson, McStay, Hughes, Crum, Buchan, Dunn, F. O'Donnell, H. O'Donnell.

The O'Donnell brothers had a good night: in 10 minutes Hugh delivered an inch-perfect cross for Frank to score with a strong header; in 30 minutes Hugh himself scored with a firm shot. After the interval (in 49 minutes) Morrison failed from penalty spot, with the goalkeeper saving both his effort and follow-up shot. In 52 minutes the Chile-Peru Select scored with a fierce shot from long range. The match was played in a most sporting manner. The visitors had substitutes waiting on the touchline throughout but none was required.

Celtic played Atlas of Mexico in their 1966 tour of the United States and won 1-0 through Charlie Gallagher's goal near the end.

On a New World tour in 1968 Celtic, badly affected by the high altitude, played Necaxa in the Aztec Stadium in Mexico City on 4 June losing 3-2.

Celtic played Cruzeiro (Brazil) at Celtic Park in the club's Centenary Match in 1988 and won 4-2.

In the World Club Championship of 1967 Celtic faced the Racing Club (Buenos Aires) in three ferociously contested matches. Celtic won 1-0 in Glasgow, lost 2-1 in Buenos Aires, and by 1-0 in a playoff game in Montevideo, Uruguay.

Celtic played the newly-crowned South American champions Boca Juniors, at the Cleveland Browns stadium in 2003. This marked the first occasion that a sport other than American football has been played there. A crowd of 20,842 saw Celtic beat the Argentinean side 1-0 in a contest where both sides struggled to gain any fluency. Chris Sutton's goal in 60 minutes decided the outcome, but the most prominent feature of the 'friendly' was the card-happy performance of the referee [a local official named Ricardo Valenzuela]. He cautioned six Boca players, and sent off one for a further offence, and booked three Celtic players.

In July 2005 Rangers and Celtic renewed a sponsorship deal with Coors Brewers/ Carling, an arrangement believed to be worth £9m to each club over the five years

Celtic were forced to remove the name of their sponsors (Carling) from their jerseys on 10 December 2003 because of a French government ban on advertising alcohol products on television. Celtic lost the Champions' League fixture with Olympique Lyonnais by 3-2.

SPONSORSHIP

Celtic's long-time chairman Bob Kelly was a traditionalist who resisted efforts by the authorities to put numbers on Celtic jerseys as he was convinced that such a development 'would ruin the appearance of the most famous strip in football.' Not surprisingly, he was equally reluctant to disfigure the Celtic strips further by allowing commercial logos. Accordingly, Celtic were relatively late in cashing in on such forms of sponsorship.

Celtic's first sponsors were C.R. Smith. In 1984 the Dunfermline-based company, best known for its double-glazing, sponsored both Rangers and Celtic believing that it was unwise for a commercial business to be involved with only one Old Firm club.

From 1999 to 2003 NTL, the cable television company also sponsored both Celtic and Rangers.

Charlie Shaw
– Celtic's shut-out king

☆ ☆ ☆ ☆ ☆ ☆ ☆ ☆ ☆ ☆ ☆ ☆ ☆ ☆

GOALKEEPERS

Davie Adams: Goalkeeper from 1903 to 1912. An outstanding keeper, Adams, a solidly-built six-footer, was a regular in the Celtic side that won six championships in a row (1905-1910). He was so highly regarded by Celtic's directors that they preferred him to Jimmy Brownlie (Third Lanark and Scotland) who appeared for Celtic in several friendly matches as a trialist. Adams was the last Celtic goalkeeper to play in the hooped jersey, and the first to wear the yellow jersey (in 1910). Till then goalkeepers were recogniseable only by their build and a cloth cap. In his career at Celtic, his only senior club, Adams made 291 appearances.

Pat Bonner: Goalkeeper from 1979 to 1994. Irish internationalist Pat Bonner was Jock Stein's last signing for Celtic and proved to be a great servant in a long career. A brave keeper, Pat was a popular player from his debut against Motherwell on St. Patrick's Day 1979, helping Celtic to a 2-1 win. He made 641 appearances for Celtic despite a long absence with a back injury in 1988. Perhaps he will be more widely remembered for his heroics with Ireland especially in three World Cup finals – in Italy (1990) his save during the penalty shootout against Romania advanced Ireland to the quarter finals, a remarkable feat for such a small footballing country.

Stars of yesteryear – Adam McLean, Eddie McGarvey (trainer) and Willie McStay enjoy a break while training at Seamill

Frank Haffey: Goalkeeper from 1958 to 1964. Haffey is inevitably associated with Scotland's 9-3 defeat at Wembley in 1961, and perhaps unfairly. A year previously at Hampden Park he had starred against England in a 1-1 draw, even saving a penalty kick taken by Bobby Charlton. Frequently a brilliant performer between the posts for Celtic with more than two hundred appearances, Haffey – like most of the so-called Kelly Kids – was prone to moments of madness but he remained popular with the supporters – who insisted that he leave his goal to take a penalty kick against Airdrie in a 9-0 rout at Celtic Park. Needless to say, his shot was saved and Frank sportingly applauded the Airdrie goalkeeper. A character!

Charlie Shaw: Goalkeeper from 1913 to 1925. Another long-serving keeper, Shaw, obtained from Queen's Park Rangers for £250, proved a remarkable buy. He was on the short side for a goalkeeper (only 5ft 7ins) but he was agile and had safe hands. He is generally credited (along with Alec McNair and Joe Dodds) for perfecting the passback but his overall record is truly astonishing with shutouts in 53% of more than his four hundred appearances. In the 1913/14 season he gave up only fourteen goals in thirty-eight matches with twenty-six shutouts to his credit. Following 'Sunny Jim' Young's retirement in 1916, Charlie Shaw was appointed Celtic's captain, an unusual distinction for a goalkeeper.

Dan McArthur: Goalkeeper from 1892 to 1903. An astonishing performer in an era when goalkeepers were considered an endangered species. Shoulder-charging was allowed, as was some forms of 'hacking' and the slightly-built McArthur took severe punishment from opponents. He was a spectacular and courageous keeper, only rarely able to complete a season because of injuries. Some consider him the club's best-ever keeper – but he made only 120 appearances for Celtic.

Ronnie Simpson: Goalkeeper from 1964 to 1970. Ronnie had perhaps the most remarkable career in football, making his debut for Queen's Park, then in the top flight, at the age of fourteen (14) in 1945, being a member of the Great Britain Olympic side at Wembley in 1948, winning the F.A. Cup with Newcastle United in the 1950s, he signed for Celtic for less than £2,000 in 1964 because 'Jock Stein (Hibs' manager) did not fancy him'. Celtic needed help with the reserve side. He made his Celtic debut away against Barcelona in the Fairs Cities' Cup, broke into Celtic's first team as a regular in 1965 and was probably the most loved of all the Lisbon Lions. To cap a wonderful career he made his Scotland debut against England, the World Champions, at Wembley in 1967 helping in a 3-2 win, and won recognition as Scotland's Player of the Year 1967. Nicknamed 'Faither' by his teammates partly because of his seniority, Simpson exuded quiet authority and confidence in his 188 appearances for Celtic.

Tom Sinclair: Goalkeeper in 1906. The strangest of all Celtic keepers, Tom came to Celtic Park on loan from Rangers in order to cover for the injured Davie Adams. He played only six league matches with Celtic, but did not concede a single goal; in addition he picked up a Glasgow Cup medal, the only goals given up in a 3-2 win over Third Lanark in the final before returning to Ibrox and winning the Reserve

League with Rangers. A footnote to the club's history.

Joe Kennaway

'Joe' Kennaway: Goalkeeper from 1931 to 1939. Montreal-born 'Joe' Kennaway's opportunity to become Celtic's keeper arose out of the death of John Thomson in September 1931. Kennaway had impressed when he played for Fall River against Celtic on the club's first American tour and he was invited to Glasgow. Kennaway was a steady goalkeeper but he also turned in outstanding performances when required, most notably in the 1933 Scottish Cup final against Motherwell (1-0), and in all three matches of the Empire Exhibition Trophy in 1938. Some doubt exists about the claim that he played for three different countries at international level: he played for Canada against the United States in 1926, allegedly for the United States against Canada in 1930, and for Scotland against Austria in 1933. He had a reputation for saving penalty kicks and, unusually for a goalkeeper in the 1930s, often preferred to throw the ball out.

The compilers have called upon three 'experts' for their help with this section. All are – or were – life-long Celtic supporters: Eugene MacBride was until he died late in 2006 the editor of *The Celt*, Pat Reilly, a graduate of the University of Glasgow and Oxford, became Head of the English Department at Glasgow and is now retired, and Pat Woods is generally recognised as Celtic's most respected and reliable historian.

DEFENDERS:

(This section includes both full backs and central defenders)

Alec McNair: A versatile player, Alec McNair could play as Celtic's right back while sitting in an arm chair. Always perfectly cool, he deserved his nickname of 'The Icicle' and was a player years ahead of his contemporaries in using the ball out of defence.

Alec McNair

Bobby Hogg: He played in the 1930s, starting off as a teenager, and was a member of the famous Empirex winning team. He also experienced the struggles of games during World War II as well as the depressing post-war seasons. All this plus the mantle of captain. Bobby was a gentleman both on and off the field and set a great example to the multitudes of players who passed through Parkhead's gates in those days. In his prime a mobile, clean-tackling, clean-kicking defender he was up there with McNair and McGrain as a Celtic great.

Willie Loney: He was Celtic's centre half between 1900 and 1913, and was an attacking pivot and could shoot but his nickname 'Loney the Obliterator', reminds us that he was a robust, no-nonsense defender as well. He was a regular and key player in the Celtic side that won six championships in a row.

Billy McNeill: Unbeatable in the air and commanding on the ground, for many Billy McNeill will always be the Celtic captain *par excellence*. A fine defender, he still managed to get three goals in three different Scottish Cup finals. An inspiring player.

Danny McGrain: A man who could play in either full-back position with ease, Danny started off as a swashbuckling modern attacking full back. Injuries and illness – he suffered from diabetes – eventually slowed him down at the end of an almost twenty-season career, but he remained a solid defender and inspirational captain.

Eugene MacBride

James Kelly: From the purely historical viewpoint he has to lead the way. After all, he was Celtic's first major signing (from Renton) and, when he signed on for the new club, other prominent players followed. An attacking centre-half, by all accounts, he was an inspiring captain.

Willie Lyon: An Englishman, an ex-Queen's Parker – and a stopper centre-half – he was a most unusual Celtic pivot in the late 1930s. But he steadied Celtic and led the team to Scottish Cup and League Championship triumphs as well as the Empirex Trophy in 1938. An important player.

Willie Corbett: Another unsung hero in defence during the dark seasons of World War II. His career was cut short because of that conflict but he was outstanding, and in one wartime international against a powerful England side that regularly inflicted humiliation on the Scots, he held Tommy Lawton and the Sassenachs to a 0-0 draw.

Billy McNeill: An inspiring leader in every sense of the word. Totally dominant, and a superb organiser in defence – and he could score important goals in cup finals! A highly successful player who came into his own under Jock Stein's tuition.

Danny McGrain: An outstanding two-footed player, who played for Scotland at both right and left back. Exceptionally fast in his early days and a tenacious tackler. Although badly affected by injury at various times – a fractured skull, and a mysterious ankle injury – he could always be relied upon.

Pat Reilly

Billy McNeill: Celtic's most dominant centre-half and captain, and an outstanding player in his own right. Unbeatable in the air, and hard-tackling on the ground, he was a model of the modern central defender. After a lifetime in football (and with Celtic) he deserves the title 'Mr. Celtic'.

James Kelly: Celtic's first captain, and a speedy attacking centre-half, as was the custom in the 1890s, James Kelly was central to Celtic's very existence. Had he not chosen to leave Renton and join the new club in 1888, Celtic might not have attracted the players necessary for their immediate success in football.

Alec McNair and Joe Dodds: Full-backs tend to work in tandem and this pair were almost telepathic in their understanding and timing. Along with the goalkeeper Charlie Shaw they developed the tactic of the pass back to an art-form, and were also adept at the offside trap. They were the organisers of Celtic's most successful defence (statistically).

Jim Craig and Tommy Gemmell: Two tall, strong and mobile full-backs, these two (and Gemmell in particular) were yet another attacking threat in Celtic's famed Lisbon Lions. They could defend when called upon to do so.

Duncan MacKay: A most unlucky right-back, MacKay was years ahead of his time in the role. He could tackle, had speed and mobility but his forte was distribution from out of his defensive position – unlike many of his contemporaries who simply cleared their lines. An unlucky player in that his Celtic career coincided with an unproductive era in the club's history.

Pat Woods

Joe Dodds

MIDFIELDERS:

(This section includes both wing-halves and inside-forwards)

'Sunny Jim' Young: He did not come from a Celtic background – at least not until and from the moment he signed in 1903. There was no more 'Celtic minded' player than this powerhouse of a right-half. He gave his heart and soul to the club as the catalyst in midfield. Jim Young was an inspiration through his commitment to the cause and there was many an occasion when he proclaimed how proud he was to be a Celt. He wasn't just a Celt. He was the greatest Celt.

Bobby Evans: Dynamic at right-half, and totally reliable at centre-half, Bobby Evans gave Celtic wonderful service for almost sixteen seasons. In an inconsistent Celtic side Bobby was the epitome of steadiness and inspiring in his refusal never to admit defeat. Celtic's 'Red Knight'.

Bobby Murdoch

Bertie Peacock

Bobby Murdoch: He was probably Jock Stein's favourite player, and Celtic'a anchor in midfield. Nobody ever passed the ball better than Bobby Murdoch, whether yards in front of Bobby Lennox or straight to Jimmy Johnstone's feet. And, when called upon to defend a lead, nobody was better at snuffing out an opposing attacker.

Kenny Dalglish: The perfect, all-round modern player, Kenny had everything: strength and stamina, ball control and positioning, the ability to hold the ball and/ or pass it; and he was a goalscorer too with more than a hundred goals in the Scottish and English leagues' top divisions.

Patsy Gallacher: Celtic's most legendary player must have done enough to warrant the memories of his dribbling, his passing and his goals. Under-weight and waif-like, Patsy Gallacher could take care of himself against the toughest of opponents in a time (1911 to 1926) when football was a physical battle. Released too soon by Celtic, Patsy went on to play brilliantly for Falkirk for another six seasons. A genuine legend!

Eugene MacBride

Willie Fernie: A delightful player to watch! He started off as an inside-forward but ended up as a stand-out at wing-half. His greatest game had to be the 7-1 demolition of Rangers in the 1957 League Cup final when he was simply unstoppable from his right-half position. A complete gentleman and sportsman, Willie Fernie could play anywhere; he ran Hibs ragged when he replaced Charlie Tully at outside-left for the Coronation Cup final in 1953.

Bobby Murdoch: Another player who started off as an inside-forward but found his perfect position in midfield when Jock Stein moved him back. An excellent passer of the ball and a powerful presence at all times. Unfortunately plagued with a chronic ankle injury throughout his career, Bobby remains a truly great Celtic player.

Bertie Peacock: An Ulsterman, Bertie started off as Charlie Tully's partner either at inside or outside left – depending on the whim of the chairman but he became an outstanding left-half when moved back to face the ball. A tremendous captain and inspirational player, Bertie was badly missed when allowed to play for Northern Ireland rather than turn out for Celtic in the 1961 cup final against Dunfermline Athletic.

Bobby Collins: A small but dynamic inside-right, Bobby Collins was another who could play several positions. Despite his size, Collins could take care of himself; in fact, his first match for Celtic was in 1949 against Rangers and 'Tiger' Shaw and he was not at all out-of-place. A great loss when he moved to Everton – to pay for the new floodlights at Celtic Park, it was claimed.

Kenny Dalglish: For several seasons, while Celtic were on a gradual decline, he was the one player who could carry the side, playing as an outright striker, inside-forward, or midfielder. An intelligent player who could control the game, an excellent passer who could create chances for his colleagues, and a clinical finisher!

Pat Reilly

Bobby Murdoch: Starting off as an inside-right, Bobby found himself as a right-sided midfielder under Jock Stein's tuition. Powerfully built, and with a strong shot, Murdoch was a constant threat to opposing defences, but his passing was outstanding:

into space for Bobby Lennox to exploit his speed, straight to Jimmy Johnstone's feet to utilise his dribbling skills. A Celtic legend!

Bobby Evans: Energetic, hard-working and one of Celtic's most whole-hearted players – despite playing in an often mediocre Celtic line-up, Bobby Evans was the best right-half in Scottish football for a decade, and later – despite his lack of height – an outstanding and inspirational centre-half.

Patsy Gallacher

Patsy Gallacher: Probably Celtic's most gifted player ever, Patsy was a dominant personality on the pitch. He could dribble, and confuse defenders, he could pass and outwit defences, and he could score goals. Simply the best, whether at inside-right or inside-left.

Jimmy McMenemy: In a Celtic side that dominated Scottish football for a considerable period, Jimmy was known as 'Napoleon'. He was the midfield general, the organiser, the dictator of the pace Celtic would play. A quiet man, but whose actions spoke volumes, he was the epitome of the classic Scottish inside-forward.

Chic Geatons: An honest, hard-working wing-half who was frequently under-rated. During Celtic's revival in the 1930s Geatons played an important, if often unobtrusive part but starred in the 1937 Scottish Cup final against Aberdeen before a record crowd.

Pat Woods

STRIKERS

Jimmy Quinn: A bustling, chasing, all-action centre-forward, Jimmy Quinn was much more than a battering ram. He developed the striker's art of anticipating the chances that would come his way, and he was brave, incredibly brave. A man who scores hat-tricks against Rangers is my idea of a Celtic hero. An automatic choice.

John McPhail: The hero of the 1951 Scottish Cup campaign although he was only half-fit with a groin injury. John McPhail when he was at his best could stand comparison with any Celtic centre forward. Good in the air, he was a man who could lead the line and hold the ball for his inside-forwards to cash in. Sadly, general unfitness hampered him throughout his career but he deserves to be remembered.

Henrik Larsson: The one modern player who would walk into any all-star team unchallenged. A predator and a team player, a forward sleek as a leopard, dangerous in the air and on the ground. Brave in the heat of battle, and equally courageous in recovering from a serious leg-break. A legend without a doubt.

Jimmy McGrory: How could you omit Scotland's greatest-ever goal scorer, and the man who carried Celtic year after year? Astonishing in the air, he appeared able to

hover for a few seconds to connect with a cross from Paddy Connelly or Adam McLean. Nobody was more respected and admired by opposing players more than this brave gentleman of a centre-forward.

Chris Sutton: A masterstroke from Martin O'Neill gave this Englishman the chance to revive his career at Celtic Park, and how well he took the opportunity! Tall and slim, he had a wiry strength and was difficult to dispossess, his forte the ability to hold the ball while under challenge. An all-round player, and a most intelligent forward.

Eugene MacBride

Bobby Lennox: Always running, always chasing – and terrifying defenders with his pace, Bobby Lennox was a true goalscorer when employed as an out-and-out striker. He could have increased his goal output more if he had been a yard slower, as linesmen tended to flag him for offside because his speed misled them.

Henrik Larsson: Celtic supporters were lucky to have seen such a world-class player performing at Celtic Park for seven seasons at the peak of his career. He could do everything in the striker's repertoire: holding the ball, netting with head and foot, panicking defences. A genius!

Jimmy McGrory: It would be impossible to overlook Celtic's leading goal scorer, and such a Celt. In 1928 he personally resisted an effort by Celtic to sell him to Arsenal, and it would be impossible to think of Celtic without McGrory in the 1930s. Astonishingly he gained only a few 'caps' for Scotland, but he was one of the great ones, and a whole-hearted Celt.

Jimmy Quinn: Apparently, a quiet man from the mining village of Croy, Jimmy Quinn was a terror on the pitch. He seemed to revel in the physical nature of the game in the 1900s, and the popular conception is of Quinn racing towards goal with defenders hanging on to him, trying to hack him to the ground but being bounced off as Jimmy finishes up his individual run with a raging shot just as he falls to the ground. It was probably true.

Stevie Chalmers: He deserves to be remembered more than as the man who poked in the winning goal against Inter Milan at Lisbon. He started off a bit later than most, having suffered from illness when young and struggled to find himself in the so-called 'Kelly Kids' in the early 1960s but he was a regular once Jock Stein took over. The manager recognised his unselfish running off the ball which opened up play for other forwards, and his courage in taking on defenders on his own – most noticeably in the European Cup semi-final against Dukla Prague

Pat Reilly

Jimmy McGrory: He could be included simply for his goal-scoring alone, but he was the spirit of Celtic in the 1920s and 30s. He was the forager, the hunter of goals and a man who never gave up. Energetic and bustling, he could upset most defences with his tireless running – and he was famed for his heading ability. Courage too in diving for hard-driven crosses from his wingers. And a gentleman, on and off the pitch!

Stevie Chalmers: Another whole-hearted Celtic player, Steve Chalmers deserves more fame than for scoring the winning goal at Lisbon. Versatile, Chalmers played in all forward positions but latterly became identified as an all-out striker and his pace and strong running throughout a match provided Celtic with an outlet when under pressure such as in the European Cup semi-final against Dukla when he was Celtic's lone forward.

Henrik Larsson: One modern Celtic player who will undoubtedly stand comparison with any of the legendary heroes of the past. A predator in the penalty box, a tireless runner into space outside of it – a striker who could take chances with both head and feet, and a forward who could provide openings for others. Courageous and strong-minded in coming back from serious injury. A wonderful player!

Charlie Nicholas: During his first spell at Celtic Park, Nicholas showed all the promise and exuberance of youth but he was also mature beyond his years. Another brave player in coming back from a broken leg in his teens, his defection to Arsenal was a bitter blow.

Joe McBride: After playing for several clubs on both sides of the border, Joe McBride – significantly – was Jock Stein's first signing. Whole-hearted and bustling, Joe was the never-say-die type of old-fashioned centre-forward and a brave man in the penalty box where he could snap up the half-chances that came his way. What a pity that his Celtic career was so short, curtailed by a knee injury that would be a mere routine medical problem at the present time.

Pat Woods

WINGERS:

Jimmy Delaney: He was the fans' hero. A fast, direct goal-scoring winger he was the focal point of the 1938 team. No game was ever lost while Jimmy was there as a goal threat. During the war years Jimmy was Celtic. He was here, there and everywhere. How much more quickly would Celtic have recovered had he stayed! To their shame the board refused to grant him a wage increase on his £2 a week. Jimmy was gone (to Manchester United) and Celtic were big-time losers. J. D. – all-time Celtic great.

Jimmy Johnstone: When you think of Celtic, you think of this brave wee winger taking on defender after defender, and delighting the supporters with his trickery and courage. So often he was a joy to watch, Jinky – the 'Greatest Ever Celt'.

Adam McLean: Jimmy McGrory considered him to be the equal of Alan Morton, Rangers 'Wee Blue Devil', at outside left. Adam played more than 400 times for Celtic between 1917 and 1928 and scored 138 goals, a good rate for a winger better known for providing ammunition to the inside forwards. He was transfrred to

John Doyle (left) with goalkeeper Peter Latchford

Sunderland, and Celtic struggled dreadfully to replace him.

Bobby Lennox: Fast wingers are almost impossible to contain, and Bobby Lennox was the fastest player in Scotland. Very often his sheer pace would terrorise Rangers in the Stein era but he learned to become a clinical finisher as shown by his goal tally in Scottish and League Cup finals against the Light Blues.

Johnny Doyle: I have a weakness for men who look like Celtic players, and touslehaired Johnny Doyle looked the part. Fast, whole-hearted and energetic he was a player who never gave up – and he was broken-hearted when he was sent off against Rangers in the league decider on 21st May 1979. A genuine Celt.

Eugene MacBride

Jimmy Delaney makes a return to Celtic Park for Aberdeen against Hibernian in the St Mungo Cup semi-final (1951)

Jimmy Delaney: A brave winger who came back after an injury to his arm that threatened his career in 1939. Unfortunately, World War II interrupted his career but he was a star, a young one in the immediate pre-war seasons – and one of Celtic's few successes throughout the war. He was tireless and a never-say-die type of winger (and sometime centre-forward) and the supporters were heart-broken when Matt Busby made him his first signing for Manchester United.

Neil Mochan: A no-nonsense player and a man who knew where the goal was. One of his ploys was to cut in from the left wing and shoot directly across the goalmouth; his shot would either be a goal, a save from the keeper, or a deflection from a defender or fellow-attacker – impossible to defend. A ferocious shot: his goal in the Coronation Cup against Hibernian from thirty yards out comes to mind, his goal against Rangers from a narrow angle in the 7-1 game on the stroke of halftime was the decider. A true Celt.

Neil Mochan

Davie Provan: He joined Celtic from Kilmarnock for a record fee between Scottish clubs at that time (1978) and resembled an old-fashioned winger with an exciting burst of speed and intricate dribbling. He was reputed to have told a Rangers full back, 'You couldn't get a touch of a beach ball from me even in a telephone box!' A memorable goal in the Scottish Cup final against Dundee United in 1985 started Celtic's comeback. Illness shortened his career cruelly when he was at his best.

Paddy Connolly: A throwback to the days when wingers hugged the touchline, gathered the ball, took on the full-back, and crossed the ball for the centre-forward to score. Paddy was the fastest winger in Scotland and could cross a ball on the run, usually intended for the head of Jimmy McGrory. Patsy Gallacher told him, when he was starting out, that was his only task, adding, 'By the way, cross the ball with the lace away from his head. Otherwise, it hurts.'

John Hughes: He could be inconsistent but this strong-running left winger could be devastating when on his game. He seemed to relish the space he needed out on the wing, and he always had an eye for goal. An exciting player, he could thrill and occasionally exasperate the Celtic support.

Pat Reilly

Jimmy Johnstone: Jimmy was probably not 'Celtic's greatest ever player', but he typified the Celtic winger more than any other. A dazzling dribbler, a scorer of goals – and many with headers – a brave wee man, on and off the pitch. Jinky was adored by the Celtic support who identified with him as with no other.

John Hughes

Jimmy Delaney: A member of the famous Empire Cup winning side, Jimmy Delaney was in the words of his great rival Willie Waddell (Rangers) 'the bravest of them all'. He had speed, the ability to cross the ball accurately and a nose for goals. In fact, he was often played as centre forward during the war-time seasons. A serious arm injury in 1939 cost him two whole seasons, but he was the first target for Matt Busby when he took over at Old Trafford. Jimmy rewarded that faith by winning the FA Cup with United in 1948, eleven years after winning the Scottish Cup with Celtic in 1937.

Johnny Campbell: Perhaps a surprising choice because he was a very early Celt but he formed a left-wing partnership with Sandy McMahon in the 1890s that was described as 'telepathic'. An important player in the development of Scottish football because of that unique understanding with McMahon, Campbell won both Scottish and English Cup medals with Celtic (1892), Third Lanark (1904), and Aston Villa (1897). For a winger (and sometime centre forward), he was a prolific scorer with 109 goals in 215 Celtic appearances.

Charlie Tully: A charismatic Irishman, Charlie Tully made an early impression on Scottish football with a dazzling display against Rangers in 1948 and followed that up with triumphs in the Scottish Cup (1951 and 1954), the league championship (1953/54), the League Cup (1956 and 1957), the St. Mungo Cup (1951) and the Coronation Cup (1953) – although he was out of action for the final of the latter. Often considered a luxury player, nevertheless Charlie Tully transformed Celtic into genuine contenders during the 1950s.

John Hughes: Surprisingly tall and power-fully-built for a winger, John 'Yogi' Hughes terrorised many defences with his strong running down Celtic's left wing in Jock Stein's early seasons. In more than four hundred first-team appearances for Celtic, he scored almost two hundred goals.

Pat Woods

STREAKERS

Streaker: an exhibitionist, who unfortunately chooses to reveal his or her shortcomings to the world.

Football has not been spared, nor have Celtic! Celtic visited the north-east to play Aberdeen in the Scottish Cup but a streaker risked pneumonia during the match. He was arrested, spent the night in jail, was fined £250 and banned for life from Pittodrie. (25 February 2002);

Just before the kick-off in Seville for the UEFA Cup final against Porto another streaker originally dressed as a referee burst on to the pitch, showed a red card to the match official, stripped and raced away with the ball (21 May 2003).

STRIPS

The famous 'Hoops' could be considered Celtic's third strip. In the first match – a friendly against Rangers in 1888, Celtic wore white shirts plus green collars and with a badge of a Celtic Cross. On at least one occasion (vs St. Bernards's on 3 November 1888) the team appeared in solid green shirts but the most frequently employed strip was green-and-white vertical stripes and dark-blue serge pants, probably first worn on 31 December 1888 vs Mitchell St. George's (England).

The now-familiar green-and-white hoops – allegedly in imitation of the junior club St. Anthony's – made its first appearance in August at the start of the 1903/04 season. However, on occasion Celtic felt the need to change strips in colour or combination clashes with other clubs such as Queen's Park, Morton, or Kilmarnock: in 1919 vs Queen's Park the players wore green shirts with a white diamond (like Airdrie); in 1925 vs Morton white shirts with green facings and a shamrock on the left breast were worn; in 1926 vs Kilmarnock this was changed to green and white quarters.

In 1927 – apparently in accordance with a Scottish League ruling – as the away team Celtic played in their traditional hoops but with black shorts even against Rangers.

The multi-ringed socks were introduced in a 1933 league fixture vs Hearts and occasional variations were introduced such as green shirts with white sleeves in a 1938 fixture vs Kilmarnock.

After World War II Celtic's most common change strip – and one highly popular with the supporters – was a white shirt with green sleeves and a huge shamrock on the breast. For many years Celtic resisted requests to have their jerseys numbered – on the grounds that such numbering would disfigure the most recogniseable strip in world football, but compromised by numbering the players' shorts for the first time in a friendly against Sparta Rotterdam.

Jock Stein is believed to have favoured the all-green outfit – similar to those worn at present like Aberdeen, Liverpool and Chelsea – but was not averse to the occasional change.

Early in the 1970s the club newspaper *The Celtic View* ran a contest to determine the most popular alternative strip, and the winner was a shirt with green-and-black vertical stripes similar to AC Milan – and virtually the same as the one most generally featured during the 2006/07 season.

With the increase in the market for leisure clothing based on football strips, clubs were not slow to realise the potential in having their change-strip vary from season to season. The result was that some bizarre outfits have been presented to the public in the past decade. They are simply too numerous to mention.

For many, Celtic are the team that wears green-and-white hoops, a fact recognised by Martin O'Neill when he had his winning Scottish Cup side change into the hoops for the presentation after beating Dunfermline Athletic 3-1 in 2004.

SUBSTITUTES

For many years the use of substitutes in a competitive match was forbidden. The implausible reason given was that it could be considered 'character-building' for a side to play short-handed through injury. It was not uncommon to see an injured goalkeeper reappear after treatment out on the wing where it was hoped he could make a nuisance of himself to the opposition or take the occasional throw-in.

Officialdom in Scotland finally gave permission for substitutions in 1966. Of course, the use of substitutes quickly became as much for tactical reasons as for injuries.

Celtic's record of 'firsts' involving substitutes is as follows:

The first substitute was Willie O'Neill who replaced Jimmy Johnstone in a League Cup victory over St. Mirren at Paisley on 3 September 1966;

In the Scottish League Steve Chalmers came on against Dundee at Dens Park on 24 September 1966, and also scored the winning goal in a 2-1 win;

In the Scottish Cup tie against Elgin City at Celtic Park on 18 February 1967 Willie Wallace replaced Bobby Murdoch to become the first Celtic substitute to score in the competition, netting twice in a 7-0 win;

In European competitions in the early days only a goalkeeper could be substituted. Thus, John Fallon was on the bench for every Celtic match on the way to winning the trophy at Lisbon – but he was never called into action;

Willie Wallace came on for lone striker Stevie Chalmers in the 1-1 draw with Red Star in the European Cup tie in Belgrade on 27 November 1968;

On 29 October 1966 Stevie Chalmers entered the history books as the first-ever sub in a Hampden Cup Final, taking over from John Hughes in Celtic's 1-0 win in the League Cup final against Rangers;

John Clark became Celtic's first substitution in a Scottish Cup final when he replaced Jim Brogan in the Old Firm match won 4-0 by Celtic on 26 April 1969;

George Connelly replaced the struggling Bertie Auld in the European Cup final against Feyenoord in the San Siro on 6 May 1970, to become the first sub used by any British club in the final of this premier trophy.

Jock Stein, Celtic's manager, never did appear willing to employ substitutes. It should be noted that Celtic had played the five previous League Cup ties in 1966 without using any, and even the humdrum Scottish Cup tie against Arbroath on 28 January 1967 passed without Celtic's using a substitute.

Most Substitute Appearances:
Bobby Lennox 81,
Shaun Maloney 69,
George McCluskey 62,
Simon Donnelly 49
Andy Walker 50

Some players during their Celtic career never made the starting eleven, but did get on the field as a substitute:
Marc Antony,
Gerry Britton,
Paul Chalmers,
John Convery,
Barry John Corr,
Bryan Coyne,
Michael Craig,
Fernando de Ornelas,
Barry Elliot,
Robert Hannah,
Dougie McGuire,
Paul McGowan,
Jim O'Brien,
John O'Neil,
Paul Shields,
Cillian Sheridan

Three others (Jeremie Aliadiere, Steve Hancock and John McCluskey) made their cameo appearances in European competition.

Best scoring rate as substitutes:
Charlie Nicholas 13 appearances, 6 goals,
Johannes Edvaldsson 10 (4),
Mark Reid 8 (3),
Murdo MacLeod 7 (4)

Chris Killen holds the record for most substitute appearances in a season – 24 in 2007/08.

SUNDAY FOOTBALL

In Presbyterian Scotland there always had been opposition to the principle of football on Sundays. What changed things was a national emergency caused by the miners' strike. The SFA sanctioned football on the Sabbath in January 1974, and it was intended as a temporary measure during the power crisis.

The first available Sunday was 27 January and Celtic took advantage of the opportunity to stage the Scottish Cup tie against Clydebank at Celtic Park and were rewarded with a crowd of 28,000. Celtic won 6-1 with Dixie Deans getting a hat-trick; two other players netted hat-tricks that same day, but Deans completed his within thirty-nine minutes and so is credited as the first player to score three goals on a Sunday.

Two weeks later (10 February 1974) Celtic fulfilled a league fixture against Dundee but lost 2-1 before a crowd of 40,000. David Hay scored Celtic's goal but it was not enough to cheer the 40,000 crowd.

In the League Cup Celtic's first Sunday game was the 1984 final (25 March) which was lost to Rangers by 3-2 after extra time in front of 66,369. Brian McClair and Mark Reid with a penalty kick scored late goals to force the extra time.

Of course, once the principle of Sunday football had been established, such fixtures have become a traditional part of football in Scotland

(CLEAN) SWEEPS

In 1966/67 Celtic won every competition in which they participated: the European Cup, the League Championship, the Scottish Cup, the League Cup and the Glasgow Cup. The Celtic squad included Auld, Chalmers, Clark, Craig, Gallagher, Gemmell, Hughes, Johnstone, Lennox, McBride, McNeill, Murdoch, O'Neill, Simpson, Wallace.

In 1907/08 Celtic won the League Championship, the Scottish Cup, the Glasgow Cup and the Charity Cup. The Celtic squad included Adams, Bennett, Hamilton, Hay, Kivlichan, Loney, McLean, MacLeod, McMenemy, McNair, Mitchell, Quinn, Semple, Somers, Weir, Young.

With the demise of the Glasgow Cup and the Charity Cup, the treble of League Championship, Scottish Cup and League Cup might be considered 'a modern clean sweep' (*see Trebles*); however, as the League Cup is no longer a passport into Europe this claim might be disputed.

T

TALENTS

Celtic players have frequently displayed talent in unexpected areas outside football:

Walter Arnott, who played briefly in 1895, was a skilled yachtsman and competed in several regattas;

Willie Maley won the Scottish 100 Yards Sprint Championship (1896);

Willie Cringan was Scottish Quoits Champion in 1926;

Robert Fisher, a wartime player in 1942, was also a cricketer with County Durham;

Sean Fallon, back in Sligo, was renowned as a long-distance swimmer;

Steve Chalmers won the Scottish Footballers' Golf Tournament in 1967 with a scratch score of 78 at Crow Wood;

Jim Craig represented the Scottish Schools in the Triple Jump and came second to Lynne Davies (later 1964 Olympic Long Jump champion);

Roy Aitken represented the Scottish Schools at Basketball, (and was also a skilled pianist).

Pat Bonner was celebrated as a Gaelic footballer as a youngster in Donegal.

TELEVISION

Television coverage of football is a relatively new phenomenon. It should be remembered that Celtic's match with Racing Club of Argentina in 1967 for the 'World Club Championship' was not covered live by the networks because it might adversely affect the attendance of minor fixtures around the country.

Celtic, however, have been involved with breakthroughs in television:

Scottish Cup final:
On 23 April 1955 Celtic and Clyde drew 1-1 in a final described as 'the worst within living memory'. The only moment of excitement for the viewers was Clyde's equaliser direct from a corner kick in eighty-eight minutes. As only 106,234 attended the match at Hampden Park, it could be argued that the TV coverage did affect the attendance;

Old Firm Matches:
7 May 1977: the Scottish Cup final, won through Andy Lynch's disputed penalty kick, was the first Old Firm contest on live television. Like the Celtic-Clyde match of 1955, it was a scrappy affair and watched by only 54,252;

25 March 1984: the League Cup final was

televised for the first time and Celtic and Rangers provided lots of thrills before Rangers triumphed by 3-2 after extra time;

31 August 1986: the first league fixture to be televised was a 1-0 win for Rangers at Ibrox Park;

Regular Games:
The first live telecast of a Scottish Cup tie outside of the final was one between Aberdeen and Celtic at Pittodrie on 1 February 1987. The match ended 2-2.

Robert Kelly, Celtic's long-time chairman, predicted in the early 1960s that excessive television coverage would distort football in Scotland. His warnings have proven prescient.

In general, attendances at football grounds have declined and, while the media money has been welcomed, the appeal of Scottish football to a larger television audience has been limited. Accordingly, the nation has lost ground financially to those countries which can offer viewers more attractive football and more compelling matches. In its simplest form, Scottish clubs get only a fraction of their competitors in England and the Continent, a fact of life which restricts the choice of footballer available in the transfer market.

Those spectators who wish to attend the matches have been put at a disadvantage because fixtures – both the dates and kick-off times – are frequently re-arranged at relatively short notice to accommodate TV schedules.

A mixed blessing, indeed.

THOUSANDS (OF GOALS)

The vagaries (and downright inaccuracy) of early football reporting has led to confusion as to the identification of players of landmark goals. Mistakes are then perpetuated until fiction is accepted as fact.

More recent research in league results shows the following list to be generally reliable:

Celtic's 1000th goal:
Davie McLean vs Partick Thistle (4-1) (1 February 1908)

2000th: Adam McLean vs Airdrie (3-2) (30 April 1921)

3000th: Hugh O'Donnell vs Cowdenbeath (7-0) (19 September 1933)

4000th: Neil Mochan vs Raith Rovers (3-1) (25 September 1954)

5000th: Tommy Gemmell vs Falkirk (5-0) (20 March 1967)

6000th: Roddie MacDonald vs Partick Thistle (4-0) (29 March 1978)

7000th: Brian O'Neil vs Hibernian (2-1) (28 November 1992)

8000th: Maciej Zurawski vs Dunfermline Athletic (4-0) (28 August 2005)

TOSS OF COIN

Not too many people like drawn matches, and various methods have been used to 'settle' the result in an acceptable manner: injury time, extra time, penalty shoot-outs, 'Golden Goals', 'Silver Goals', corner kicks and astonishingly by tossing a coin! This latter method has been used frequently in the Glasgow Charity Cup with mixed fortunes for Celtic:

10 May 1930 FINAL lost (to Rangers)

3 May 1952 lost (to Clyde)

2 May 1953 won (over Third Lanark)

9 May 1956 lost (to Third Lanark)

7 May 1958 lost (to Rangers)

2 May 1959 won (over Rangers)

7 May 1960 won (over Clyde)

9 May 1960 lost (to Rangers)

1 May 1961 won (over Queen's Park)

The venue for the League Cup semi final between Rangers and Celtic on 22 September 1993 had to be decided by the toss of the coin with Hampden Park being unavailable through reconstruction. Rangers won the toss and eventually the match by 1-0.

For the Scottish Cup semi final in 1998 a similar procedure had to be followed because of construction at Hampden Park. This time Celtic won the toss and the match was played at Celtic Park, but Rangers won 2-1 to advance to the final.

Perhaps the most important match to be settled by tossing a coin took place in Lisbon on 26 November 1969 when the European Cup quarter-final between Celtic and Benfica ended up 3-3 even after extra-time in the second leg.

More drama was provided when the coin rolled under a table in the referee's room and Jock Stein, according to eye-witnesses, scrambled quickly to retrieve it shouting out as he did so that Celtic had won!

TOURS

There have been frequent trips by Celtic to North America but only three deserve the title of 'Tour'. They took place in 1931, 1951 and 1966.

1966
This was the platform from which Celtic launched the astonishing 1966/67 season, in which they swept everything before them. Jock Stein felt that such a tour would have a positive effect on morale, and he was proved correct. He had arranged competitive fixtures against Tottenham Hotspur (thrice), Bayern Munich and Bologna, as well as 'exhibition matches' against local opposition which gave opportunities to tinker with new formations. The games were played in Bermuda, the United States and Canada.

13 May 1966 Bermuda Select 10-1
Lennox (4), Auld (3), Gemmell (2), McNeill

15 May Bermuda Young Men 7-0
Lennox (3), Gemmell (2), McBride (2)

18 May New Jersey All-Stars 6-0
Lennox (3), McBride (2), Murdoch

22 May Tottenham Hotspur 1-0 Lennox

27 May Bologna 0-0

28 May Hamilton Select 11-0 Lennox (4), Murdoch (3), McBride (2), Gemmell, Clark

29 May CYC All-Stars 6-1 McBride (2), Chalmers, Lennox, Auld, Hughes

2 June Tottenham Hotspur 2-1 Lennox, Auld

5 June Tottenham Hotspur 1-1 Lennox

A gangster film set? No, the Celtic squad on their 1951 tour to USA and Canada

10 June Bayern Munich 2-2 Lennox, McBride

12 June Atlas (Mexico) 1-0 Gallagher

16 June Fulham 1-1

17 June Kearney Select 2-0

21 June Fulham 2-3

1951

As in 1931, Celtic travelled to the United States and Canada as holders of the Scottish Cup. It proved an exhilarating experience for the players who were undertaking foreign travel for the first time.

20 May New York All-Stars 5-1

27 May Fulham 2-0

30 May Eintracht Frankfurt 3-1

3 June Philadelphia Stars 6-2

5 June National League 2-1

8 June Chicago Polish Eagles 4-0

1931

23 May Pennsylvania All-Stars 6-1

24 May New York Giants 3-2

30 May New York Yankees 3-4

31 May Fall River 0-1

6 June Pawtucket Rangers 1-3

7 June Brooklyn 5-0

13 June Carsteel Montreal 7-0

14 June Hakoah 1-1

21 June Chicago Bricklayers 6-3

25 June Michigan All-Stars 5-0

27 June Ulster United 3-1

28 June New York Yankees 4-1

29 June Baltimore 4-1

TRANSFERS

It would be sensational news if Charlie Tully or Pat Crerand had been transferred from Celtic to Rangers . . . but that is what happened on 11 March 1959.

A Rangers/Celtic Select were due to play at Telford Park to hansel Inverness Caledonian's new floodlights. However, SFA rules demanded that all players fielded had to belong to the same club; accordingly, Dick Beattie, Jim Kennedy and Jim Conway, along with Tully and Crerand, signed for Rangers and then re-signed for Celtic the following day. To ease the minds of Celtic zealots, the players did not wear Rangers jerseys, turning out instead in red, white, and blue hoops.

It is sad to relate but every player has his price. Celtic have lost some outstanding players, idolised by the support; similarly, they have brought in players established at other clubs.

Neither the clubs nor the football governing bodies are obliged to reveal the financial dealings involved in such transfers. Accordingly, many transfers are shrouded in mystery and the sums mentioned are only intelligent guesswork.

The following are some landmark deals within the transfer market, and the amounts listed are an indication of how much football has changed within such a short period. They represent the first five-figured, six-figured, and seven-figured amounts paid to or given to Celtic.

IN

1948: Leslie Johnstone (Clyde) £12,000

1978: Davie Provan (Kilmarnock) £120,000

1991: Tony Cascarino (Aston Villa) £1,100,000

OUT

1937: Willie Buchan to Blackpool £10,000

1973: Lou Macari to Manchester United £200,000

1989: Frank McAvennie to West Ham United £1,250,000

One of the most painful was the departure of Kenny Dalglish to Liverpool in 1977 for a sum estimated at a little more than £400,000 – laughable in that Liverpool had received almost double that for Kevin Keegan from Hamburg only weeks before.

With Martin O'Neill's arrival as manager in 2000 Celtic became a major dealer in the transfer market. O'Neill purchased several high-priced performers from England such as Chris Sutton (£6M), John Hartson (£6M), Neil Lennon (£5.5 M) and Alan Thompson (£4.5M) – and it should be stressed that all of these figures are estimates. The brightest star in that Celtic side was Henrik Larsson, picked up from Feyenoord by Wim Jansen for a bargain £600,000.

Most recently the highest priced transfers have involved Stiliyan Petrov to Aston Villa for a fee estimated at £7m and the purchase of Scott Brown from Hibernian for £4.4m.

The reality of modern football finance means that in the recruiting of top-class players no Scottish club can compete effectively with the major European sides and the English Premiership outfits.

TREBLES

Celtic have won the domestic treble (League Championship, Scottish Cup and League Cup) three times: 1966/67, 1968/69, and 2000/01. The first two were won with Jock Stein as manager; the third with Martin O'Neill.

Celtic have never won the Scottish Cup three times in a row. They came close on a number of occasions:

in 1900/01 Hearts beat them 4-3 – and Celtic had won the two previous finals, against Rangers (2-0) and Queen's Park (4-3);

in 1908/09 after the SFA withheld the trophy after an Old Firm riot at Hampden Park – and Celtic had won the two previous finals, against Hearts (3-0) and St. Mirren (5-1);

in 1912/13 after a defeat by Hearts at Celtic Park (0-1) – and Celtic were the holders having won the trophy in successive seasons, against Hamilton Academical (2-0) and Clyde (2-0);

in 1972/73 by losing 3-2 to Rangers, after winning in 1971 (Rangers 2-1) and 1972 (Hibernian 6-1);

in 1975/76 after losing 3-2 to Motherwell in Round Three, after winning in 1974 (Dundee United 3-0) and 1975 (Airdrie 3-1);

and heart-breakingly to Aberdeen on penalty-kicks in 1989/90, after winning in 1988 (Rangers 1-0) and in 1987 (Dundee United 2-1).

TRICOLOUR

In honour of the club's founders and original support, for many years since the club's foundation Celtic flew the tricolour of the Irish Republic from the flag-pole at the Celtic End of the Jungle. It flew without much comment from anybody, Celtic-minded or otherwise, until one Scottish official (almost certainly George Graham, the SFA Secretary) suggested that it might be offensive to a visiting Northern Irish League select in the 1930s.

Following outbreaks of hooliganism involving Celtic supporters – and in particular after the 1952 New Year's Day clash with Rangers at Celtic Park, Glasgow Magistrates made a number of recommendations for the SFA to consider. Among them was the suggestion that the flying of the tricolour inflamed sectarian violence.

Celtic were ordered by the SFA to stop flying the flag or face sanctions which included a possible expulsion from football in Scotland.

After receiving legal advice Celtic decided to ignore the SFA edict and the battle escalated. Opposition to Celtic was widespread, an opposition orchestrated by George Graham, and Celtic's chairman Bob Kelly was relatively isolated in the administrative chambers – apart from unexpected support from Rangers. Eventually, Celtic's position was accepted but it was a struggle which convinced the club that a lobby within the SFA was prepared to act in a hostile manner towards it.

On 30 October 1968 Rangers played Dundalk in Fairs Cities Cup and (allegedly) borrowed an Irish tricolour from Celtic Park for the occasion. However, the tricolour remained unfurled on the flag pole, apparently because the Irish club had not specifically asked for its use.

TUNNELS

The tunnel at Celtic Park has been the scene of some unseemly incidents, and oddly enough often involving Spanish clubs. On 10 April 1974 Celtic entertained Atletico Madrid in a ferociously contested European Cup semi-final in which three visiting players were ordered off and seven booked by the referee. After the whistle there was considerable jostling and fighting among players from both sides in the tunnel;

In the Celtic vs Barcelona UEFA Cup tie on 11 March 2004 the Celtic goalkeeper Rab Douglas and the Barcelona midfielder Motta were involved in an incident as they were leaving the pitch and both were ordered off.

Unsurprisingly, given the volatile nature of many Old FIrm clashes, incidents have occurred after the whistle:

On 16 March 1997 Paolo di Canio and Iain Ferguson of Rangers were involved in a highly publicised incident on the way to the dressing room, and it has to be admitted that the Celtic player seemed the more at fault;

on 16 April 2008 Gary Caldwell (Celtic) and David Weir (Rangers) became embroiled in a scuffle after the whistle and apparently the incident continued as the players headed towards the tunnel. Both were issued red cards for the offences.

'TURNCOATS'

Several players have turned out for both members of the Old Firm, although direct transfers between the clubs are rare:

Tom Sinclair,

Robert Campbell,

Willie Kivlichan,

Hugh Shaw,

David Taylor,

Alec Bennett,

Davie McLean,

Scott Duncan,

James Young,

Alfie Conn,

Mo Johnston,

Kenny Miller,

Steven Pressley.

Mark Brown, Craig Beattie, Gordon Marshall and Barry Robson were once on Rangers' books though not making the first team.

Power and strength – Celtic captain Roy Aitken towers above
his Hearts opponent John Colquhoun in a match at Tynecastle.
John Colquhoun had previously played for Celtic

U/V

UNATTACHED PLAYERS

Pat Bonner played for the Republic of Ireland in the World Cup of 1994, held in the United States shortly after his registration with Celtic had ended; so, technically, he was a free agent at the time.

Henrik Larsson played for Sweden in the 2004 European Championships but he had already left Celtic at the time; he did not sign for Barcelona until after the championships.

UNIVERSITY GRADUATES

Not too surprisingly, given the demands of full-time football, the number of graduates who have completed their degrees while playing for Celtic is small.

John Atkinson: a medical student at Glasgow, John played one game for Celtic in 1909 – and scored two goals in a 5-1 win over Morton. He qualified as a doctor the following year.

Frank Brogan: Frank qualified as a CA and played on the left wing for Celtic.

Jim Brogan: Frank's younger brother is also a CA and played as a valued member of the Celtic side that won nine league titles in as many years.

Jim Craig: a graduate of Glasgow University, Jim was a fully qualified dentist and practised in Scotland for a number of years as well as briefly in South Africa.

John Cushley: Highly regarded as Billy McNeill's understudy, John was a graduate in Modern Languages from Glasgow University. He acted as translator for Jimmy McGrory when Celtic's manager was despatched to Spain in a vain attempt to sign Alfredo di Stefano.

Andrew Davidson: Andrew played five league games for Celtic in 1914 while a medical student at Glasgow. He qualified as a doctor in 1916.

John Fitzsimons: John played five times for Celtic in 1935 but was unable to replace the regular left winger Frank Murphy. He qualified as a doctor in 1940 and became Celtic's medical officer in 1953.

Mike Haughney graduated with a B.Comm. from Edinburgh University in 1953.

Tony Hepburn: Tony, an outside right, made only six appearances for Celtic in 1952, but graduated MA at Glasgow University, and later attained a law degree.

Frank Kelly: The son of Celtic's first captain, James Kelly, and brother of Bob Kelly, Celtic's long-serving chairman, Frank, another CA, made two league appearances for Celtic during World War I. He was killed in a train accident in France just after the conclusion of the Great War.

Alex Kiddie: An outside right, Alex played briefly as an amateur for Celtic before moving on to Aberdeen in 1945. He graduated with a B.Sc. from Aberdeen University in 1948.

William Kivlichan: Willie played ninety-two times for Celtic, mainly at outside right, between 1907 and 1911. He gained an MA from Glasgow University in 1908, and later retrained as a doctor in 1917.

Matt Lynch: He graduated with a B.Sc. from Glasgow in 1942 and played for Celtic during the wartime seasons, as well as briefly before and after the conflict. His academic career was as a teacher of mathematics.

Joe Riley: Joe played ten league matches in 1928 as a possible replacement for the inconsistent Tommy McInally, and also graduated from Glasgow University with a B.Sc. to become a teacher in 1931.

Leigh R. Roose: an amateur and Welsh internationalist goalkeeper, Roose played one Scottish Cup tie against Clyde in 1910. He was also a doctor who won the Military Medal during World War I in which he later died.

John Weir: A midfield player who made a number of appearances in 1980/81, and studied Civil Engineering at Strathclyde University after he left Celtic in 1982.

'UPSTARTS'

Celtic were deeply resented in some quarters when they first burst upon the Scottish football scene in 1888. The new club was identified as being predominantly Irish and Catholic, but additional resentment was felt when it embarked on an aggressive signing policy, openly flouting the rules against professionalism.

Perhaps, some older clubs were jealous of the immediate success attained by 'the upstarts from Glasgow's East End' who reached the final of the Scottish Cup in their first season.

Clubs already in existence at the time of Celtic's start – and who are still active in football – include the following:

Albion Rovers (1882),
Alloa (1883),
Arbroath (1878),
Berwick Rangers (1881),
Clyde (1878),
Cowdenbeath (1881),
Dumbarton (1878),
Dunfermline Athletic (1885),
East Stirlingshire (1880),
Falkirk (1876),
Forfar Athletic (1885),
Morton (1874),
Hamilton Academical (1874),
Heart of Midlothian (1874),
Hibernian (1873),
Kilmarnock (1869),
Montrose (1879),
Motherwell (1876),
Partick Thistle (1876),
Queen's Park (1867),
Raith Rovers (1883),

Rangers (1873),
St. Johnstone (1884),
St. Mirren (1877),
Stenhousemuir (1884),
Stranraer (1870).

The Scottish League was inaugurated in April 1890 with the following membership: Abercorn, Cambuslang, Celtic, Cowlairs, Dumbarton, Hearts, Rangers, St. Mirren, Third Lanark, Vale of Leven and Renton. There were three notable omissions: Queen's Park and Clyde who declined the overtures made to them, and St. Bernard's who were not accepted by the original members.

Of those founding members only Celtic, Dumbarton, Hearts, Rangers, and St. Mirren still function as members of a Scottish League.

URUGUAY

Celtic have played only one match in Uruguay – on 4 November 1967 at the Estadio Centenario in Montevideo. This was the infamous play-off match for the World Club Championship against the Racing Club of Buenos Aires.

In this World Club Championship, Celtic and Racing had won their home legs. Celtic, in view of the violence seen in those matches, seriously considered withdrawing from the play-off game. They eventually chose to compete but with unfortunate consequences. The match was lost 1-0, six players (four from Celtic) were sent off by a referee out of his depth and the eleven Celtic players who had participated were each fined £250 by the club.

V

It would seem unlikely that many surnames begin with this letter but Celtic, especially in recent times, have had a share:

Joos Valgaeren, Pierre van Hooijdonk, Stanislaus Varga, Rudi Vata, Ramon Vega, Mark Viduka, Jan Vennegoor of Hesselink

VALENTINES

Several fixtures down the years have been scheduled for 14 February (St. Valentine's Day).

1903 St. Mirren H SC 4-0 Murray, McMahon, Watson, Campbell

1914 Morton H SL 3-0 McColl, Gallacher, Browning

1920 Albion Rovers H SL 3-0 McLean (2), McInally

1922 St. Mirren A SL 2-0 McInally (2)

1923 Albion Rovers H SL 1-1 Cassidy (pen)

1925 St. Johnstone A SL 2-1 Connolly, Thomson

1928 Dundee H SL 3-1 Thomson, McInally, McLean

1931 Morton A SC 4-1 McGrory (3), Napier

1948 Queen of the South A SL 0-2

1953 Hearts H SL 1-1 McPhail (pen)

1968 Stirling Albion H SL 2-0 Gemmell, Wallace

1981 Stirling Albion H SC 3-0 McGarvey, McCluskey, Burns

1984 St. Mirren H 2-0 PL McGarvey (2)

1987 Hearts H PL 1-1 McClair

The only club to beat Celtic on St. Valentine's Day (14 February) has been Queen of the South; similarly, the only club to beat Celtic on a Christmas Day was Queen of the South.

Perhaps some Celtic followers will recall that Rangers' centre half on 19 October 1957 was named John Valentine, recruited amid great fanfare from Queen's Park. The 7-1 defeat by Celtic in the League Cup final hastened the end of his Ibrox career.

A referee named Bob Valentine (Dundee) took the 1977 Scottish Cup final and awarded Celtic a highly controversial penalty kick from which Andy Lynch scored the game's only goal. Rangers' defenders protested at length about the decision.

VERSATILITY

The ability to play well in more than one position has always been prized at Celtic Park.

Bobby Evans: Signed as a teenager from St. Anthony's in 1944, Bobby was more recognised as a utility forward in his early days. Certainly, he played at inside or outside left most frequently although he may have been fielded in other forward positions on occasion. He made his first start as a right half in the relegation battle at Dens Park in 1948 and, following the arrival of the celebrated English coach Jimmy Hogan, made the position his own in the following season with international honours coming his way. After Jock Stein's ankle injury in 1955 Evans played regularly at centre half, having already played in that position for Scotland in a previous emergency. Whenever a Celtic goalkeeper was injured – prior to the use of substitutes – Bobby Evans was the designated keeper, most notably in the St. Mungo Cup final of 1951.

John McPhail: Another wartime signing (from Strathclyde in 1941), John played regularly at right half although he was occasionally switched to left half, and sometimes at centre forward. Shortly after the war he alternated between right half and inside right. In 1950 he was moved to centre forward and heralded the move with a hat-trick against Falkirk. For two seasons McPhail was the regular centre forward and performed admirably both on the ground and in the air until weight problems and injury slowed him down. His career looked over but he was restored to the side in 1953 as a left half and played outstandingly in the Coronation Cup. John McPhail performed creditably for Celtic in all three midfield positions, and in every forward position between 1941 and 1956.

Willie Fernie: A gifted and gentlemanly player, the problem lay in deciding his best position. He started off as inside right but was frequently switched to inside left. However, he made at least one appearance (unsuccessfully) at centre forward and several at outside left, most famously in the Coronation Cup final against Hibernian in 1953. He was granted a new lease of life when he was moved back to right half, from which position he engineered the 7-1 rout of Rangers in the 1957 League Cup final. He proved equally versatile in his Scotland appearances.

Chic Geatons: A hard worker in midfield after signing for Celtic from Lochgelly Celtic, Fife-born Chic, starting off as a right back, played in all three positions in the half-back line. He may well be best remembered for the forty-odd minutes he played in goal when John Thomson was injured at Ibrox on 5 September 1931. After retiring as a player Geatons returned to Celtic Park as trainer, and later as a coach to give up that role in 1950.

Alec McNair: Described inadequately in some Celtic histories as 'a utility player', Alec joined Celtic in 1904 from Stenhousemuir as an inside-forward but he was moved around regularly to cover for absent players – he made his debut at outside left against Queen's Park in 1904 – but by 1908 he had established himself as the best right back in the country, his coolness under pressure earning him the nickname of 'the Icicle'. His manager Willie Maley reckoned that the long-serving McNair – his last appearance at the age of 41 was the 1-0 win over Hibernian in the 1923 Scottish Cup final – could have played any position equally well, including that of goalkeeper. For Scotland he earned eighteen 'caps' (including three unofficial Victory internationals in 1919) turning out for his country in three different positions: right back, right half and left half.

Peter Dowds: Signed from Broxburn Shamrock in 1889, Peter Dowds is a largely forgotten player but he is recalled as being Celtic's best all-round player in that during the club's early seasons – when organised football was in its infancy – he was fielded in virtually every position: in defence and attack, and on the right and on the left. Unusually, for such a 'utility' player, Dowds could score goals as his tally of twenty-one in forty-nine appearances attests.

Some players have made interesting changes in position: Tom McAdam from centre forward to centre half; Neil Mochan from centre forward and outside left to left back and Chris Sutton from centre forward to centre half and also midfield.

War hero Sgt. Willie Angus, VC, was paraded round the track of Celtic Park at a game in 1917 to encourage spectators to enlist for the final push to end World War I. James Kelly supports Angus in his walk round the track, accompanied by Willie Maley

W

WARTIME FOOTBALL

Football found itself in an awkward position during the two World Wars: 1914-1918 and 1939-1945. Morale at home may have been boosted by the continuation of the football schedule, but with many footballers (and supporters) absent on war duties the atmosphere could be unreal.

During both conflicts the SFA discontinued the Scottish Cup, but the Scottish League struggled on after a fashion.

As a belated recognition of the situation the Scottish League decided that the league competitions during the World War II would be considered 'unofficial'.

WORLD WAR I (1914 – 1918)

A powerful Celtic side were in the ascendancy at the start of the Great War and remained so for most of the duration, mainly because the nucleus of the team found employment in war-related industries such as mining or munitions rather than in the armed forces. Celtic won the league championship in 1913/14, 1914/15, 1915/16, 1916/17 and finished only one point behind Rangers in 1917/18.

No doubt Morton owed much of its prominence during these seasons to its important strategic position as a port and ship-building centre, factors which attracted extra thousands to Greenock.

The cumulative league tables for those seasons during World War I make interesting reading as an illustration of the relative strength of the top clubs:

	P	W	D	L	F	A	Pts	(Position)
Celtic	182	139	31	12	423	113	309	(1 1 1 2 1)
Rangers	182	123	26	33	381	158	272	(3 2 3 1 2)
Morton	181	99	45	37	361	204	243	(4 3 2 3 3)
Hearts	181	89	30	62	293	246	208	(2 5 14 10 7)
Partick Thistle	182	79	42	61	278	222	206	(7 5 9 6 4)

Similarly Motherwell – recognised as an important centre within the industrial heartland of Scotland – showed steady improvement in its football fortunes throughout the war years, finishing successively in 17th, 13th, 8th, 5th and 5th positions.

Players throughout Scotland were called up for military service or volunteered – as in the celebrated case of Heart of Midlothian whose first team players joined up en masse at the start of the war. Footballers on leave from the services turned out for their clubs on a random basis, or made guest appearances for other (closer) teams. Football had reverted largely to a part-time arrangement. It was agreed that for the sake of morale the sport should be allowed to continue but no player was to make a full-time living from football (allowing him to work in a war-related industry). No close-season wages were permitted, and pay rates ranged from a minimum of £1 per week to £2 but players were not permitted to turn out for their clubs on the Saturday if they had not completed their regular week's work beforehand; fixtures were scheduled only for Saturdays or holidays to prevent any absenteeism from the war effort.

In the season immediately preceding the war Celtic had won the league title comfortably enough with a six-point margin over Rangers – and incidentally with an identical record to the first wartime championship (P38 W30 D5 L3 Pts65). For that season Celtic were well grounded in defence with the following rearguard: Shaw, McNair, Dodds, Young, Johnstone, McMaster. The goalkeeper Charlie Shaw had established a telepathic understanding with his two full backs, the always unruffled Alec McNair and the energetic Joe Dodds. Outstanding individually, they had perfected the new art of the passback to the goalkeeper as a means of escaping trouble.

'Sunny Jim' Young, although nearing the end of his career, was an outstanding right half. Apparently ungainly, he was a difficult player to round and his tireless enthusiasm was a constant inspiration to his team-mates. Peter Johnstone, who had started off as an inside left, had developed into a reliable centre half, strong in both air and on the ground while John McMaster had filled gap left by the departure of Jimmy Hay to Newcastle United to everybody's satisfaction. This unit conceded only fourteen (14) goals in the thirty-eight (38) match league programme.

Celtic dominated Scottish football during the years of World War I in much the same way as Rangers were to do in World War II – and were subject to much the same criticism, the suggestion being that the players were shirking their patriotic duty by not serving in the armed forces.

The accusation is worth scrutiny and seems ill-founded. One former player Willie Angus received the Victoria Cross, the military's highest award for gallantry, for rescuing an officer during trench warfare in France being wounded seriously in the course of his action and losing the sight of an eye. Peter Johnstone, a regular at centre half, was killed in action at Arras in 1917. Willie Maley, the club's manager and the son of a soldier, volunteered for service but was turned down on the grounds of age and devoted much of his energies as manager to helping the war effort. Celtic sent footballs to the men undergoing military training and to soldiers at the Front; men in uniform were admitted free to the ground for fixtures; support was extended to wounded soldiers at Stahl Hospital and to British prisoners-of-war; the Celtic Sports in 1915 were virtually a recruiting rally.

Like footballers elsewhere in Scotland, Celtic's served in the forces, worked in the shipyards, in the steel forges, and down the mines. For example, Patsy Gallacher worked in the shipyards, Joe Dodds in munitions at Beardmore's, and Andy McAtee in the mines. However, the football authorities were rightfully vigilant and Patsy Gallacher became an early victim when he was fined £3 by the Glasgow Munitions Tribunal in November 1916, and suspended by the Scottish League from 19 December 1916 to 27 January 1917 for 'bad timekeeping as an apprentice shipwright' and Celtic were also fined £25.

Throughout the next four seasons Celt attained a remarkable level of consistency. Winners of the coveted double of Scottish Cup and League Championship in the last pre-war season, Celtic simply continued their success with a group of players reaching their peak. The defence has been praised already but the forward line contained two of the best -ever inside forwards to play in Scotland: the youthful Patsy Gallacher and the veteran Jimmy McMenemy. They were assisted by two outstanding wingers, Andy McAtee and Adam McLean, forceful men who could cross a ball and score frequently themselves. The only problem appeared at centre forward where Celtic were seeking an adequate replacement for Jimmy Quinn. 'Trooper Joe' Cassidy and Jimmy McColl between them filled that gap but Cassidy could appear only when on leave and McColl, prolific scorer as he turned out to be, was inexperienced and at times injury-prone.

What was Celtic's secret? For one thing, Celtic's squad, although limited in number, was a versatile one with several players able and willing to accommodate the team's needs by playing in different positions: McNair could play in every defensive position, Dodds could play equally well at centre half or left half, Cassidy could be fielded confidently in every forward position, Gallacher and McMenemy could switch from inside left to inside right with ease, 'Sunny Jim' could play every half-back position – and even in goal on one occasion!

Willie Maley was at his prime during this period. He was probably the epitome of the football manager of the era: astute at spotting raw talent, and later picking players' best positions, authoritative in dealing with matters of discipline, energetic in every matter that concerned Celtic's best interest, he inspired his players to greater efforts through his enthusiasm or through the authority he wielded.

Hearts provided the main opposition in the 1914/15 season but the absence of so many starting players caught up with them as the season reached an end, Celtic running out winners by five points.

In the following season Celtic strolled to the championship to win by eleven points from Rangers. So confident were this Celtic side that they could afford to fulfill two fixtures on the same day (15 April 1916). They defeated Raith Rovers by 6-0 at Celtic Park after kicking off at 3:15, and travelled to Fir Park to defeat Motherwell by 3-1 – with only one change from the previous match.

In 1916/17 Celtic remained in charge throughout the campaign to win by ten points from a strong Morton side – and during this season completed a record run of sixty-two league matches without defeat (from 13 November 1915 to 21 April 1917). So dominant were Celtic then that some critics nicknamed them 'the Huns', comparing them to an all-conquering German army.

In 1917/18 Rangers interrupted Celtic's string of league titles, scraping through by a single point with the outcome in doubt till the last seconds of the season. Celtic, despite exerting pressure on Motherwell's defence throughout, were held to a 1-1 draw at Parkhead at the same time as Rangers were beating humble Clyde 2-1 at Ibrox. A Celtic victory would have meant another play-off match between the Old Firm as had happened in 1905.

Celtic partisans pointed out, ungraciously, that 'Rangers' had won the title with the aid of guest players from Queen's Park, Oldham Athletic, Hearts, Hibernian, Clyde, Dumbarton, Raith Rovers, Dundee, Morton and Sheffield Wednesday.

Celtic struggled at the start of the last wartime season (1918/19). By December 1918 Rangers had moved five points ahead, including a 3-0 win in November at Celtic Park against disorganised opponents. Celtic, however, rallied and embarked on a run of twenty league matches without defeat to regain the title by a single point.

The following list of players with Celtic connections served in the services during the Great War:

William Angus, VC was a Celtic reserve player briefly before the war;

Tom Barber fought with the Footballers' Battalion while with Aston Villa and, after being invalided out of the army, worked in a munitions factory in Glasgow making five appearances for Celtic in 1918;

Alex Bennett, who played for both Celtic and Rangers, joined the Scottish Rifles;

James Blessington served in the Merchant Navy;

Robert Boyle served in France with the Canadian Field Artillery;

John Brown, an outside left who served in the Royal Navy, was invalided out in 1916;

Joe Cassidy served in the HLI from 1915 on and gained the Military Medal in 1918;

Joseph Clark also served in the Armed Forces;

John Coleman, by 1914 overage for the forces, wangled his way into uniform;

Robert Craig a full back from 1906 to 1909 who served with the South Wales Borderers and died in action 1918;

Willie Cringan served in the Royal Flying Corps;

Andrew Davidson, a doctor, played for Celtic at the outbreak of war and served with the RAMC from 1916 on;

Joe Dodds acted as a driver with the Royal Field Artillery in France;

Scott Duncan, who 'guested' briefly for
Celtic, also served with the Royal Field
Artillery in 1917;

William Ferguson served in the Army in
1916;

James Fisher served with the Royal
Engineers;

Michael Gilhooly was a reserve player
who joined Celtic in 1913 and served
in the 17th HLI;

James Hay served with the RFA;

John Jackson served with the Royal Scots
Fusiliers;

Peter Johnstone, Celtic's regular pivot,
served with the Argyle & Sutherland
Highlanders and was killed in action
at the Somme in 1917;

Frank Kelly, an outside right and brother
of Bob Kelly, joined the Cameronians
Scottish Rifles and died after a train
accident in 1919 while still serving in
post war France;

Willie Kivlichan, another doctor, served
with the King's Own African Rifles,
and was wounded in 1918;

George Livingstone served with the
KOAR and RAMC in East Africa;

Allan Lynch, an outside left, served with
the Scottish Rifles;

Andy McAtee, a stocky outside right with
Celtic, served with RFA as a gunner in
Italy with the 29th Division;

Thomas McAteer, centre half and Celtic
goalscorer in the 1911 Scottish Cup
final against Hamilton Academical,
served with the Cameron Highlanders
in 1914 and was wounded in action;

Patrick McCabe joined the Scots Guards
in 1916;

Dan McCann served in the Army from
1914 to1917;

Tom McDermott was in the HLI Black
Watch in 1916;

William McGinnigle served in the Army
before joining Celtic in 1918;

Tom McGregor served with the Argyll &
Sutherland Highlanders;

James McIntosh was in the Scots Guards
at the start in 1914, and had
transferred to the US Army by1917;

James McKay served with the Royal Scots
Fusiliers; he was still patriotic enough
to drive army lorries during World
War II;

James McLaren, an ex-Celt of 1891,
served in the Canadian Army;

Donald McLeod of the Royal Field
Artillery died in Flanders in 1917;

John McMaster, Celtic's regular left half,
was with the Royal Engineers and was
wounded in France in 1918;

William McOustra played for Celtic from
1900 to 1902 and joined the Scots
Guards in 1915;

James McStay, a long-serving Celt in the
1920s and 30s, joined the Royal Scots
Fusiliers in 1918;

William McStay, Jimmy's brother and
another long-time Celt, served with
the North Irish Horse in 1917;

James Murphy joined Celtic in 1920 after
service with the Royal Scots Fusiliers;

William Nicol, an Englishman from
Durham, played for Celtic in 1911/12
and had been a professional soldier
pre-war with the Seaforths. During
the conflict he won the DCM
(Distinguished Conduct Medal), rose
to rank of lieutenant, and was
wounded in action;

Joe O'Kane served with the Royal Irish
Regiment and Royal Engineers in
1915;

Ebenezer Owers served with the Footballers' Battalion;

David Pratt of the Cameron Highlanders won the Military Medal, and joined Celtic in 1919;

William Ribchester served with the OTC Machine Gun Corps in 1917, was promoted to Lieutenant and wounded in action in 1918;

Leigh Roose, yet another doctor, made one appearance for Celtic as an amateur. He joined the Royal Fusiliers in 1914 and was killed in action in 1916 at the Somme. During the war he was decorated (Military Medal);

William Semple, an outside left from 1907 to 1909, later fought with the Ist Battalion 7th King's Regiment;

John Shaughnessy, a Celtic director, held the rank of Lt. Colonel with the HLI;

Thomas Sinclair played six league matches for Celtic while on loan from Rangers in 1906 and did not concede a goal. He also picked up a Glasgow Cup medal when with Celtic. He served with the army from 1914 to 1916;

David Taylor joined Celtic in 1919, having played for Burnley twice against Celtic in 1914 at Budapest and Turf Moor. He had just served his time with the RA;

George Whitehead, a centre forward, signed from Hearts in 1913 but in 1915 he joined the Royal Naval Division and was torpedoed twice and rescued twice;

James Young played briefly for Celtic as an outside right in February 1918, but later the same month he joined Rangers, and served in the Army from May 1918.

WORLD WAR II (1939 -1946)

Several reliable historians consider that the period of World War II coincides with the most dramatic decline in Celtic's footballing fortunes – and there is much to substantiate this claim.

In 1938 Celtic won the Empire Exhibition Trophy against English and Scottish opposition. It could be said that this competition – described as an unofficial British Championship – might be considered as an equally unofficial World Club Championship as Britain still led the world in football.

The Celtic side which defeated Everton – packed with internationalists from England, Scotland, Wales and Ireland – in the final at Ibrox Park on 10 June 1938 was as follows:

Kennaway, Hogg, Morrison, Geatons, Lyon, Paterson, Delaney, MacDonald, Crum, Divers, Murphy.

During the first part of World War II most of these players were still available for Celtic, but on-field performance was at an all-time low.

What went wrong?

Three outstanding players were missing: Joe Kennaway, the American/Canadian goalkeeper, returned to North America shortly after the start of the conflict; Jimmy Delaney suffered an arm injury so serious that the surgeon considered amputation and he was out for more than two seasons; Willie Lyon, the captain, was quick to volunteer for active service and was largely unavailable 'for the duration'.

Willie Maley, a stalwart as Celtic's secretary and manager for so many years, was summarily dismissed at New Year 1940 after a series of poor results but that was a mere pretext for the directors who had viewed the 70 year-old's increasing authoritarianism with ever-deepening resentment. Their choice of replacement, Jimmy McStay – a former Celtic captain – hinted at a stop-gap solution from the very start and he was hamstrung in his team selection as players came and went, or were available then unavailable.

Lastly, and perhaps more importantly, the Celtic board of directors gave no real committment to football throughout the war – and were uninspiring to a man.

None of the players seemed too aware of the privilege of playing for Celtic – admittedly under the unreal and unofficial seasons of the war.

Other clubs were able to make use of star players stationed in Scotland with the Forces: Rangers were able to field on occasion such English-based luminaries as Stanley Matthews (Stoke City), Frank Swift (Manchester City), Torry Gillick and Jimmy Caskie (both of Everton); Hibernian fielded Matt Busby (Liverpool) and the distinguished amateur Bob Hardisty (Bishop Auckland); while humble Morton could sometimes field Stanley Matthews and Tommy Lawton (Everton). No doubt these 'guests' received some extra remuneration for their appearances, but Celtic consistently declined the opportunity to display this calibre of performer in their colours.

The case of Matt Busby is a fine example of their shortsightedness. Busby, born near Bellshill and of a Celtic-minded family and background, turned up at Celtic Park to offer his services but he was turned down. He promptly went through to Edinburgh where he gave Hibernian two outstanding years, and laid the foundation of that club's period of success immediately following the war.

Those players who had represented the club so well in the pre-war seasons – and who were still available – simply lost interest at playing for £2 a week and training part-time after their essential war work. Several went to clubs prepared to appreciate their talents: Johnny Crum and John Divers for example, went to Morton, a most enterprising outfit during the years of the Second World War.

What made it infinitely worse for Celtic's long-suffering support was the fact that Rangers dominated Scottish football during the years of World War II. In fact, so dominant was the Ibrox club that they fielded a side in the North-Eastern League. This was virtually a reserve side but it competed against the first-teams of such as Aberdeen and Dundee, going so far as to win their league championship in 1941/42.

Several Celtic historians have suggested that Rangers' wartime football success was based on their having secured employment for many of their players in 'reserved' employment, such as in shipbuilding, and suggest that the Ulster connection with Harland & Wolf was convenient for the purpose. Certainly, their long-time manager Bill Struth was determined to preserve the standards of football at Ibrox and did much to ensure that success by retaining so many players on his staff.

Does he – and Rangers – deserve criticism for this policy? During the war the morale among Rangers supporters was at an all-time high, and the Ibrox club deserves some credit for those on-field efforts. Significantly, when the war ended, Rangers were able to retain their leadership in the Scottish game – while Celtic continued to drift. Hibernian, who also had made an effort to maintain football standards, were the main rivals to Rangers during the immediate post-war years.

Celtic appear to have made little effort to ensure keeping their players and left them to fend for themselves. Johnny Crum originally worked at constructing air-raid shelters but was able to find work in a Govan shipyard – but only after the intervention of Jimmy Smith, Rangers' centre forward (*Weekly News*: 10 February 1940)

To be fair, Celtic did improve during the war-time seasons, 'rising to mediocrity' as one critic acidly put it. In 1940, after beating Rangers somewhat luckily 1-0 at Ibrox in September Celtic picked up the Glasgow Cup. Almost three years passed before the next piece of silverware headed to Celtic Park – the Charity Cup of 1943, after a convincing 3-0 win over Third Lanark at Hampden. The last trophy – the Victory-in-Europe Cup was gained by the narrowest of margins – by a single corner kick – over a youthful Queen's Park side in May 1945. (See War-Time Trophies)

As in World War I, many players with a Celtic connection went off to join the Armed Services:

Seton Airlie served in the Royal Artillery;
Oliver Anderson also served in the Royal Artillery, serving from 1 September 1939 onwards;

Alec Boden was called up in 1943 and served as a PT Instructor before being demobbed in 1946;

John Cantwell after serving in the Royal Navy joined Celtic in 1946;

Joe Coen a goalkeeper who played briefly for Celtic in 1931 joined the RAF and was killed in action in 1941;

Austin Collier another PT instructor – and an English-born left half – made three appearances for Celtic in 1941;

John Conway served in the RAF from August 1942;

Willie Corbett served in the Royal Navy from 1942 onwards;

Thomas Doyle who played briefly for Celtic in pre-war days was in the Armed Forces between 1940-1946;

Robert Duffy was a wing half with Celtic from 1935 to 1947 but his football career was badly affected by the war as he made only four appearances with the first eleven, leaving Celtic to join the RAF in 1940. He acted as a PT Instructor;

Willie Dunn, a centre forward from 1932 to 1935, joined the RAF in 1941;

Willie Fagan, a pre-war (1934 to 1937) inside forward was with the RAF from 1939. He made later appearances with Celtic as a guest player from Liverpool;

Cornelius Ferguson was borrowed from Alloa Athletic in 1940 but had made only two appearances before he joined the RAF in 1941;

Robert Fisher was a soldier with the Royal Engineers and was with the BEF prior to the mass evacuation from France and Belgium in 1940. He joined Celtic in 1942 and made three wartime appearances as a centre forward;

Willie Gallacher, Patsy's son and Celtic inside forward, served with the Royal Engineers;

George Hazlett was a sailor with the Royal Navy before joining Celtic in November 1945;

Gil Heron, born in Jamaica but a resident of the United States served for three years with the RCAF. He joined Celtic after being spotted on the club's tour of the United States in 1951;

Mike Haughney, who scored the winning goal against Rangers (3-2) in his debut in 1949, served as a Captain in the Seaforth Highlanders and trained as a Commando;

John Hunter, who made seventeen appearances as a goalkeeper in 1941, joined the Royal Navy in 1942 serving until 1945;

Walter Jones, a guest player from Port Vale, was stationed with the Army in Scotland, and made three appearances as a centre forward in 1940;

John Jordan served with the Scots Guards while a player with Queen's Park, and joined Celtic in 1946;

Konrad Kapler, Celtic's promising outside left, was spotted by the club while playing with his Polish Army unit;

Charles Kelly, an outside left with Cambuslang Rangers, was an outstanding junior player before and after his time with Celtic in 1944 and 1945. He joined the Royal Navy in 1945 to serve in the Far East;

Tommy Kiernan joined Celtic in 1945 from Albion Rovers after serving with Royal Engineers;

Willie Lyon, Celtic's pre-war captain and centre half, joined the Scots Grays in 1940, and was awarded the Military Cross in 1943 for gallantry in Tunisia. He started off as a private and emerged from the war as a Major;

Tom Lyon, Willie's brother and part-time Celtic player, served with the 14th Army in Burma;

Henry McCluskey made four starts for Celtic in 1943 before joining the Royal Engineers;

Joseph McCulloch, a competent left back, had made twelve appearances for Celtic before joining the Royal Scots Fusiliers in 1941. He was killed in action in a tank battle in Holland in 1945;

Pat McDonald, a useful left back, served with the Royal Navy;

Tommy McDonald after serving with the Royal Navy joined Celtic in 1947;

John McInally played for Celtic between 1934 and 1937 and served with the RAF;

Jim McKay was with the Cameronians in Burma;

James McLaughlin, a centre forward with Renfrew Juniors, joined Celtic after three years in the Royal Navy;

Roy Milne, who made his debut at left back in 1940, was stationed with the RAF in India;

Frank Murphy, outside left in a famous pre-war Celtic forward line, joined the RAF in 1943;

David Nelson, a corporal in the Wiltshire Regiment, joined Celtic on loan in 1942;

Hugh O'Donnell, an outside left for Celtic with twenty goals in seventy-five appearances, left the club to join Preston North End in 1935 and served with the RAF from 1940 onwards;

George Paterson, Celtic's left half in the Empire Exhibition side, joined the RAF in 1941;

Johnny Paton served with the RAF from 1943 as a navigator and bomb-aimer; also served as a Flying Officer

Joe Rae, a hard-working centre forward, signed for Celtic in 1942 but made only 45 appearances (21 goals) as he joined the Navy in 1943, missing to the club for several years;

James Shields signed for Celtic in March 1939 but served with the RAF between 1941 and 1946;

Willie Waddell joined Celtic on long-term loan from Aberdeen in 1940 but was serving in the 8th Army against Rommel in North Africa by 1942;

John Watters was with Celtic from 1935 to 1947 as an inside forward but his career was badly interrupted by his Royal Navy service starting in 1940. He took part in the Normandy landings in 1944;

Jock Weir, popular Celtic right winger and centre forward in the late 1940s and early 1950s served with the Royal Navy in the Fleet Air Arm from 1941;

Desmond White, Celtic's secretary, was involved in an accident in Canada while serving with the RAF.

Abbreviations:
BAOR; British Army on Rhine,
BEF; British Expeditionary Force,
HLI: Highland Light Infantry,
PTI: Physical Training Instructor,

RAF: Royal Air Force,
RA: Royal Artillery,
RCAF: Royal Canadian Air Force,
RFA: Royal Field Artillery,
RAMC: Royal Army Medical Corps,
RN: Royal Navy.

WAR-TIME APPEARANCES (1939 – 1946)

An often neglected aspect of Celtic's history, this section contains details of players' appearances in the Regional League, Southern League Cup, and the War Cup. Each player is given his total appearances and goals scored; goalkeepers are credited with shutouts. A short-hand description of the player's regular position is indicated.

Seton Airlie cf 17/5
Oliver Anderson or 3/1
Tommy Bogan or 8/1
Bill Boland ir 4/2
Willie Buchan ir (loan) 1/0
Joe Carruth cf 14/5
Austin Collier lh (loan) 3/0
John Conway ir 25/5
Willie Corbett ch 39/0
John Crum cf 69/23
Jimmy Culley gk 22[5]
Jimmy Delaney or 145/87
John Divers il 115/44
Harry Dornan lb (loan) 66/1
Davie Duncan ol 14/3
Bobby Evans rh 14/1
Willie Fagan if (loan) 2/1
Neil Ferguson lb,lh (loan) 2/0
George Ferguson fb 6/0
Robert Fisher cf 3/1;
Willie Gallacher ir 18/3
Jackie Gallagher cf 83/69
Chic Geatons rh 26/2

George Gillan il 30/10

Hugh Gilmartin ir 3/0

John Gould or 17/5;

George Hazlett ol (loan) 7/1

Dennis Hill ol 2/1

Bobby Hogg rb 216/0

John Hunter gk(loan) 17[1]

George Johnstone gk (loan) 37[8]

Maurice Jones cf loan 3/1

Charles Kelly ol 4/0

Frank Kelly fb 2/0

Johnny Kelly ol 29/3

John Kelly fb 5/0

Alex Kiddie or 2/0

Tommy Kiernan ir 32/4

Hugh Long ol 24/3

Matt Lynch rh 143/28

Tom Lyon if (loan) 3/0

Willie Lyon ch 24/0

Gerry McAloon if (loan) 28/16

Tony McAtee ol 4/1

Pat McAuley lh 113/23

Harry McCluskey wh 6/0

Joe McCulloch lb 12/0

James McDonald or 7/3

Malcolm MacDonald if 188/18

Pat McDonald lb 75/1

Hugh McFarlane ch (loan) 5/0

Charlie McGinlay if 11/1

Jimmy McGowan il 23/5

Johnny McIlhatton ir 1/0

Donald McKay gk 17[1]

Jim McKay cf 3/2

Joe McLaughlin d/m/f 150/35

Duncan McMillan ch 20/0

John McPhail m/f 131/13

Jimmy Mallan lb 70/0

Willie Miller gk 142[36]

Roy Milne lb 33/0

John Morrison lb 22/0

Frank Murphy ol 82/27

David Nelson ol (loan)1/0

Jimmy Nelson ol 14/3

Hugh O'Neill ch 11/1

Pat O'Sullivan ol 13/0 ;

George Paterson lh 88/2

Johnny Paton ol 36/13

Robert Quinn rh 3/0

Joe Rae cf 19/12

John Riley or 22/10

Pat Rodgers ol 19/1

Jimmy Shields if 3/0

Jimmy Sirrel if 10/2

Bob Smith gk (loan) 15[1]

Willie Waddell ch 53/0

Jackie Watters if 9/0

John Wylie rh 1/0

Andy Young ir 3/0

The careers of some players were badly affected by the war and among them might be included Jimmy Delaney, John Divers, Bobby Hogg, Matt Lynch, Pat McAuley, Malcolm MacDonald, Joe McLaughlin, John McPhail, Willie Miller, and George Paterson – each of whom made a significant number of appearances during these 'unofficial' seasons.

Other players made only fleeting appearances for Celtic but went on to have respectable careers with other clubs after the war: Davie Duncan (East Fife), George Johnstone (Aberdeen and Raith Rovers), Johnny Kelly (Morton and Barnsley), Hugh Long (Clyde), Johnny McIlhatton (Albion Rovers and Aberdeen), Joe McLaughlin (Aberdeen and Raith Rovers) and Andy Young (Raith Rovers).

WAR-TIME TROPHIES

During World War II (1939-1945) Celtic simply went through the motions of competing in the 'unofficial' seasons of the conflict. Their manager, former captain Jimmy McStay, had been lured from Alloa Athletic to replace Willie Maley but the newcomer was hamstrung in his efforts to field a competitive side. The Celtic directors declined to use the services of some outstanding footballers stationed in Scotland with the Armed Forces and this contributed to the club's falling away.

However, under the managership of Jimmy McStay, Celtic did manage to gain some silverware: the Glasgow Cup (1940), the Charity Cup (1943) and the Victory-in-Europe Cup (1945).

The first was won at Ibrox Park on 28 September 1940 against the clear favourites Rangers, a perennial powerhouse during World War II. Celtic's side included two Aberdeen players (goalkeeper George Johnstone and pivot Willie Waddell) and the only goal was scored in 61 minutes, although the newspapers suggested a suspicion of offside.

The second – the 1943 Charity Cup – was won at Hampden Park on 22 May 1943 with an eventually comfortable win over Third Lanark by 3-0 with goals from Charlie McGinley (2) and Hugh Long before a crowd of 26,000. Celtic looked strong down the right side with Bobby Hogg at full-back, Matt Lynch at wing-half, and Jimmy Delaney and John McPhail on the right wing – but all three goals (the last a solo run by Long) came from the left.

The last – the Victory-in-Europe Cup – was won on 9 May 1945 at Hampden Park in a narrow win on corner kicks over a gallant Queen's Park side, called into action at the last minute when Rangers withdrew from the event organised by the Glasgow Charity Cup Committee. Johnny Paton equalised in 27 minutes and the match ended 1-1 but Celtic scraped through by the narrowest of margins – three corners to two.

These were probably the only highlights of a most depressing period in the club's history.

WESTERN REGIONAL LEAGUE

Throughout World War II football in Scotland was in crisis. However, it was quickly agreed that some form of the sport would contribute to maintain morale, and so the sport operated on a part-time 'unofficial' basis.

Unlike World War I the Scottish League decided to suspend the season after a few games in 1939. The League decided to organise two regional leagues – an Eastern and Western – probably because of the difficulties in travelling during wartime.

Celtic featured in the Western League in its only 'season', but did not distinguish themselves ending up with a mediocre record – P30 W9 D6 L15 F55 A61 Pts 24. This meant they ended in thirteenth place, well behind the champions Rangers who accumulated double Celtic's points' total.

At the end of the campaign Celtic recorded a heavy financial loss of £7,155 caused by several factors: an unusually cold winter, the make-shift nature of the league, and the club's obvious lack of ambition during the war.

After this 1939/40 'season' Celtic participated in the marginally better Scottish Southern League.

WHISTLE

When Celtic played Morton at Cappielow on 23 January 1965, they were leading 3-0 with only thirteen minutes left but they surrendered that lead before the end. Celtic could be considered lucky as another shot was heading into the net as the referee blew for full time.

WIND DELAY

Celtic's Scottish Cup tie against Inverness Caledonian Thistle was scheduled for 4 February 2000 but high winds caused parts of the guttering on the roof of one stand to be dislodged. For safety reasons the fixture was postponed until the following Wednesday (8 February) – and Inverness Caley won 3-1!

WORLD CLUB CHAMPIONSHIP

In 1967 Celtic as European champions faced Racing Club (Argentina) for the glory of being recognised as 'the best club side in the world'. The first leg on 18 October 1967 was held at Hampden Park to accommodate a larger crowd and about 90,000 attended the match. It proved to be a brutal encounter with the Buenos Aires side making little effort to attack, and attempting to frustrate Celtic with cynical and physical tackles. They succeeded until 70 minutes when Billy McNeill, despite being jostled and elbowed in the face, headed in a corner kick from John Hughes.

Because of the tactics and approach of Racing Club, Celtic gave some thought to not completing the fixture in the Avellaneda, just outside Buenos Aires but decided to travel, having invited the president (Tom Reid) and the secretary of the SFA (Willie Allan) to accompany them as observers.

The atmosphere in the Estadio Avellaneda on 1 November 1967 was terrifying, and Celtic's veteran goalkeeper Ronnie Simpson was struck on the head by a missile hurled from the terracing behind the goal during his warm-up. He was unable to take any part in the game, John Fallon being hurriedly prepared for the match. Tommy Gemmell scored with a penalty in 21 minutes, awarded when the Racing goalkeeper rugby-tackled Jimmy Johnstone. But inspired by a fanatical home support Racing equalised through Raffo in 33 minutes, and took the lead through Cardenas in 49. Once more the tactics adopted by Racing were chillingly intimidating, and the bedlam inside the ground – with more than 70,000 packed in – seemed to intimidate the Uruguayan referee into favouring the home side.

Celtic reluctantly agreed to play a deciding match in Montevideo, in neighbouring Uruguay, but this proved a fatal mistake. Racing were as always cynical and ruthless; Celtic determined to stand no more nonsense from them. The match – mishandled by a Dr. Rodolpho Osorio from Paraguay – was a fiasco: six players, four from Celtic, and two from Racing were ordered off by the hapless official – and several more should have been dismissed. Uruguayan policemen, heavily armed, had to be called on to the pitch several times to restore a semblance of order among the players. In 57 minutes Cardenas scored the only goal of the game to give Racing a tarnished victory, his swerving shot from thirty yards leaving John Fallon helpless.

The sequel was equally disturbing: Bob Kelly and his fellow-directors levied a fine of £250 on each Celtic player – with the exception of Simpson who had been unable to participate in the matches – while Racing rewarded theirs with a bonus of more than £2,000 each and a new car; the BBC patched together a highlights programme which showed Celtic in a very poor light, concentrating as it did on the dismissal of the four Celtic players (Lennox, Johnstone, Hughes, and Auld – all of them forwards) and ignoring the offences of the Argentines, and indeed not indicating the excesses of the South Americans in the two previous matches. It was left to the prestigious French magazine *Miroir du Football* to describe the winners as 'the World Champions of thuggery, cheating and play-acting'.

A later SFA report written by the secretary Willie Allan did much to explain the circumstances of Celtic's uncharacteristic fall from grace in Montevideo, and help Celtic escape further punishments from the football authorities.

18 October 1967 Hampden Park, Glasgow
Celtic 1, Racing Club 0
Celtic: Simpson, Craig, Gemmell, Murdoch, McNeill, Clark, Auld, Johnstone, Wallace, Lennox, Hughes;

1 November 1967 Estadio Avellaneda, Buenos Aires
Racing Club 2, Celtic 1

Celtic: Fallon, Craig, Gemmell, Murdoch, McNeill, Clark, O'Neill, Johnstone, Wallace, Chalmers, Lennox;

4 November 1967
Estadio Centenario, Montevideo
Celtic 0, Racing Club 1
Celtic: Fallon, Craig, Gemmell, Murdoch, McNeill, Clark, Auld, Johnstone, Wallace, Lennox, Hughes

WORLD CUP CELTS

An appearance at the World Cup finals might rightly be considered the pinnacle of a player's career. Some with a Celtic connection have featured in this event, although only one has actually gained a World Cup winning medal:

1930: Jimmy McGhee, an outstanding Celtic player of the 1890s, emigrated to America in 1910 and his son Bobby played for the United States in the first-ever World Cup (and scored the second-ever goal in the competition in a 3-0 win over Belgium). Incidentally, he also played at outside-left for the New York Giants against Celtic in the 1931 tour of the United States.

1934: Julius Hjulian, although a Swede by birth, played in goal for USA against Italy (1-7). Julius had turned out for Celtic Reserves in 1925/26 including a Second XI cup tie against Rangers.

1954 (Switzerland): Willie Fernie and Neil Mochan represented Scotland against Austria (0-1) and Uruguay (0-7). Former Celt Tommy Docherty also played. The Celtic squad were taken to Switzerland to watch the competition and to learn from it.

1958 (Sweden): Willie Fernie made his second appearance in the finals when he played against Paraguay (2-3); Bobby Evans and Bobby Collins played in all three matches against Paraguay, Yugoslavia (1-1) and France (1-2). Evans was the first Celtic player to captain Scotland (vs France) in the event while Collins was the first Celt to score (vs Paraguay). This was the 500th goal netted in the history of the competition. In the same tournament Bertie Peacock appeared in every match for the surprisingly successful Northern Ireland team.

1974 (Germany): Danny McGrain, David Hay, and Kenny Dalglish played for a Scotland side undefeated against Zaire (2-0), Brazil (0-0), and Yugoslavia (1-1). A fourth Celtic player, Jimmy Johnstone, did not participate in any match although he had left the bench to warm up as a substitute in the closing minutes against Yugoslavia. Wim Jansen represented the losing finalists (Holland) in all their matches. Accordingly, three future Celtic managers played in this tournament.

1978 (Argentina): Ex Celts Lou Macari (Manchester United) and Kenny Dalglish (Liverpool) represented Scotland as did future Celt Alan Rough. Wim Jansen again played for Holland, and once more reached the final.

1982 (Spain): Jock Stein was the Scotland manager; Danny McGrain, ex-Celt Kenny Dalglish (Liverpool) and future-Celt Alan Rough played for Scotland. Also in the Scotland squad were Gordon Strachan and Joe Jordan, and John Robertson, later to be coaches at Celtic Park, while

Martin O'Neill captained Northern Ireland in their march to the quarter-finals. Dr Josef Venglos was the coach/manager for Czechoslovakia.

1986 (Mexico) Paul McStay and Roy Aitken represented Celtic at this tournament; ex Celt Charlie Nicholas (Arsenal) and future Celt Frank McAvennie (West Ham) also played for Scotland. Gordon Strachan was to be remembered for his aborted celebrations when he scored against West Germany. Dariusz Dziekanowski played for Poland.

1990 (Italy): This was a vintage year for Celtic representation for Scotland with Paul McStay and Roy Aitken. Ex Celts Mo Johnston, Allan McInally and Murdo MacLeod also featured and Gary Gillespie came on as sub. Pat Bonner, Chris Morris, Mick McCarthy and Tony Cascarino played for the Republic of Ireland while Lubomir Moravcik turned out for Czechoslovakia (managed by Dr. Venglos again) and John Harkes (who had been fielded for Celtic reserves) played for the United States.

1994 (USA): Pat Bonner and Tommy Coyne were stand-outs for Ireland and ex Celt Tony Cascarino made a cameo appearance as did Roy Keane. Sweden finished in third place with Henrik Larsson making five appearances for them. John Harkes turned out again for the United States, and Russia was captained by their goalkeeper Dmitri Kharin (who would join Celtic six years later from Chelsea).

1998 (France): Tom Boyd, Craig Burley, Darren Jackson, Tosh McKinlay and Jackie McNamara played for Scotland while former Celts John Collins (Monaco) and Derek Whyte (Middlesbrough) were also in the squad. Marc Rieper and Morten Wieghorst turned out for Denmark. Pierre van Hooijdonk played three times for Holland and scored once; Norway's goal in a 1-1 draw with Scotland came from Vidar Riseth.

2002 (Japan/South Korea): Two Celtic players, Henrik Larsson and Johann Mjallby played for Sweden, and Larsson scored three times; the Swedish goalkeeper Magnus Hedman later joined Celtic. Henri Camara played for Senegal and his 'golden goal' eliminated Sweden. Shay Given played for the Republic of Ireland, who were coached by Mick McCarthy while Roy Keane withdrew from the squad just befoe the tournament. Du Wei was in the Chinese squad and Maciej Zurawski played for Poland. Juninho came on as a late substitute for Brazil in the World Cup final and picked up a winner's medal.

2006 (Germany): For Poland Artur Boruc and Maciej Zurawski played well as did Shunsuke Nakamura for Japan. Henrik Larsson was still scoring goals for Sweden, while his former strike partner Mark Viduka turned out for Australia. Jan Vennegoor of Hesselink came on as a substitute for the Netherlands as did Thomas Hitzlsperger for Germany (who played two pre-season games as a trialist for Celtic in 2000).

X/Y/Z

X

The Treble Chance was once the aim of every punter who did the coupon religiously every week. The draws were to be marked with an 'X'.

During 1895/96 Celtic went through their league season of 18 matches without a single draw; in 1989/90 they managed 14 draws in the 36-match schedule.

The highest-scoring draw is a 4-4 result, accomplished on several occasions:

1894/95 H Third Lanark SL 23 February

1925/26 A Hibernian SL 16 January

1928/29 A Queen's Park SL 27 October

1936/37 H Motherwell SC 17 March

1948/49 H Falkirk SL 27 November

1951 N Clyde St. Mungo Cup 19 July

1956/57 H Rangers SC 16 February

1959/60 H St. Mirren SC 24 February

1961/62 H Third Lanark SC 10 March

1963/64 H Third Lanark SL 14 September

1985/86 A Hibernian SLC 4 September (Hibs won after penalty shoot-out)

1985/86 A Rangers PL 22 March

Surprisingly, Third Lanark featured in three out of these twelve matches, and all were at Celtic Park.

XMAS

When Christmas Day was not celebrated as much in Scotland, often football matches were scheduled. Celtic have lost only one of their fifteen Scottish League fixtures played on 25 December:

1897 Clyde A 9-1 Allan (5), Russell (2), McMahon, Campbell

1909 Kilmarnock A 1-0 Quinn

1915 Airdrie H 6-0 Gallacher (3), McColl, Browning, McMenemy

1920 St. Mirren A 2-0 McInally, Cassidy

1926 Kilmarnock H 4-0 McInally (2), W. McStay, McGrory

1933 Queen's Park A 3-2 F. O'Donnell, Napier, McGrory

1934 Queen's Park H 4-1 Delaney (2), Crum, McGrory

1937 Kilmarnock H 8-0 Crum (2), Divers (2), Murphy (2), Delaney, MacDonald

1946 Queen's Park H 1-0 Rae

1947 Hearts H 4-2 McDonald (2), Bogan, Walsh

1948 Aberdeen H 3-0 McPhail, Paton, Johnston

1954 Clyde H 2-2 Boden, Collins

1957 Queen of the South H 1-2 Conway

1965 Morton H 8-1 McBride (3), Chalmers (2), Hughes (2), Murdoch

1971 Hearts H 3-2 Johnstone, Deans, Hood

Jimmy McGrory had mixed memories of Christmas Day fixtures; he scored in all three matches he played in, but was also Kilmarnock's manager when Celtic beat them by 8-0 in 1937.

YOUNGEST

The youngest player to play in a competitive match for Celtic is Mark Fotheringham who was 16 years and 204 days old when he appeared against St. Johnstone on 13 May 2000.

Other contenders might include John Kennedy, who was 16 years and 231 days old on his appearance against Motherwell on 5 April 2000, and Roy Aitken at 16 years and 290 days when he came on as a substitute away against Stenhousemuir in a League Cup tie on 10 September 1975.

Other young debutants include Adam McLean and John Hughes. Adam was 17 years (and nine months) old when he turned out for Celtic at Parkhead on 20 January 1917; John was 17 years (and four months) old when he scored on his first appearance in a 2-0 win over Third Lanark on 13 August 1960.

Brian McLaughlin was given a chance to impress in the second leg of a League Cup quarter-final against Clydebank on 22 September 1971 after Celtic had won the first leg by 5-0 at Clydebank. At the age of sixteen years (and 350 days) he helped Celtic to a 6-2 win at Celtic Park.

Paul McStay made an early debut for Celtic at seventeen years (and 93 days), appearing for the club in a Scottish Cup tie against Queen of the South at Parkhead on 23 January 1982.

On 21 May 2000 Celtic fielded seven teenagers against Dundee United in the last fixture of the league programme, and won by 2-0 before a crowd of 47,586 at Celtic Park. The youngsters were Goodwin, Kennedy, McColligan, McCann, Fotheringham, Burchill, Lynch; another teenager (Liam Miller) was on the bench, as was Covery, and both came on as substitutes. The side was balanced somewhat with a leaven of experience in Gould (31), Mjallby (29), Lambert (30) and Berkovic (28) while Henrik Larsson (28) made his first appearance after recovering from his leg-break as a late substitute. It is doubtful if any aggregate fielded by Celtic during the time of 'the Kelly Kids' could match the youthfulness of that side.

It could also be claimed that Michael McGlinchey was the youngest Celtic player of them all at 14 years and 335 days, but his debut was against Wycombe Wanderers in a Testimonial Match on 22 Oct 2002.

ZAIRE

Scotland opened their 1974 World Cup finals in Germany with a 2-0 win over Zaire. Three Celtic players (Kenny Dalglish, David Hay and Danny McGrain) were in the Scots line-up.

ZURAWSKI

Not too many players have a surname beginning with 'Z' but Celtic's Polish international striker Majiec Zurawski was a notable exception.

Celtic's huddle was proposed by captain
Tony Mowbray in the early 1990s to
promote team spirit